To George

2009

Best Wishes

· BETTER LATE THAN NEVER ·

Jack Berry

·

In support of

The Injured Jockeys Fund

·

Ashgrove Publishing
London

First published in Great Britain by:

Ashgrove Publishing

an imprint of Hollydata Publishers Ltd
27 John Street
London WC1N 2BX

ISBN 978 185398 150 0

First edition

Book design by Brad Thompson

Printed and bound by Butler Tanner and Dennis, Frome

Contents

•

Foreword – 7

Preface – 9

The Injured Jockeys Fund – 13

Chapter One
Better Late Than Never – 15

Chapter Two
No Better Man for the Job – 25

Chapter Three
Forty Years to the Day – 45

Chapter Four
Rough Justice – 69

Chapter Five
Who Would Want to be A Starter? – 91

Chapter Six
Start of the Injured Jockeys Fund – 109

Chapter Seven
Beneficiaries in Tenerife – 137

Chapter Eight
Holiday Over – Let's Kick On – 149

Chapter Nine
Sharp Lads – 171

Chapter Ten
Some Operator – Mouse – 201

Chapter Eleven
Tickets and a Dicky Bird – 211

Chapter Twelve
The Big Day – 235

Index of Names – 251

•

The Horse's Prayer

I'm only a horse, dear Master, but my heart is warm and true,
And I'm ready to work my hardest, for the pleasure of pleasing you.
Good corn and hay and water are all that I wish to ask,
And a warm dry bed to rest on when I've finished my daily task.
Don't strike me in needless anger if I'm slow to understand,
But encourage my drooping spirits with a gentle voice and hand.
Finally, O my master, when my health and strength are gone –
When I'm getting old and feeble and my long life's work is done –
Don't sell me to cruel owners to be slaved to my latest breath,
But grant me the untold blessing of a quick and painless death;
That, as you have always found me a patient and loyal friend,
The years of my faithful service may be crowned by a peaceful end.
I plead in the name of the Savior,
Who cares when the sparrows fall,
Who was born in a lowly stable and knows and loves us all!

Foreword

•

If Jack Berry had been a horse, he would be standing at stud getting four hundred mares a year to cover, and still looking for more! At seventy years of age he has got more energy, drive and enthusiasm than anyone else I know. While most people are still thinking about doing something, Jack has already done it and is on the next task. This is the tale of how he sets out to raise £30,000 in a year for the Injured Jockeys Fund and, not surprisingly, ends up with double the amount. It will restore any wavering doubts you may have had about the racing community. Their generosity when it comes to looking after their own is something we can all be proud of, and when it comes to having proper people to help and support those in need, we are blessed. There are stories that will make you laugh and many that will make you realize how lucky we are to be healthy, but overall I will be surprised if it doesn't make you want to be a better person.

John Francome

Picture Credits

•

Efforts have been made to contact to contact holders of of copyright material. The publishers would be grateful to hear from holders of copyright material who have not been previously contacted.
Contributors are listed below.

Nigel Brunyee
John & Ann Crossick
Vicky Dobin
David Drew
Robert Elliot
Fotosport Ltds
David Hastings
Les Hurley
The Injured Jockeys Fund
Mark Johnson
Will Lack
Peter Mooney
Willie Newton
PA News Photo Library
Provincial Press Agency
Alec Russell
Jan Scott
Colin Turner
Edward Whittaker
RH Wright

Preface

•

I'm not trying to make excuses about why there's been a delay getting this book published and off the ground in the year of its greatest relevance.

When I was training horses at Cockerham with plenty of staff, Helen was one of our office girls. In fact, I know Helen would prefer it if I used her proper title as my secretary.

When I wrote my last book, *One To Go*, and the copy for my weekly articles in the *Daily Star* and the *Sporting Life Weekender*, Helen would enter my words on a computer and print them out in the office. I would knock them about until we got the wording right, or at least to my satisfaction, before I rang it through or faxed it to the papers.

When I retired in January 2000, it was a different ball game, as I couldn't just pop into the office and say 'can you do this for me, mate?' Now, the office I have at home is more a retreat for me and my pack of dogs.

My missus, Jo, is brilliant with animals and shopping but, like me, she cannot use a typewriter. To compound the problem, my handwriting is worse than a doctor's! Ten minutes after writing down the words, even I have difficulty reading my own writing. I don't do the internet, dot coms, texts, or play with other gadgets. If it's got four legs, a tail and breathes, it's got half a chance.

In this book I frequently refer to 'my old pal' or 'my mate' and you, dear reader, may think 'wow, he has a lot of mates'. Well, thankfully, I have, and one of these is Brian Robb, with whom I have kept in touch for many years since the time we had a licence to train before starting our three decades at Cockerham. Brian now works for a telesales firm called Ventura. One of the girls who worked there, Karen, took on the mammoth task of translating my scribble, typing it beautifully and printing it out in legible form.

This was all pretty straightforward until a problem arose out of the blue. Karen decided she was going to take a year out and go to Australia, when the copy and amendments were still unfinished. Karen did not work for me, so she was free to do as she pleased, but I was extremely grateful to her for the work she had already done.

Brian Robb quickly found someone to take over the copy editing role and Brian and I arranged to meet him at the Bridge Inn on the A1 near Wetherby. Sean was his name. He turned up in a pair of well-worn dungarees, with hair down his back, long enough to make it into a ponytail. It's common knowledge that under every ponytail there's an arsehole. He was also wearing an earring. I was not impressed, but I was eager to move my book on, so took him on. He crammed three of Karen's pages into one and there wasn't a full stop, capital letter or even a comma in sight. Only once did he send me part of the manuscript, and then I never heard from him again.

After some months, Brian managed to obtain the data disc onto which Karen had been able to transfer my copy. At that time I was rather disillusioned about carrying on, as I didn't have anyone to knock it into book form.

Again, out of the blue and well over a year since Karen took her trip 'down under', she returned and called me. I told her of my plight and she asked for everything to be sent back to her and she'd try to sort it out. The weeks went by, the months went by, and Karen didn't get back in touch. Karen had changed her mobile number and neither I nor Brian Robb could get in touch with her. After several enquiries Brian managed to contact her; the poor girl must have thought things were in a mess. Eventually the copy on data disc was sent to me in a registered parcel, but with no covering letter or contact details. One would be amazed at the equipment needed and the knowledge of how to use it to complete a book.

Months flew by and my manuscript was doing nothing but gathering dust on the shelf. Then, another friend introduced me to a former journalist, Patrick Lavelle, who was willing to take on the task of finalizing things. Patrick travelled to our home and we had a brief chat about what was needed to be done. But when, a few weeks later, a sample first chapter arrived in the post, he had completely re-written my words. I was surprised because that was not what I wanted. Patrick explained he thought I wanted him to ghost-write my book, something he had done successfully in the past for other people, but I pointed out that I just wanted my manuscript proofread and checked for spelling and grammar, errors, punctuation and literals.

With the misunderstanding out of the way, the work in progress began to progress. Progress, that is, until yet another hurdle arrived. This was in the form of the data disc on to which I was originally told the manuscript had been transferred. Imagine my dismay when, after handing the disc to Patrick, he told me there was nothing on it. Nothing other than a 'shortcut' to the manuscript which could only be accessed on the original computer it had been worked on. With only a hard copy to work from, Patrick then took it upon himself to hire a typist to get the manuscript into electronic form. The material was handed over to Patrick on a memory stick. Picture his frustration when he plugged the memory stick into his computer only to find the stick wouldn't power up! He made a few frantic calls to the typist hoping that she had had the foresight to save the manuscript on to her own computer so it could be transferred onto another memory stick – one that worked. Eventually, the fully typed manuscript on a working memory stick arrived, and he got to work on knocking it into book form – something quite foreign to me. There were times when I thought this book would never happen as if there was something working against it getting into print. That was damned frustrating. I also posted the rough manuscript for Jonathon Powell to have a look. He in turn showed it to Brough Scott. The outcome was they thought I touched a bit near the bone with my naming and shaming, as Jonathon called it. But I was determined not to let technology, or anything else, beat me. So in the face of all that adversity I persevered. I've never been the type to give up easily.

I had dedicated my first book, *It's Tougher at the Bottom,* to Andrea Campion, a lovely, young, blind and disabled girl, who lived in Cockerham Village where we then trained. Andrea's father, John, often brought her to our yard on a Sunday afternoon to see the horses and have a bit of banter with me.

She loved it. She would laugh and giggle and very much enjoyed her time with us. I mentioned Andrea in *It's Tougher at the Bottom* a couple of times, so forgive me if I am repetitive. It took me a long time to come to terms with it when she died. I loved that little lady to bits. Although she was wheelchair-bound, she was very curious and wanted to know everything. Her laughter and enthusiasm were infectious and when she asked a question I would sometimes say, 'I'm not telling you, you're too nosey.'

'Go on, Jack, go on,' she would say.

'You want to know everything that happens here,' I would say to her.

'You never tell me anything about that great big brute you have in training with David Chapman. I don't know why David keeps kidding you on about the crab, it's useless.'

She could retaliate with far more verbals that I could muster. For the record, her horse, Sobering Thoughts, won six races in one season, including the Ayr Silver Cup in 1993, breaking the six furlongs course record. At that rate, he could have won the Ayr Gold Cup.

My second book, *A Year in Red Shirts,* was dedicated to Wilfred Sherman, who now lives in Spain, the Founder and Trustee of the Stable Lads' Welfare Trust, on behalf of all the stable lads and lasses who look after our wonderful horses every day. My latest book, *One to Go,* was dedicated to our son Sam along with the rest of the injured jockeys whose injuries have ended their careers.

I am honoured and privileged to be a Trustee of the Injured Jockeys Fund and in that capacity I have met and had dealings with many injured jockeys. No matter how badly hurt they have been, or whatever hardship they have suffered, I can say, hand on heart, that I have not heard one of them say they would not have been a jockey if they had their time over again. Many jockeys have suffered injuries in racing – some serious and some fatal, as have many horses.

All of us are so lucky to have worked, or to be still working with animals; especially racehorses. While looking in the mirror when having a wash and shave on a morning, I say to myself, 'good morning, Jack. You're still here'. If I were in a supermarket, I would be amongst the bargains nearing their sell-by date. With racehorses in mind, if this book ever makes it to the printers – as the late trainer Bob Ward said, I have stopped buying long-playing records – I will dedicate this book to the horse and all profits will be donated to the Injured Jockeys Fund.

When you have read the book, even if it doesn't come up to your expectations, don't give it away; charge whomever a fiver for it and send the fiver on to the IJF or a charity of your choice. By doing that you will have helped someone.

P.S. A long time after finishing the book a very good friend of mine, Joseph Heler, rang to have a chat and I told him I could do with a sponsor to get the book published and thereby 100% of the book's profits would go to the Injured Jockeys Fund. Joe said, 'leave it with me and I will have a think about it.' Half an hour later he rang back and said, 'I have thought about it and I will sponsor your book.'

To say I was chuffed would be an understatement.

Joe Heler makes the most wonderful cheese in Cheshire and has owned some very good sprinters that I have had the good fortune to train. He has been a great supporter of racing. He has sponsored the prestigious Joseph Heler Lilly Agnes Two-Year-Old Stakes at Chester for many years. A landowner of prime Cheshire grassland with 300 pedigree Holstein cattle and followers, he started making cheese in 1957. Today, his company is one of the leading independent cheese-makers in the UK, manufacturing over 17,000 tons of prize-winning cheese annually, with forty varieties which includes Cheshire, Red Leicester and Double Gloucester.

In 1981, Joe won the Queen's Award for Enterprise for his low-fat cheese and in 2003, he was awarded the Dairy Industry Prize for his lifelong contribution to the dairy industry.

May I suggest that to repay Joe for his generosity he has shown to the IJF, we should each buy 2lbs of his cheese, eat 1lb of it and give the other to a friend? You will be pleased with it and will more than likely buy it every week!

The Princess Royal and JB having a chat at the races.

The Injured Jockeys Fund

•

Providing care, compassion and financial help to injured jockeys.

The Injured Jockeys Fund was the brainchild of our President and founding Trustee John Oaksey and came about following the horrendous accidents of Tim Brookshaw and, four months later, Paddy Farrell in the 1964 Grand National. Both falls resulted in severe paralysis and immediately ended two careers.

With virtually no compensation available at the time to help injured jockeys, the Farrell-Brookshaw Fund was created. Support was instantaneous and following several name changes, tireless work by many for over forty-five years, the IJF has become what it is today – a fund that has spent over £16m in helping over 1,000 jockeys whose injuries have forced many to give up riding. It has maintained this ethos with continuing support for existing beneficiaries and provides immediate and effective help to all newly injured jockeys in whatever way is appropriate.

In all cases, from the most severe which require life-long ongoing changing care and assistance, to those that need short-term help and support, there are no time or financial limits on assistance that the IJF provides in order to ensure a reasonable quality of life for beneficiaries and their families.

Furthermore, the IJF has heightened awareness of the risks of race riding resulting in the racing authorities implementing many safety initiatives for the protection of Jockeys, training schemes for those wishing to become jockeys and re-training for those unable to continue as jockeys.

The Trustees, who carry the responsibility for strategy and governance of the IJF, are: Brough Scott (Chairman); Jeff Smith (Treasurer); Jonathan Powell (Vice-Chairman); Peter Scudamore MBE; John Fairley; Simon McNeill; Jack Berry MBE; William Norris QC; Ian Balding LVO and Pamela Deal.

We are also hugely indebted to our Patron: Her Royal Highness, The Princess Royal for her great interest and support, and to our Vice Patrons: Clare Balding; John Francome MBE and AP McCoy ME for their interest in and enthusiasm for our work.

The Injured Jockeys Fund
1 Victoria Way
Newmarket
CB8 7SH

Telephone: 01638 662246
Fax: 01638 668988
Email: kh@ijf.org.uk
HYPERLINK www.ijf.org.uk

*Jeremy Richardson and the Princess Royal discussing the model
of the proposed development of Oaksey House in Lambourn.*

Chapter One

Better Late Than Never

•

When training for three decades at Moss Side Racing Stables at Cockerham, Lancashire, we had lots of fun when we staged our Open Days for various charities. Above all, it's important to have a laugh and a bit of fun and, when possible, bring in the beneficiaries of any cause to share it. I will mention a few later on.

When Jo, my Bride, and I retired, we held our first charity barbecue at our new abode, just outside the village of Hunton, North Yorkshire, on 18 August 2002. It was a great success, earning our cause, The Injured Jockeys Fund (IJF), a cool £21,000. I decided then that the next year we would go for the big one, raising £30,000 or at least surpassing the previous total. I consider reaching this target no mean achievement, as the hub of the fund-raising activity was our house with just a few acres, unlike the big yard we owned at Cockerham. There we had a vast platform to work from, training more than 100 horses on as many acres of land.

Being realistic, it was quite a mammoth task working from our small spread, but it was a challenge, and I do love a challenge. In order to achieve our goal, we needed to start the ball rolling straight after 18 August. We would have lots of fun doing it, and I do enjoy a bit of fun! There wouldn't be a suitcase big enough to hold the memories of the fun, excitement and enjoyment we had at Cockerham in raising money for good causes.

The money we raised during the year would directly benefit and better the lives of a lot of people. The idea of me writing this account is to give you, out there, an insight into what we needed to do to reach that magical figure. I do not wish to bore you with elaborate detail and bog you down in statistics, so I will endeavour to make this story informative and interesting, with a bit of tittle-tattle, a few of my own anecdotes and a few stories and opinions of mine and others from the racing world, which might prove illuminating and perhaps a little controversial. Above all, this will be a true and detailed account of how much money we raised, who donated, and where, when and in what spirit those gratefully received donations were made.

However, whatever is said, hopefully no one will bear any malice, as none is intended. I know we live in a litigious culture, but, please, don't be knocking on our door! As my old training pal, Mick Easterby, would say, 'we've got nowt'. There are more pages to get through and pictures to view than in the average book, but you can do it. It's a very light read. Pour yourself out a sizeable drink and get stuck in!

On 24 August 2002, in order for us to get some good saleable racing memorabilia together for an auction on a chosen day the following year, I started by writing to Henry Candy, the trainer of Champion sprinter, Kyllachy, the

Irish Trainer, Dr MVO O'Brien – my hero.

winner of the season's Group 3 Palace House Stakes at Newmarket. The horse was grossly unlucky to be beaten in the King's Stand Stakes at Royal Ascot and had recently won the Group I Nunthorpe Stakes at York – the top Northern sprint. This was a race I would dearly have loved to have won, but never managed to, although our Paris House was second in it twice. I asked Henry if he could kindly supply me with a photo of Kyllachy signed by himself and the horse's jockey, Jamie Spencer, so we could put it up for auction the the following year. It would be even better, I said to Henry, if he could donate to our cause one of the sprinting champ's actual racing plates he wore when he won the Nunthorpe, along with a letter of authenticity to prove it wasn't a ringer.

One of my former owners, Sir Alex Ferguson, loves his racing second only to his football. From leaving our yard, Alex went on to greater heights, seeing his colours carried by the all-conquering Rock of Gibraltar, originally named by Gary Moore, the son of Middleham trainer, George. How the horse got the name was like this; every year staff at the Coolmore Stud are invited to name a yearling. They each pick a name and it goes into a ballot box. Gary, who worked at Coolmore at the time, chose the name Rock of Gibraltar. The horse was trained by the Irish maestro, Aidan O'Brien at Ballydoyle – no relation to Dr MV O'Brien, a much older version born in 1917, who trained at Ballydoyle before Aidan. That name was a legend if ever there was one; he was definitely my hero in the training ranks.

Not only did he train three Cheltenham Gold Cup, three Champion Hurdles and three Grand National winners in successive years; he trained the winner of every big race in the calendar. The Doctor's successor kindly sent me a lovely photo of Rock of Gibraltar in a very smart frame, signed by himself, to auction at one of our barbecues. It was bought by Sir Alex for £2,200. Trainers Barry Hills, David Nicholls and John Dunlop had photos of some of their good horses in our auction, which raised big money.

One of the most touching items auctioned was a picture of Shane Broderick driving a sports car. The photo was bought by Middleham trainer George Moore for £200. For anyone unaware, Shane broke his neck in a racecourse fall on Easter Monday in 1997 at Fairyhouse, on a horse called Another Deadly. Shane was only twenty-two at the time and the fall left him paralysed from the neck down.

Shane drives the car with a device fitted to his helmet by way of a switch and a straw for braking and accelerating. He sucks in to go faster and blows out to stop. Fair do's to Alex Ferguson, who took time out from his busy schedule as Manchester United's manager on 18 July 2002 to travel from his home in

Shane Broderick, in his specially-adapted sports car.

Cheshire to Hunton to sign the photo of Rock of Gibraltar before the auction. Alex would have stayed for the day but for his concern for his daughter-in-law, who was heavily pregnant and had fallen at home. His stay was therefore understandably shortened, but he still had time for a cup of tea and a bacon butty. That was something we often did when we trained for him at Cockerham.

When watching Alex on the box chewing gum, looking pensive, howling at his players and grumbling at a referee, he might appear to some to be a real horror. Let me put your mind at rest. Alex is committed to any cause he associates himself with 100 per cent. He is very kind and a real family man to boot. Over the years, he has given our charity days thousands of pounds. A few years ago at Cockerham, when we had our Open Day in aid of the International Spinal Research Trust Fund, Sir Alex sent Fred the Red, his own Old Trafford Park mascot, over to entertain the punters and it was a great success. The first racehorse he owned was Queensland Star, named after a ship his father helped build in the Clyde shipyard. As you can see in the photo overleaf of Queensland Star, Jane Molloy and yours truly, as good as Sir Alex is at managing his football team in the main yard at Cockerham, even he needs a bit of help.

By 27 August 2002, Champion National Hunt Jockey Tony McCoy had ridden no less than 1,698 winners; forty-one more than I have trained in thirty years. Tony was only one winner behind the record holder Richard Dunwoody. Later in the day at Uttoxeter, AP McCoy rode a double to make history. The first win was on Dream With Me, for Martin Pipe, for whom AP was stable jockey. Half an hour later, the mighty McCoy won on Mighty Montefalco, trained by another ex-Champion National Hunt Jockey and a good friend of mine, Jonjo O'Neill. That day's victories made the Irish-born jockey the world's most winning jump jockey of all time. Knowing AP as I do, I knew he would not consider burning out or entering a comfort zone; I knew that the following day he would be as hungry as ever to ride more winners.

*J.B. & Queensland
Star. Jane Molloy
picking the team.*

Everything was going great for Tony, but the jumping game can be hazardous, as demonstrated during the week of Tony's historic wins when Richard Johnson, the jockey then in the runner-up spot to AP, had a fall and broke his right leg. Even more serious than Richard's fall was that of nineteen-year-old Irish Conditional National Hunt Jockey, Jimmy Mansell, who suffered serious head injuries from a fall at Ballinrobe Racecourse and had to be put on a life-support machine at a hospital in County Mayo. For me and everyone else who loves the jumping, Jimmy was very much in our thoughts. It's difficult to get everything you want when there's such a high price to pay. For some jockeys and horses, it's a very high price indeed.

At the time, I felt in my water that AP would do the business, so I wrote to his personal secretary Gee Armitage – who had ridden one of our rare jumpers one day previously at Sedgefield and finished second, and whose brother Marcus rode Mr Frisk to win the Grand National in 1990, breaking the course record. Gee was a very good lady jockey in her day. She had claims to fame with riding in the Grand National and, more importantly, in 1987 at the Cheltenham Festival, she rode a double on The Ellier and Gee A. In my letter I asked Gee if she minded getting me a nice big photo of the historic event signed by AP, so that when the time arrived we could auction it at our barbecue the following year.

The barbecue of 2002 had a limit of 150 people at £35 per head. Our local trainer, Anne Duffield, not in any sense a dumb blonde – for she is as sharp as a needle and a true entrepreneur to boot – helped us with the barbecue. Years before, when her mother, who owned an old people's home died, Anne, at the tender age of just seventeen, had to leave boarding school and run the home. She matured into a shrewd and astute businesswoman.

Anne, with The Bride, Jo, rang round many people and soon all the tickets for the barbecue were sold. We put a ticket limit on because we attempted to get everything sponsored, and there is a limit to what you can ask people for! Pete Fawcett and his business partner Roger Towner agreed to supply all the steaks, sausages and beef burgers from their firm Fawcett's Fresh Foods. Jack Clayton, John Stephenson, John Forsyth and Anne Duffield financed the wine and beer. Jim Andrews supplied the salmon, salads and boiled potatoes. In addition, Jim brought his barbecues and utensils and, with his wife, cooked the lot for us.

My missus made the trifles and apple pies. Anne Fawcett and Christine Sellers supplied the fruit and cream and served on the sweet table. I was overwhelmed by the generosity of all concerned and could not have asked for more.

There was a little room for improvement on the ticket sales. I sold two to Pat Haslam, the trainer, but didn't collect the money and he returned them by post after the event. Jo sold twenty-four to another trainer, Ferdy Murphy. (He started training in 1990. On his first day with runners he trained three winners, all at Huntingdon.) Ferdy assured Jo he would have no trouble selling the tickets. Two weeks before the event Jo rang his secretary, to be told everything was in order. But on the big day itself there was no sign of the trainer or his punters and in the post the Tuesday that followed were seventeen unsold tickets with a message from the secretary on a compliment slip 'please find enclosed the tickets we couldn't sell'. My missus was fuming, as she and Anne could have sold the tickets twice over! Paul and Yvette Dixon and the Dowager Lady Bolton donated valuable auction prizes but, due to other commitments, they could not attend. But they kindly sent in their ticket money.

By 28 August, the day after Tony McCoy's record-breaking achievement, the bookmakers had the champ priced at 50/1 for him to be crowned the Sports Personality of the Year. To me, that was just pathetic. For everything he had done in racing in such a relatively short space of time, a 10/1 shot would have been a more sensible price. It was just as bad the previous year, considering that Tony smashed Sir Gordon Richard's fifty-four-year-old record of 269 wins in a season when the young living legend even failed to make the nominees!

By the time September arrived I asked Jackie, the wife of Jonjo O'Neill, if she could possibly get me a framed photo of Mighty Montefalco signed by Jonjo, the owner, and AP. While in the begging mood, I also wrote to trainer Henrietta Knight asking her if she could do the same for our cause with her horse Best Mate when he won the Cheltenham Gold Cup. Hen rang me back to tell me she had three complimentary prints of Best Mate jumping the last, and she would get one, nicely framed, up to me.

It may appear bold of me to have asked some of these kind people not just to donate valuable photos, but also to frame them. But I was loath to dip into the funds for anything unless I really needed to or we would never have reached our target. That's why we tried to get everything sponsored. That way the Injured Jockeys Fund would get all the money raised, and not just a percentage of it. I think many more people would give more generously to charities if they knew all the cash was going to the cause, instead of huge amounts going on administration and the like.

By this time, Henry Candy had yet to reply to my request for a photo of Kyllachy, but that didn't surprise me. Following his great triumph in the Nunthorpe, Henry's poor horse was found to have a cracked bone and would not be able to run again. The unlucky man must have felt gutted. It's at times like these, if you are not careful, that the training can grind you down. Luckily for Kyllachy, he was still a full horse and would stand as a stallion. Half of him was sold to the Cheveley Park stud before the Nunthorpe, the same stud that owned his father, Pivotal; the very horse who beat our Mind Games half a length in the 1995 King's Stand Stakes at Royal Ascot when ridden by George Duffield and trained by Sir Mark Prescott Bt.

When 7 September arrived, our son Alan had two runners at Thirsk and, as he was at Haydock Park, he asked me to tack up. When I arrived in the car park at Thirsk, ex-trainer, Peter Easterby, a class act, pulled in behind my car. When he approached me he dipped his hand in his pocket, pulled out £100, handed it to me and said, 'this is for your IJF to get them lads and lasses away on holiday.' For the record Peter has given £100 every year towards our fund-raising Red Shirt Night at Pontefract Racecourse. Peter, father to Tim, is no stranger to success, having trained winners of most big races, both flat and jumping, in the north as well as down south, including five Champion Hurdles with Saucy Kit, Night Nurse and Sea Pigeon. In addition to that amazing feat, he trained Alverton to win the 1979 Cheltenham Gold Cup and won again two years later with Little Owl. Although Johnny Greenaway, one of our past top Northern jockeys to whom I was talking at an IJF beneficiaries day at Doncaster told me, he rode Shamrock Star to win the top Redcar sprint and the Gosforth Park Cup from the only two rides he had for Peter. Feeling miffed and disappointed when challenged about the reason no more rides were forthcoming, Peter said, 'you were always engaged.'

On my return from Thirsk after having a chat with Jo, we arranged to open a building society account in the Injured Jockeys Fund name via Hunton Post Office in the village, so that all monies for the cause could go in and earn interest.

The following morning in the mail was a cheque for £20 from my old school pal Eddie Foster, who sent it as I had forwarded him a copy of my book, *One To Go*. With Peter's £100 and Eddie's £20 we could put £120 into the new account. That left us with only £29,880 to go!

While I was at Thirsk races, David Pipe, the visiting tailor who holds a stall there and has made suits for me, wrote a letter enclosing a voucher for a tailor-made suit as an auction prize the following year as he heard we were to hold a barbecue again. Invincible Spirit won the £200,000 Stanley Leisure Group One Sprint at Haydock Park the day before, ridden by my old apprentice John Carroll. It goes without saying that I was really chuffed for John. In the twelve years John rode for our yard, riding more than 500 winners, we had never managed to win a Group One race. I rang John the following day to say well done. His wife Tracey answered the phone as John was in the sweatbox trying to lose a few pounds before setting off for a meeting at York. That just goes to show what these jockeys have to go through. When he rang me back later, I asked him if he could get me a framed photo of his win on Invincible Spirit. As always, John agreed. JC has done a lot for our charity days over the years. He and his wife are a sensible couple, and, instead of frittering money away, they invested in property in the Morecambe Bay area. At the time they had about thirty-five properties on their books, and this was during the property boom. I was very pleased for them.

Trainer John Dunlop, OBE. A great man in the cause of racing welfare.

I wrote to Invincible Spirit's trainer John Dunlop, who, in 1966, trained his first winner Tamino in the Group Three Palace House Stakes at headquarters. Three years later, J Berry trained his first winner Camasco in a selling hurdle at Kelso. John, who handles one of the biggest strings in England, and who has an OBE for his charitable work for the Stable Lads' Welfare Fund, asked him if he would kindly send me one of Invincible Spirit's racing plates, accompanied by a letter of authenticity that the horse had worn at Haydock the day before.

Watching the Group One Irish Champion Stakes from Leopardstown in the Tote Credit at Thirsk Races, I thought it was a long time before, if ever, that I had seen a better finish to a race. It was the shortest of short heads in favour of Grandera, ridden by Frankie Dettori, over Aidan O'Brien's Hawk Wing, ridden by Irish Champion Jockey, Mick Kinane. It was obvious neither jockey knew who had won; it had been that close. Frankie got his horse's head in front on the line.

On my return home, putting pen to paper, I wrote to Simon Crisford, the manager of Godolphin, who owned the winner. I asked Simon if he would do the honours and grace our day with a signed photo.

It was good news the following day for Aidan O'Brien when the all-conquering Rock of Gibraltar breezed into the record books by winning the Prix du Moulin at Longchamps in France, becoming the first horse to win seven consecutive Group Ones.

In the auction the previous year, as an extra lot, James Blackshaw, of Cantor Sport, kindly donated four tickets for the Audley Harrison vs. Wade Lewis fight to be held at the Olympic Theatre in Liverpool on 5 October. Cantor Sport sponsor jump jockeys AP McCoy, Carl Llewellyn and Mick Fitzgerald. In addition, they sponsored the heavyweight boxer Audley Harrison. Cantor

Fitzgerald occupied several floors at the top of the World Trade Centre Towers in New York, where thousands of innocent people lost their lives in the world's worst terrorist atrocity. There were 658 of their own people amongst them.

Peter Fawcett bought the boxing tickets for £450. However, Peter called me later to tell me he would not be able to attend the fight as he would be in Spain that day. He asked me if I could sell the tickets on. I mentioned it to Dave Armstrong and David Bowes and we decided we could invite a neighbouring farmer, Brian Muir, who likes a bit of sport, to join us and we would each donate £50 to the next barbecue fund-raiser. By this time the account stood at £29,680 to go!

On a day in early September, Eddie O'Leary, the Irish breeder, from whom I had bought a few yearlings in the past, told me at Doncaster St Leger Yearling Sales to fax him a list of the donated items so far for the barbecue the following year so that himself and some of his boys could put in bids for them. Eddie is the son-in-law of the ex-Irish-Champion-National-Hunt-Jockey Timmy Hyde, which makes him the brother-in-law to Norman Williamson, the crack jump jockey. Eddie is a really smashing, generous, fellow.

I gave the second day at the sales a miss, having bought three yearlings the day before, two for Brian Robe. The previous week I was with Brian at the Stadium of Light to see his team Sunderland draw 1-1 with Manchester United. The other yearling I had bought for Lilo Blum, the sister of my old mate Gerry, the ex-Newmarket trainer.

Rather than go to the second day of the sales, I went to Old Trafford to watch Manchester United get beaten 1-0 by Bolton. That result was a bit of a turn-up! Before the kick off there was a minute's silence, as there was at most sporting fixtures throughout the country as a mark of respect on the first anniversary of the World Trade Centre attack. Cantor Sport, on behalf of the Cantor Fitzgerald UK Charitable Relief Fund, who set up support for the families of the 658 employees of the parent company who lost their lives, sponsored the entire day's racing at Hereford.

As my wife Jo isn't a football fan, I arranged to take Ann Hewitt to the match for company. Ann was a Champion ladies point-to-point rider in her heyday and is a family friend. At the time she was training a few jumpers in Cheshire and loved Man United. Sir Alex arranged a nice meal for us before the match and we were to meet him after the game, as I normally do. While waiting for him in his lounge to arrive, John Smith, York's Clerk of the Course, Mike Dillon, of Ladbrokes and Channel 4 racing presenter and ex-jockey John Francome came in. Thinking about our cause, as ever, and not wishing to miss an opportunity, I scrounged a day for two with breakfast thrown in with John and the rest of the crew at Channel 4 Racing. I knew it would fetch a tidy sum, as most women go bananas over John Francome! Mike Dillon promised he would arrange three £100 Betting Vouchers for the raffle, just as William Hill did for our previous barbecue. A lot of racing women are not into football. Gee Armitage on the box once asked Bryan Robson, the England captain, what sport he was involved in. Mind you, some can go the other way. Racecourse judge Sandra Arkwright, a staunch United fan, and her husband Philip, once went to Old Trafford to see a game with me and an old pal of mine, Steve Allen. She was like a hooligan, shouting and cheering. Yes, Sandra the judge, was as near as you could get to an embarrassment.

13 September arrived – considered unlucky for some – proved lucky for me, as in the morning post there was a letter from the National Savings with a £50 Premium Bond. 'Every little helps', I thought, like the old lady said when she peed in the sea. It was not an unlucky day, either, for the well-over 100 beneficiaries of the Injured Jockeys Fund as, at Doncaster Racecourse, we have an annual get-together in a marquee sponsored by Chris and Antonia Deuters, great supporters of the IJF. As well as sponsoring the marquee, they serve, along with The Bride, behind the bar all day.

St Leger Day was a great occasion for the North as Bollin Eric won the 226th running of the St Leger, Britain's oldest classic. He was trained by Tim Easterby at Malton and owned by Sir Neil (born 1917) and Lady Westbrook, two of the nicest people you could ever wish to meet, and a very loyal couple as they have owned horses with the Easterby family for more than forty years. (As some owners change yards often, in racing circles it is said of some hot-arsed owners that the only stable they haven't been in is Bethlehem.) Quite rightly, Sir Neil and Lady Westbrook were rewarded by winning Racehorse Owners' Association/Weathery's Award for Horse of the Year.

Eric was ridden in the Leger by Kevin Darley. A lot of water had run underneath the bridge since 5 August 1960, when Kevin on his seventeenth birthday rode his first winner on Dust Up at Haydock Park, the same place where, as a twelve-year-old boy, the legendary Lester Piggott (born in Wantage Hospital, Berkshire) rode his first winner on The Chase in 1948.

In the years to come as a turf trivia question this is sure to come up: 'What was the great jockey's last British win also at the same venue?' It was Palacegate Jack on 5 October 1994, and I am extremely proud to say that the horse was trained by yours truly.

Bronze of Lester Piggot riding his first and last British winners – The Chase in 1948 and Placegate Jack in 1994.

The photo is of The Chase and Jack, the bronze William Newton sculpted for Lester's birthday, commissioned by Lester's wife Susan. As a kid, Kevin was the leading apprentice while in the care of Rugeley trainer, Reg Hollinshead. In 2000, he was the country's leading flat jockey. Bollin Eric credited the North with its first St Leger victory since 1973, the year Peleid won, trained by Bill Elsey and ridden by Frankie Durr. Frankie was a good boxer as a kid. He rode a number of classic winners before he went on to train the speedy Ahonoora.

The North's previous winner of the St Leger was in 1959, Cantello, trained by Captain Charles Elsey, Bill's dad, and ridden by the North's champion jockey Edward Hide.

Earlier in the year of our second major fundraising drive for the IJF, leading up to the following year's barbecue, on Sunday 14 July, I was guest for the day with Attheraces at Haydock Park where I tipped Bollin Eric to win the MEN July Trophy Stakes. He had won two races at a mile and being by Shamit, I thought he wouldn't have a problem staying the Haydock one-and-a-half-mile. Incidentally, I was standing with David Metcalfe, the racing manager of Shamit's owner, K. Dasmal, when the horse won the 1996 Epsom Derby. Shamit was ridden by Michael Hills, and trained in Newmarket by Willie Haggas, Lester Piggott's son-in-law.

At Haydock it was great to see the Andy Turnell-trained Jelani win a good race, when he beat Bollin Eric, as Dr and Mrs Hollowood are such great supporters of racing. I don't want to take away Jelani's glory, but I didn't think Bollin Eric, ridden by William Supple, ran his best race in the MEN that day. Needless to say, I was soon writing letters to Kevin and Tim for signed photos and a shoe from the Classic winner to auction the following year at our barbecue.

By mid-September, with so many framed photos about to arrive and more requests made, a racing plate of the Vernon Sprint winner Invincible Spirit, along with a cheque for £50 to get the plate mounted, arrived in the post, kindly sent by John Dunlop. It was marvellous to think that John was listed in the year's Horse in Training as having 172 horses in his care. As busy as he was, the man had found time to help us. It was little wonder that John received the OBE from the Queen; he should have been given a knighthood, as he certainly deserved it.

Chapter Two

No Better Man for the Job

•

When 16 September arrived, I was at an IJF Trustee and Almoners meeting in London. Ex-jockey, now racecourse starter and fellow Trustee, Simon McNeill, gave me two Oaks and two Derby 2002 Racecards with every jockey's signature beside the name of the horse that they rode in those races. Each of these will be rare collectors' items in time, as they are in mint condition. Derek Blake, the Clerk of the Scales – he's the man who weighs the jockeys out before and after the race – arranged to get all the jockeys' signatures for our big day. I was sure the cards would raise a lot of interest at our auction. In addition to the cards, Lady 'Chicky' Oaksey, the President's wife and Northern Almoner Sarah York promised me a framed print to auction of an original painting by Sue Crawford of 'The Three Kings': Arkle; Desert Orchid and Red Rum.

For the record, Lord Oaksey has been a Trustee of the IJF since it started in 1964, when Paddy Farrell broke his back on Border Flight in the Grand National. John, born in 1929, was a very capable amateur rider for twenty or so years. He was made Chairman of the IJF later on, and a very good one at that, without a shadow of a doubt. Lord Oaksey is Mr IJF.

Whilst in Tenerife, at Mar y Sol, where we took around sixty-five beneficiaries and carers, at suggestion of our Chief Executive Jeremy Richardson, we

Mr Injured Jockeys Fund himself – Lord Oaksey OBE.

trustees got together and asked the great man if he would become our president. He was very moved to have been asked and happily accepted. He made sure the job carried a dictat with it. He continues to attend Trustees' meetings and over the last forty years with an average of twelve meetings per year. John, no matter what crops up, has never missed a single one. Could you imagine a Trustee meeting going ahead without him? Following all those years of service it was decided that the noble Lord should be relieved of some of his workload. Therefore Sir Edward Cazalet was made our Chairman and Brough Scott the Vice Chairman. This all works very well. 2002 saw the departure of two dear and close friends of our fund. Our much beloved Patron, Her Majesty Queen Elizabeth the Queen Mother, and a fellow trustee Dick Saunders. Dick was born in 1933 and is famous for riding the 1982 Grand National Winner, Grittar, at the age of forty-eight. Returning to the unsaddling enclosure with Grittar, Dick said, 'It can't get any better than this', and he retired straight after the race. He couldn't have gone out on a better note. Dick served the IJF well for over twenty years.

Karen Hatton, the IJF Secretary to Jeremy Richardson, told me they had some nice, rare, framed prints in stock ready for auction or raffle for our big day. The problem with goods stashed away in the office was that no one got a chance to see them. It's not like a shop where items are on view; goods are only sold on when they have been asked for. While I have the chance, I must say the Injured Jockeys Fund had a great deal to thank our Chief Executive Jeremy Richardson for the many years he tirelessly worked for the Fund. It has grown from strength to strength with his guidance.

Setting off for the three-day Western Meeting at Ayr, we met our postman Rob. I took the mail from him which I read while Jo was driving. Talk about people being generous. Lady Westbrook sent a lovely letter and a cheque for £1,000 to boost our fund. Whilst at Ayr and staying with Willie and Wilma Burns at Dunlop just a few miles away from the racecourse, Wilma gave me a cheque for £30 for one of the unframed prints Karen sent from the IJF; reducing our target to £28,650. It was early days but we were getting there.

Whilst at Ayr, I was asked by the racecourse management to place a plaque to commemorate wheelchair-bound former Ayr race-goer, Mario Gillon, whom I got to know well over the years. Mario, who sadly died a couple of years ago, campaigned for a wheelchair ramp, and it's a shame that it wasn't installed in his lifetime. As we have been for the last three years, on Ayr Gold Cup day we were invited to lunch before racing started at Tony Collins' lovely home in Troon. AK, or 'the Colonel' as Tony is called, is a real character who is either loved or hated. AK is famous for the 'coup' at Cartmel several years ago with Gay Future. My dealings with AK go back even further than Gay Future, as I had several rides for him some thirty-five years ago when I rode for Harry Bell, who then trained for him.

Talking to AK, he gave me for our fund-raising cause, a very nice framed and signed, limited-edition print of Colonel Collins, the Classic-placed colt he shared with Robert Sangster, the man who graced our yards with its first horse good enough to become a stallion at stud, Distinctly North. 'Sid', Distinctly North, won the Group Two Flying Childers at Doncaster in 1990, was second to Mac's Imp in the Group One Heinz 57 Stakes at Phoenix Park in Ireland and to the French horse Lycius in the Group One Middle Park Stakes at headquarters. As good as the horse was, RE Sangster never once rang up to enquire when or where we intended running the horse. The only thing he did say once when I saw him racing was, 'John Carroll has done really good on Distinctly North but, if it's at all possible, would you mind letting Pat Eddery have a ride on him', as he was friendly with Pat. Robert was such a good owner. He never interfered with the training of his horses, he trusted his trainers 100%. He once said when the passengers want to fly the aircraft, it's time to get off. In 1990, Distinctly North won at Sandown which meant that our yard had had a winner on every British flat course. That meeting was Hong Kong Day. Robert's winner's trophy was a huge Onyx Chinese horse valued at £500. RS didn't like it, so he gave it to me. I think it's great.

John Stephenson was one of our owners a few years ago, and he owned a decent sprinter called Stephenson's Rocket. John also helped to sponsor the wine and beer at one of our fund-raising barbceues. He also sponsored the alcoholic bottle tombola, which was a great success. Talking to John, he said he would not only sponsor the tombola again if we were struggling, he would also sponsor the whole bar. Wasn't that great? John and his wife Gail always attend the Ayr Western meeting as part of their holiday.

Still at Ayr, Thirsk trainer David Nicholls won the Ayr Gold Cup with Funfair Wane, owned and bred by the then Manchester City's manager's wife, Jean Keegan and ridden by David's son Adrian. The Ayr Gold Cup, a six-furlong handicap is one of the hardest races in the calendar to win. My racing ambition to win it was thankfully achieved with So Careful in 1988, after many attempts.

Remarkably, David Nicholls had won the race three years running. Well done Dandy, as he is affectionately known. He was a very good jockey before he started training and rode the odd winner for our yard. He has proved to be an even more successful trainer. David rode his first winner at Chester on Hunting Tower in 1973. Possibly the best two horses he has ridden were Soba and Chaplains Club. BHB Chairman Peter Savill owned the latter; both horses were trained by David Chapman. When Soba won the Stewards' Cup at Goodwood, Lester rode our horse Touch Boy, who we really fancied, as he had already won a Portland Handicap. I said to Lester, 'Soba runs a bit and she has got to be our biggest danger even though she is drawn one.' He said, 'You can't win from that draw', but even the great judge LP was wrong as she popped out of the gate, never looked like getting caught and won easily!

Sprint king Dandy Nicholls. One of the most likeable trainers in the game.

The 22nd September 2002, marked the day of the Countryside March when over 400,000 country folk walked through London to Hyde Park to protest about having too much interference in their way of life from the Government – a way of life that nowadays is controlled by red tape and authority. Recently, someone who must have thought our politicians of the day were losing control, posted me the new emblem.

The Government announced today that it is changing its emblem to a condom because it more clearly reflects the government's political stance. A condom stands up to inflation, halts production, destroys the next generation, protects a bunch of pricks and gives you a sense of security while you're actually being screwed.
DAMN, it just doesn't get more accurate than that!!!!!

It was also an Open Day for Turf 2000 at the local training yard of Anne Duffield, where George Duffield, her jockey husband, launched his autobiography called *Gentleman George*?. George signed and gave me the first book off the press to auction at the next year's barbecue. I don't know about George being a gentleman. There has already been a bit of a stir up as there was a story that came out of the book in the newspapers where, in 1991, 'the gentleman' hit the BHB Chairman Peter Savill. George said his only regret was that he didn't hit him hard enough!

The trouble arose because Peter was holding up a booked private plane that was taking him, George and some more jockeys from a day meeting at Beverley to an evening meeting at Hamilton in Scotland. GD lost his rag and thumped Peter. As you can gather, George Duffield is no fan of the BHB boss. In fact, George told me that in his opinion, Peter Savill couldn't run a bath, never mind the BHB. Mind you, a bunch of sour grapes could account for that statement. There are times when I wish George would not sit on the fence and speak his mind. Some joke. Jo and I were going out to lunch with him and Anne, his other half, later on that day. I made sure I sat on the opposite side of the table in case the little bugger turned nasty! Hamilton, even for us Northerners is a long way to travel. Newmarket trainer Sir Mark Prescott who retained George for many year, sent a horse to run at Hamilton. Mark said to the owner Mr Haggas, who hails from Yorkshire, and whose horse finished third running on, 'The horse ran well but needs stepping up in trip. We'll have to find him a race a bit further.' The owner said, 'I didn't think you could go much further than Hamilton.' For the record Hamilton staged the very first British night meeting and 18,000 people attended. For such a small racecourse that's a huge crowd.

I made a phone call to Sarah Cousin's house. Sarah lives in Lockerbie and runs a livery yard. She has broken many horses in for us and cared for some animals that were out of training whilst we were at Cockerham. Sarah is the daughter of the late John, and the niece of the late handicap specialist of his day, Eric Cousins. Both brothers were trainers of many winners. Sarah recently had the most horrific riding accident; the poor girl got very badly kicked in the face. So terrible were her injuries that she lost all her top teeth, several of her bottom ones and broke many facial bones. In addition to that, she had the roof of her mouth kicked out. Unfortunately for Sarah, she didn't ride in any races, if she had she would have qualified for the Injured Jockeys Funds help. Sarah is a great tough girl and I desperately hope everything goes right for her. She was in the operating theatre for twelve hours on the day of the accident. Sadly, Sarah had yet another bad hand dealt to her. She had to undergo another operation to remove an eye a couple of days later.

I decided to put my charity hat on when I went to the Children's Outpatients Ward at St James Hospital in Leeds with Sister Eileen Cullen. Eileen is the daughter of Paddy Farrell. The reason for our meeting was that we were trying to get enough money together to refurbish and redecorate the Children's Outpatient Department of the hospital. Would you believe that it hadn't been refurbished or even had a fresh coat of paint on the walls for over thirty-two years. It looked so depressing and uncared for.

After my visit, Anne Cunningham from Yorkshire TV got on the phone to me, and we made some headway in getting a fund started to finance the clean-up. Frank, one of my younger brothers, lives in Leeds. He drives a mini coach set up for wheelchair passengers. He would take a load of kids to school and back, hospital appointments to Jimmy's or wherever else they needed to go every day. One day on an outing, a driver of a car cut him up in town so at the next set of traffic lights at Poole, Frank stopped his coach, wound down his window and asked the offending driver what his grief was. All the youngsters in Frank's vehicle were shouting, 'Chin him, Frank.' When the other driver saw Frank, who must have looked a bit like Alex Ferguson in a bad mood, he shot straight over the lights on red. The kids were saying to Frank in unison, 'what's he say? What's he say?' Frank's reply was, 'I don't know, you were making that much noise you frightened him away!'

I have two other brothers. Harry, the eldest, who is now retired, devotes most of his time as a Trustee at the Birtley Boxing Club, near Sunderland, and he voluntarily maintains the building. Geoff is the youngest, also now retired. He worked all his life in hunting, starting off Second Whip with the West Percy, then Second Whip for three years with The Belvoir. He then moved on to be a First Whip for The Cheshire (these hunt servants have more homes than gypsies), then on to become First Whip and Kennel Huntsman for the Southwold in Lincolnshire, and eleven years as First Whip and Kennel Huntsman

One of my hunters, Trigger. JB & Shane Broderick.

with the East Sussex and Worcestershire Hunt. For eleven years in two sessions, he was Huntsman to the Romney Marsh. Now that George Duffield and I have retired, we ride with the Bedale every Wednesday and Saturday. Had I not been in racing, I wouldn't have minded a hunting job. Shane Broderick stayed with us and I showed him Trigger, one of my hunters.

Jockey Michael Tebbit had a horrendous fall at Nottingham which landed him in the intensive care unit of the Queens Medical Centre with a punctured right lung, seven broken ribs, internal bleeding, two fractured bones in his left hand and a broken thumb on his right. Thankfully, he made progress and was soon out of the intensive care unit. It's a tough job being a jockey. There are not many other jobs where the ambulance follows you around while you are working.

I was speaking to Joy Hawkins, the equine artist, in the marquee of the IJF get-together at the Leger meeting at Doncaster. She painted the year's IJF Christmas Card of yearlings being broken at Ian Balding's yard, at Kingsclere in Berkshire. There were a number of yearlings being driven in strings on a very snowy and cold winter morning. The drivers were taking the yearlings in different directions; it was really life-like. I think it was brilliant, dead original. As I was talking to Joy and telling her how I liked her work, I got around to asking if there was any chance of her donating a print for the auction, which she readily agreed to. I didn't have the balls to ask for the original painting. Joy has to earn a living painting and she needed to sell that. However, she later rang for a chat to arrange the promised print and a couple more from the paintings she had been commissioned to do. When I told her Rock of Gibraltar's blown-up photo that Aidan O'Brien donated raised £2,200 at our barbecue, she said she would love to paint Rock of Gibraltar. Jokingly, I said I would ask Sir Alex if he would allow her to do so. Quite seriously, Joy said if

I did she would make a run of prints from the original and we could have all the money from them for the IJF.

When 26 September arrived, the postman brought us a nice present of £500 in the form of a cheque from Brett Oils Ltd, as they had also contributed to a race on a Red Shirt Night at Pontefract. This left us with £28,150 to reach our target.

I rang Sarah Cousins as she had been allowed home from hospital to see how she was following her horrendous accident. When I said to her, 'I thought you might be riding out so I rang early', she was laughing like a good'un and then even more so when I said she could borrow a spare set of my teeth. In addition to all the other things that had happened to her, most of her other teeth had been kicked out except for four at the bottom. What a brave lass. Typical of Sarah, she said when she learned of the tragic accident earlier in the week to stable girl Rebecca Davis of James Given's yard, who had been killed on a horse, it made her feel quite sick and realised how lucky she was to be alive.

On the last day of September, I met Hilary and Dr Kerr. Hilary was the first Northern Almoner of the IJF and a very good one too, now retired. We met, along with present Almoner Elaine Wiles, at Bob North's home near Catterick, an ex-jockey whose wife Phyllis suffers with a crippling muscle disease. She had difficulty standing up. Dr Kerr's mother had recently died, therefore, they had no use for the sit-on motor scooter she had used.

We met at the North's house to see if his wife Phyllis could cope with the scooter. Thankfully, after taking her in it for a spin, she was able to so that the scooter found a good home. Dr Robin Kerr, a northern racecourse steward officiated at some of our Open Days at Cockerham in case of any emergencies. Hilary's input organising the first IJF Tenerife holiday, was immeasurable. In fact, without her the holiday wouldn't have got off the ground.

I had just been reading the *Racing Post* and sadly it wasn't good news for Irish jockey Jimmy Mansell. It stated that he was back on a life support machine

My brothers, l to r, Harry, JB, Frank & Goeff.

after suffering a setback in his recovery from serious head injuries following a fall. It also said that Jimmy had developed a complication related to the ventilation of his lungs and had been moved to a chest hospital in Galway where the poor lad was to undergo surgery.

The morning of 1 October came with glorious sunshine, just like a midsummer day as we made our way to Sedgefield. The reason Jo and I were there is that every year Sedgefield Racecourse kindly stage the Sam Berry Novice Steeplechase. It was at Sedgefield on 5 March 1985 when our son Sam had a fall from Solares that ended his career as a jockey – the blackest day of my life. Sam now lives in Sparsholt with his girlfriend Carole, but couldn't be with us at Sedgefield that unusually warm October day as Carole worked for Wantage trainer, Henry Candy, looking after the hostel. She didn't like asking for more time off work as they had recently attended the IJF gathering at the Doncaster St Leger meeting. Trevor Taylor, part owner of Solares, presented the winning owner Brian Padgett with a race trophy, as he does every year. Sorrento King, the winner, was trained by the only lady trainer to have trained 100 winners in a season, Mary Reveley. Hopefully, if Sedgefield continues with the race we will make sure Sam goes in future as no end of people, especially the jockeys, always asked where he was.

Sam Berry (with the red tie) presenting the trophy in the Sam Berry Novice Chase at Sedgefield.

Reading George Duffield's book one night in bed, I nearly wet myself laughing at the story about Newmarket trainer Sir Mark Prescott leading GD out of the paddock on Lily Augusta at Carlisle. When Mark let go of the horse, it flyjumped and hit George with her head right smack in his face, dislodging some of his some teeth. George sat on Lily's back, holding his hand to his mouth with blood oozing between his fingers. Sir Mark ran up – he had probably had invested a few quid on the filly – grabbed hold of her and steadied George by gripping his leg. Then he said, 'How are you George? You'll be alright won't you? This filly can win. Ride her and we'll get you to the hospital right after the race.' This was way out of the question as George was concussed and couldn't even speak. Still in his breeches and boots, Sir Mark ferried his jockey to Carlisle Infirmary to the Casualty Department.

Picture the scene on a Saturday night when the pubs are beginning to close, punters coming in with broken arms, bottled faces and the like, and every time they got near the front of the queue another life or death case comes in to shuffle them further back. Just as they were nearly there to get attended to, a mother came in with a little kid who came in with a saucepan stuck on his head. He had been playing soldiers, telling the nurse he had wedged the pan on his head for a helmet and he couldn't get it off. As you can imagine, Sir Mark was rolling about laughing, tears were pouring down his cheeks and it started George off. Even with the pain of broken teeth and a smashed face he couldn't help laughing. Sir Mark said, 'Hold on George, won't be long now it's your turn next.' Just as he said that the double doors swung open and in staggered an old tramp with a ruddy great kitchen knife sticking out from between his shoulder blades. By then it was 1.30 a.m., and Sir Mark says 'George it looks as though we could be here a bit longer.' After that long wait, all they could do for George was give him a tetanus jab. For the record, George is the most winning flat jockey who has never been a champion. Up to the time of him writing his book *Gentleman George?*, he had ridden no less than 2,372 winners. George tasted his first success on a filly called Syllable in a seven-furlong apprentice race for his old guv'nor Jack Waugh. It's quite some time ago, 31 August 1982 to be exact, when the old timer rode our hundredth flat winner, in the Paddock Handicap on Bri Eden at Epsom.

I couldn't help feeling chuffed for Kevin Darley when he won the Group One Queen Elizabeth Stakes at Ascot on the Terry Mills-trained Where or When. After winning Kevin jetted off to race the following day at Woodbine

Trainer Terry Mills with his Group I winner of the Queen Elizabeth Stakes, and Jockey Kevin Darley along with the colt's groom, Karen Jones.

in Canada where he rode the ex-John Dunlop-trained Fraudlein to win another Grade One race to win a cool £216,659. The following day, the much travelled jockey was brought down to earth when he was carted a full circuit of Hamilton Racecourse by the Donald Nolan-trained Square Dancer. I was watching this happen on Attheraces TV at home. As soon as KD got the animal stopped, he couldn't get the saddle off it quick enough and dived back into the weighing room for cover. It was so funny watching Kevin explaining to the ex-journey and hard man, jump jockey Don Nolan. Kevin went on to give up his remaining rides on account of exhaustion.

For a laugh, the following morning I rang his home. Debbie, Kevin's wife answered the phone. In an altered voice I asked her if Kevin was all right to ride a horse for me at Catterick next week. Debbie asked who was speaking, 'Donald Nolan,' I said. Straight away she said, 'You will have to ring his agent.'

I couldn't stop laughing, then Debbie realised it was me. She went on to enlighten me about the horse of Nolan's. She called it many names but never once by its racing name Square Dancer!

In the paper, there was a very nice photo taken by Edward Whitaker of winning trainer and stable lass Karen Jones watching Kevin Darley plant a kiss on Where or When after the QE 2 Stakes. I don't think Square Dancer had to worry, as there was no chance of KD kissing her!

It had been a right job trying to find the Olympia Theatre in Liverpool when we went there on 5 October. The Theatre was the venue of the Audley Harrison v. Wade Lewis fight. Bill Robinson and Brian Muir in the back of Jo's car and Dave (J) Bowes riding shotgun to me driving, were not a bit of help with directions. In the end, I stopped to ask a taxi driver to give us a lead to the theatre and we paid him. I didn't take my Jaguar, as I heard about the evils that happen to cars in Liverpool. (The Lancashire comedian, Bernard Manning. used to joke when he went to Liverpool at least once a year to visit his hubcaps!) We got a bit of a fright during the Super Featherweight title fight between Nicky Cook, the champion and Gary Thornhill, when the damned fire alarm inside the theatre went off, but no one took any notice of it and the fight carried on.

Boxer Audley Harrison

At the main event when Wade Lewis had been in the ring for ten minutes or so, the ringmaster announced for the third time, 'in the red corner from Wembley England, Audley Harrison'. Of course everyone was cheering and rooting for Audley and still no sign of him. Then, just as if it had been rehearsed football-fashion, all the Scouses in harmony, 'Audley where the f... are you?' When the star finally came into the ring, he wasn't there for long. Audley knocked the Yank out stone cold in the first round.

On Arc day, above all days, seeing as George Duffield wasn't going over to ride at Longchamps, his stepson AJ rang to see if I fancied a game of golf. You can count on one hand the times I have played a round of golf. To see us kitted out on the course with the proper gear would have made Tiger Woods proud. The last time I played before then was in Barbados and I had bought a new pair of white golf shoes. George had the first shot, which trickled on the ground for about six yards, followed by a few choice words. The jockey said, 'I will take that again', which wasn't any better! The first two holes went to me after George had lost a few balls and delivered a few more swear words. I don't know whether he kicked or knocked his trolley over, but his clubs were all over the place. On a bad day he can be like an underfed pit bull terrier. I have heard people say before that golf is an infuriating game. As this one proved, Mr Duffield showed little sign of being a sport and by his antics he was certainly no gentleman. On the eighth hole, I got to the green in three, he said he also got there in three. Counting must not have been his best subject at school. By the time we arrived back at his house with only one ball left between the three of us, the racing from France had finished.

It was good news for us British; Frankie Detorri had won the Prix de L'Arc de Triomphe on Marienbard, Godolphin-owned and Bin Suroor-trained. A great result was the David Nichols-trained Continent winning the Prix de L'Abbaye. The horse was owned by one of our ex-owners, Edward St George, owner of Lucayan Stud and was ridden by Daryl Holland. I decided I would definitely get round the connections for something for our auction, especially from David 'Dandy' who is just like a little banty cock, forthright and sure of himself. Not everyone's cup of tea, you take him as you find him. There is no kinder man. Dandy doesn't know how to say 'no' to a good cause. A few times I had been to charity events organised by his late secretary, Sarah Lunn, who invariably roped me in as auctioneer. Whatever the cause, it has always been richer for Dandy's presence. Sadly, Sarah was killed in a car crash. Aged only thirty-two, she was a lovely, outgoing girl, very popular, as was proved at her funeral at St Joseph's Church, Wetherby, when £3500 was donated in Sarah's memory towards a Bolder wheelchair, which was presented to George Fowler, a beneficiary of IJF, at Catterick Races.

'Sarah Lunn 1971-2003' was engraved on a silver plaque and fixed on the back of the chair. It was only just over a year since her young brother died and the church collection from his funeral went to buy some garden furniture for a hospice at Boston Spa, Yorkshire. The Lunns are a lovely family, but have been so unlucky.

On the evening of Arc day, although I missed seeing the race on the box, I did manage to see the Great North Run on TV, which is a half marathon. I was speaking to Eileen Cullen as we had another meeting at St James Hospital the following day at 9 a.m., where we were hopefully going to come up with ways and means to refurbish and decorate the kiddies part of the building mentioned earlier. In conversation, Eileen said that she and a nurse at the hospital would run for the kids. Jo chipped in that she would too. When I arrived home, I rang Anne Duffield to ask if she would also do the run, as she has long legs that start from her armpits and wouldn't need to take as many strides as

Local girl Helen Davey, who ran in the Northern Marathon in support of the St Jame's kids.

the other girls; she declined as she has a breathing complaint. I would have willingly run for the kids but my knees were absolutely knackered as I was waiting for new ones. However, I gladly agreed to manage the team. We agreed we would start fundraising right away, get a charity number and the relevant forms for the next run. Although we hadn't lived here very long in our village of Hunton, on occasion I had seen a young lady by the name of Helen Davey, who is a serious runner in this area. Asking her one day what it was all about, her reply was she just enjoys running to keep fit. Thinking of channelling her sterling efforts into a worthwhile cause, I asked Helen if she would consider running in the next Northern Marathon in support of the St James' kids. Thankfully and readily, she agreed. I told Helen I would set about getting her some sponsors to make it worth her while so that the Leeds youngsters would benefit financially.

My birthday arrived, 7 October, but I wasn't complaining as I spent it at our meeting at St James' Hospital in Leeds. It went very well. We had the pleasure of the company of journalist John Morgan, plus the Yorkshire Post photographer and our plan to raise £50,000 to redecorate and refurbish the Outpatients' Department of the children's ward went out on Calendar TV. Everything went smoothly and according to plan, but I must admit a chill ran down my spine as one of the last times I came to St James Hospital was when I was an apprentice at Charlie Hall's Towton near Tadcaster yard some 50 years ago.

I went to visit my mum who was in there and very poorly. It was on her forty-eighth birthday and she died the same night. That was very sad; so young. I couldn't even say goodbye to her as she was in a coma.

At Catterick Races the day after my birthday, Jo and I went to saddle the horses up for our Alan, as he was on duty saddling Frascati to win at Southwell. We drew a blank at Catterick; the horses ran well having two seconds and two thirds. One of the seconds was Bonny Lad, who is owned by the England and Liverpool football star Michael Owen. Michael couldn't be there as he was attending a luncheon at No. 10 Downing Street. Following a chat to his mum, she told me she would get her famous son to send me a big signed photograph to auction later on at our barbecue. Even the following day the friendly punters at Catterick kept saying 'Happy Birthday for yesterday', as they had read the date in the *Racing Post*.

We were getting some very favourable feedback from the TV slot on Calendar and from the Yorkshire Post in connection with Jimmy's children's outpatients department. ASDA In The Community, from Normanton near

Wakefield went to look around the department. They said they could and would paint the place up; in addition they would also provide the paint. As Jiminy Cricket says: 'There's more.' ASDA were also giving two Christmas hampers to raffle for the cause. The Variety Club also rang to make an appointment for Monday 14 October, to see how they could help. Lesley Hallis, a freelance artist from Crossgates, Leeds, rang to give her services in helping to decorate the walls with paintings of Mickey Mouse etc. Kind people also donated cheques to the tune of £5000. Wasn't that just great? When Eileen Cullen rang me to tell me all this, she was ecstatic. We knew that if the trend continued, we would reach our target very soon.

At Newmarket Yearling Sales on 15 October, I had arranged to meet Joy Hawkins, to pick up some prints to benefit our big day. There were some very nice signed hunting prints, a dozen in total, which she gave me. There were also some racing prints, which she normally sells for £75 each, and she only charged me £300 for ten. Plus, she gave me several other prints to sell at auction. As the ten prints were from a Limited Edition of 275, it made them quite rare. I also bought from her a very nice framed 3'6' x 3' print of her famous IJF Christmas Card, and various other framed prints as well which she let me have for £400. In total I owed Joy £700 for our purchases but I knew we would make a tidy profit for the cause from them. I told Joy I would pay her when we had sold some and banked a few quid. She said she wasn't in a rush. Instead of selling them the same day at our barbecue and creating a glut of much the same, I decided to take the occasional one to functions to auction for our cause. I would also sell some on privately for a profit before our event. For good measure, Joy also gave me a Limited Edition framed print of racehorses walking around at the start of a race called 'Cheltenham in the Snow' to auction or sell on.

The following day Dave, (J) Bowes gave me £80 for one of the hunting prints and one of the racing prints. Dave Armstrong also gave me £40 for Joy's print of Dublin Taxis, which got our target down to £28,010.

England, Liverpool & Newcastle football star Michael Owen.

In the same week we saw the death of a lady at fifty-three who holds a permanent place in racing history. Meriel Tufnell, MBE, rode Scorched Earth to victory at Kempton Park in 1972 to become the first woman jockey to ride a winner in Britain. Muriel went on to become Lady Champion in England. She also rode winners in races all over Europe. Unfortunately, the lady developed the 'Big C'. Although she knew about her disease, and coped and handled it well, she declined treatment. The last time I had spoken to her was at

Goodwood Races the previous August. She was there as the Guest of Honour and to present the victor of the Lady of the Month Award with champagne. She was only a shadow of her old self, bravely and slowly getting around with a stick. At an hour-long funeral service, which she had planned herself, there was a 550-strong congregation at St Michael and All Angels Church, Lambourne. While planning her funeral, Muriel asked John Francome to do the reading. She had said to him, 'Make sure you brush your hair and don't drop your h's'!!' She was a tireless campaigner on behalf of the children's charity 'Sparks'. Two years previously, Muriel raised more than £4000 by playing 180 holes of golf in one day over seventeen hours. It's a good job it wasn't my jockey neighbour George Duffield playing 180 holes. It would have taken him seventeen weeks or maybe even seventeen years and seventeen tons of balls.

Henry Candy, the Wantage trainer, sent me a couple of nice photographs and in addition kindly posted me a racing plate worn by Kyllachy, the Champion Sprinter when he won the Nunthorpe Stakes at York, the last time he raced. The next season Kyllachy was to take up stud duties and stand at the Cheveley Park Stud in Newmarket. If I had had a suitable brood mare, I wouldn't have hesitated to send her to go visit him. The horse had lots of fans while racing, so I knew Henry's precious gift would create a lot of interest at our auction. Henry is no stranger to Group One success, as his horse Time Charter won the 1982 ridden by Billy Newnes.

On Monday 21 October, I attended one of our Trustees and Almoners meetings held at the Montcalm Hotel in London. We welcomed Jonathan Powell as a new Trustee. The IJF panel of Trustees are now: Lord Oaksey; Brough Scott; Sir Edward Cazalet; John Smith; Peter Scudamore; Simon Tindall; Simon McNeill; John Fairley; Jonathan Powell and yours truly. Not only is Jonathan Powell a very good racing writer, he and Bob Champion wrote *Champions Story* about Bob the jockey who made a comeback from cancer to win the 1981 Grand National on Aldaniti. A film was also made starring John Hurt, who played Bob.

To show all you kind people who send donations in to the IJF, buy Christmas cards and calendars or hold functions, give donations, leave legacies and so on, how we spend your money, one of the cases that came up was that of Dennis Wicket. His wife, Jane, wanted a surgical bed to ease her ex-jockey's bedsores and make their life a little better. In 1987, Dennis and Jane, who was pregnant at the time, were both riding in the Hunt Race at Crimp point-to-point in Cornwall. Dennis was in front when he and his horse fell. Jane went on and won the race without knowing the fate of Dennis, who was badly hurt. It took him ages to struggle around with the aid of a stick, then one day out walking he had a fall. Since that day Jane, who was having her best season point-to-pointing with seven winners, had to pack up riding to look after Dennis. Their son Oliver had never seen his Dad before the accident. Dennis had not spoken to or recognised anyone since the fall and had also been confined to a wheelchair. Needless to say, it was a unanimous vote with the Trustees, he got the bed. Another sad case was that of seventy-four-year-old Roy Carter, a jockey for many years, who lived in Wood Green, London, in the centre of a highly multi-cultural environment alongside many asylum seekers. He lived in a flat owned by the Council for thirty-eight years and was the only white person left on that street. Roy became vulnerable due to the high population of young people in the area and had recently been mugged twice outside his house, threatened at knifepoint in the local park and had his home broken into while he was in it. It all shows what some of today's society is like; even the internal doors in the living room were heavily bolted. We were able to move him into a smart flat with a really nice view looking across the Newmarket gallops.

It's a great life being retired, as Jo and I proved one Sunday in October (it was the 20th). More than likely, punters think we crawl out of bed at nine or ten a.m., mooch about in pyjamas reading the papers while eating breakfast waiting for Attheraces to come on the box. I can honestly tell you that is not so. We got up at 7 a.m., fed the ducks and the fish in and on our pond, the nine horses we have stabled at home and the three-and-a-half couples of dogs, three cats, twenty-five pigeons, two guinea fowl, twenty-two hens, bantams and the wild birds. Then we feed a further four retired racehorses, a pony and six heifers in two fields we rent in the village. We then came back and put five yearlings on our horse walker while we mucked them out, hayed and watered them. Then we brought them back off the walker and tidied them up, as they belonged to trainer Anne Duffield. (Thankfully, they were only here for a couple of weeks in quarantine, they then moved on to be broken). Then we put the other four horses on the walker, which are in two paddocks with a field shelter in each. Lastly, we dived into the house at around 9 a.m. to have our first cup of tea and an egg-and-bacon sandwich. Ten minutes later, we would be

Some of my pack of dogs at Cockerham – always pleased to please.

sweeping up and doing the rest of the stable duties until about 12 a.m., when we finally finished. Then it would be in the bath to be changed and ready for Anne to bring some of her owners along to see the yearlings.

When Ann and George were showing two quite expensive colts to the hopeful new owners, they fed them a fair proportion of bullshit. For instance, if one of the colts did well as a racehorse, he had a good enough pedigree to breed with. They were so convincing, I very nearly got my cheque book out to beat them to buying it. The Bride was dishing out coffee and biscuits and I thought Anne was going to choke on hers when I asked her if I should ring the vets to cut the colts whilst they were here.

We're still kept busy, but now we are retired we can go down the road we choose; we love it. I couldn't imagine me being without animals, especially horses and dogs. Here's a photo of my pack when we were at Cockerham.

A day, a week, a year; it just all flies by so quickly. To speed the job up a bit, for The Bride's birthday, I considered buying her a pair of Hunter Wellingtons and a wheelbarrow. If we got any more horses in for Christmas, I thought about getting her a wheelbarrow with an engine. Looking back it's marvellous how we managed to fit the workload in when we were training. Busy as we were when training, every year we spent three weeks holiday in Barbados with Michael and Gay Jarvis.

One evening while waiting for dinner to cook, Jo and I watched the Dales Diary on the box. Pete Edmonds, employed by the NFU in London was posted up here to the North of England as Secretary of Northallerton NFU. He enjoyed the life so much that in his lunch breaks he would go to some remote place on the hills or in a village and practise playing his clarinet. In due course, he formed a jazz band, which he named the 'Swale Valley Stompers'. On telly they were brilliant. Pete said on the box that he had played on trains, in village halls and at many other different venues. If he's that keen, seeing the Swale Valley Stompers perform on the telly, I decided I would try and get hold of Pete and his band to see if they would perform at the following year's barbecue. Peter Stewart, along with Gary Gibson, the John Lennon lookalike, sang for us at the previous barbecue. Unfortunately Peter recently suffered a brain haemorrhage and was taken to the Intensive Care Unit of Middlesborough Hospital.

On the last Saturday in October, although I had to decline the invitation to George Duffield's book launch, as it was on the same day, I was very privileged and proud to have been asked to open the new grandstand at Carlisle Racecourse, from which the IJF benefited by £1000. There was also a parade of champion racehorses which included the almost white Better Times Ahead; Bindaree (2002 National Winner ridden by Jim Culloty); Direct Route (Mumm Melling Chase Winner); Earth Summit (1998 winner of the English; Scottish and Welsh Grand National ridden by Carl Llewellyn); Jodami (1993 Gold Cup Winner and three consecutive Hennessy Gold Cups wins, who was trained here in Yorkshire by Peter Beaumont; Red Marauder 2001 National Winner ridden by Richard Guest; Sparkey Gale, Cheltenham Winner; The Grey Monk and others.

Carlisle is a track where I have ridden winners as a jockey and trained quite a few over the years. Many a good day out has been had on the Cumbrian racecourse. However, things there have not always been rosey. At Carlisle many years ago, 13 April 1968 to be precise, having my first ride after returning to race riding from breaking a leg in five places at Wetherby (which took nine months to mend), I rode a horse called Oban Bay that fell, breaking my left wrist. On another occasion while still training, we won with a filly named Frisky Miss, ridden in a sprint by Paul Roberts, one of our apprentices. However, the filly was unjustly disqualified. I am not one to throw toys out of the pram without good reason, but I felt like a farmer I knew in Berwick-in-Elmet where a burglar visited his goose hut just four days before Christmas and left a note which read: 'Maurice Wood, your geese are good, but not so very fat. Out of the eleven I took seven and what do you think of that?' On account of the Stewards' injustice, I named a horse Carlisle Banditos. They must have forgiven me for that as in my retirement year, Clerk of the Course, Johnny Fenwicke-Clennel named a race in my honour – The EBF Jack Berry Stakes. I would have loved to have won the race with our runner Red Sonny, but 'sods law', it ran like an absolute prat and finished last, just in front of the ambulance! Also, to commemorate the Course's former local trainer, GW Richards (simply known to everyone as 'the Boss'), who died in 1998 aged sixty-eight, the Carlisle Executive unveiled a statue of him. Since Gordon passed away, his son Nicky, the former amateur jockey has

GW Richards. A great Trainer of Jumpers and Jockeys.

successfully taken their yard over. Gordon was a great trainer of jumpers and of jockeys too. Champion Jockeys Ron Barry and Jonjo O'Neill both rode for him. It was fitting for the day as, now a leading jump trainer, Jonjo ran seven horses and three of them won. If the Boss had been looking on, he would have been very proud.

Amongst some of Gordon's best horses were Lucius and Hello Dandy, both Grand National Winners, plus Playlord, Titus Oates, Sea Pigeon and Man Alive. But whenever I spoke to Gordon, his pride and joy was the winner of the Queen Mother Champion Chase in his final year, One Man. The Boss's total tally of winners over jumps was a colossal 1911. It was a hard man that didn't have a lump in his throat or tear in his eye on 29 September 1998, when the ex-Champion jockey and now Inspector of Courses, Ron Barry, rode the almost white Better Times Ahead in front of the hearse that took the Boss to his final resting place. Fittingly, he was the last winner Gordon trained.

I drove fairly urgently back from Carlisle to see the Breeders Cup Meeting on TV, coming this year from Arlingdon where the first Breeders Cup Distaff took place. Winner of nine out of of ten races, Azeri was running in the same colours as the famous Arazi who had also won a Breeders' Race. The filly flew the gate and never looked like getting caught. Imperial Gesture, the Godolphin-owned filly ran third to net the 'boys in blue' a cool £164,684. One would have to win a fair few Novice Hurdles around Carlisle to earn that kind of money!

Racing now, though, has hit a bit of a bad patch. On 27 April 27 1990, we won a crap maiden race at Carlisle with a two-year-old named Time for the Blues ridden by Kevin Darley, which earned his owner £2,451. Fifteen years on, we often don't race for much more. It's often less, and it's not just Carlisle, it's everywhere. Those days costs, wages and expenses bore no relation to what they are now. What's it all about?

The procedure in America is totally different and it gives the impression that no expense is spared. Every runner has a lead horse and is ponied to the start, and there's no end of stall handlers down at the gate – at least one per horse. It takes seconds to load the horses into plush stalls that really do make ours look like claustrophobic traps. The build-up for the Breeders' Cup Mile, Rock of Gibraltar's race, nearly had me in a muck sweat. He looked a picture. Let's hope he makes it eight Group Ones on the trot.

Unfortunately, it wasn't to be. Landseer, Rock of Gibraltar's stable companion, broke a leg in the race and impeded her stable pal's challenge at a time when the Rock was really getting into top gear. Rock was really travelling at the finish, but ran out of distance to finish second to the French horse, Dome Driver. It was too late to push the champagne back into the bottle, but I did feel sorry for the horse. He looked as if he should have won. Had Rock of Gibraltar won his race it would have been a good result for our brood mare, Bolshaya, which we own in partnership with the Deuters and the Brown, a half sister to Bolshoi and our Royal Ascot winner of the Kings Stand, who had been covered by the Rock's father, Danehill. I thought the stud fee at the time was a fortune at £70,000. However, because Danehill had sired so many Group One winners around the world, his owners Coolmore Stud increased his stud fee to £200,000. At this time we part own a lovely colt foal by Danehill, and, in view of that, for us, Danehill can't sire enough winners. In the richest race of the night, The Filly and Mare Turf, Zenda trained by John Gosden ran no sort of race after being hampered several times. Islington, ridden by Kieren Fallon, finished third and was surely the unlucky one in running. He got pushed all over the place. I must say, if I ran a good horse in America, I would consider letting one of the American jockeys ride the horse, as the jockeys from our shores get no favours done to them. However, John Gosden trained in America with a lot of success, so he knows what he's doing. Aidan O'Brien's horse, Hold That Tiger, ridden by Kieren Fallon finished third in the Breeders' Juvenile nine-furlong race. The British horses were running well, but they just couldn't win. Thankfully, High Chaparral, the colt who had previously won the English and Irish Derby's and finished third in the year's Arc, won the John Deere 1½ mile Breeders' Cup Turf, the second highest prize of the evening. I didn't want to appear brash and greedy, but I decided I would ask Aidan if he would favour our barbecue with a photo of High Chaparral. For the record, Rock of Gibraltar, the horse Aidan donated the photo of to the previous year's barbecue, was retired to stud and stands with his father, Danehill, at the world famous Coolmore Stud in Ireland.

The final race at Arlington was the world's leading flat race, the 1¾ mile Breeder Cup Classic with a purse of £1,424,658 to the winner and was won by rank outsider Volponi. This kind of money is obscene. Think of the stakes we raced for when I was an apprentice at Charlie Halls in Yorkshire. In the 1955/56 season, the year the Doorknocker ridden by Harry Sprague won the Champion Hurdle, our yard was the country's leading National Hunt Stable with forty winners, which added up to £15,573 in total prize money.

After watching the end of the Manchester vs. Aston Villa drawn game, I opened the mail – it was good news as there was a parcel with the St Leger winner's shoe and an accompanying letter of authenticity stating Bollin Eric had worn the plate on the 14 September, when he won the St Leger. Tim Easterby, the trainer, and Brian Greenly, who was Eric's blacksmith, signed it.

John Carroll, true to his word, sent a really nice photo of Invincible Spirit signed by himself and John Dunlop of when the connections won the valuable Group One Stanley Leisure Sprint race a few weeks earlier at Haydock Park. Bollin Eric was a very popular win in the St Leger, being a northern-owned, ridden and trained horse.

David Bowes 'joiner' (I put that in as there is a David Bowes 'farmer') now retired, has been a family friend for years. In fact, forty years ago he was best man at our wedding. So you could say we've been good mates for a long time. Dave said he would make a mount for the racing plate to be then taken to the jewellers where the horse and his connection names would be engraved on a silver plate. It was really exciting and it gave me a great buzz touching the very same racing plate Eric took round Doncaster when he won the St Leger, the oldest classic in the world. Even the soil was still in the grooves which I left in! John Carroll is also a very popular northern jockey who has come a long way since he rode his first winner at Pontefract in 1981, on Heliva. I knew the connections fans would bid well when these two gems come up for sale. Out of decency and appreciation I put pen to paper to thank John and Tim for their contributions. There was a lot of hype over the great horses that ran at the Breeders' Cup Meeting at Arlington. It wants noting at this early stage that we could have seen a horse at Doncaster out of the top drawer in the winner of the Trophy in Brian Boru ridden by Kevin Darley, trained by the all-conquering Aiden O'Brian and owned by Sue Magnier. He is aptly named after a brilliant Irish warrior who kicked out the Vikings in Cashel in around 1002 AD. At this stage, I didn't want to say, 'I told you so', as the proof of the pudding is in the eating. I knew it would be around next June, Derby time, when we

Adrian Maguire with his family, recovering from the broken neck which forced his retirement.

might have heard a lot more about this colt who is by the great sire of great horses, Sadler's Wells.

On 20 October, it was shown just how dangerous a jump jockey's life can be. It was announced Adrian Maguire would be forced to retire after breaking his neck in a fall at Warwick in March. Adrian surely must have been one of the best jump jockeys never to win a championship; he certainly was in my time of racing. His British record of wins over jumps is a staggering 1024, which puts him in sixth place in the winning jump jockeys to date. There are only six other jump jockeys today who have ridden over 1000 career winners. They are: Tony McCoy; Richard Dunwoody; Peter Scudamore (one of our IJF Trustees registered his 1,000th at Worcester in 1989 on Baluchi); John Francome; Stan Mellor (the first to reach 1,000) and Peter Niven. Adrian Maguire missed out being Champion jump jockey, but as a man he was already a champion. Not many people in racing have a bad word to say about him. Adrian's best moment was probably when he won the Cheltenham Gold Cup on the Toby Balding-trained Cool Ground in 1992 – a great day for Toby.

It's nice when some lesser lights get a mention, as did seventy-nine-year-old Mary Howey. She was voted Champagne Victor Lady of the Month. The award was for her extraordinary care and devotion over the past three decades to her son, Gordon, a fifty-four-year-old tetraplegic with paralysis of all four limbs. Gordon was one of our most promising conditional jump jockeys until a car, in which he was a passenger, went off the road and into a ditch. At first, he thought he had broken a collarbone, then both collarbones. Then he realised he couldn't move. The driver of the car wasn't insured, so there was no compensation as is so often the case. The Injured Jockeys Fund provided the lifeline. We tried to get him to come to Tenerife on one of our holidays. However, he declined because since he broke his neck, he cannot bear hot weather. Gordon can swivel his head and upper shoulders and slightly move an arm and a few fingers. Mary has cared for him without any outside assistance since he was discharged from Mandeville Hospital that year, 1973. Mary, you're a star.

Chapter Three

Forty Years to the Day

•

On 30 October, it was forty years to the day Jo and I got married at the Doncaster Registry Office. As stated before, Dave Bowes ('Joiner') was best man. To celebrate the occasion of our fortieth anniversary, we invited him down to the house to share a bottle of Laurent Perrier Rose Brut champagne. A lot of water had gone under the bridge since our wedding day. We had the occasional 'domestic' during that time, but I have no intention of trading her in. Many times I have said there are two things I wouldn't sell: one is The Bride, and the other the old horse, OI Oyston, who won twenty-four races for us when we trained. But not just because he won all those races; he was a pal. The old fella is still here with us looking great. A competition was held in the inviting racing personnel and celebrities to choose their favourite racehorse. No guessing the horse I chose. Arkle won the competition beating Red Rum and Desert Orchid. Arkle was a great horse, winner of twenty-seven races, which included three Cheltenham Gold Cups. In the same competition was Golden Miller, the horse that won five successive Cheltenham Gold Cups and the 1938 Grand National. Best Mate was the most exciting chaser around at the time and the winner of the previous two Cheltenham Gold Cups. His trainer Henrietta Knight was very economical putting miles on the horse's clock, always having him cherry ripe for the Festival.

The Bride, OI Oyston and the dog, Olly.

*Jo and JB –
forty years ago.*

Remember the group of owners Anne Duffield brought down to our spread to see the yearlings? Well, Tim Townsend and his wife Linda were amongst them. For our barbecue the year previously they went to France to get the wine, the pair of them also helped in other ways and were good bidders at the auction. However, the day after the visit Tim told Linda he didn't feel very well. He was shaking as if he had the 'flu and Linda packed him off to bed. Sadly, the next morning he died, he was only forty-eight years old. What a sad occasion it was going to his funeral. Tim was such a nice fellow. As would be expected, the crematorium was packed. Recently I seem to be attending more funerals than christenings.

On a much brighter note, we all start off in life the same with a blank sheet of paper. I am delighted to say our ex-jockey Kevin Darley has done particularly well for himself. Reading *The Post,* there was a good picture of Kevin, fresh from riding his 2000th British winner at Nottingham. He was on the John Dunlop-trained Heir-to-Be that marked Kevin the third most winning jockey then currently riding, behind Pat Eddery and George Duffield.

What a day to be out on the road as I was on Friday 18 November, the volume of traffic was horrendous. I was guest speaker at the Yorkshire Sport House Annual Dinner at the Livestock Centre in York. Digby Law, a neighbour and his wife Cynthia were going, so I scrounged a lift with them. It took just under three hours to travel the fifty miles on account of an accident on the A1. We were an hour late, which was a bit embarrassing but they waited for us. As you can imagine, I opened up my speech as all the horsey people there knew Digby, by telling them it took us three hours to travel the fifty miles in Digby's car and that I used to have a car like that. Thinking I had better not let the opportunity slip to do a bit of good for our cause and for the St James Outpatients children's ward, I took a couple of Joy Hawkins's unframed hunting prints to auction. The first in aid of the IJF made £150 reducing our target to £27,860, and the other fetched £170 to benefit the St James kids. The night went really well and we had a lot of laughs. I finally ended up back at home at 1.30 a.m.

I know footballers are often dubbed as overpaid, over-rated and over-sexed prima donnas, but speak as you find. A lot of worthy causes would be much poorer without them. I went to the Sunderland v. Tottenham match and Sunderland legend Niall Quinn announced his retirement. It wasn't long before Niall's testimonial, where he received £1,000,000 and he gave the whole lot of it to charity. £450,000 of it was donated to the Sunderland Royal

Hospital towards building a new children's outpatients unit. The year before the Sunderland v. Spurs match, Niall gave trainer Kevin Ryan one of his Irish International Caps to be auctioned in aid of the IJF at our BBQ which made £1,000 for the cause.

Brian Robe, one of our Alan's' owners, himself a Sunderland supporter and whose firm Comtec helped to build the London Eye, bought it with a successful bid of £1000. Just think how many charity functions you go to and see a signed football or shirt being auctioned off for various causes given by footballers or their clubs.

For the BBQ the previous year, David Bowes (the farmer) kindly lent us a very big bull that we put in our field shelter

Sunderland legend Niall Quinn

and closed the gates so that the punters could get close to the beast to guess his weight. Colette, the daughter of Laurie Dolan, a retired York bookmaker I have known for many years who is a neighbour and was a friend of Paddy Farrell's, told me as a pet she had a huge Clydesdale carthorse which stands over eighteen-hands high and weighs around three-quarters of a tonne. As you can imagine I soon had him booked for the following year's BBQ – not to eat of course but to guess his weight.

It was an early start on Remembrance Day, as I had to catch the 7 a.m. train from Darlington to Kings Cross to attend a Trustee away day of the IJF at the Montcalm Hotel at 10 am. On the agenda were plans to talk about things to better the fund in general and to elect a Vice-Chairman and a Treasurer, two positions we had never had in the past. It's all getting more technical. I suppose it's up to us old farts with our old fashioned ways to get a bit more up to date, but hopefully not to take away the personal touch and the feeling we have for our beneficiaries. We hold IJF meetings at various venues across the country and we are also getting some younger faces on board, which is a good thing. We don't want a reputation for being like Dad's Army!

John Smith, the retiring Clerk of the Course at York, and fellow IJF Trustee and I travelled back on the 4.30 p.m. train together. On the opposite seat sat an old boy and what looked like his daughter. When the food and drink trolley came round he shouted real loud as he must have been deaf: 'Two coffees and a sandwich,' to the young man serving from the trolley.

'How much?'

'That'll be £5.60 please.'

'How much?' 'What!' He yelled, 'take it all back,' pushing the goods back to the lad, '£5.60 it's a bloomin' disgrace, how much is a sandwich?' '£3.40,' was the reply.

'How much is coffee?'

JB, Sir Edward Cazalet & Princess Anne share a joke at a IJF function.

'£1.10.'
'For the two?'
'No, each.'
'Go on then, I'll have the coffees, but it's an absolute bloody rip off!'
Needless to say not only we were laughing but the whole coach was.

The following day, Jo and I were invited to attend Lord Zetland's beautiful home Aske Hall near Richmond to see and help financially, a demonstration of assistance dogs called Canine Partners. The dogs are trained to help disabled people mainly those in wheelchairs. They fill up and empty washing machines, help their owners to dress, bring the paper, the portable phone and many more things. They were brilliant, and most importantly on account of the help from the dogs, their handlers enjoyed a much better quality of life. Also in attendance were Fred Trueman and his wife Veronica. I knew Fred quite well as he was one of our owners at Cockerham. Fiery Fred was possibly the fastest bowler in cricket ever. A very tough and hard man, but his heart was in the right place. He told me he would do a guest speaker event for the Canine partners. It's great how lots of cricketers like racing, as we also trained in the past for David Brown, Bob Willis and Ian Botham.

I couldn't help to admire the success of Media Puzzle, when he won Australia's richest race the Melbourne Cup for the second time for his trainer Dermot Weld. I put pen to paper to ask the Irish crack trainer if he could see his way to give our cause a photo or plate to auction at our BBQ. Media Puzzle was ridden by Damian Oliver, which was quite an emotional event as his brother Jason died seven days earlier following a fall from a horse called Savage Cabbage, trained by Steve Wolf. He was crushed by the horse in a barrier trail at a racecourse school for young horses in Perth. The horse broke a leg and had to be put down. Damian was in Perth with his mother following his brother's accident as he lay there on a life support machine, and had given thought to missing the Melbourne Cup. As in Damian's own words, it was hard to take watching his brother lay there so helpless, but deep inside him he knew Jason would want him to ride. Damian flew straight back to Perth to attend his brother's funeral and in doing so missed the last two days of the Flemington Carnival. Following the samples taken from Savage Cabbage, Phenylbutazone and Oxyphenylbutazone, both non-steroid anti-inflammatories were found in the horse's system. Needless to say, West Australian Turf Club stewards held an inquiry into Jason's fall. They suspended trainer Steve Wolf for two years for improperly administering a drug to Savage Cabbage.

On 15 November, Jo and I got up early to get all our jobs finished before we set off for a couple of days racing at Cheltenham. When we arrived there the place was really buzzing with a large record crowd, good weather and great racing. We were late in getting off to Cheltenham as, 1) I forgot my pills for arthritis; 2) I forgot my binoculars (and that's important as you need a good pair of bins to sight most of the horses I back) and; 3) we forgot the invitation card to the Open 2002 Champions' Dinner. Any one thing and we could have hacked it and kept going, but not all three! Luckily, we had only travelled about six miles and it's a good job we did turn back, as on the invitation for the dinner and dance for the Saturday night after racing, it stated Black Tie, which we hadn't accounted for.

At Cheltenham, it was great to see so many old faces of the jump world. After the racing we stayed with Chris and Antonia Deuters as we always do when we visit Cheltenham. During the course of a lovely meal prepared by Chris, he told me he had filled up three jars with 1p, 2p, 5p and 10p pieces and in all they weighed in all about four stone. I asked him if he would like a good home for them. As Chris and Antonia are great supporters of the IJF or any other good cause, I told them about Jimmy's kids. They readily gave the coins to me for them. I thought it would be good fun for the kids to count the money and get it ready to bank. However, Sister Eileen said not as they might nick it!

'You're joking!' I said

'No, it's a fact,' she said.

When I mentioned that to my old pal John Morgan, who received the MBE from the Queen for his charity work and who writes for the *Yorkshire Post* and is a bit of a comedian, he said, 'Oh yes, that'll be right, in that part of Leeds it's so rough that Alsatians walk round in pairs.'

John, who says there is more fun at a Lancashire funeral than at a Yorkshire wedding, depending which county he is in as it gets reversed, invariably, at whatever function, always tells the same jokes and has done for years. Here is a couple that spring to mind:

Two Irish jockeys were killed when their car hit a tree in Dublin. The IRA said they planted the tree.

Michael and Paddy were staying at a Hotel in Belfast one night when it was blown up while Paddy had gone to buy a paper. On his return Paddy was searching for Michael in the rubble and hears a noise.

'Is that you Michael?'

My old pal, John Morgan MBE at a Red Shirt Night in Pontifract.

'Michael can you hear me?'
'Yes, yes, I'm here!'
'Where are you?'
'Here.'
'Where?'
'Here in room 137.'
Paddy phones home.
'Is that Dublin 3, 33, 33, 33, 3?'
'Yes it is.'
'Will you ring 999 for me. I have my finger stuck in the 3.'
To be fair, not all of John's jokes are about Irishmen.

Anyway, back to the jars of money. I couldn't resist the temptation to weigh the money on our bathroom scales when I got home – 4st 8lbs. I think that should be about right, but my missus always says the lying beggars are weighing heavy!! Nothing to do with what she puts down her neck!

In between races on Saturday I helped 'Chicky' Oaksey (Almoner), Jeremy Richardson and Karen Hatton (Secretary) to sell Christmas Cards and Calendars from the IJF stall. In the first two days at Cheltenham, the sales amounted to over £20,000. Henrietta Knight gave me the very nice big-framed picture that was signed by the connections of Best Mate, the previous year's Gold Cup Winner, as she promised it for our auction.

I really rated this fellow, I knew he had a fair way to go to beat Arkle's three times winner of the Cheltenham Gold Cup, 1964-1966 and Golden Millers fine 1932-1936 record, but Best Mate was only seven with very little mileage on his clock. Under Hen's care he had every chance, he oozed class and jumped for fun. The Open Dinner 2002 was to celebrate the season's champion to jumping. The first three went to eight consecutive years' Champion AP

*Best Mate oozed class
and jumped for fun.*

McCoy, with no less than 289 winners he had ridden in the season, to his credit even beating Sir Gordon Richards' record of 269 wins set in 1947. The award crowned Tony Champion of Champions. Next was a special award to Adrian Maguire for his outstanding bravery and last but not least was to our founder member and now President of the IJF, Lord John Oaksey.

Adrian and John received a well-deserved standing ovation. Looking down the list of Champion Jockeys since 1945 there were some very famous and formidable names. To name just a few of them; Tim Molony, Fred Winter, Dick Francis, Josh Gifford, Ron Barry, Tim Brookshaw, John Francome, Tommy Stack, Peter Scudamore, Jonjo O'Neill, Bob Davis, Graham Thorner, Brian Marshall, and the 1946-1947 Champion Jockey Jack and his wife, Betty Dowdeswell who were in attendance and looking good. But, note the difference in totals, Jack, who was born in 1917, was Champion Jockey with just 58 winners. Today, with the increased fixtures, leading jockeys ride well over 100 winners in a season.

As you can see here on the list, there were some characters there. I thoroughly enjoyed every minute of the whole two days but all good things have to come to an end. Jo and I took turns at driving home, although I must admit The Bride did have the lion's share. By the time we retired between the sheets after emptying all the gear and taking the shopping she bought at Cheltenham out of the car, it was 4.30 a.m. As everyone who knows me will know, that wasn't much of an excuse to lie in bed the following morning, so with eyes like piss holes in the snow, I was up and about before 7 a.m. feeding all the mouths that were glad to see their old mate back from his vacation.

Talking about vacation reminds me. A few years ago whilst we were training at Cockerham, Geoff Dawes, one of our owners, a lovely man who was a partner in a Banana Farm in South Africa, asked me if I would like to accompany

The Bride: Jo, my wife.

him to visit the farm. We would also spend ten days or so, with friends of his in Rhodesia first, which was great and we had a marvellous time. Every day, I rode out at Barrowdale Park Racecourse for an English trainer who had gone out there to train. On our return from Johannessburg, Geoff had very bad stomach pains. While we were in the Duty Free Shop at the airport, Geoff broke wind quietly.

Well, I have never smelt anything like it in my life! The released gas travelled so fast it got everywhere. To be fair, the Duty Free Shop wasn't particularly busy, but every single person except for the poor ladies who were working being the counters vacated the building. Geoff kept telling me how bad he felt. I must admit I was worried because I had to sit next to him on the plane and if he did that again while we were in the air, the pilot would have to do an emergency landing. What would happen if we were flying over water? On the plane on the way back home, he honestly messed himself. He asked me if I would tell a crew member. I rang the bell and an air hostess came. Being quite embarrassed (she probably thought I was related to Norman Collier), as I struggled with my words, as the hostess was a real good looking young 'piece'. Geoff helped me out in his Cockney accent and very bluntly said, 'Ay love, I've shit myself.' Was I embarrassed?!

'Pardon sir?' She said

'I've shit myself.'

Had there been a hole to bolt down I would have. She had a chat to Geoff, sprayed him with a deodourant and told him to 'stay put and hang on for a couple of hours, as when we arrive in Luanda we will be stopping for fuel and we will get you cleaned up then'. 'Effing hell, I thought … two hours!

When we reached Luanda, Portuguese soldiers with guns escorted the passengers who had chosen to disembark from the plane across the tarmac to a big Nissan hut type of building, where there were lots of tables and chairs. Needless to say, I was one of the first off! When we were all in the building, the soldiers closed the door and stood guard on the inside. In the corner were a couple of women with a counter, something like our WI ladies in hospital selling tea, coffee and bits of things and there was also a post box. I bought a post card and a stamp and wrote a few words like 'had a great time and on my way home'. I addressed it to The Bride and posted it. The soldiers held us there just like prisoners, or for a better word, hostages, for nearly three hours until the plane was allowed to take off again. Thankfully, Geoff had recovered and was no more trouble. The card I posted never arrived home. However, at the next Doncaster yearling sales I bought a yearling colt – unfortunately it wasn't very good. And what do you think I named him? – Jo'burg Special. Geoff has since died, but I'm sure he wouldn't mind me telling you this tale, as many was the time I reminded him he would only have laughed. He was a great sport and loved a bit of fun.

Jo and I met quite a number of Tim and Linda Townsend's friends at Anne Duffield's for a rather sad farewell to Tim. George, riding Anne's hack Stripey, scattered Tim's ashes on the gallops. I am sure Tim would have liked that as he and his wife Linda were great friends of the Duffields and were down at the yard most weekends. They both loved the place. Linda donated the collection money from Tim's funeral for our cause, which amounted to £1,026 – a sum proving how popular a man he was. The funds were banked into the IJF account. Tim worked hard for our cause when he was alive and continued to do so in death. Our target now stood at £26,855.

Scott Taylor, the northern jump jockey, got very badly hurt in a fall while riding T Kay Dan in a novice chase at Perth in 1999, which finished his career. The IJF will be there to help Scott for the rest of his life, but quite rightly his fellow jockeys wanted to help. So they staged many events of all kinds, up and down the country. The southern jockeys played their northern colleagues at football. Jockeys Richard Johnson, Xavier Aizpur and Robert Thornton got sponsors and dyed their hair for Scott's cause. If you saw the flat jockey George Duffield at the races with blue hair, it was nothing to do with the Scott

L to r, Stan Mellor, Trevor Hemmings, Scott Taylor, JB & Jonathon Haynes at Haydock Park in aid of the Princess Royal Trust for Carers.

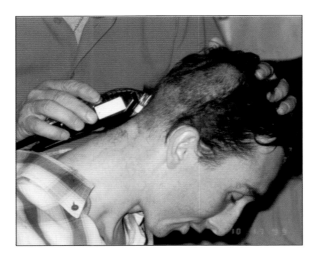

Tony Culhane gets the treatment in aid of Scott Taylor.

Taylor Appeal Auction at the Under Whitestone Cliffe pub near Thirsk. It was a colour rinse that went wrong. I conducted the auction, which raised over £10,000 for Scott. A fair amount of it was raised by a top northern jockey Tony Culhane's head shave, performed by a man in a red shirt.

Johnny Bradbourne, father of Mark the National Hunt Jockey, arranged a dinner dance in Edinburgh; he even got the brilliant Irish band, The Dubliners, over to entertain. It was a cracking night, jockeys and ex-jockeys, Norman Williamson, Robbie Supple, Jonjo O'Neill, Brian Harding, Peter Dunn, Tony McCoy, Tony Dobbin, Seamus Durak and myself got up on stage with The Dubliners and sang their famous song, 'The Seven Drunken Nights'. It was a great honour to be in the same room as them, never mind being allowed to perform with them, as they are brilliant.

Whilst attending the Champion Diner at Cheltenham, I was talking to Seamus Durack and he mentioned what a night it had been and asked if I had a photo of us all as it had appeared in a newspaper at the time. John Grossick, the Scottish photographer, took the photo so I rang John to get a big copy from him to send to Seamus – who had said he would get all the boys in to

The Dubliners in full flow at the Scott Taylor Appeal in Edinburgh.

sign it and send it back to me to get it framed for our shindig to auction. The jump jocks are very popular, so I knew it would go down well and raise quite a bit for our cause.

For many years, Jo and I had been invited to Ruth and John Barrett's (and John's sister, Ann Hartley) House, friends of ours who live together near Cockerham, for a new season's Beaujolais party. We sampled the wine, had a good feed and a good chat mainly about racing. We always stay overnight and it's great. Whilst we were there this time, on 21 November, John and Ruth bought one of Joy's prints for £60 and John's sister, Ann, bought one for £100, bringing our target down to £26,680.

Gee Armitage sent me the photo she promised me for our auction, of AP McCoy breaking the all-time most winning jockey record on Mighty Montefalco at Uttoxeter. She sent it via our Sam and his partner Carole when we stayed the weekend with them at The Village in Dudley. It's signed by Tony and mounted in a really nice mounted frame with a gold edge. It should go down a bomb and benefit the IJF quite a sum. It was funny, on the way home from Sam's we passed a big dirty wagon, and some bright spark had written through the dirt 'Bin Laden's in here'. Jo cracked up laughing when she saw it, as every morning as soon as I have fed all the animals on the place I make a cup of tea, then I turn on the telly to listen to the news and say, 'Let's see if they've caught Bin Laden'.

On November 26, Jo and I went with George and Ann Duffield to Newcastle Races as George had only got himself a National Hunt Licence to ride Anne's bumper horses. Wouldn't you think he would take off to Spain in the winter and get a break? At his age, you would think so, but I can tell you G Duffield, who was fifty-six a couple of days after our trip to Newcastle, doesn't act or feel his age and is forever messing about. Fancy, at that age, taking the bread out of the poor jump jockey's mouths. He should be ashamed of himself. Once, when he and the leggy one Anne were attending a boring seminar and got separated in the room, Anne sent George a text message on his yuppie telling how boring and what a waste of time the gathering was, and asked 'do you fancy a shag?' Only inadvertently, the silly mare had sent it to someone else's mobile number that was stored in her phone. She must get the hots on impulse. I know for a fact she is having it off with her gardener. All will be revealed later. On another occasion we were at the Bedale Hunt Ball and George, the silly beggar, got the band to announce and play 'Happy Birthday' for my seventieth birthday. It wasn't even the same month, and at the time I was a good bit off being seventy!! The horse that George rode at Newcastle was called Nailbiter and having his initial race. George was like a young apprentice having his first ride.

The following day we went to George Moore's Middleham stables to pick up some horseshoe nails he said I could have to get the Bollin Eric, Kyllachy and Invincible plates mounted. Carol, his missus, gave me a framed-signed photo of Steve Cauthen and Lester Piggott. She also gave me a black and white photo of jockeys and trainers taken many years ago at some function in York. One man in the photo is her father, Steve Nesbitt, who was a good pal of mine but he sadly died aged only fifty-one in 1982 after losing a long battle with cancer. You never heard anyone say a bad word about Steve; he was a lovely fellow. In the photo are trainers and jockeys past and present. I knew that no doubt it would create a lot of interest at our 'do' and I would be putting a bid in for it that's for sure. Some of the guys' names from the photo are: Mark Birch; Alan Horrocks; Steve Norton; Willie Carson; Eric Eldin; Clive Eccleston; Kevin Leason (before he had a sex change operation); John Lowe; Frank Carr; Jimmy Etherington; John Higgins; Brian Connorton; Chris Dwyer; Gerry Kelly; John Seagrave and others. It really is fascinating. George and Anne were coming to our house for dinner so I thought I'd show it to George to see if he would place a bid.

I showed George the photo and he thought it was great. He was over the moon reminiscing, telling me who was who. The bottom line is that he likes it a lot and said he would start the bidding with £100. While we were having dinner, we decided to hold the BBQ on 20 July, as this is the only Sunday without any racing.

Eileen Cullen came over late after work with 100 badges that said, 'I'm supporting Jimmy's Outpatients' on them and took away the jars of money that Chris and Antonia Deuters donated to Jimmy's. Eileen rang the next day to tell me it amounted to £131.40. That cost me five pounds, as I bet Jo I would be nearest, she said £100 and I said £180.

Although she had been ill for such a long time, it was a sad time for Malton trainer Jimmy Fitzgerald, as on Friday coming up it was the funeral of his fifty-four-year-old wife, Jane. It was taking place at St Mary's Church Old Malton at 1p.m., followed by cremation at York at 2.30 p.m. Jimmy had always been a good friend of mine. I knew him years ago when he worked for Ted Gifford and I worked for Charlie Hall, before we both started riding in races. But I possibly knew Jane before Jimmy did. When I was a jump jockey, I actually received a £500 retainer from Mr and Mrs Leggat, her mum and dad, which in those days was quite a sum, especially in the north of England. Periodically, I went to their home at Biggar in Scotland to school their horses. Jane was a very good rider having ridden show-jumpers, cross-country and point-to-point. Jane was an invaluable help to Jimmy, in and out of the yard. As a trainer, his first win was Archer in 1969, the same year Camasco gave us our first training success. Jimmy's biggest win was in 1985 when Forgive 'n' Forget won the Cheltenham Gold Cup when ridden by Mark Dwyer. I was just hoping he coped all right without Jane as I knew it would be hard for him. It wasn't possible for me to go to the funeral, as I had to attend a Trustee Board and Almoners IJF Meeting in London. My train didn't get back to Darlington in time and I had no chance to get to Malton without a car, although I must confess that knowing her so well I did feel guilty not going. However, I felt let off a bit, as the same evening we went to the Grove and Rufford Hunt Ball as guests of Mr and Mrs Paul Dixon and that had been arranged quite a while before the funeral date was announced. It was great at the Hunt Ball to see people I hadn't seen for so long. Years ago, I rode for Ben Bealby at Worksop, a really nice man. The Hunt point-to-point was on his land. We used to school the horses over the course and I often had a day's hunting with the Grove and Rufford Hunt. On a couple of occasions I acted as the starter's assistant at their point-to-point. Happy days.

On the last day of November I had a pleasurable task to perform in aid of the IJF when I received a cheque from Peter Dunn in the winning enclosure at Newcastle Races for £7,777.77, for him running in the Northern Marathon. Peter put the 77p to it to keep it all the sevens! He worked so hard to get all the sponsorship money by working at the northern races collecting in a bucket. On 13 May 1985, Peter had a terribly bad fall from a horse by the name of Stand Back in a race at Hexham, when he received severe head injuries, which put him in a coma for quite some time. He was taken to the intensive care unit and put on a life support machine at Newcastle Hospital. Thankfully, Peter made a remarkably near 100% recovery. He has since got married to a lovely girl called Kim and they have a smashing daughter. Peter and Kim have been helped by the IJF in the past, and he is so appreciative. Between the two of them, they run the horse ambulance at most northern racecourses. Peter doing the marathon was his way of saying thank you to the Fund.

There is nothing to beat a day's jump racing and there are not many better racecourses to go to than Wetherby. Now we have moved back to Yorkshire it only takes three quarters of an hour to get there. Jo and I went there on Saturday 7 December. Sarah York, one of the Stewards and also one of our IJF Almoners for the week, had invited Jo and me for lunch before racing. She also wanted me to meet Dr Bruce McLaine who was a very nice fellow and he willingly agreed to attend our BBQ as doctor in charge on 20 July.

At Wetherby, the luncheon in support of the Epic Challenge for Epilepsy was organised by northern trainer Tim Easterby's wife, Sarah. Sally Kettle who is the skipper and Marcus Thompson the first mate accepted Sir Chay Blyth's Atlantic Challenge to row and race 3,000 miles from Tenerife to Barbados starting in October 2003. The 24-foot boat, which was on view in the paddock area, was to be Marcus's and Sally's home for three months the following year. There would be around thirty starters for the race across the Atlantic Ocean, a challenge that only 100 people have attempted. The object of the race was to raise £1,000,000 to fund a new permanent training post to find the causes of and cure for epilepsy. I had a chat to Sally about her challenge and she was really bubbly, very enthusiastic and confident. Many sports people suffer from epilepsy, a disorder of the central nervous system, including quite a few Flat and NH Jockeys, usually following head injuries.

In the evening after Wetherby, we travelled on to the Green Hill Hotel, Wigton in Cumbria, for the first Annual IJF Dinner Dance. It was organised by Vicky Dobbin, wife of Tony who had ridden four winners at Wetherby that day, Linda O'Hara, wife of Johnny the ex-jump jockey who is now confined to a wheelchair, Nita Eubank, wife of ex-top amateur jockey and northern racecourse steward and last but not least, Jackie Williamson, a retired very good point-to-point rider. The event was a sell-out and it was really good to see it so well attended by lots of the north's top jockeys and trainers. Following an excellent traditional Christmas dinner, I was in charge as auctioneer and Master of Ceremonies.

Nine excellent lots came up to sell. The first being a day for two at Carlisle Races raising £250. Second came a day on the gallops plus breakfast, with top northern trainer Len Lungo (who as a jockey rode record-breaking trainer

Martin Pipe's first ever winner), raising £650. For a laugh, I told them that thrown in with the package was a ride on Lenny's good horse, The Bajan Bandit. A commissioned painting by Vicky Dobbin raised £750. Many National Hunt fans will remember Vicky painted the IJF Christmas Card in 2001, which sold record numbers that year.

Another lot was a lavish dinner party for eight served in one's own home, which was bought for £775. A framed Limited Edition Print by Joy Hawkins came in for £400; it was one that was in the £700 deal with Joy. A Manchester United signed football raised £550 and an oval hand-made rug made £125. A pair of pictures of old jockeys and horses raised £225 and, finally, a Scottish Premier League signed football shirt raised £225. The cost of the tickets to the event was £20 each. Gary Gibson played and sang for us into the early hours. We old jockeys did a fair bit of reminiscing and we had a great time. David 'joiner' Bowes fed and looked after all our flying, water and ground stock in our absence while we stayed overnight at the hotel. The next day we had lunch at Pat Fullalove's house, with Johnny and Linda O'Hara and another old ex-jump jockey Pat Hurley, and his wife Miriam. When we waved our farewells to everyone there wasn't a single person who wasn't wearing an 'I'm supporting Jimmy's children's outpatients' badge, which they had purchased from us. This part of the world has some very game and generous people.

A few years ago I conducted the auction in aid of the IJF at a barbecue put on by the Lockerbie trainer, Colin Parker, and his wife Janet in their local village hall. At that time jockeys were having sponsored head shaves wholesale in aid of Shane Broderick, who had been badly injured. Out of the blue a middle-aged lady by the name of Isobel Parker, a farmer's wife from Hawick, with beautiful hair, said she wanted me to announce for the highest bid, provided

The Injured Jockeys Fund's Christmas card for 2001 painted by Vicky Dobbin which sold in record numbers.

it reach £50 or more, she would let that person shave off her hair. The final bid reached £500. Colin's main owner Raymond Anderson Green stepped in and said he would give £500 to the fund if we let the lady off the hook and let her keep her hair on. Isobel and myself had a word with Raymond and the result was Raymond gave the fund £500 and the other guy also paid £500. The top bidder bottled it and wouldn't do the hair job. Janet produced some horse clippers. Needless to say, the brave lady had a hairdo! However, note the barber in the photo; he had already had one from a previous function!

Over the years I've been asked many times to do various things at functions, and if at all possible I have always obliged. The year I retired, the Vicar of St

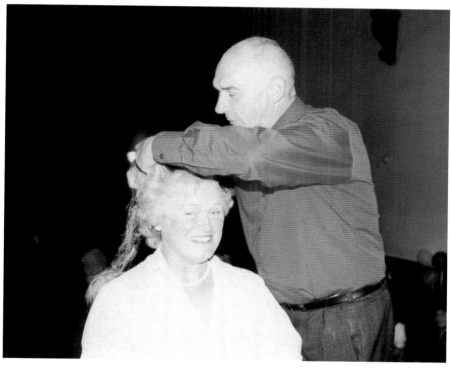

Brave Isobel Parker raised a grand for charity by losing her hair.

Peters Church in Heysham, Morecambe, very near to where those cockle pickers were drowned, asked me if he could borrow a horse so he could take the annual service, which was out of doors, on horseback in Heysham and also would I read the horse's prayer on horseback. The vicar said he could ride, and taking him at his word, I said that I would sort him out a quiet ride. I chose Palacegate Touch (Archie) for him and Palacegate Jack for me, both greys. When we got loaded up on this bit of a park, Archie started to jog and I must tell you I was inwardly panicking. The vicar didn't seem a bit concerned, his robes were flowing around Archie's belly and legs and he was riding one handed as he had some books under the other arm. I thought if the horse takes off with the man of the cloth, where on earth would he go? And worse still where would he finish up? It wouldn't have been so bad if the vicar had sat still, but he was a bit hot-arsed. There were dozens and dozens of kids

Jo and her mother.

on ponies, punters with dogs on leads, one with a goat, kids and women with rabbits, cats, hamsters, bird in cages and all sorts of creatures in their arms all milling around close to our horses. Both horses were used to seeing cats, dogs, sheep and cattle, but to be honest, Jack and Archie's eyes were nearly popping out of their heads, although we have plenty of animals at home they had never seen the like of this lot before. Olly, my old Jack Russell came with us but I left him in the box that brought the horses.

We all sang the hymn. 'All Things Bright and Beautiful' from a sheet we had been given and my little missus was giving it some welly, I think she gets it from her mother. On the occasions her mother came to stay with us when we first got married, we would go to Owston Church on Sundays and Jo's mother and the lady organist would sing so loud one could hardly hear the choir! Then the vicar read from one of his books, by now I had beckoned The Bride to catch hold of Jack's head.

I then read the 'Horse's Prayer' but not before saying one to myself to get both horses back home safely which, thankfully, we did. The vicar said how much he had enjoyed the service and mentioned something about 'next year' to which I played a deaf'un thinking, 'let our Alan sort it out now he's taken over'. One can burn up enough nervous energy with the ups and downs of racing without looking for trouble. It's rather like asking the same girl out; if she keeps saying no, one gets a bit disillusioned. Every year at Cockerham the carol singers came round. We always invited them in for mince pies, drinks, and a bit of a warmth and we would sing a couple of carols or so around the Aga in the kitchen. One particular Christmas when we were in full cry, Hardy, the black Labrador dog, cocked his leg and peed down Auntie Molly's leg. Molly Billington drove the local school bus for years and years and everyone no matter what age affectionately called her Auntie Molly. Luckily, she saw the funny side of it and laughed.

Watching the box on a Sunday night, it was great to see Tony McCoy, flat jockeys Lester Piggott and Frankie Detorri making into the finals for the prestigious BBC Sports Personality of the Year Awards. The other finalists were runner Paula Radcliffe, footballer David Beckham, boxer Lennox Lewis, and the previous year's winner and rugby player Johnny Wilkinson. The Bride and I phoned in and voted for Tony but unfortunately it wasn't enough to secure him being the place of winner. That went to Paula Radcliffe. David Beckham came second and Tony McCoy third. This was the time of year is a time for awards. As was the case for the Horserace Writers and Photographers Association Annual Derby Awards, held at London's Royal Lancaster Hotel the following day. No less than 650 guests attended the function, a record. The Clive Graham trophy for the Journalist of the Year went to the writer Tom O'Ryan. Tom went with our IJF party on holiday to Tenerife a couple of years ago to report on it for the Post; he was brilliant and I'm sure it did the Fund a lot of good. Edward Whitaker was awarded the Photographer of the Year for the second time, he also came out with our crew to Tenerife. Flat Jockey of the Year Award justifiably went to Richard Hughes who rode some great races to finish second to Kieren Fallon in the Jockeys' Championship title. Middleham trainer Mark Johnson won the Trainer of the Year. If he got the same feeling as I did when I, as head of our team, collected the trophy in 1991, he would know it was to be cherished as it is absolutely great. It was a formality for AP McCoy to be voted National Hunt Jockey of the Year, and rightly so. Tommy Cullinan in 1930 was the only jockey to ride the Champion Hurdle, The Gold Cup and the Grand National winners in the same season. That must be the only record Tony hasn't broken. However, knowing Tony it is certainly possible. He is so keen and dedicated, he keeps himself super fit and hasn't an ounce of fat on his bones as you can see on the photo where he's cuddling up to my missus at a charity function at the pub in Sparsholt, near Lambourn.

Looking at him, I bet he's never tasted a McDonald's in years! He has set the bar so high riding winners, it will be hard for anyone to ever better him.

AP McCoy, possibly the most dedicated jump jockey of all time, with Jo at a charity function in Sparsholt near Lambourne.

National Hunt Trainer of the Year went to the Cheltenham Gold Cup's handler, Henrietta Knight. That was the first year for some time that the legendary Martin Pipe hadn't carried off this prestigious prize. Martin has a great record in buying horses and he buys a lot of them in France. Mind you, he is always on the lookout for horses he thinks are decent in claimers and sellers. Like when he claimed his good gelding Make A Stand for just £8000, which must have paid him back 50 times over. Martin has made a few people unhappy by claiming their horses but in fairness we all know the rules. I once had a run-in with Martin when he claimed a two-year-old filly of ours called Dear Glenda that finished second first time out in a seller at Doncaster. On the owner's behalf, I rang him up at night to offer a profit but he wouldn't take one, yet later he contacted the filly's owner Richard Green and he sold her back to him. So I lost the horse and the owner. However, thankfully since then I have grown up. I have nothing but admiration for Martin and to be fair to him, via Martin's father, his vet helped me no end once when our horses at Cockerham were not right and were running in and out on account of a virus. International trainer of the Year, justifiably, went to the globe-trotting man from County Kildare, Dermot Weld, mainly on account of his superstar Media Puzzle winning the Melbourne Cup. In the 1991 Irish Season, Dermot broke Jim Bolger's 148 record of winners with his then flying machine Vintage Crop.

Owner of the Year Award went to the Manchester United Football Manager, Sir Alex Ferguson, in whose name another flying machine, Rock of Gibraltar, runs. Dave Goodwin from Jeremy Noseda's yard and Tom Townsend of the Stuart Williams outfit shared the Stable Staff of the Year Award. A position Rachel Hume, one of our girls who looked after Bolshoi when we ran him in Japan, held a few years ago which was a great boost for the whole yard. The Outstanding Achievements in Racing went to Ian Balding. Ian has trained some superstars in his time, e.g. Mill Reef the Winner of the 1971 Derby and Champion Sprinter Loch Song whose backside was familiar sight to some of our top sprinters, especially in 1993 when our good sprinter Parris House was second to her in Goodwood's King George and the Group 1 Nunthorpe Stakes at York, a race I would dearly loved to have won. She was some machine. On the year of my retirement it was I who carried off the prestigious prize. This time of year reminded me of the Orange Men marching in Ireland, its seasonal and like the awards, just goes on and on. The next night it was the 'Daddy Dinner' of them all, a real honour to be invited, where 117 guests sat around the famous horseshoe table in the Gimcrack Room at York Racecourse.

The Gimcrack Stakes is a prestigious two-year-old race run over six furlongs at York. It was run for the first time in 1846 and was won by Ellendale, ridden by Tommy Lye and trained by Tom Dawson here in Yorkshire. That platform gives the chance for the owner or representative to make a speech at the dinner and to air his or her views uninterrupted. The 2002 winner was Country Reel owned by Godolphin and Sheikh Maktoum al Maktoum. Michael Osbourne, the Irish vet, spoke on behalf of His Highness Sheikh Maktoum, who said pathetic rewards for owners damaged the whole industry and on account of our prize money being so low it was inevitable we would see less and less of their blue silks in Britain. The York Gimcrack Club was celebrating its 232nd Annual Dinner.

John Francome proposed the toast for the success and prosperity of the Gimcrack Club and told a few tales and jokes with a few choice words thrown in to lighten up the evening. John Francome is a good mate and a really nice fellow, a wonderful man for any kind of a good cause, and, although he loves his long hair more than most women, he doesn't know how to say no when asked to help a worthy cause. I know for a fact he visits people in hospital and also keeps in touch with them by phone. While I was talking to him during the interval remembering we wanted a celebrity to have his or her hair shaved off for the Jimmy's kids at a function that was coming up in York, tongue in cheek I said, 'John mate, will you do me a big favour?' 'Yes, if I can,' said the greatest jockey, as the hairy man John McCririck of Channel 4 calls him, then I popped the question Without any hesitation whatsoever, straightaway he looked me square in the eyes and said, 'F... off', so that was one time when the greatest jockey jibbed! He's some man J. Francome; he told a joke once on the 'Morning Line' only he could get away with – 'What can a cow do that a woman can't? Walk in water deep enough to cover its udders without getting its backside wet!!'

Having driven home after the Gimcrack Stakes dinner, I don't need to tell you at 8.00 a.m when I was feeding all the faces of my stock, I have felt better. Amongst the junk mail and a few Christmas cards that day was a letter from Reg Griffin from Timeform that really perked me up. In it was a cheque for £4,000, a staggering amount that I credited to our BBQ account, leaving us with a target of £22,680, not bad? Oh! Also in the post was this letter from the Rev. Harold Knight, which I thought you would like to read. Mind you, I did look at the address on the envelope twice to make sure the Postie hadn't mixed it up with a trainer I know from Sheriff Hutton.

> The Reverend Harold Knight
> The Rescue Mission
> 182 Elliot Street, Clerkenwell
> London SW1
>
> Dear Jack,
>
> Perhaps you have heard of me and my nationwide campaign in the cause of temperance. Each year for the past fourteen years, I have made a tour of Scotland and the North of England, including Manchester, Liverpool and Glasgow and have delivered a series of lectures on the evils of drinking. On this tour, I have been accompanied by a young friend and assistant, David Powell. David, a young man of good family and excellent background, is a pathetic example of a life ruined by excessive indulgence in whisky and women.
>
> David would appear with me at lectures and sit on the platform, wheezing and staring at the audience through bleary, bloodshot eyes,

sweating profusely, picking his nose, passing wind and making obscene gestures, while I would point him out as an example of what drinking etc. can do to a person.

Last summer, unfortunately, David died. A mutual friend has given me your name and I wonder if you would care to take David's place on my next tour.

Yours in faith,

Harold Knight,

Rescue Mission

Still on the social circuit, the next Thursday found yours truly and The Bride at the Racehorse Owners' Association Horseracing Awards 2002. It was held at the London Hilton and we went as guests of Brian and Donna Robe. Seeing as the event didn't start until 7.45 p.m. and we were staying at the Robe's flat in London, we weren't in a big rush. We parked our car at Northallerton station and caught the train to York to then change for the train to London. My missus is brilliant! With just four minutes to countdown she told me she was going to the toilet, 'Ok love,' I said 'but you have just four minutes' and off she goes. The train pulls in and there's no Jo. Then a message came over the tannoy system, 'Stand back please as the train doors are about to be closed' —still no Jo! Just as the guard blows his whistle, waves his little bat and the train sets off, one could just see its arse end leaving the station, my little missus saunters up with a magazine under her arm that she'd made time to buy in the station shop. 'That's the train' I said, 'Is it?' she asked, 'What time's the next one?'

At the award ceremony, Rock of Gibraltar rightly won the Horse of the Year. Hunter Chaser went to Gunner Welbourn, the year's Best Hurdler Award went to Barracuda, Novice Hurdle winner was Like A Butterfly and Chaser of the Year was Best Mate. Moscow Flyer received the award for best Novice Chaser. Handicapper of the Year went to Scots View, Prix de L'Arc de Triomphe winner; Marienbard won the prize for the Outstanding Older Horse. Although I got that one wrong, I went for Kyllachy, who in my opinion was the best sprinter in Europe and so unlucky to have been retired following the injury he sustained after winning the Nunthorpe at York. Although I could have been biased, loving sprinters as I do, Kyllachy's trainer Henry Candy had some compensation from his two-year-old Airwave winning the Juvenile Filly of the Year which was sponsored by Chris and Antonia Deuters' Slatch Farm Stud. The two-year-old Colt of 2002 was voted Tout Seul, the Dewhurst Stakes winner, trained by Fulke Johnson-Houghton, a very popular winner, It was particularly nice to see Fulke get back into the limelight, as Tout Seul was the best horse he had trained for some years. In the past, he trained some real good horses, the likes of Ribocco and Ribero to win the 1967 and 1968 St Leger's. Islington received the award for the Best three-year-old Filly from very strong opposition beating the likes of Gossamer, the Irish 1,000 Guineas Winner, Kazzia, our 1,000 Guineas Winner and the Royal Ascot winner of the Coronation Cup, Sophisticat and Zenda, who was beaten by a neck in that race. Racecourse of the Year went to Cheltenham and possibly the most popular win of all, was Best Mate's owner Jim Lewis, when he was announced Owner of the Year.

On my return home, I had to write a cheque for £150 from our IJF BBQ account to pay for some more of the pictures I had framed to auction off. With that backward step, it brought our target back to £22 830. When attending our IJF meeting I usually catch the London train from Darlington, which is a bit further from home than Northallerton, but not all London trains stop at Northallerton, although Darlington station does bring back memories of when I was apprentice jockey at Charlie Hall's way back in 1957. The year after, I looked after Doornocker when he won the Champion Hurdle ridden by the crack hurdle race jockey of the day, Harry Sprague. It was at the end of the season and we had two horses running at Towcester, which were both owned by our main owner Clifford Nicholson, who also trained a few jumpers himself on a permit. As it was both horses' last run of the season, after they had run they were returning home to Willhoughton Manor the home of Mr Nicholson, near Gainsborough, to be turned out for the summer. Mr Nicholson sent his head man and a horsebox driver to Towton, where we trained, to pick up the horses and me and to take us to Towcester the day before racing. Paddy Farrell, our stable jockey, was riding both horses, only he travelled down in his car on the day of the races. I was to go back with him and my gear in his car. Would you believe the first of our runners fell and Paddy broke his collarbone? I wasn't aware Paddy was injured until I led my next runner up and Michael Scudamore was chucked up on the horse in the paddock. I asked Michael what had happened to Paddy he told me that the racecourse doctor had sent him by ambulance to hospital for an X-ray. As soon as I let the horse go to canter down to the start, I legged it to the weighing room to get the full run down on Paddy, but more importantly my lift home. The valet didn't know how bad Paddy was but said he was certain the hospital would keep him in and told me to take this bag of Paddy's clothes, his saddle, watch, whip and wallet, telling me that with him being a southern valet he didn't know when he would see Paddy again. To be honest, I had the same thought! These two old boys of Nicholson's were as much good to me as a one-legged man in an arse kicking competition. No offer of help at all. They wouldn't even get Paddy's gear off the valet in the weighing room. I had to go back for it after I had done my horse up. When I suggested that they could take all the horse's gear back to Willhoughton and bring it over for me in the car the following day, it was ruled out of the question. All they could come up with was that they could take me with my gear to Grantham railway station on their way home, from there I was on my own and not a train in sight when we arrived at the station. By the time I had carted my gear, the two horses' gear and Paddy's gear to the right platform to catch the train to York, I was absolutely knackered. I had to take everything in relays and keep everything in view so that nothing was nicked. Mind you on reflection, who would have wanted any of it? I'm lucky I didn't end up in hospital with big balls after all that. There was so much of it I could have half-filled a Pickford's truck.

What a prat I must have looked with my flat cap, sweater, jodhpurs and boots, as that was the dress for us at Charlie Hall's. Ben Robinson, our Head Man, would go bananas if we lost the smallest piece of equipment at the races, so there was no chance of me dumping anything. No, it all had to come home. There was I, miles from home, with about £2 of my own in my pocket – I didn't look to see how much there was in Paddy's wallet – having to return to Towton. I had two horse rugs, two blankets, two buckets, 'metal' at that, two head collars, paddock sheets, rollers, bridles, grooming kit, colour bag, Paddy's kit and my own gear. I had travelled a horse on the train to Ayr once before. On my return from Ayr at the now defunct Newton Kyme railway station, where we unloaded the horse, when Ben came to pick me up he asked me if I had used up all the hay and oats. He threw an absolute wobbler when I told him I had given the spare feed to the stableman at the racecourse for his kid's rabbits. 'Do you think our boss is an 'effin' millionaire?' he raved. 'Do you realise we work for a man called Charlie Hall not Charlie de Fucking Rothschild?' Therefore, I dared not leave anything! I wish I could say that was the end of it and I got home OK, but I can't. By the time the train reached Doncaster I was so tired I fell asleep.

When I woke up with the noise of screaming brakes, the train was just stopping. I asked a punter on the train if we were at York yet, he said, 'York? We were there half an hour ago. We're in Darlington.' In a flap and panic, all the gear was thrown off the train and dumped on the platform. By now, it was getting on for midnight. The only train back to York was a Royal Mail train that only stopped to pick up mail, which was about 4 a.m. I was very hungry and freezing cold. I went into the waiting room where someone had lit a fire earlier, but it was nearly out. In those days stations weren't as clean or as comfortable as today. The only other person in sight was a man generally tidying up and looking after things. There was no more coal to be seen for me to stoke up the fire. So to keep it going, I emptied all the rubbish bins and burnt that. I was cold and miserable. I felt like putting Paddy's saddle and the horse's bloody rugs on just to keep warm. Only the thoughts of the wrath of Ben Robinson would be worse than having to put up with the cold and hunger. To relieve my mind of all my problems, I told the man at the station all that had happened to me; that I had been on the go since 6 a.m when I fed the horses at Towcester racecourse stables. He must have felt sorry for me, as he said he would turn a blind eye to getting me on that Royal Mail train, but I would need to be quick as it doesn't stop long. Moreover, if I was caught I wasn't to squeal on him at any price.

When the Mail train arrived, no sooner had it stopped than I had a door open and threw all the gear in with all the mail bags, and dived in after it. No chance of kipping on the way back to York for fear of a repeat performance! When the train pulled up, I knew we were at York, as the man at Darlington had marked my card and told me it was the first stop. It's a good job he did, as I couldn't see a thing in the box wagon! The journey seemed to last forever. Was I glad when the train finally stopped and I pushed the door open and saw a bit of daylight. I threw all the gear out onto the platform in much less time than it took me to load it at Grantham! The train went on its way. I found a trolley on the platform, put all mine, Paddy Farrell's and the bosses gear on it, and wheeled it towards the exit.

A railway worker, or porter asked me where I had come from, I came clean and told him I was a stowaway on the Mail train. Thankfully, he was good about it. When I had explained, he made me a cup of tea and I had a warm in his own little room. He even arranged me a lift with the paper van that was going to Leeds! The driver of the van originated from Leeds as I did, and in view of being in charge of half the tackle in his van, he must have felt a bit sorry for me looking bedraggled, weak and pathetic, (which was more than those two prats of Nicholson's did). Instead of going through Tadcaster, he went via Towton and dropped me and all the gear off right at the stable yard gate.

By now it was getting on for 7 a.m. Sunday morning. Ben was just starting to feed the horses. I gave him a hand and said nothing about my ordeal, and the only thing he said was it was a bloody waste of expenses going all that way and not having a winner. Me, thinking like Fred on Coronation Street: 'You can say that again, I say, you can say that again.' Paddy Farrell had somehow got back to the course from the hospital and one of the northern jockeys who were riding at Towcester drove his car back for him. The keys to Paddy's car was the only thing of our old jockey's the valet didn't give me; the only thing that would have been any good to me, even if I hadn't passed my test. At least I could have asked that pair of Nicholson Samaritans to load Paddy's car up with the freight I had to haul to Towton.

Later on in the day when I saw Paddy, he had his wing in a sling. All PA Farrell was concerned about was 'are all my belongings safe? Did you bring my clothes back? Did you get my wallet off the valet? Did you get my saddle back? Have you got my watch?' 'Yes Paddy I did,' 'Did you get my whip?' 'Yes, I brought back everything.' He then went on to tell me he had a right fecking job (Paddy always spelt that word with an 'e' not a 'u') having treatment at the hospital and getting himself and his car home.

It was only seven more days to go to Christmas and Sam, our son and his partner Carole, plus Lilo Blum the sister of my old Newmarket pal Gerry Blum the ex-trainer (probably the best horse he trained was Venus of Streatham), were staying with us for a few days. Gerry told me he once ran a horse that finished second to a Richard Hannon' winner just beaten by a head in a photo finish. Richard was presented with a bottle of champagne, and he immediately gave it to Gerry saying, 'You have this mate, you were unlucky to get beat.' Richard is a good sport always ready to have a bet on anything. One day he was going racing with one of his owners who said to him 'what do you think will win today Richard?' 'Not easy today, it's a hard card,' but his owner kept on as he was sickening for a bet. 'Look,' said Richard, 'if you want to bet, I will bet you £20 Jack Berry, if he's there today, will be wearing a red shirt.' 'Don't be so bloody silly, how would you know that?' and he took the money. Needless to say, Richard finished a score to the good. Lilo Blum liked the Joy Hawkins prints so much she bought one for Gerry's Christmas box and another for a friend of hers for £80, bringing our target to £22,750.

Our Aga cooker has been playing us up. The man came from Bedale Services to give it a service. We were just finishing our breakfast when he arrived. As this house is no different from the one we owned in Cockerham (Jacks Café), everyone who comes visiting, making deliveries, whatever or whoever gets invited to share with us a tea or coffee. As the man was drinking his tea and I was putting my dirty pots in the washer, I looked out of the window and noticed the passenger seat was occupied. Without hesitation, I said to the man, 'Don't leave that lady in the car, mate, bring her in for a cup of tea and a warm.' He nearly dropped his cup with laughing, 'That's not a lady, it's my dog. He thinks he's a human though, he sits bolt upright like that all the time and when I look right and left at crossroads, so does he. One of these days, I'm convinced he's going to speak and say, 'you're all right, there's nothing coming.'

As the saying goes, I lost my shirt at Haydock Park Races.
Only this one was auctioned by John Lavelle in aid of
the Princess Royal Trust for Carers. It made £1,200.

Chapter Four

Rough Justice

•

Following the BBC Panorama programme and the controversial episode of the 'Kenyon Confronts' investigative series, entitled 'They fix the races don't they?' where trainer Jamie Osborne was secretly filmed telling an undercover reporter that he would be prepared to cheat, there followed a hearing at the Jockey Club in London where Jamie pleaded guilty and was relieved of £4,000 by way of a fine. A similar fine was handed to trainer Ferdy Murphy for infringing the rules and bringing racing into disrepute. Whatever rules the Jockey Club puts on your plate, like it or not, you have to eat. Racing was going through a bad time at the time. A number of other punishments had been dished out. One in particular was very harsh, when Graham Bradley had an eight-year ban imposed on him by the Disciplinary Committee on corruption charges. Talk about give a dog a bad name; personally I would term his charge 'youthful exuberance' rather than corruption. Possibly on occasions he has mixed with the wrong characters, as he was found guilty of passing on privileged information for reward.

In the past, John Francome was handed a short suspension and fined £150 in 1978. Jockey Billy Newnes was banned for three years in 1984 for accepting £1,000 from a professional gambler.

Both cases seem quite lenient compared to Brad's eight years, which stopped him going racing, being a bloodstock agent and managing horses as he had done successfully since he retired as a jockey. Brad had appealed. In this modern age information is given so freely, and daily on Attheraces and other channels via jockey and trainer interviews. So what makes the information privileged if it's so-called tips? I can assure you, most of the tipsters couldn't successfully pick their nose.

When jockeys appear on Morning Line on Channel 4 on Saturdays and the other racing channels, they are invariably asked to give a run down on the chances of the mounts they are to ride. As they are paid to appear on the programme, they are being paid for passing on information. Nowadays, jockeys have 'mikes' thrust under their noses, with only one purpose; 'how will the horse go and what chance has it got?' as Derek Thompson asks. No doubt if the jockey convinces D T that it will win, he will probably convey the message on his tipping line that he charges punters for when they ring in! At a function where I attended at York one day Derek ran down the card for the guests. You couldn't have sighted his selections with the telescope from Jodrell Bank! All sport needs rules and regulations, but officialdom for some can be intimidating and OTT. Hopefully the letter I faxed on 19 December may have given Brad a bit of support by stressing a few good points in Brad's favour that most people didn't know or have forgotten about.

Dear Sirs,

There has been an awful lot said and written about Graham Bradley recently, most of it not in his favour. Some of the withering comments I have heard on 'at the races' and remarks in the press have made me wonder whether in fact they were discussing Brad, ex-National Hunt jockey and a man of true courage, or Osama Bin Laden.

Speak as you find. I don't see, or hear, any reference to the day in 1985 when Brad single handedly organised a charity day at York Racecourse in aid of two jockeys who had each received serious head injuries from race riding falls. One of them being my son Sam Berry, the other Peter Dunn.

He organised a gathering of Sir Bobby Charlton, Mike Sommerbee, Bobby Collins, Francis Lee, Peter Lorimer and others to play in a charity football match against top flat and jump jockeys.

A parade of great horses which included Badsworth Boy, Sea Pigeon and Night Nurse. A question of sport followed between top trainers, jockeys racecourses, sponsors, in fact everyone you could imagine connected with racing, to raise money for the boys who had been injured, solely to give them a holiday. He gathered a huge amount of items, racing memorabilia etc for auction.

When Shane Broderick was left paralysed following an horrific fall, Brad organised a golf day which raised a staggering £35,000 for Shane's cause.

During all this time Graham Bradley was riding at the top of his profession, he didn't need to do all this and he certainly didn't have the time to do it but, unlike most of us, he made the time. Just like he did for all the kids just starting to ride when they needed help and guidance in the weighing room. No doubt that is why you can't find anyone in racing who actually knows the real Graham Bradley to say a word against him. They all stand by him and it's not out of sentiment.

I have known Brad for years, even before his days with the Dickinsons, when I trained mainly jumpers. He came to me for a job, full of confidence and bravado. I put him on one to school over hurdles and the useless bugger fell off! I told him he should drive a horse box like his dad as he didn't have what it takes to be a jump jockey! How wrong I was.

There is one thing I am right about, there is an awful lot more good in Brad than bad. When the powers that be pass judgement please remember Brad's good points.

Jack Berry

Hunton,
Bedale,
North Yorkshire.

Brad rode his first winner on Talon at Sedgefield in 1960, and by 2002 had retired from horse racing. There is no point in waking up Sleeping Beauty, or we could have said Brad was fined £500 by the Ludlow stewards in 1988 for dropping his hands on Trout Angler. I appreciated Brad is a bit of a character and probably wouldn't make the ideal Avon Lady, but he was no threat to anyone. It isn't as if he's auditioning for Blue Peter or Songs of Praise. If we are not careful the so-called characters left in racing will be to what Boy George is to boxing. You can take a man out of racing, but you can't take racing out of the man.

The powers that be don't get it right all the time. In 1928 when races were started by flag or starting gates Charlie Smirke was warned off for five years allegedly for making little or no attempt to get his mount Welcome Gift to jump off and start in a race at Gatwick. The same horse consistently refused to start, proving a miscarriage of justice had taken place. No compensation was given to Charlie by the Jockey Club or even an apology, which makes the system so unfair. If a paid official of the Jockey Club stepped out of line (they are human so it has happened) the offender doesn't get dragged through the same open channels. It's dealt with internally. Seldom do they get warned off; they either resign or get sacked but are free to take up similar positions abroad. Can that be fair?

Racing has always retained a certain amount of mystique and optimism if it wasn't so, it could be quite boring. Many years ago I bought a lovely three-year-old gelding by Deep Run at Doncaster Sales which I sold to Geoff Dawes, one of our owners when we were into jumpers and the money was quite scarce. Once we broke the horse in I often popped him over poles, little baby jumps and then hurdles; the horse jumped for fun and he loved it. I told Geoff what a nice horse we had and the next time we had a runner I would put him in the horsebox and I would give him a school around the course. Those days schooling on racecourses after racing on most northern tracks was allowed. We were charged a nominal fee of somewhere in the region of a fiver per horse and some trainers would send their own horses up together but often a bunch of everyone's would go in the same gallop.

Our man had his first test of a racecourse at Catterick where I rode him with a bunch of others. I only took him quietly round but he gave me a real good feel. On my return, I told Geoff that another one of those outings would put our horse right so kick on and get him named, which he did. A couple of weeks later I did the same with him at Teesside Park after racing where I gave the horse plenty to do in the trial and he beat the others effortlessly. Quite a few of the wide-heads in the gallop asked me for the horse's name and so on, which in all honesty I didn't tell them, as, at the time, he hadn't one.

However, I did tell his owner he would be very hard to beat in a 3-year-old Maiden Hurdle especially if we aimed at a small course where the opposition wouldn't be great. Geoff named his animal Kas, after his son Keith and our two sons Alan and Sam, and we chose to run him at Wolverhampton the day after Boxing Day in 1975. Also when I was looking at the race, I said to Geoff the horse could fall down, get up and still win as the race entries looked so moderate with very little form at all from any of the horses which had ran. With our fellow going so well I couldn't see him getting beaten.

In the Bingley Building Society, Jo and I had invested £1,240 which was the proceeds from the sale of our small terraced house we lived in when we first got married. In those days £1,200 was a fortune. Geoff and his wife Landa came up to Cockerham to stay with us as they often did. Going through the race form of the entries many times I couldn't see Kas getting beaten. I thought it would be as easy as taking sweets from young kids. Over a few drinks we decided we would have a coup. Those days we only trained a few horses, mainly jumpers and we hadn't trained many winners (not yet); we hadn't really got going so the horse would be a big price as he had never raced under rules. I drew the money out of the Building Society gave it Geoff to put on the horse as Geoff was into betting. Geoff placed our money on the horse which averaged 14/1. He opened up 16/1 and returned 5/2 joint favourite.

At Wolverhampton on 27 December 1975, when Kas jumped the last hurdle six lengths in front I picked the missus up and jumped about with her I was so chuffed, all of a sudden I could hear the crowd getting excited as the other horses were catching Kas. With all the noise and cheering from the excited punters which also included Jo and me, the poor horse shortened his stride as he lost his concentration and finished third, beaten two short heads by Jimmy Miff and Jack's Mate. The winner received £340. Kas for finishing third collected £40. His jockey Richard Evans must have thought I was allergic to money. He said that had he been a bit harder on him and given the horse a couple of cracks, he would have won. It was only on account of the noise of the crowd that brought out his 'greenness' or for a better word, inexperience that got him beaten. The jockey said this lot would never beat him again and the experience, I can tell you, certainly taught me a lesson. To bet in moderation and above all make sure newcomers to racing have a thorough education, a point we have later on proved with our two-year-olds. I was treating my fingers for burns weeks later.

Seamus Durack duly sent me the picture of the Dubliners and the jockeys all signed it ready to frame. It looked good. I knew that it would hopefully go down well at the auction. I decided to get Jonjo O'Neill, Tony Dobbin, Norman Williamson or one of the boys on the photo interested in bidding for it. I thought more than likely it would be Jonjo, as he seemed to have plenty of money. Or should I say the Jockey Club do? Only a day or so before my prediction, Jonjo was fined a record £4,200 for giving a couple of horses easy races. Malcolm Wallace, Director of Regulations at the Jockey Club, said with of one of the horses, it was as bad a case as he had seen for some time. The race report in the *Racing Post*, just said 'tenderly ridden'. Probably the reporter didn't want to make a big fuss so that it didn't shorten the price when he put a few bob on in the future. If that was the case, I bet the *Post* reporter thought 'what a big mouth that Wallace has'.

In the run-up to the festive season more post was arriving. One day just one letter and a dozen or more Christmas cards. One card was from Tom and Jill Durcan the mother and father of our former apprentice Ted, the leading jockey for the previous couple of seasons in Dubai. Ted was one of our star apprentices at Cockerham. Never one to shirk work, always level headed, punctual clean and tidy, well mannered, a perfect gentleman and above all gifted

Happier times for Jongo
(at back), *giving his son*
on a ride on Hardy,
our Labrador, in the
kitchen at Cockerham.

with exceptional talent. He could ride really well. No-one was more pleased for Ted doing so well than Jo and I. In his early years Ted was apprentice along with Champion Tony McCoy with Jim Bolger in Ireland. So I am not going to claim I taught Ted much about riding! It was a pleasure having him at the yard. When either Tony or Ted did anything wrong at Bolger's, where it was difficult to pull any kind of stroke, as JB seldom missed a trick. Jim very cool and collected with ice cold eyes cutting into them and without raising his voice would say, 'You're some fool.' I bet he doesn't think that now of the pair!

Sir Gordon Richards was the only jockey ever to be knighted, it's high time we had another in AP McCoy. However inside the letter from Tom and Jill was a £50 note to go towards our cause, which wasn't the first time they have sent us money for the IJF. We were getting there. The total now stood at £22,700.

Recently I read in the *Racing Post* that a rake of horses in Britain and Ireland were to be disqualified as prohibited substances were found in their systems. In December 2002, there were over twenty horses screened for morphine and that figure seemed certain to rise. The findings were of grave concern on both sides of the Irish Sea, but there was no evidence of any wrongdoing. The con-tamination seemed to come from the Irish based feed company Red Mills. The Jockey Club vet, Peter Webben, stated eight British trainers had horses that had tested positive, some with more than one horse, It is not a case of 'if you dip your nib in the office ink, someday you will get caught' no yard can police how feeds get contaminated, so how can they be blamed? It's hard enough to win races without losing them on account of feed products or sup-plements. To be honest trainers don't have a clue what compounds go in the feeds, they can only rely on what it says on the bag. My heart went out to the owners, trainers, jockeys and staff of the horses involved. I knew how they felt, as a few years previously we lost two races because traces of theobromine which is residue from the cocoa bean, was found in the horse's system. It was traced back to dirty containers carrying compounds to the mills where the horse feeds are made up. At the time we were reimbursed with the prize money and expenses, but it is not the same at the end of the season. It's how many winners you train that's important.

Our two horses were called Houghton Weaver and Boardman's Glory. The latter was owned in partnership with Major Jack Rubin and Willie Stephenson. Jack Rubin was a grand fellow who owned Boardman's furnishing shops in most towns in Lancashire. Willie Stephenson was the former trainer from Royston. Willie is one of the few trainers to have trained a Derby winner as he did with Arctic Prince, when ridden by Charlie Spares in 1951 and a Grand National Winner, Oxo 1959, partnered by Michael Scudamore, father of Champion jockey Peter, the first jump jockey to ride 200 winners in a season. I felt honoured to have trained a winner for Willie Stephenson, with him being the great trainer he was, but a right prat when I lost the race for him on a technicality. See in the photo Willie Stephenson, Lionel Edwards, along with ace flat jockey Willie Nevitt, who rode three Epsom Derby winners and was runner-up in the Jockeys' Championship no less than six times, and me.

Willie Stephenson (at left), *Lionel Edwards* (in back), *Willie Nevitt* (in front) & *JB with Broadmans Glory in the Winning Enclosure.*

Christmas is always a busy time and it's a worrying time for trainers placing horses with the threat of bad weather without losing races through no fault of their own due to contaminated feed. I was hoping the feed companies would soon get things sorted out and back to normal.

Unfortunately, some jockeys also tested positive for prohibited substances. A few weeks previously, jump jockey Dean Gallagher lost his licence for eighteen months following the failure of a second test for cocaine. Just before

Christmas 2002 Newmarket-based Franny Norton was the latest jockey to test positive. He was facing a long suspension if found guilty of deliberately taking drugs. Franny was adamant he was innocent and claimed the source of the banned substance was an exotic tea he was drinking to help keep his weight down. Franny is a super lad, a former eight times stable lads boxing champion. In around fifty fights he only had one defeat. Boxing promoters were mad keen to sign Franny up professionally, but he stuck to racing, which has been good to him. He is as good a lightweight jockey as any riding today. Among his big wins are the Cambridgeshire Magnet Cup, Northumberland Plate, the Ebor and the great St Wilfred Handicap. The season prior to Christmas 2002 alone, he rode twenty-two winners for our Alan. The authorities now test jockeys for alcohol. In my day it was unheard of. The crazy thing is, many times when a jockey rides a winner, especially for sponsored races, they are invariably presented with a bottle of champagne. Many jockeys because of their hectic schedule and wasting have been known to hit the bottle. Giving jockeys drink is putting temptation in their way.

You can imagine the scene. Three or four of the jockeys have travelled up to say, Carlisle from Newmarket. They possibly have ridden a couple of horses at work before they set off for the races, not had a bite to eat, passed every car in sight as they are pushed for time and rushed around all day, riding and sweating their cobblers off. If they are lucky grabbing a sandwich out of the weighing room run to the car with their gear that's parked at the nearest available point so as to get a flyer. Still in their riding clobber, off, as they call it to 'do the two'. Possibly somewhere like Beverley's night meeting. Not even in the same direction as home. What do you honestly think they will do with that bottle of champagne? In the main we're talking about teenagers and young men who enjoy a bit of fun, not reformed old–age pensioners. It would do more good if sponsors gave them gift vouchers for new clothes, by the look of some of the clobber a lot of jockeys turn up at the races in, or the jocks with vouchers could exchange them to kit them out their kids' clothes. During the season they don't see very much of them, on account of this sort of routine happens every day, and if the jockeys miss out on the almost every Sunday racing at home then they are flying off to somewhere like France, Germany, Italy or even further to ride. It's a great life but a busy one.

Christmas Day arrived and Jo arranged with Anne Duffield to have Christmas dinner at their house as we did the previous year. The arrangement was that we would supply and cook the turkey and take it down at 1 p.m. to the Duffield's house. At about twelve noon I rang them up. AJ, that's Anne's 12-year-old son by her first marriage, answered the phone. He said 'Happy Christmas Jack, how's the turkey?' 'That's what I'm ringing about, mate', I told him. 'Jo put the turkey in the Aga and we went off to see to the horses which took us longer than normal as we had to repair some rails that they had broken. When we got back to rescue the bird from the oven, it was too late. It looked like Nat King Cole, as black as the ace of spades. In fact it's ruined, but tell your mother not to worry, Jo said she's put a chicken in the oven to cook and she's got about 2lbs of sausages which we will also bring down.'

I made a parcel up and wrapped it up in tin foil, which looked as if it could be a chicken. When we went into the Duffield's house I put the chicken look-alike on the table in the kitchen with the sausages on a tray. In the kitchen were Arthur, Anne's father, one of her owners Betty Duxbury, Nicky, George's son by his first wife Gill and Linda Townsend. Linda said, 'We'll manage.' We all had a glass of champagne until I thought I'd better get the turkey out of the car! When I did they all said they knew I was kidding, but I can assure you there were some relieved faces when the big bird was produced. We had a great lunch with a lot of laughs.

On Boxing Day, The Bride and I, as usual, went racing at Wetherby, the venue where I rode my first winner, Sasta Gri in 1957. I was to pick up the picture from Jonjo's box driver of his Mighty Montefalco. However, it didn't happen, as Jonjo's intended runner didn't run because of the heavy rain. I have got to admit although we earned our living by training flat two-year-olds and sharp sprinters, I absolutely love my jumping. At Cockerham latterly I only trained the odd jumper. The reason was not because we were not offered jumpers to train, if we had trained more I would never have had a day off to go jumping, but to be honest the Cockerham gallops lacked hills which jumpers need to get them super fit. One day we had a winner at Edinburgh on the flat and runners elsewhere, but I sneaked off to have a day jumping at our local course, Cartmel with no runners. I think it's the norm with a lot of flat trainers. You always see them in full force at the Cheltenham Festival.

It was great to see Best Mate win the King George at Kempton, ridden by AP McCoy on heavy going, which he didn't like. The way he beat Marlborough I thought he will take all the beating in the Cheltenham Gold Cup again. In my book he had to be the best Cheltenham type chaser around since Arkle and only a seven-year-old to boot with very little mileage on his clock. The only threat I could see to Best Mate was the Irish horse of Michael Hourigan's, which won the Ericsson Chase at Leopardstown, Beef or Salmon. It was so sad and unjust; Jim Culloty the horse's regular jockey didn't have the ride on Best Mate on account of serving a suspension. The Doncaster Stewards must have thought Jim was an unscrupulous operator and gave it to him for not riding a horse out to finish second in a Bumper race worth a couple of grand. Pity they weren't on duty at Wolverhampton on 27 December 1975 when Richard Evans may have given Kas a crack. Bumper races were supposed to be to introduce younger horses to racing without giving them a hard time. In the past most trainers schooled horses after racing as previously stated, but Clerks of the Course now don't like extra horses cutting their courses up. And, of course, health and safety have stepped in and course need to have vets, doctors and the like present, which is more expense. Bumpers were originally ridden by conditional jockeys and amateurs, but let's be fair, what on earth will novice horses ridden by novice riders learn? I feel the Stewards sometimes go over the top in these races and forget what they were put on for. The game today is all about betting, nothing at all about introducing young horses to the racecourse.

The Grade One race at Kempton was worth a cool £87,000, which made Jim's Doncaster suspension unreasonable in fact, a complete joke. I watched the Doncaster race and it did not merit Jim a suspension. The punishment did not fit the crime. At the time there were far too many jump jockeys out of action with unnecessary interruption of their livelihood. If stewards need to punish jockeys they should fine them. Only if the infringement of the rules was without a shadow of a doubt intentional should they suspend them. You would need a magnifying glass to find some of our stewards' hearts. Every year there are more and more rules to adhere to and I am surprised no-one has yet been on Mastermind with their specialist subject being Rules of Racing! One would need to have a good memory or have a big head to store all that knowledge.

The New Year, the dawn of 2003, was arriving and the authorities needed to get with it; there were less jump jockeys around than there used to be. There is far more racing and the jockeys have a far greater work load than in the past with PR work interviews, enquiries. In the short time they have between races they don't have a minute to themselves. It isn't only horses people go to see racing, they also go to see the jockeys. Harsh and long suspensions are not always the answer, there needs to be and has to be a reasonable solution (which is not just directly read from a rule book). The Stewards at times could do well to remember a thin coat of whitewash would last for years; a thick coat often flakes off in no time. It's like if you kick the dog for being naughty. How many times do you kick him before he has learned his lesson? Often in murder cases I am sure had the culprit not hit the victim as many times, the victim would have been badly injured, but not dead. Where do you draw the line? There are not many people who work harder, longer and put more effort into their work than jockeys.

Boxing Day 2002 at Wetherby two horses couldn't run in the first race, as there were no jockeys to ride them. Temple Dog was declared, trained by Tom Tate; the horse had only ran once that season and he had won. In the *Racing Post,* Temple Dog was the 9/4 Fav and was tipped all over. The other intended runner was Fryup Booster trained by Peter Niven. Temple Dog was to have been ridden by Richard Guest but he was re-routed to Wincanton to ride of Henrietta Knight's good chaser Cordon Bleu. No doubt the trainer would have been frantically ringing round to get a replacement jockey hours before the racing started, proving it was time the Jockey Club addressed the problem in a different way and not lay-off jockeys for minor offences. It's not easy for the trainers to ring the owners on the day of the race, saying they can't run their pride and joy because they can't get a jockey to ride it, and even worse if they have actually turned up to see their animal run. We are talking about decent horses not bone-breakers here. Fortunately for the Ivy Syndicate, the owners of Temple Dog, were able to run and win two days later at Haydock Park with their intended jockey R Guest aboard. Richard was on board Beach Road for trainer Toby Balding when he won the 1989 Champion Hurdle at 50/1 and Red Marauder to win the Grand National for his boss Norman Mason in 2000 at 33/1. All's well that ends well. As it did years ago when one day at Wetherby I had a few rides. I got a fall in the handicap chase. This was the days before ambulances followed the horses around, tending to and picking up jockeys. The horse fell at the last fence round the back. I ran all the way across the middle of the course as I had a ride in the next race, a novice chase.

On my way back, feeling a bit sore, blowing like a train, I knew I needed the ride as I needed the money, what with having a wife and a kid on the way to support. But this particular animal had only had the one run over fences at Southwell and it ended up on the deck. Southwell's fences in comparison to Wetherby's jumps were like dandy brushes. Game, or stupid, I arrived back in time to weigh out and pass the doctor, as one did after a fall. As there were only a few runners in the race my trainer said sit on him, hunt him round early on and when you get him jumping well and he gets a bit of confidence, quietly put him in the race and go from there. There are twelve fences in a two-mile chase and, to be honest, the horse didn't take any holding up. He was flat to the boards as soon as we jumped off. It's not a very long run to the first fence at Wetherby. My fellow walked straight through it. How on earth he stood up was a miracle. Needless to say by the time we recovered we were last. I gave him a slap to make sure he wasn't taking the juice out of me, and I wasn't taking the owner's riding fee off him on false pretenses. The horse ballooned the second, having had such a fright at the first. Had I known which direction to look in we could have seen Ferrybridge Power Station. In the paddock the owner of the bike told me the horse was a good jumper and the trainer agreed. When he last schooled him he was brilliant, ask so and so, which I thought was a bit Irish as, 1) I didn't even know the man he told me to ask, 2) I was in the paddock about to get a leg up on the crab after only scrambling over the jumps so far. I can tell you I wasn't looking forward to facing the huge open ditch in the straight where one of the horses in front of me fell. My lad hit the guard rail so hard he turned a complete somersault. As I lay on the floor looking under my elbow to see if my yoke had got up, he wasn't in a rush, but when he did when hacked away. I thought thank goodness for that. As I was walking up the straight with (I think) Owen Brennan, who fell at the same fence, I looked up and saw a man had caught my horse and was trotting it towards me. Had it been an ordinary punter I would have told him to mind his own business and let the bloody thing go, but it was Captain Crump, one of the most respected trainers in the business, who must have been walking the course, telling me there were only two horses still standing. Before I knew, it the captain had given me a leg up and I was facing another circuit of Wetherby's formidable fences. Somehow we got over them, all except the last, where down he came again. However, this time, as we didn't have any more fences to jump, I was on my feet before him where we reunited to finish second.

Reading the the day after Boxing Day it was not a happy ending, in fact it was very sad to read that twenty-year-old apprentice Phil Greally, who had just fourteen rides to his credit, died in Leeds Infirmary on 27 December. He was kicked in the head by a horse turned out in a field while working for Sheriff Hutton-trainer Mick Easterby the previous Saturday. Apparently, a strap on a New Zealand rug had come loose on one of the horses turned out in the field; Phil and a stable girl went to put it right. Phil slipped and one of the other horses in the field lashed out and kicked him on top of his head with its hind legs as it cantered past. The youngster was taken to York hospital then later transferred to Leeds. For his mother, who is disabled, it was an emotional time. Elaine Wiles our Northern Almoner of the IJF forsook all her seasonal festivities and kept a bedside vigil throughout the five days he was in hospital, but he never regained consciousness. The family had an exceptionally dire hand dealt them. Phil's father John was laid up recovering from a fractured hip and pelvis he sustained in a recent car crash. Elaine told me on the phone, John was in absolute agony as he was in no fit state to travel. However, the Leeds doctor said if it was at all possible the father should come as his son was so ill, and would not last much longer. Therefore, John went. So sad. It was only three months since eighteen-year-old Rebecca Davis suffered fatal head injuries after being dragged by a horse. The pair of them just kids. Phil's parents, as you can imagine, are not going well and nor are they wealthy. Thankfully for them, the IJF will at least pay for Phil's funeral and help the family along until they get sorted out.

New Year's Eve arrived. I bet when the BHB Chairman Peter Savill looked at his that morning he nearly choked on his cornflakes when he read that jockey George Duffield had been awarded the MBE in the New Years Honours List. In the paper it said that, 'the award goes to an archetypal Yorkshire man whose grit, determination and persistence have helped carve a successful career in a sport far removed from the mining area in which he was born'. And it should boost sales of his autobiography *Gentleman George*?'. Having looked up the word archetypal in the dictionary, as was mentioned in his book it means 'original'. I thought he might have got his gong for swearing or fighting! Also, it said the veteran rider was on holiday with wife Anne in Tobago, and therefore was not available for comment. What it didn't say was that while he and Anne were drinking champagne and burning their backsides on the beach in the beautiful sun out in Tobago, I was out every morning in the freezing cold and pissing rain keeping an eye on their yard for them in Constable Burton, North Yorkshire. While they were away not only did the old jockey ask me to look after his wife's horses whilst they were gallivanting about, he brought his car for me to look after and garage it for him. As with everything with G Duffield, it is absolutely immaculate regardless of what George says; he loves it to bits. When they were halfway through their hols, I got Ian, Anne's secretary to send George a text message to tell him I'd painted his Merc white and it looked a lot better now!

No wonder George wanted me to look after his car in his absence. Most racing lads don't always behave like choirboys; some tend to get in a spot of mischief. On occasions it can be like working with the Taliban.

A young Welsh lad worked for us at Cockerham and one afternoon, while most of us were away racing, Taffy thought he would take one of the tractors out for a spin up the gallops. I don't know how, but he managed to drive it through a hedge and finished up in a ditch, three or four fields past our boundary fence. The boyo also ended up in hospital with a broken leg.

Another of our apprentices, Steve Houlker, a real nice, clean, well-mannered lad, rode us a few winners. All of his spare time, he spent at our local parachute club. He loved it. One day, he and a Para pal only parachuted off Blackpool Tower! They must have been seen by many people. By the time they landed and legged it to the getaway car which Steve had parked as close as he could to the Tower to get a flyer as soon as they hit the ground. The police, sirens screaming, were frantically winging all over Blackpool looking for the culprits. Steve and his mate were stopped by the police for speeding six miles away from the scene. They were only found out when the lawmen spotted the parachutes had been thrown in the back of the car.

When Anne told the owners she was going on holiday the previous year, and that I would be keeping my eye on things and would ring them every other Sunday, one owner said 'Ok, that's good – Jack coming in. If that's the case don't be in a rush back.' Alan, Anne's gallop and handyman, knows I am a Leeds United supporter and was telling me one day, when he was a kid that he had always wanted to be a footballer and a goal keeper in particular. As he was reminiscing about when he played for his local town team as a young man, he told me he once let in eighteen goals in one game! With no shame he said, 'I think eighteen is a record.' Mind you, he went on to say we didn't have a very good side, no mention about the goalie. He sounds a bit like that Gary Sprake who played for us a few years ago. He had a habit of dropping the ball.

Talking of Leeds, Eddie Foster my old school mate, as seen in a redder shirt than me, reminded me recently of the picture house we used to attend in Easy Road when we were kids living in Leeds. We christened it the 'Bug Hutch', as it was renowned for being scruffy. Eddie in later years became quite friendly with the two Jewish brothers who owned the joint, they were called Issy and Abby. Like many people of that breed they were not renowned for throwing their money about. One day a traveller came to the picture-house telling them he could for a 'good price' re-cover all the seats. With this particular cloth it would be so much, in this other cloth it would be a bit more expensive. It didn't take the brothers long to chase the traveller away telling him the only thing they wanted to cover their seats were people's backsides!

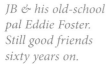

JB & his old-school pal Eddie Foster. Still good friends sixty years on.

The final night of the year arrived and I wrote Michael Hourigan a nice begging letter asking him if he could see his way to letting us have a racing plate, shoe or signed photo of his good chaser Beef Or Salmon, either worn or taken when the horse won the Ericsson Grade 1 Chase at Leopardstown on 27th. I knew Michael fairly well as, in the past, he had bought horses to go jumping from our yard. One in particular was called Honey Trader. Michael bought him at the sales for little money and he was owned by Chris and Antonia Deuters. Although we did win with Honey Trader on the flat he wasn't much, but Michael had bought him to go jumping, seeing as the minimum distance over hurdles is two miles.

Honey Trader was sired by Beveled out of a sharp mare. The horse lived on its nerves. The only way I thought the horse would stay two miles would be travelling in a horsebox. I was wrong yet again! The horse never stopped winning for Michael. Little wonder he always had a good look at our horses when they were in the sales. I bet he thought I couldn't train ivy up a wall or even pigs to be dirty. It seemed a bit slow at the time making money for our BBQ to reduce our deficit of £22,700 as not much was happening. Although we were getting a few good items collected up to auction on our big day. My granddad taught me never get anything you can't pay for, and whatever you do, make sure you don't owe anyone a penny before the first day of a new year. Mind you, granddad wasn't a racehorse trainer. But taking the old gentleman's advice whenever possible, as we would be going into the New Year, I knew I must pay the £700 we owed to Joy Hawkins as I told her I would as soon as we have enough money in our IJF account. So our fund target now stood at £22,400. It was only a temporary setback; I could feel it in my water. Joy's pictures, I knew, would earn us plenty of profit.

New Year's Day 2003 arrived. It was happy birthday horses, especially our Ollie, OI Oyston who was twenty-seven that day. What do you buy for a horse that has everything? Last Christmas I bought him a new Rambo turnout rug. He gets as much food to eat as he can, he has an en suite paddock stable bedded up with straw to his belly and a pony for company. I give him carrots and Polos every day plus lots of TLC; he could also have my dinner every day if he wanted it. I would give him anything I have in my power to make him look, feel or be better. I love the old lad to bits and what a star he has been. I bought him as a yearling at Doncaster Sales for £2,600. Ever since we broke him as a yearling I rode him just about all the time he was in training and he didn't retire till he was twelve. That must be thousands of miles. Until he was five years old, he was owned by the Oyston Estate Agency. Owen, one of the bosses wrote and told me to sell Ollie and their other two or three older horses, then buy more yearlings to replace them. It made sense for their firm as all their horses had Oyston somewhere in their name which couldn't be changed once the horses had run, making it good advertising at someone else's expense. Jo rang Owen and asked him how much he wanted for Ollie as Jack didn't just like him, he idolised him and wouldn't want him to go to the sales – and that if he went to the sales Jack would buy him back even if it meant selling the place. So Owen gave him to me as a present. Therefore, most of Ollie's twenty-six wins have been for yours truly in the patriotic red, white and blue colours. Ollie was such a good ride in races and a complete gentleman; often I would put up our inexperienced apprentices on him in races. By popping out as soon as that gate opened and grabbing the inside rail he would make a moderate kid look good. All he had to do was sit still and let him run.

One of my favourites, Ollie in his paddock at our house in Hinton.

One night after tea, I tacked Ollie up to ride round the gallops and check the cattle that were turned out, a thing I often did. I noticed there was a sheep on the bank of the ditch near our schooling ground at Cockerham with its two lambs on the opposite side of the fence. I jumped off Ollie and tethered him cowboy-style by the reins to the fence, as I had often done before. This particular sheep was a real idiot, as most of them are, flighty and scatty as hell, scuffling about as I am trying to catch it, we had travelled about two furlongs down this dike bank when the crazy beggar jumped in the dike that had at least a foot of horrible stinky, thick black slimy mud in the bottom of it. By the time I got the crazy animal out it was pitch black. I was wet through and stank awful. Taking a short cut across our fields and gallops I dropped all my stinking wet clothes off at the back door and galloped bollock-naked upstairs to have a hot bath. Jo was watching the telly sitting round the fire. Half an hour or so later I poured Jo and myself a whisky and dry ginger and got stuck into my entries, which I did whenever I had a spare minute. About 11 o'clock, 'Bloody 'ell Jo', I said. 'Ollie's still tied up where that stupid sheep went into that dike!' Jo took me over in the car and I rode the old fella back and put him away. Next morning he had eaten up and I rode him out with the first lot; he was as fresh as paint and not a bother on him.

It had been a poor start, in fact, one could say a disastrous start, to the New Year for the Cullens and Farrells. I had just settled down reading my and checking the racing and football results when Eileen Cullen rang to tell me her brother Christopher, who worked for Securicor, had just been killed in a car crash. She and her husband PJ would go straight to tell Mary, her mother who lives near York and who will no doubt be gutted. In fact the whole family were; they are so close. It was hard for Christopher to take it when his Dad died in 1999. Since Paddy Farrell's injury on Border Flight in 1964 Grand National, which left him in a wheelchair, with his mother's help Christopher used to bathe him and dress him and took his dad racing, especially to Wetherby. He went there most meetings or wherever Paddy wanted to go. Having said that, he was also his mother's right hand man, as Mary is not a strong lady and suffers terribly with a bad back. She will also miss him around, as he tended her garden and did most of the heavy jobs around the house. The funeral was arranged for 1 p.m. the following Monday, 13 January, at Haxby, the same church where the service was held for his father.

On Tuesday, 7 January, I attended the funeral of retired trainer Bob Ward. On my way there I picked up Walter Wharton at Wetherby. Walter is renowned for being smart and proper, especially for his immaculately polished shoes, bliffed up Army-style, so you could see your face in the toe-caps. Although one day at the Yorkshire Show, he noticed his shoes were a bit dirty as he had been walking around the show ground. He went to someone there who was polishing shoes to rub them over, only to learn the wretched man had cleaned them with dubbin, which soon took the shine off them completely, and it took him ages to get the shine back. Walter trained Vaguely Noble to win the Observer Gold Cup at Doncaster now called the Timeform. The horse was sold on for the record amount at the time £136,000 guineas and later won the 1968 Prix De L'Arc De Triomphe, and trained by E Pollet in France. Although Walter and I are both retired we are not exactly roughed-off. Walter, whose son Wally described his recreations as eating and smoking cigars, in his late 70s rides out just about every day, we, along with another former trainer Eric Storey and his wife Lily, Cockerham farmers Bill and June

A scene reminiscent of Last of the Summer Wine *television series. On our annual day's following fell hounds in Cumbria.*

Robinson, ex show-jumper John and Anne Warmsley who are farmers, and John and Norah Earnshaw who follow the fell hounds and stay for a few days each year in Cumbria. Don't we look like the 'Last of the Summer Wine' cast?

Walter and I have been great pals for years. Being a King's Trooper, I must say like Walter, I like things nice and ship-shape, but proving it doesn't always work out for the best. One day as the horses were walking around the yard at Cockerham, thinking the exercise sheets could do with a clean as they looked grubby, I said to our head lad: 'Gather all the sheets up, some forty or so, make an appointment to get them dry-cleaned, all in one go at the cleaners in Garstang.' God only knows what they did to them, but when they came back they had shrunk so badly they would have fitted greyhounds, certainly not racehorses. They must have boiled them. They were no good at all and we binned them. The cleaners were going to compensate us but never got on with it. We certainly never took any more for them to work the debt off.

JB & Walter Wharton relaxing in Barbados.

The above photo shows Walter and I relaxing on holiday in Barbados. In the other photo I am not trying to drown Walter, as he is a non-swimmer; I am teaching him to swim. When we were there we also met up with trainer Bill Marshall, the island's twelve times champion trainer, who trained a very good sprinter years ago called Raffingora in England. He was a fighter pilot in the Second World War. On two occasions, he was shot down and survived, and was awarded a DFC for his skill and courage. In 1972, he and Joe Mercer the jockey were involved in an air crash where Bill rescued Joe from the wreckage. Bill and his wife Pam emigrated to Barbados a number of years ago. I'm not sure who gave me the poem, Walter or Bill, but thought you might like to read it.

The Trainer

'I envy the life of a trainer'
Said a chap I met on a plane,
'A lucrative life in the open
Surrounded by birds and champagne!'

JB giving Walter Wharton swimming lessons in Barbados.

'High living at Ascot and Deauville
At seasonal times of the year,
Then home for a healthy old gallop
Why, it's life at ten thousand a year!'

Amazed at the stranger's delusions,
At a loss if to laugh or to cry,
I wondered if I should correct him
And thought it at least worth a try

The 'open'. My God, have you tried it
In winter with snow on the ground
At seven o'clock in the morning,
And more wrinkles than inches around?

Our social life may seem all roses
But the birds aren't for us, and the 'Fizz'
You use for reviving an owner
When he finds out how bad his horse is

Peers, prostitutes, pansies and punters,
Does that sound a pretty odd bunch?
On the turf they are prominent owners
And we have the whole boiling to lunch!

You'd get quite a new view of Ascot
In tails, a top hat on your head,
Sprinting up hill to the paddock
With a saddle and two stone of lead!

Deauville has many attractions
Your owners adore them, of course
They go out to dinner with Pollett
And you go home minus your horse

Your Head Man awaits your arrival,
With relish he tells you his news
The Travelling Man's broke his leg, Sir,
The box driver's gone on the booze

Bert's had a row at his digs, Sir
The new girl is pregnant, of course
Sir Harry is coming round stables
There's ringworm all over his horse

The wages are up thirty bob, Sir
And I'm going down with the 'flu
You thank him and try to look cheerful
Goddamit, what are you to do?

The telephone never stops ringing
It's Sunday but you'll get no rest
The owners consider it their day
For getting complaints off their chest.

Then there're jockeys, those Knights of the Pigskin!
A look at their ladies will tell
For your winners they get all the credit
And most of the presents as well!

The betting boys bunch us at Christmas,
By day they're extremely polite
But spend all their spare time conspiring
To get at your horses at night

The Press have the last word in all things
As Trainers they'd all top the tree
The fact that they haven't a licence
Is terribly lucky for me.

The Stewards demand explanations,
But listen with cynical looks
It's obvious in their estimation
That Trainers are all licensed crooks

It's wonderful how we continue,
In spite of complaints from our banks

To render such service to racing,
For peanuts and damned little thanks!

In normal, in other professions
To prosper, retire and die,
But trainers go on training horses
I'm buggered if I can think why!

Christopher Farrell was only forty-one-years old, just in his prime. Bob died at the ripe old age of ninety-five; he was a real character. The strokes he pulled and the jokes he told were endless and really funny. Bob was so amusing, even in his last few years when Gill, his wife, pushed him around the occasional race meeting in a wheelchair. For humour he would have qualified for the Guinness Book of Records. As a trainer he was renowned for getting sharp two-year-olds ready. Mainly in sellers as in his day there were a lot of two-year-old selling races, which earned him the title that he was very proud of 'The selling plate king'. Bob would run two or three youngsters in the same race, many owned by his principle owner Mr EA Brown, who also owned horses with several other trainers. Bob would sometimes win with the long priced one. He did in 1962, at the Lincoln Meeting when Lester Piggott rode the short-priced favourite Ione and Bob won with the other horse, Polly Macaw. The stewards took a dim view and warned Bob off for a long time and also Lester, for a period of time.

The service was held at All Saints Church, Owston Park. If there is such a thing as heaven and Bob could be looking down on us, I thought he would have approved as there was a full house in church and he arrived in a hearse drawn by two black horses. The church is set amid the beauty of the Owston Estate almost hidden by the trees with its eighteenth-century Hall and its hamlet of seventeenth and eighteenth century houses. The only building erected in modern times was the vicarage in 1926. The setting is tranquil and beautiful – I know, as I was the stable jockey and head lad to Harry Maw in 1960 when he trained at Owston.

Although the yard is now defunct and has been turned into a nursing home, it has not lost its character. It was at the same time that I met and married Jo. The guv'nor (Harry Maw) was as good a character as Bob and they were great mates. If you get the chance to read my book *It's Tougher At The Bottom*, one could read a few tales about Harry Maw and Owston.

Following the service, Gill put on a lovely spread at Bob's local pub. I have some fond memories of Bob, the loveable rogue. In 1969, when I was just starting training from a small yard I rented from John Massarella, who owned the famous international show jumper Mr Softee at Arksey near where Bob lived. There was a man called Harry Lindley, the very man who founded the Northern Apprentice Racing School at Doncaster, who was also setting up training locally and Bob was getting him a few clients together and generally helping him. When Harry's licence to train came through, he held a house party and I was invited. His home was quite a small bungalow, as you can imagine it was packed with horsey people. The ladies did what they had to do

Bob Ward.

inside the house whilst us men peed outside up a fence in the garden. Bob and I were letting out some of the booze only he was a bit worse for wear and he fell down. That wouldn't have been so bad only it was blowing a gale and snowing like mad. Bob had his trousers round his ankles and I was doing my best to get him on his legs but it was impossible. He kept saying 'do you like my underpants?' To be honest in the blizzard I couldn't see anything. I was saying, 'come on Bob stop tinkering about and let's get in the house its 'effing freezing.' He was rolling about in the four to six inches of snow and his trousers were now off completely. I picked them up and took them into the house and got a couple of men from inside to give me a lift in with Bob. We put him in front of the fire. It was no wonder he said 'do you like my underpants?' They were red white and blue with the same pattern as the Union Jack. To his last days Bob told people I had pushed him down in the snow!

At the wake, Walter and I met up with quite a few old pals we hadn't seen for a while reminiscing about old times. There, a friend of Bob's told me a tale about his old mate. It happened when one of Bob's owners part paid his training bill by giving Bob a greyhound that was in training and was due to run at Sunderland dog track. The trainer of the dog was very bullish about its chances and told Bob that he had been doing some healthy fiddling with the dog in its last few races, and tonight the dog was off and was an absolute certainty. In the trainer's opinion the dog could break a leg half way round, finish the race walking on three legs and still win, 'make no mistake, tonight he will do the business'. Then he told Bob to put his maximum wager on. Although Bob arranged many gambles on horses, he did it for his owners, not for himself, and his punters would put the money down and look after Bob if and when the touches came off. Therefore Bob himself was not a great big hitter, so he said to the trainer, 'You put the money on' 'How much' said the trainer. 'I will have the same as yourself' was Bob's reply thinking the trainer would be in the £20-£50 bracket. Just before they put the dogs in the traps the dog handler told Bob he got Bob £500 to £200 on and the dog was now even money favourite. You could imagine when he said to his mate who told me the tale; 'let's get near the exit, just in case the dog gets stuffed so we can do a runner.' As it happened, thankfully the dog did win and Bob collected the money. John and Coral North were also present at the wake as they were friendly and lived locally to Bob and Jill.

When we first trained at Almholm near Arksey Doncaster, John and Coral were one of the first to send us a horse to train. We have been friends ever since. In fact, before we moved to Cockerham, John and I were going to buy a 300-acre farm in a village called Sykehouse for only £30,000 each. It was a rambling, run-down, old house, all down to grass, which badly needed draining, re-seeding and some TLC. It also had a couple of miles of derelict railway track that also went with it, that would have made a brilliant all-weather gallop. John decided that it would be too expensive and drawn out for us to make a go of it. I have often wondered about how we would have shaped up had we gone for that with John, instead of buying Cockerham but having trained a good few winners at Cockerham we can't grumble.

There was a letter of thanks in the post, which I felt I must add to this summary. It was from John Stephenson, the Lancashire lad who did our bottle tombola at the previous year's BBQ and for the last few years we were training at Cockerham He raised money for all kinds of charities. Although John made out in the letter that it was mainly down to me that Rebecca got her wheelchair, I can assure you he played a big part in it.

06 January 2003

Dear Mr Berry,

I am writing to you to thank you for your help in purchasing a new custom made wheelchair for a beautiful little nine-year-old girl. Rebecca is a lovely girl who I had the great pleasure of caring for while on this year's HCPT Pilgrimage to Lourdes. Becky is registered blind and profoundly deaf and wears bilateral hearing aids, she takes no solid food and is fed via a tube into her stomach. Becky can stand for short periods and can only walk short distances – on a good day!
I must apologise for the delay in writing to thank you, but I wanted to wait until Becky had her 'all-singing, all-dancing' wheelchair. It cost to buy £2,000.00 and the £1,500.00 you raised at your open day was marvellous. We managed to raise the balance from our local Rotary group. She has a lovely family, cared lovingly for by her Mum Linda and Father Jim. Becky has an older brother Andrew (11) and younger brother Callum (13 months). The wheelchair purchased for Becky has been a great bonus for the family. It has an electric motor for her mum's ease and the wheelchair itself is very funky, painted a bright metallic green and purple, very trendy for a nine-year-old girl. She looks a proper young lady in it. I enclose a photo of Becky taken at the recent HCPT Christmas party.

Once again, many thanks of behalf of the Stephenson's and especially Jim and Linda who were so very grateful and extremely moved.

Hope you are keeping well.

John Stephenson

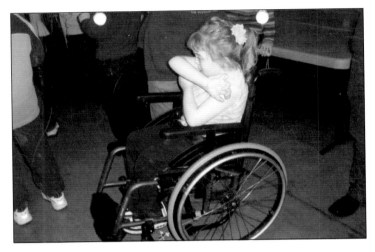

Becky in her new wheelchair.

Chapter Five

Who Would Want to be a Starter?

•

Jo and I were invited to the racecourse starter Gerry Scott's retirement party. It was at his house in a village called Healy near Masham, just a few miles from our house. Gerry, before he was a starter, was a northern jump jockey and he rode for the Middleham trainer Captain Neville Crump. In 1960, Gerry was aboard Merryman II when he won the Grand National. He can also claim to be, along with Paddy Farrell, Stan Hayhurst, Nimrod Wilkinson, Jumbo Wilkinson, Jack Boddy, Larry Major and yours truly, a founder member of the Northern Jockeys' Association. This was before north and south amalgamated, which is now the Professional Jockeys' Association. At Gerry's gathering there were lots of racing officials, ex-jockeys, owners and trainers, and we had plenty to drink and eat. Gerry and his other half, Avril, put on a splendid spread. I have known and been friendly with Gerry Scott just about all my racing life. He was a good jockey, a first class starter and a gentleman to boot.

Although four-times Champion jump jockey Fred Winter was a top class jockey and a gentleman who everyone looked up to in the weighing room, I for one, as a struggling northern jockey called him 'Mr' Winter – and that was when I picked up the courage to talk to him. In addition to his riding career he was the first jockey to be awarded a CBE. On retiring from the saddle, would you believe, his application to become assistant starter was turned down. Fred went on to become a champion jump trainer and the first jump trainer to win £100,000 prize money in a season. You could say the authorities got it wrong. As a starter, Gerry Scott knew exactly when to let the tapes go. All the horses and jockeys were given the same chance and he commanded so much respect from the jocks, he didn't have to put up with any flack or nonsense. With him being so good a horseman and a past jockey, he knew the script and the jockeys knew he did, as would FT Winter. (Unlike the old boy who started races years ago on the Isle of Man, when Jo, myself and our apprentices used to ride over there at Great Meadow.) The island's main trainer, Dizzy Righall, would send a small private hire plane from the Isle of Man to Blackpool Airport, which picked us all up to ride the horses at the races. On one occasion I rode a treble there. Once, in the weighing room, I heard bits of gossip that two of the local jockeys plotting how to stop me from making the running in the feature race, Monarch's Gift, the mare I was riding who was a bit of a cow if taken-on, and they knew it. If she wasn't allowed to bowl along in front, she would down tools and sulk. They would know all these things because, if we couldn't get to the meeting due to commitments on the mainland, these 'Herb's' would ride the horses in our places. To be honest, they didn't welcome us riding their horses and taking the bread out of their mouths, so to speak. Mind, in all fairness not many of them would have been good enough to have ridden in races on the mainland. So we never received much help from them. In the previous race, I rode a horse called Billy Bond. No horse race is just a walk in the park, no matter how cramped the odds, they all need 'sussing out'; but I thought Dizzy's mare was a good thing. As we were all getting our girths checked at the start, I made sure the starter did mine. I told him what a grand job all these part-time officials do on the day and so on. 'Oh sir,' I said, 'in the next race I ride this old mare, Monarchs Gift, of Dizzy's and she's a bit of a bag at the gate. I don't want to cause you problems but I would like to make sure she gets off. Could I suggest I take her on the wide outside and try to be trotting approaching the start?' (He let the horses go by a flag when he got them in some sort of line.) The starter thanked me for telling him of the problem and said he would keep an eye on her. Down at the start I reminded the starter that this was the bitch I told him about earlier. I kept the mare out of the back and with the two local jockeys being on would-be front runners. Also, they were bang on the inside so as not to lose an inch looking all over for me.

As the starter was climbing on to his DIY rostrum, he shouted, 'Are you alright Berry?' I gave her a kick in the belly, galloping in. 'Yes sir,' I shouted, and poached about six lengths on everything. I never saw another horse in the race. Martin Pipe and AP McCoy would have been proud of me.

Part of the riding arrangement with Dizzy was that we were supposed to help and teach the local jockeys as best we could to race ride, as they were keen to get racing going on the island. We probably taught them most of what they knew, but we kept a bit up our sleeve and didn't teach them all WE knew! In fact to be fair, we put them away whenever possible because we wanted to ride the winners.

The funeral of Christopher Farrell was very moving, the church being the same one as his father's funeral, St Margaret's, Clitheroe. It was a repeat performance of his Dad's day in 1999. The church was absolutely packed. In fact, so full that I, along with quite a few mourners, had to stand at the back, as

Paddy Farrell and myself at one of our Open Days at Cockerham. It took me a long time to get over the loss of Paddy and I still often think of him.

every seat was taken. The collection was shared between the IJF and the Children's Outpatient Unit at St James Hospital, Leeds. It's awful really how it takes a funeral to meet up with old friends and acquaintances. It had been years since I saw Johnny Markham, who lodged for years with Paddy Farrell's mother in Ireland when I met him there as an apprentice. Also there was ex-jockey, Jimmy Power, who rode Freebooter to win the 1950 Grand National, Gerry Kelly, Paddy Guiry and Owen Brennan, all of us who were friends of Christopher's father and rode with him.

Jimmy Byrne, another pal of mine fell off his perch aged sixty-three. Jimmy knew everyone and everyone knew Jimmy. He helped me for years at the sales. Whenever I bought yearlings in England or Ireland, I just handed Jimmy the pass outs. Jimmy saw that each yearling I bought went down to the vet to get wind tested and arranged all the transport and documentation. He also sang at our Open Days and anywhere else there was any kind of a jig or party. He was famous for his rendition of 'The Crystal Chandelier' and was the life and soul of any gathering; he was a great lad. The bloodstock sales will be poorer for his absence, I will certainly miss him. The funeral took place on Friday 11 January at Newmarket Catholic Church of our Lady at 1 p.m. As one could imagine with Jimmy being so popular with the horsey fraternity, the large church was crammed full with some people even standing at the back and sides. If one can say the service was very good, this one was with two rousing hymns, 'Amazing Grace' and 'Oh Lord My God, When I in Awesome Wonder'. Jimmy would have loved it. The first reading was read by Jimmy's sister Jose, who struggled quite a bit, being upset as you would expect. The collection again benefited the IJF, a charity very close to Jimmy's heart. During some of the prayers we prayed for all those who had been injured and disabled during their work as jockeys and riders in the horseracing industry. We prayed in particular for the work of the IJF. Jimmy was then taken to the Cambridge Crematorium for cremation (the very same one Myra Hindley the sixty-year-old 'Moors Murderer' was cremated at following the refusal of several others). Jimmy's ceremony was followed by a lively wake at Tattersall's Sales Paddock at 4 p.m., where a lovely spread fit for a king was put on by the sales company with every type of food and as much drink as one wanted. I bet there were some thick heads by about 10 p.m.

Seeing lots of the mourners brings a lump to one's throat. With the likes of Grand National jockey Tommy Stack who won the great race in 1977 on Red Rum, now a trainer, and who had recently recovered from meningitis after being desperately ill for such a long time. In order to be there he had journeyed from Tipperary in Ireland. Like the song goes, 'It's a long way to Tipperary'. It was also a long time since I visited the former jockey in Hexham hospital in 1977, when he was recovering from a horrendous fall. His horse slipped and fell when walking round the paddock, smashing Tommy's pelvis. However, Jimmy's sister travelled further than Tommy. She came all the way from Canada, where she had lived for the past twenty-two years. As I said, Jimmy was a great man for a singsong and didn't take much encouraging to get up. He also made a couple of recordings, including one song he was famous for singing wherever he went, 'The Crystal

The popular Jimmy Burns.

Chandelier', which was definitely his favourite. Once, at Newmarket Sales, there had been a number of horses withdrawn for one reason or another. The brilliant auctioneer, David Pym, announced from his rostrum that they were at least half an hour ahead of themselves. To skive away a bit of time, 'we will ask Jimmy Byrne to come up to the rostrum and sing 'The Crystal Chandelier'. Imagine walking up all those steps to the rostrum in the vast Newmarket auditorium to sing a song with no accompanying music, with everyone's eyes glaring at you. You need to have some bits to do that, which he had. The crowd went mad, they loved it.

At the wake, Don McCain (Red Rum) called for some order to say a few words, and to thank Tattersall's for putting the magnificent spread on, then he announced, 'Jack Berry will now sing you one of Jimmy's favourite songs as those two were always singing wherever they went.' So I sang the 'Jolly Farmer', which was also one of Jimmy's favourites. At least I had some music, as I sang it over the tape from a recording. Jimmy's sister liked the song a lot and said she would like a copy, therefore I gave her the cassette so she could take it back to Canada with her.

A week before the funeral, Maurice Gibb of the Bee Gees singing group from the seventies died. At Jimmy's wake, Tommy Stack said if the Bee Gees ever make a comeback, I could take Maurice's place! You have to laugh sometimes, even on tragic occasions. Tommy Stack is 95% deaf since his illness and every time anyone spoke to him, he would say to his mate Paul, who came over with him from Ireland, 'what's he say?' even though Tommy read lips well. I may just name a yearling that – What's he Say? – after Tommy. Whilst at the wake, Len Wilkinson gave me a fiver, I'm not sure whether it was for me to not sing anymore or for the IJF, but I will give the IJF the benefit. Martin Pickering gave me a cheque for £30 which brought our total needed to reach our thirty grand target to £23,370.

I must also say a sincere thank you to Tattersall's for putting on such a good feast for Jimmy. The sales play a very big part in the lives of trainers and racing people. Although mainly it's hard business, we do have some fun at times. One very hot day many years ago, I was in attendance at Ascot Sales. Ascot Sales very rarely attract big pundits or good horses. In fact, a majority of the horses were moderate to say the least. For all that, there was always a good feeling to the place, one could have a laugh and it always buzzed. One day, there was an exceptionally good-looking girl there wearing a white sweater with the biggest pair of tits you ever did see. The horse she was looking after had no form at all. In fact, as equine greatness goes you could say it was of no account. However, that day at the sales you could have mistaken it for a Group horse as the animal was pulled out for inspection more than any of the other horses at the sale that day!

When the potential 'buyers' (or should I say 'tyre kickers', because they had no intention of buying the animal) asked her to walk it up and trot it back, you can imagine it created a lot of interest; no sooner had the poor girl put the bike back in its box than some other berk would ask her if she minded pulling it out to do the same all over again. I bet her ribs fair ached with her cleavage bouncing about all day. In the ring, even with all the interest shown in the preliminaries, it realised just a few hundred pounds. A few days after Jimmy's funeral, Jo and I took the plinths David (joiner) Bowes made for the racing plates of Kyllachy, Invincible Spirit and Bollin Eric, to the jewellers to get the owners, trainers and jockeys names engraved on square silver plaques to get ready for the big day.

I busied myself designing the BBQ tickets, as we needed them to look good. We also intended to have some raffle tickets properly printed up. Therefore, I was still working on accumulating some decent prizes, such as a couple of tickets with lunch thrown in at York races, a day at Manchester United ground and meals at top restaurants, plus the likes of a paid up share in a racehorse, a box of good wine, or £100 worth of bet vouchers from bookmakers etc. I wanted to get them listed on the raffle tickets in really good time and send them out early. My intentions were to give plenty of time and send chosen people, say, £50 worth to sell weeks before the event itself to make sure we succeeded in fulfiling our target.

On 21 January, I had a meeting with Peter Mason of Sporting Fine Art at our house. Peter gave me six very nice prints of Rock of Gibraltar and one of dual Champion Hurdle winner Istabraq for our big day in July. I waited for it, and yes, there was a catch. In return he left me with 20 of the same prints of Rock of Gibraltar for me to get signed by Sir Alex Ferguson. Although it actually meant me going to Alex's house in Cheshire to get them signed, as I didn't see much of him at the time with us now living in Yorkshire, and I didn't train for him anymore. When I was training for the soccer legend, he loved to come to the yard to see the horses work, it was a nice retreat for him. Alex is a good mate, so I couldn't see a problem with getting the prints signed, it was just a case of catching up with him. When I was talking to him at the Racehorse Owners Association Awards in December 2002 at the London Hilton, I told him he takes more getting hold of than the Queen with his new found fame with Rock of Gibraltar; he just laughed.

The next day my old training pal Ken Ivory and his partner Val came to stay with us for a few days. Ken, who retired from the art last year, trained that very sharp mare, Dawn's Delight. We intended to visit Coolmore Stud in Ireland to see Rock of Gibraltar, High Chaparral and many more great horses that stand there. To say Ken and the rest of us were looking forward to the trip was an understatement. For a couple of weeks we had been really revved up and talked of little else.

At 10 a.m. we arrived at Leeds Airport where we learned to our horror that the Cork plane was cancelled due to a fault in its engine and it was the only plane going to Cork that day. The only alternative on offer was that we could get a flight to London and then on to Cork, which would arrive at 4 p.m. However, our appointment at Coolmore was at 2 p.m. and it would take at least one-and-a-half hours to get there from the airport. So we had to cancel our hotel rooms, the hire car and abort our trip. As we arranged for Dave (joiner) Bowes to look after the livestock, the two women suggested we make the most of it and go shopping to Harrogate! I thought that's all we need, my missus let loose with her plastic cards shopping in Harrogate. It was bad enough the Irish hotel saying they won't refund our money as we didn't cancel

What a privilege for Jo and I to have our photo taken with the famous Sadler's Wells on our visit to Coolmore.

at least two days prior to the scheduled time of arrival. Now that was really Irish, as we didn't even know the plane wasn't going until we got to the airport. No! I suggested we went to see Harvey and Sue Smith as they only lived a few miles from Leeds airport. They were both in and they were really pleased to see us and we were made very welcome. Harvey gave us a tour around his gallops and schooling ground in his Range Rover. It was fantastic and we had a great day. Harvey had the trophies he won from show jumping over the years in one of their rooms and it has to be seen to be believed. There are literally hundreds from all over the world. We were in stitches laughing at the things Harvey said. It was a pity when we finished our guided tour, as it was so good. Afterwards, we went down to the Smiths local pub for lunch where there were some horsey people who knew us all and we thoroughly enjoyed our day. However, Jo and I at a later date did visit Coolmore and Ballydoyle, as seen above with the brilliant Sadler's Wells and chatting to Aidan O'Brien.

On our return home, I showed Ken the Joy Hawkins' prints and he bought a couple. I told him they stood us at £30 each. I said, 'Whatever you give us over that it is profit and goes to our cause.' Being the generous man Ken is, he gave me £220 leaving our goal to reach at £23,150. We were getting there. Although we would have to fork out £120 for the plaques, when they got back from being engraved at the jewellers the following week; you can't have your cake and eat it. On occasions you have to speculate to accumulate, and if you remember, early on John Dunlop sent us £50 with Invincible Spirit's racing plate to help with costs. We were also due another bill from the printers as I had ordered the 400 tickets to be printed up for our do and I asked the printer to put numbers on each ticket to enable us to have a draw. I thought about getting one of Joy's prints framed as the prize.

On 1 February – for a welcome change from funerals – Jo and I had been invited to a wedding at St Mary's Church Ashbury, which dates from the

Aidan O'Brien having a heart-to-heart chat with JB at Balydoyle.

twelfth century. It was the wedding of Dana Mellor, who is the daughter of three-times champion jockey Stan Mellor. Stan was the first jump jockey to ride 1,000 winners. There's more; Dana's mother Elaine, was also the Lady Amateur Champion three times. Dana herself was a very good little 'jockette', who was apprenticed to me and rode quite a number of winners when lady jockeys were not given quite as many chances as they get today. Having said that, there are still lots of owners and trainers with a bias. Personally, to give female riders the chance to ride more winners, I have always been of the opinion lady riders should receive a 5lb allowance from the males, as do fillies from colts and geldings in races. St Mary's Church Ashbury is a quaint old church with a belfry that contains a peal of six bells that were wonderful to hear before and after the wedding. The church was full to capacity. However, one of the most important men there was declared a non-runner in the morning, but managed to pull a few strings and got a re-instatement. That was The Bride's father, Stan. Stan started to feel unwell just after Christmas and two weeks previously he had pains in the back of his arms and was also suffering from chest pains. He went along to the hospital for a check up where his heart was monitored while he was on a treadmill. Expecting to be on it for five or ten minutes they urgently took the old jockey off after 40 seconds and they inserted a drip. When he was told he had come as close to a heart attack as one could, Stan's surgeon Bill McCrea, told him under no circumstances could he go to the wedding. Although the old champion couldn't give his daughter away, it was Stan Mellor sitting two pews in front of me as Dana and Philip Brown were taking their vows.

On the right side of the aisle where Linda, Dana's sister, was sitting was a woman with two young kids about three and four years old and they were playing up. No one seemed to bother until Linda gave the mother such a look that she very soon gathered the pair up and took them out of the church. To be fair to Stan, he went home to lie down following the service instead of attending the reception, which was held at the Corn Exchange in Hungerford. It was brilliant. Plenty of drink, a good spread and the country and folk dancing to live music was great. It reminded me of my days as an apprentice which I mentioned on page 38 of my book *It's Tougher at the Bottom,* where Mr Mottram played the fiddle in the Ulleskelfe Village Hall Band. Philip, Dana's husband is a flute and harp maker, and as you can imagine he was well into the music and dancing. We did enjoy it although I did feel sorry for my old mate, Stan, missing out.

Our son Sam lives with his partner Carole at Sparsholt, in a lovely house, only about twenty miles from Hungerford. So Jo and I stayed with them overnight. It was nice to have a chat with Sam and Carole as we don't see enough of them. Also staying at their house for a few days was Ronnie Singer. Ronnie suffered head injuries quite a few years ago from a fall.

On our way back home, Jo was driving and I couldn't help raise a smile when passing the Wayside Café on the A1 near the Pontefract turn off. Once, when we were training from Arksey near Doncaster, I was driving our horse-box returning from a race meeting. John Spouse, who worked for us and was actually the first person we employed and a real good lad, was with me. John was at the time of writing, Clive Brittain's Travelling Head Lad. We pulled in at the Wayside Café car park, as we hadn't eaten for hours. The boss of the café came tearing out waving his arms about. 'Not here, no not here, it isn't a transport café,' he was telling us. 'Yes it is,' I said, 'I have stopped here before.' 'Maybe,' he said, 'but not anymore, I have just recently bought this place and I am turning it into a first-class restaurant. We've done it all up inside and we're going to start on the outside next week. We're going to fill these potholes in and re-tarmac the whole of the car park. You won't recognise the place when I've finished with it. You look nice tidy lads, put your wagon in that corner out of the way.' It wasn't difficult to notice the horsebox was a bit of an embarrassment to him, 'I'll show you what's been done inside.' 'No need to bother with that boss,' I said, 'as we want to get back home and get the horses bedded down for the night.' By then he had settled down and was all over us like a rash. 'You won't be a minute,' he insisted, with me thinking, 'now we're in hopefully he will soften up and at least make us a bacon butty.' But he didn't. Well I can tell, you I'm no decorator, but I can appreciate a good paint job when I see one and that was a real DIY effort.

A woman came into the room looking something like a sumo wrestler carrying a jug, your man said to her, 'Marion', or whatever her name was, 'can you get a couple of clean spoons please so these young men can taste the quality of the food we serve here?' With that the old girl staggered back in with the spoons, still holding the jug, which didn't look safe as she was shaking it quite a bit. Giving John and myself a spoon, he said, 'taste that. What do you think? Is it good or is it good? What do you really think of it?' As we hadn't eaten all day, I was thinking I wish it was a bloody sandwich they had made for us. Had it been today not some forty years or so ago, I would have thought we were on a game show or Candid Camera. 'It's gravy,' I said. 'Yes, I know its gravy, but have you ever tasted gravy as good as that before?', like it was some big deal.

Then he went on telling me he'd got stock cubes in it and whatever else. I told him, 'my missus makes gravy as nice as that every Sunday for our Yorkshire Puddings. I have mentioned to her the odd time that this is a nice bit of meat, but I can't ever remember saying about the gravy being nice. Gravy's gravy!' I shouldn't have bothered as it went right over his head. He finished up giving me a card and showing me an advert they had put in the *Yorkshire Post* saying that the place was now under new management and was one of the best eating houses in Yorkshire.

That night, Jo and I had arranged to go out for a meal to the Hippy Chippy Restaurant in Barnby Dun with John and Coral North. During the conversation I told them about my run in with the boss of the Wayside Café, now Restaurant. We all agreed we would go and pay a visit on Saturday then go onto the dogs at Elland Road. So I booked for the four of us at 6.30 p.m., as the greyhound stadium was only half an hour away. We went in and no one came for ages. Two more couples arrived and still no one served them. Then the boss came in and said, 'good evening' and had a little tinkle on the piano that was in the corner on a bit of a stage. He wasn't very good as he played a few bum notes, like the late Lancashire comedian Les Dawson used to do, only this fella was for real. A waitress asked us what we wanted to order and we told her, as did the other clients. I asked her how long it would take and told her we had to kick on as we were going to the greyhound stadium in Leeds. It got to about 7.15 p.m. and the starter arrived. When we were about halfway through it, the boss came back in and hopped onto the stage and I couldn't help but think for Pete's sake, don't start playing again. He picks up the mike and welcomes us to his restaurant, telling us we wouldn't believe the trouble he has had getting the place ready for the night. He then reached down near the piano and held up a curtain that had been badly burnt. By now, I was nearly pissing myself laughing. He went on to tell us all that the night before he had a couple of thugs in and they lit the curtain as they were waiting for their food. Then he started crying. By now Coral had had enough and stormed out of the place and after five minutes hadn't come back. She was only walking home down the bloody A1 in the dark! I went after her in the car. I could have done with a couple of stall handlers to give me a hand, it was an awful job getting her loaded back into the car. When I did she said 'no wonder that punter burnt down the bloody curtain, it's that cold and miserable in there. He possibly did it to raise some attention and keep warm.' We never did get the main course, I don't know what time that would have been due, but it was already too late to go dog racing. We paid for the soup and went to the local for a pint and a sandwich. Coral laughed about it afterwards but we never went back there again. Later I noticed the place looked very rundown and depressed, so it appeared the boss never did make a go of it.

I was up really early on Monday 3 February to catch the 7.30 a.m. train from Darlington to London to attend an IJF meeting. Jo was driving me to the station. We try not to leave our cars in the station car parks as on two occasions we have had the windows smashed and the culprits stole the radio and cassette player. Mind you, that was at Lancaster station. There were two or three inches of snow on the ground and it was very frosty underfoot. As we approached the mini-roundabout near Catterick Garrison, a lorry had skid-ded and shed its load that had completely blocked the road. It looked as if it would be there for quite some time and I didn't have the time to do a detour. For the first time since I became a Trustee, I couldn't make it to a meeting. Later on in the day I went to the Northallerton jewellers to pick up the engraved silver plates for Bollin Eric, Invincible Spirit and Kyllachy's plaques ready for Dave (joiner) Bowes to nail up and mount. They looked very good and I was sure the £120 the jeweller charged was money well spent. But it knocked our figure another backward step to £23,270. When Postman Pat arrived, amongst the junk mail there was a bill for £152.75 from Castle Print, the firm in Richmond who printed the 400 entry tickets for 20th July. I had them printed early to be on the ball and get some sold. Thinking that's a lot of money for 400 tickets, I rang the boss of Castle Print up and reminded him that the BBQ was for a good cause and asked him if he had made a mistake? Assuring me he hadn't and there was a lot of work involved with the tickets being red, white and blue, the artwork and me wanting them individually numbered. Being the nice fellow he is he finished up telling me to make the cheque out for £115 instead; which increased our target to £23,385.

The idea of numbering the tickets was to make sure we knew who had paid for them, and who hadn't. Also, as previously stated, we would draw a ticket and give the winner a good prize. After my call to the printers, Ken Ivory called me up. I had just sold him two BBQ tickets and I had £75 of his for the Irish hotel that he left with me. After all the grief my missus gave them, the hotel actually rang to say they would reimburse us after all, seeing as the plane couldn't take us over. This left us at £23,315 to achieve our goal. As you can see it was no penalty kick reaching our target. Although we still had five months to go, I knew it would hopefully be all right on the night. It's always paying for things that hold good causes back. I was loath to pay for anything I didn't need to, in order to reach our £30,000 target.

On 20 February, my £500 to £30 for Rhinestone Cowboy to win next month's Champion Hurdle was looking good, since he had run three times unbeaten since I struck the bet with Mike Dillon at York's Gimcrack Dinner. The horse was now 2/1 favourite ante post. At this time, Jonjo O'Neill's horses were absolutely flying. Already that season he had trained 84 winners from 411 runners, with prize money totalling £970,491, from his state of the art yard Jackdaw's Castle near Cheltenham. For the record, Thanks Keith was Jonjo's first winner that he trained from Jackdaw's Castle. Jack Clayton, a for-mer owner and friend of mine, owned him. It wasn't long till Jonjo passed the magical 100 winners, and at the time of writing this book, it made him the only person ever to ride and train 100 winners in one season.

I put the phone down after ringing Steve O'Sullivan, Jonjo's farrier, to ask him if he could get me one of Rhinestone Cowboy's racing plates that he was to wear in the Champion Hurdle whether he won, lost or drew. To make sure I got Rhinestone Cowboy's plates was the reason I rang Steve and not the trainer. I didn't want a ringer like I got for a charity auction from Phil Tuck when I asked him for the whip he used when he rode Burrough Hill Lad to win the 1984 Cheltenham Gold Cup. He gave me an old whip that looked like one kids would use at a riding school. (Unless it was the whip he took with him to Newmarket as a kid to work for Noel Murless, where the soft boy only stayed a few days and came home as he missed his mummy). Racing officials, like men of the cloth, all kosher like, you don't expect them to tell porkies. 'You never rode Burrough Hill Lad with that,' I said to him and he started laughing when I asked for a letter of authenticity. Phil Tuck is now a steward's secretary for the Jockey Club. I would have had held a steward's enquiry regarding its authenticity! Before that whip went through the auction, Phil actually rode ten winners on the trot, to equal Johnny Gilbert's record, only two behind the all-time record set by Gordon Richards. It's a wonder he didn't tell me to took the same whip round on them too. Jonjo is a lovely lad and will do anything within his power to help any good cause, but Steve was in a better position to get the shoe than Jonjo as he could just pick up a plate and say 'give him that, he won't know the difference!' Which is true.

Whilst we were staying at the Caledonian Hotel when attending the Ayr races with some of our owners, Terry Holdcroft and John Forsyth, I looked through the window of the lounge and there was a barber's shop opposite. John said, 'I'll pop over and get my haircut as there's nobody in.' I told him he was to get the brakes off as we were meeting up with some more racing friends to go out for a meal. Above the shop window was the barber's name and phone number. On my mobile I rang it as soon as he left the room. When the man answered I told him where I was staying and asked if he would cut my hair, 'I am in a real rush and could you please take plenty off?' 'Yes, no problem sir, come straightway. There's no one in the shop at the moment.' John was out in less than ten minutes telling me 'the barber's more like a bloody butcher, look what the prat's done to my hair!' I agreed with him; the prat had taken a lot off and made a right balls of it!

Brian Robb, an animal feed traveller and friend, whom I bought Spillers feed from when I first started training, called at our house. He wanted to see

JB and Brian Robb.
We go back a long way.

if I was interested in buying any of his wares now that he travels part-time for the Newark feed firm Creature Comforts. Unfortunately, he didn't make a sale but I didn't do too badly! I sold him a Joy Hawkin's print for £50, which he paid for there and then. Also, two BBQ tickets, which he promised to send a cheque for, and he even bought a badge for Jimmy's kids. On leaving, Brian shook hands with me and said how nice it was to have a cup of tea and a chat about old times again as I hadn't seen him for quite some time. He would call again when he'd had time to save up for another visit! There was now only £23,265 to go!

Jo and I returned from a two-week holiday in Spain. We went with Dave and Trish Brown to the apartment we bought there when we retired. Those of you with good memories will remember that the Brown's owned Bolshoi our multiple group-winning sprinter. We have a couple of shares in brood mares with them at their Furnace Mill Stud. While we were having a drink on the balcony in Spain, Dave's yuppie phone rang. It was Christy Grassick from Coolmore Stud wanting to know if Dave had any broodmares this season to send to the Coolmore Stud. In conversation, Dave told Christy he was in Spain at the moment having a drink with yours truly, so Christy told Dave to put me on. Chatting away and not being too far from the pace, I asked if it would be possible to get a really nice big photo of their dual Derby winner High Chaparral to auction off at our IJF BBQ. Right away, and without any hesitation, 'consider it done, and in addition,' Christy said, 'you can also have for your auction a tour round Coolmore Stud and the Ballydoyle racing yard of Aidan O'Brien.' Imagine that at an auction? It should fetch quite a sum.

On one of the days while still in Spain we went to Ken Ivory's, the Radlett-retired trainer's villa. There we met Sean Coughian the very man who bred High Chaparral and he was also the proud owner of Ridgewood Pearl, the winner of the Coronation Stakes at Royal Ascot, the Irish 1,000 Guineas, and the winner of the Breeders' Cup Mile in 1995. What a nice fellow he was. Afterwards, when Sean left for his villa, Ken put on a video of the life of Ridgewood Pearl. In addition to seeing her win the races, she had a huge fan club back in Ireland and a song was made about her, which was great. Sean, John Oxx, her trainer, and dozens more fans and punters were celebrating in a pub, singing away. Never mind Barbados being called Little Newmarket, as there are so many racing folk there, in our two week visit to Spain visit we came across many people connected with the racing world. Among others there was my old mate Gerry Blum, the former Newmarket trainer, Colin Tinkler the ex-Malton jockey, who now trains at the new track at Mijas in Spain, Bill Watts the ex-Richmond trainer who trained the 1975 Arlington Million Winner, Teleprompter and John Forsyth, the boss of Countrywide Freight Limited and one of my ex-owners who has sponsored a race on Red Shirt Night for a number of years and who now has horses with our Alan. Over the years John has given hundreds of pounds towards our charities. One year on the Pirate Ship, The Jolly Roger, whilst holidaying in Barbados, John dropped his packet of cigarettes, which landed over the seats in an out of bounds area. Desperately, John said, 'make sure none of the crew are looking' while he climbed over the seats to retrieve the smokes. On our return home on the plane and in his company,

I was telling someone the tale. John said he could stop smoking if he wanted to. He finished up betting me a sizeable wedge he would stop for a year. Which he did a year to the day, or so he told me. When the year was up, he bought a packet and smoked nearly all of them in one go. To be fair to John, he gave me his winnings back as a donation to our charity Open Day. John smokes like a chimney. He is a great lad full of fun.

Jonjo O'Neill was in the news for giving one or two of his horses an easy race. As it was his third breach of the running rules, on 13th February, the Jockey Club hit the old jockey with a £6,000 fine and thirty days' suspension for one horse. I read this while I was in Spain and I also read that Jonjo intended to appeal. Although this was his third offence that season, and it looked bad, to be fair it wasn't as if the horses were short-priced, well-fancied favourites and were being stopped to organise coups. One of them hadn't run for almost two years and had been plagued by leg trouble. Surely, a nice racecourse gallop would do him more good than knocking him about and jiggering his legs up. The fact of the matter is the horse's adrenaline gets going when they get to the races and sometimes it runs better than expected. Quite rightly, following a long lay off, especially if the horse has been absent on account of injury, the trainer tells the jockey to look after him. Hence the reason some horses benefit with a racecourse gallop. Some people only know two things about horses; one end bites and the other end kicks. After we arrived back from Spain, I arranged to pick up the framed photo of Mighty Montefalco via Tony Dobbin at Catterick races.

True to his word, our postie dropped off a £70 cheque from Brian Robb. It was for the tickets. We are getting there, only £23,195 to go. On 28 February, I donned my auctioneer's hat at a Charity Race night at Richmond in aid of the local church getting central heating installed. There was a good crowd, with quite a few racing lads in attendance, as Richmond isn't far from the racing centres of Leyburn and Middleham. MC for the night was Bill Wardby, known in some circles as Billy Wizz. He is the type of man that wouldn't see another starve; he would turn his head and look the other way! Only joking, but the things Billy would do to make money would make Derek Thompson, of the Channel 4 Racing team, blush. He is a lot like Del Boy. Very sharp and witty, he had the punters laughing and he got them in a good mood and they really let go of their money. The organisers agreed to sell some of our tickets, so I left forty between them and they promised to forward the money on when they sold the tickets.

The first day of March our postman brought another £70 cheque for tickets I sold to Digby Law. That, along with the cheque Brian Robb sent, left us needing £23,055. The previous week, I rang my mate Shane Broderick in Ireland to remind him to ask the trainer Michael Hourigan, who Shane rode for, if he could see his way to give me to auction, either a framed photo of his good chaser Beef or Salmon or ask his farrier for one of his racing plates accompanied by a letter signed by both the farrier and Michael to prove that it was kosher. Shane rang me back on 6th March to say he had got me a signed photo and one of the very plates Beef or Salmon wore when be won the Leopardston Chase the month before. Beef or Salmon was a lovely horse and

I thought that if Best Mate could be beaten in the Gold Cup next week, it could be by this fellow. Unfortunately, lots of owners don't own horses that are good enough to run in top races on the best courses. It must be marvellous to own a horse of that calibre. It reminds me of the day at one of the early meetings at Southwell all-weather course. I ran a horse belonging to a very nice Chinese man by the name of TC Chang who, as I write, still owns horses with Linda Stubbs. The animal was only moderate; therefore, to try to win a little race, I ran it in a seller first time out. I explained to TC if his horse won he would have to be auctioned, if he got beaten anyone could claim him. 'Do you understand?' I asked him. All excited, he said, 'yes, yes let we have a winner, we meet at Southwell, me have a nice bet.' 'Alright,' I said, 'but don't go mad it's not very good.' 'Yes, very good.' 'No it's NOT very good,' I said. At Southwell, no sign of my man TC and in the race his animal finished second, would you believe? Someone only claimed it. Having given the horse's passport to the Clerk of Scales as was the procedure, TC turns up knowing his horse had finished second. Over the moon he was. 'My horse ran well Jack, I saved my money, I back him cash each way. Take me to see my horse.' 'Sorry,' I said. 'I told you what could happen, someone has claimed him, he isn't your horse anymore.' 'No, I don't want to sell him,' said TC. 'It's too late for that now and we've covered that ground before, he's already been sold!' It took forever to settle TC down and get through to him. His last request was could he go over to the racecourse stable yard to say goodbye to his former pride and joy. Thankfully when we arrived at the yard stable security told us the new owner had already left with him. I don't know if he ran abroad or left racing but I never heard of the horse again.

Jo Bower had an appointment with me to see what she could do to help us with the fund raising on 20 July. Personally, I had a few things in mind. One idea was for her to pay for the raffle tickets and commemorative brochures to be printed. In return, we could print on them that her firm was the sponsor. We had another idea, as her firm Creature Comforts supply the best possible quality shavings, a fact I have been assured of by a good source that told me Aidan O'Brien had ordered some. Aidan he would bed his horses down on £10 notes if he thought it would make them gallop faster. The idea was that they supply us with enough shavings to set fair our eight boxes for our Open Day with a board up advertising them. The reason being that hopefully we would have an abundance of horsemen there. So all in all, I was very much looking forward to meeting Jo. Jo turned out to be a lovely lady full of fun and with a great sense of humour. No problems at all in getting enough shavings to bed down on our boxes. In fact, she said she would donate a 450-bale-wagon load of the bedding for our auction. Imagine that – a value of around £2,000. In addition to that, she said she would be prepared to provide the hog-roast spit and cooker. She also offered her husband Colin plus a friend to do the carving and serving. She could also bring the young pig with her thankfully ready for cooking, which was a good job as it would be a ripe old age if they waited for me to kill it! I told her I would get someone to sponsor the pig as she had already done enough. She also happily agreed to pay for the raffle tickets and commemorative brochures to be printed, seeing as we had agreed she could have her firm's name printed on as the sponsor. Jo also took ten BBQ entry tickets to sell on for us and left a £140 cheque for me for four tickets. This reduced our target figure down to £22,915. Although Jo Bower's a very kind lady and was like meeting up with Mother Christmas, we shouldn't get carried away by thinking she's a soft touch. For starters, she worked for a number of years for the newspaper magnate, Robert Maxwell, so she's a very keen and capable businesswoman, as you would imagine. Her wares are good and well she knows it. Our day on 20 July will hopefully be frequented by a number of trainers and horse people who will no doubt see her products. Hopefully, Jo will get a good spin off with punters that will carry on trading with her indefinitely.

My friend the postman delivered a letter from another old friend of mine with £140 cheque enclosed for four BBQ tickets that I sold him when The Bride and I visited him at his home, Dinkley Old Hall, which dates back to thirtenth century, near Blackburn. The senior occupant of the hall is entitled to be called Lord Dinkley, not bad for a retired scrap man. The jackpot now stood at £22,775. Colin Bradford-Nutter and I go back a long way. He was one of our owners when we first started training at Almhome, Arksey, near Doncaster, in 1969. In fact when we moved over to Cockerham in 1972 Colin was a partner in the yard with another two, David Hall and James Kearsley, until we got on our feet. Then we, Jo and I, bought them out with the help of the Midland Bank, who were partners for much longer. Also, when I was writing my first book in 1991, *It's Tougher At The Bottom*, and needed to get a bit of peace and quiet away from, as I called it, the ever-ringing telephone to finalise things, as a retreat Colin lent us his beautiful home, Elm Lodge, in Ravensdale near Kirby Stephen in Cumbria. As, hopefully you can appreciate at the time, I was quite busy. In fact, that year we were very busy training over 100 horses sending out at least one winner to every flat track in Britain in the one season and finishing up the leading trainer with 143 winners, making our yard numerically the leader for the second time. What a year that was. Having trained the fastest 50 winners ever, we then went on to train the fastest 100 when on 17 July, Our Fan, ridden by John Carroll, won the five furlong Handicap Sprint with the welterweight of 10st 3lbs at Hamilton Park. The training record beat the previous holder Henry Cecil, by six days and it still stands at the time of writing.

When I was invited to ride in a Golden Oldies Race at Wetherby on 17 November, 2002, in aid of the International Spinal Research Trust, I replied, 'yes I would love to.' Having a chat over a cup of tea after the race with Rachel Wright who used to be a Botterills (Ascot Sales Pedigree expert), herself a paraplegic after a fall in a point-to-point 1960, she asked me if there was any help our yard could give to their cause during the year. In other words, could we have an Open Day? She was so excited telling me that they are on to, and hopeful for a cure for some of the wheelchair bound people. Seeing the young folk that attended the races that day at Wetherby in their chairs and struggling with the simplest of chores, the majority of injuries were caused by accidents; mainly car crashes. Whatever the cause, they were stuck and confined to wheelchairs. It would have taken a very hard-faced or thick-skinned person not to have felt for them. Rachel's enthusiasm was contagious and I agreed we would and also try to get lots more people involved instead of just the same old faces, and we would go for the big one, £100,000. Sadly, Rachel has since died. Wetherby annually stage a race in her memory at the October meeting.

Our table at the Wetherby Race in aid of International Spinal Research. L to R: Howard Rainbow, Sue Rainbow, JB, Lisa Rainbow, Tom Wood, Jo Berry, Bill Robinson, Auriol Robinson, June Robinson & Walter Wharton.

The International Spinal Research Trust hold a luncheon in a marquee. At the auction, lots of money is raised for the fund. One of the auction items is a box at Wetherby Racecourse for 20 people. On a couple of occasions, a few of us jump enthusiasts shown on the photo club together and buy it, including Howard and Sue Rainbow, J and Jo Berry, Lisa Rainbow with boyfriend Tom, Auriol Wharton, Bill and June Robinson and Walter Wharton.

Having visited my old pal Paddy Farrell in the Spinal Units at Liverpool, Southport, York and Stoke Mandeville many times since he was injured. I can tell you, I have seen a few horrific sights. One that comes to mind was at Southport Hospital. A young man had just been brought up from theatre to the ward who had dived into an empty swimming pool and broken his neck. When he woke up, he started to scream as he found he had been fitted with a halo fastened with a swivel to the bed so he couldn't move. He was absolutely petrified. Imagine it yourself. What a thing to wake up to. All these past years I have often thought of that young man and wonder how he is. He and people like him are those we are setting out to help, so after the chat with Rachel I decided to ask quite a number of people to perform various fund raising activities. I asked people to buy raffle tickets, donate prizes or be a sponsor.

Geraldine Rees, the first lady jockey to ride around the Liverpool Grand National Course, for the benefit of the Trust agreed to doing a bungee jump at the Kings Fold Pub, Penwortham, Preston on 5th June. Trainers Mike Heaton-Ellis, and Jimmy Harris were having a wheelchair race around the paddock in between races at Nottingham racecourse on June 12th. Both of them had their riding careers cut short through race riding falls on the same day, but in different years at Huntingdon. However, although we had sold many sponsor tickets for this unique event, I hoped I didn't fall foul of the Stewards at the Jockey Club as I would have to run a ringer in the race for the previous week Jimmy Harris, as if he hasn't suffered enough, fell out of his wheelchair and broke his left leg. How about Jonathan Haynes, who broke his back in a fall at Southwell in 1980 (he was at the time Jimmy Harris's conditional jockey), and is confined to a wheelchair? Call it brave, stupid what you like, but Jonathan was doing a parachute jump from a plane at 10,000 feet on our Open Day on August 8. By the end of that day, I knew we desperately needed to – sincerely hoped to, please God – reach our mammoth target. I must thank the owners, trainers, race clubs, and syndicates who have bought and sold raffle tickets for us that I cheekily posted to them to sell on. I know this procedure hadn't pleased everyone as some people returned the tickets. However, at the time I couldn't think of a better way of getting the tickets out to raise a substantial amount, as raffle tickets and sponsoring Geraldine, Micky the 'ringer' and Jonathan were the main source of income for the cause. Nottingham, Haydock, Newmarket, Hamilton and Chester all offered to help by indicating they were prepared to stage races. However, they needed some firm or kind persons to sponsor the races. Johnny Fenwick-Clennell, the Clerk of the Course at Carlisle, decided to put the ISRT race on over hurdles for jump and flat jockeys to ride in as they did at Chepstow the year before, which was very successful. The Patten Arms pub at Winmarleigh was putting on a sponsored Pro-Am Bowling Match. The directors and staff of the newly formed High Flyers did a sponsored run to the tune of £500 and were sponsoring the marquee on our Open Day. Alan Smith, a pensioner from Blackpool gave us a gallon whisky bottle full of pennies that took him years to

Harry Sprague (standing on left) *was one of the best hurdle jockeys ever to sit on a horse. I led him up on Doornocker when he won the 1956 Champion Hurdle. The other old jockeys in the photo are:* (left to right) *Billy Stott* (standing next to Harry), *John Oaksey, JB, Bill Shand Kydd, David Mould, Marion Mould, Lady Cazalet and Bill's carer.*

collect. Reg Morris, George Leatham, David Pickering, Brian Buckley, Ken Higson, Murray Grubb, Alan Finley, and Roy Peebles had all given or promised substantial donations. Paris House Restaurant was putting a meal on in aid of the Trust. Pat Eddery kindly gave me to auction the whip he used in the 2,000 Guineas when he won on Zafonic. Unlike the ringer of Phil Tuck's, this one was kosher, as Pat gave it to me at Newmarket after the race, as John Carroll did likewise the day when Paris House won the Palace House Stakes. Willie Carson gave two pairs of his goggles. Timeform were auctioning my new book, *It's Tougher at the Bottom* at their event at York, former England fast bowler David Brown was donating a cricket bat autographed by the then current England and Australian teams, and there was more.

I had been talking to the ex-jockey Bill Shand Kydd at an IJF function. Bill is in a wheelchair with spinal injuries from a riding accident. He told me they were just around the corner with a solution to cure, or somehow mend spinal cords, just as Rachel Wright had said. I hope so, and I hope it happens soon.

Chapter Six

Start of the Injured Jockeys Fund

•

On my rounds as a guest speaker at various functions around the country, this was the general gist of my speeches: 'the downside is, we are still just around the corner from a cure.'

Jack Berry's International Spinal Research Trust pledge is this: 'Break your leg and the broken bones knit back together again. Cut yourself and the skin heals up naturally. But break your back or your neck and sever your spinal cord, the damage is, at present, irreparable. The result is permanent paralysis and because the average age at which people are injured is just nineteen, the chances are that life will be very different from the one they had been dreaming of before the injury. But today, international medical research is poised on the brink of a cure for paralysis caused by spinal cord injury. As members of a caring society, there is almost an obligation, given the great advances in medical research, to look for and find a cure. Because people will keep having car accidents, they will keep colliding on the rugby pitch, they will keep being thrown from their horses on the racing track; they will keep breaking their necks and backs. Support for this research is very much needed in order to take the next crucial step. Here's a typical pitch:

'How can I help? You may ask. Quite simple really! Our racing stables are very keen to raise £100,000 for the International Spinal Research Trust, which we appreciate is a mammoth task, but without the help of everyone, including people like yourselves (remember the widow's mite), it will prove impossible. So please give this effort your full support.

'There are going to be several fund raising events, like Geraldine Rees, the first lady jockey to complete the Grand National, who will be doing a 'bungee jump' at the Kings Fold Pub, Penworthan, Preston on Saturday 5 June. Ex-jockeys Jim Harris and Mike Heaton-Ellis will be having a Wheelchair Race on June 12 at Nottingham Racecourse. Bloodstock Agent David Minton is doing a sponsored slim. Sponsor tickets for these events are available.

'Also our yard has an Open Day on Sunday 8th August to which all are warmly invited. At the event ex-jockey Jonathan Haynes, himself a paraplegic, will be doing a parachute jump from 10,000 feet and there will also be a Grand Raffle, (tickets now available!) as well as all the other goings-on. So there is something for everyone. Either give sponsorship for the individual events or buy some raffle tickets or attend the Open Day in August, the entry fee is £5... or even be rash and do all three!

'I do hope that you can help us to raise this enormous amount for this very worthwhile cause.

Thank You.'

At a sportsman's aid function in Blackpool, Bernard Manning, a Manchester City fan, was the comedian and before he came on I did my bit for the ISRTF appeal which went as follows: 'Good evening gentlemen. The last time I saw as many men together was in a gay club in Manchester. Nice to see so many of you have turned up here tonight. Don't tell Bernard that one when he comes on, he'll say I've been nicking his jokes.'

Bernard must have been listening in the back as the first joke he told when he came on stage was, 'Good evening gentlemen, the last time I saw as many men together was in a gay club in Manchester etc…' which raised huge laughs. I am well aware that lots of people say Bernard was a foul-mouthed racist git. That was his act. He would also do anything in his power to help any charity or good cause and, I can assure you, our cause benefited on account of him that night.

In my speech I continued: 'The International Spinal Research Trust's aim is to find a way to repair the spinal damage caused to people after accidents. Wherever a person's spinal cord has been severed from the neck downwards, the person is paralysed and therefore confined to a wheelchair. In the past it has been accepted, tough as it seems there has been very little done for these people. In fact, it would be fair to say there has been no attempt to even try to repair the spinal cord until recently. To stress this point to the full, imagine yourself for just one whole day in a wheelchair with your partner to tend to your needs. When you think lots of them cannot feed, bathe or wash themselves, go to the toilet or even swat a fly away, it would drive most people round the bend. In fact, many people could not hack it. The International Spinal Research Trusts aim is to end the years of misery for these people. Research and tests are so progressed they are very close to a cure. One of the fund's Directors, Simon Barnes, is paralysed from a motor accident he sus-

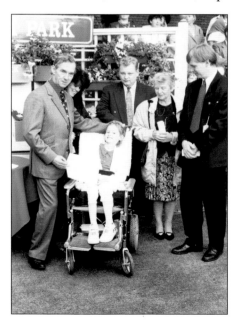

This little girl at Haydock Park Races gave me a cheque to go towards our fund raising for the International Spinal Research Trust.

tained years ago. Rachel Wright who originally asked me if I could help their cause was paralysed following a fall from a horse in a point-to-point. The pair of them work endlessly for the ISRT and are excited with the thought that they and people like them, may one day discard their wheelchairs and walk. Simon and Rachel could be here talking about us down there in their chariots. To help the ISRT our yard pledged we would go through fire and water to get them £100,000. Through your generosity from various functions like this, at this moment we have £91,621.49 in a high-interest account at the Midland Bank in Garstang that earns interest every day – so only

£8,378.51 to go! With your support this evening we will get even nearer to the magical £100,000. So on behalf of every quadraplegic and paraplegic in the land, many thanks for your help.'

From November 1990 to November 1991 through various stunts, functions and Open Days with the help and generosity of many people our yard sent a final cheque for £131,000 to the International Spinal Research Trust Fund.

At Haydock Park races, one could hardly say it was a chore receiving this cheque from the little girl from Cheshire, who had spinal injuries due to a car accident. With her parents, she presented me with the cheque, a proportion of her money from a fund that had been set up for her, to go towards finding a cure for spinal injuries. God love her.

In March 2003, I received a phone call from Carole, our Sam's partner. Sam had had a seizure through the night and was in hospital. Jo and I were going for all three days to Cheltenham, only the next day I had an IJF meeting at the Lords of the Manor, Upper Slaughter 12 noon and we intended setting off about 6 a.m. for we were to stay with Chris and Antonia Deuters. In view of Sam's set-back, we went that day to stay the night at his house in Sparsholt to see how he was.

When we arrived at his house, Sam had come out of hospital and was at home. He was a bit weak and slurring his words more than usual. Also, he suffers from being a bit slow and restricted on his right-hand side through paralysis which resulted from his injury following his original fall. Following a seizure, it tends to get worse for a while. However, Sam takes it all ever so well. As soon as he wakes up in hospital, he gives the staff such a hard time telling them he wants to go home, and they nearly always give in. Sam makes some remarkable recoveries, but fair do's, when he gets home never ever does he

complain about his illness or anything. A real tough nut is our Sam. It's sad he and many others have to suffer fits following their injuries. Carole works for Henry Candy, cooking for his lads. I was wishing she would pack it in, as often she had to leave Sam on his own when he wasn't very well. The thought of him having an epileptic convulsion and no one being there didn't bear thinking about. There was no need for her to work and she worried herself stupid over him, but to be fair she liked her work and on many occasions she took Sam with her and he enjoyed the craic with the lads in Henry's hostel. When I went to our IJF meeting in Upper Slaughter, Chicky Oaksey gave me a list of Joe Mercer's racing memorabilia that he gave to her for the Trust to auction or sell as best they could.

JB's son Sam doing his exercises with some of our dogs in attendance.

Chicky arranged for me to take charge of it the following day at Cheltenham. Some of the items weren't in good nick. A couple of pictures wanted re-framing, which we would get done, but on the whole I had no doubt they would earn our fund quite a sum of money. Joe rode his first winner at Bath as a fifteen-year-old on Eldoret and became champion jockey in 1979. His last ride, Bold Rex, was a winner on 9 November at Doncaster in 1985. Joe is a star and no doubt he will be glad to know that when I went back to Chris and Antonia Deuters house after racing the first day, I sold the framed and metal badges to Chris for £1,000. Our target figure now stood at £21,775.

Cheltenham Races and the Festival meeting are absolutely brilliant. You can feel the vibes on entering the car park. I have had a love affair with the place since I led up Doorknocker to win the 1956 Champion Hurdle. I haven't missed many Cheltenham Festival meetings since that day and every year stakes get higher and racing gets better. As a kid in 1954, I remember the opening race was a selling hurdle and was won by a horse called Mull Sack, ridden by the legendary Lester Piggott. LP was a decent jockey over hurdles, too, having ridden 20 winners. His last was on a horse called Jive at Sandown Park. Seeing so many old faces and jockeys I rode with gives me a real buzz. Though often a graveyard for gamblers, I was in the position of being able to afford to lose the money I could put on. Gambling is one job from which I wouldn't attempt to make a living. I was taught my lesson a long time ago with Kas at Wolverhampton. Being Champion Hurdle day, Jackie and Jonjo O'Neill, the Deuters, Jo and I went down to their state of the art yard, Jackdaw's Castle for breakfast, which was fascinating. Work was going on under the biggest barn I have ever seen. It must have been a furlong long. Big enough for a swimming pool, three horse walkers and an indoor ride. If a horse got loose, it could have taken forever to catch it.

In the lounge where we ate, it was like a Hall of Fame – chock a block with photos and trophies the great man had won. All credit to Jonjo, he has worked for his success and he is a good fellow. Talking to his staff, they were all very pleasant and happy, working with a real sense of pride, which was good. Happy staff, happy horses. And happy horses win races.

Michael Hourigan left me a very nice framed photo of Beef or Salmon signed by him at the stable yard at Cheltenham for me to collect, which I duly did for our big day's auction. It was such a shame Beef or Salmon fell quite early on in the Gold Cup, which was won for the second year running by the superstar Best Mate. The style in which Hen's horse won the race was unbelievable; he just sauntered in by ten lengths, jumping foot perfect, to enable Jim Lewis, Best Mate's owner, to add £152,215 to his bank account. Looking at an old Cheltenham race card from 1956, the year Limber Hill won the race ridden by Jimmy Power, and trained by Bill Dutton, Mr Dewey the proud owner, received £3,750. It could be that Best Mate could be the best Gold Cup winner of all time and was definitely going in my ten to follow. He was certainly the best Gold Cup horse I had seen since Arkle. As he was only an eight year old, as I've said before, I thought he could win the next two or three Gold Cups. Best Mate was the first back-to-back winner of the Festival crown since

L'Escargot in 1971. He went on to win the Grand National. However I couldn't see Best Mate running at Liverpool. If he did, Henrietta Knight would need to take some 'Pampers' with her! Poor Hen, gets wound up like a spring and is so nervous she can't watch her pride and joy even jump a racecourse fence. I don't think Jim Lewis would risk his horse around Aintree, as he isn't much better with his nerves than the trainer. With a record that reads; from sixteen starts, eleven wins and five seconds, I don't think I would risk him either.

Speaking to Jim one day, he assured me he leaves all the decisions of where and when to run to Henrietta. Many owners like to have a bit of a say or involvement with their horses. Others leave things for the trainer to decide. As he has dealings with the horse daily, on the whole he should know best. But some trainers are not approachable and don't like to suggest their plans even to the owner. One of Charlie Whittingham's owners rang him up during training times at the track asking Charlie, 'if we were running in a particular race'. 'Yes, we're running, yes we are definitely running.' Trying to be as quick as possible, as he had a lot to get through. Then the owner, who must have been listening to one of his advisors said, 'I am asking you a question, Charlie, as I have heard a rumour that my horse isn't doing too well.' 'You did, did you?' said the trainer, 'Well Frank, I heard a rumour that you're an asshole, but I don't believe everything I hear.'

David Fish, a great man to help any good cause, who sells racing photos on the racecourse, promised us a limited-edition print of Rock of Gibraltar, which I took up to the box of JP McManus, for Sir Alex to sign, which he did, as he was a guest of JP. I then took it back to Dave to re-frame it for the auction. Not only did Michael Hourigan have the misfortune of Beef or Salmon falling, he had a terrible hand dealt to him in the Foxhunter Chase when his old stalwart Doran's Pride was killed. The horse was fourteen years old. In 1995 he won the Stayers' Hurdle at Cheltenham and was placed in two Cheltenham Gold Cups. Doran's Pride won no fewer than twenty-seven races. My old pal Shane Broderick was his regular jockey before he got smashed up. Shane loved the horse to bits and I knew he would be upset. I decided to give him a ring a few days later. Losing any horse is distressing and it saddens the whole yard, but to lose one of the yard's stalwarts, especially on the verge of retirement, is a bitter pill to swallow.

It was just like top Irish jump jockey, Ruby Walsh said, 'if you can manage to ride a winner at the Festival meeting and walk away sound, you've cracked it', and it's the same for the horses. Looking at the mail on my return from Cheltenham, there was a £210 cheque from Ian Bolland, our accountant at the yard, for the six tickets I sold him while attending the Arnold School Sports Dinner at St Anne's, near Blackpool a few days before Cheltenham. The evening's purse went towards sending the schools hockey and netball teams to play in Barbados. The guest speaker was Tarleton racehorse trainer, Geraldine Rees. At the auction I bought a meal for four people to be cooked at our house by a top Lancashire chef. Nothing to do with Jo's cooking!! The target was now £21,565 to go. We can then ring the bell.

Among the items from Joe Mercer's memorabilia, were some framed photos of the Eclipse winner, which was of course at Sandown. There was another of the same horse breaking the track record at Royal Ascot when winning the Prince of Wales Stakes, both in the same year, 1978. The horse was Gunner B, trained by Henry Cecil. Unfortunately, they were only small photos in poor frames and the glass of one was cracked. In view of Gunner B dying only a few weeks earlier at Shade Oak Stud in Shropshire where he stood, I thought Dave Hockenhull, the stud's owner, might like to buy them, as the horse had been very successful standing at Dave's stud. Gunner B sired Red Marauder, the 2001 Grand National winner and many more good horses. Therefore, even though the photos weren't brilliant, I asked him just £100 for them. I thought as it could still turn out to be a chance to swell our kitty making our cash target £21,465. For the record, we trained Gunner B's first winner which was a little filly called Conveyor Belle. She won on her first run at Newcastle as a two-year-old. We also bred the 1987 November Handicap winner, Swingit Gunner, trained by Colin Tinkler, and sired by Gunner B, out of I Don't Mind. So the old fella did us quite a bit of good as well.

Our nice postman also delivered a cheque from Brian Robb for three more tickets, which he had ordered earlier by phone; plus a cheque to the value of £70 from Dave Whiteman, one of the Royal Bank of Scotland's bank managers, for the tickets which I sold to him at the St Anne's Sports Dinner. The new target was thus £21,290. On Wednesday, the 19 March, Jo Bower, along with her sales rep Tracy, came along for lunch and to discuss how her firm could sponsor the costs of tickets and the commemorative brochures etc. At the meeting we finalised the BBQ and decided we would definitely have a hog roast, especially as she has the equipment to cook a whole pig right there on

JB presenting Mrs Connie Marshall of Sutton-on-Trent with a print of our crack sprinter Mind Games for her 90th birthday celebration at Southwell Races.

the premises. While Jo was there, I rang Jimmy Andrews, who did the cooking for us last year, for his views and he thought it was a great idea. We would still have sausages, plenty of potatoes and salads, not to mention the salmon as well. Therefore, Jimmy boy still had plenty to do on the day. We sorted out most of the auction and raffle prizes, so they could kick on and get the tickets printed. Never before have I seen so many valuable prizes in a raffle.

For starters our top prize was a nomination to Mind Games, valued at £3,500. Mind Games was our first Royal Ascot winner (see the print of him where I present Mrs Connie Marshall of Sutton-on-Trent with it on her ninetieth birthday at Southwell Races where a party was held in her honour).

Then there was a wagon load of shavings from Jo's firm Creature Comforts and lots more great prizes. Hopefully, we would sell around £10,000 worth of tickets. I intended asking all the trainers I thought would support us, if they would sell £50 or £100 worth for me, I didn't want them to buy them, just sell them, as we did for the ISRT a few years previously. I knew lots of trainers had a poor reputation with some owners, by treating them like mushrooms; keeping them in the dark and feeding them plenty of shit. In this instance, I can assure you that this is not the case. Trainers I had seen just before writing this book, such as Harvey and Sue Smith, Mark Polglase, Brian Smart, Jamie Osborne and Derek Shaw all said they would sell me £100 worth, so that was an encouraging start. However, we thought we would print the tickets in different colours in thousands, because if one bought a ticket and it was, say, number 4963 they would straightaway say they had no chance of winning anything or that we were ripping them off. Then, Jo Bower had an even better idea. As we were all to have our stationery printed in red, white and blue, she suggested we keep the same artwork and colours, only instead of changing the colour of the tickets, the first thousand we would make 1000A, then 1000B and so on. Also, at the meeting it was decided we would use paper plates so we could burn them instead of hiring porcelain ones as we did the year before.

Creature Comforts, as promised, sent the load of shavings to set fair our stables, so potential punters would see them. I must say the shavings were brilliant, not a single bit of dust in them. That's because they had gone through 13 processes to eliminate it. If I were still training, I would certainly put my horses on them. That same night, The Bride and I had an invitation to Paul and Yvette Dixon's pre-season party at their huge home in Retford, which was once a hotel. Anyone who knows Paul will appreciate he is a very big man, but wouldn't have thought he needed 30 or so rooms to live in! It's a lovely place and the Dixon's make everyone welcome. There were probably around 100 people attending, all made up from jockeys, trainers, owners and the Dixon's friends. The John Lennon lookalike, Gary Gibson would be there to entertain us. Drinking goes on until near breakfast time, Paul and Yvette are very good people and help a lot of good causes. In fact, it was the Dixon's who gave a computer to auction at the previous year's barbeque. Their kindness during the evening was still in evidence as Yvette gave me an envelope with £130 inside for our big day as they had sold a box of Foster and Allen' CD's. The Irish country singers, Foster and Allen made the record in aid of the IJF with the backing singers being a group of jump jockeys. These included Tony McCoy, Ruby Walsh, Adrian Maguire, Mick Fitzgerald, Seamus Durack and a few other jockeys called the Fields of Athenry. The Dixon's sold the CDs in commemoration of Jimmy Byrne. If you have never heard of the Field of Athenry, then you didn't go to the 2003 Cheltenham Festival. The singers there certainly gave it some welly. Our target figure now stood at £21,160 to go. Malton trainer and former champion conditional jockey Richard Fahey sent me a cheque for £70 for two tickets he had ordered on the phone. Chipping our figure down to £21,090. Richard also presented me with a £1,000 cheque for the IJF from the proceeds of a recent function at Doncaster Races, which was sent directly to the IJF office.

Richard Fahey presenting JB a cheque for the Injured Jockeys Fund.

Thursday 20 March was the opening of the flat season at Doncaster. One of my favourite races is the two-year-old Brocklesby Stakes, a race I had been lucky enough to train the winner of a couple of times in the past with Great Chaddington and Mind Games. However, this 2003 season I gave it a miss, as my old friend Colin Bradford-Nutter (Lord Dinkley) with his wife Jean were coming to our house for lunch. We would therefore watch the racing on the box. While Colin was there, as a prize for the auction, he gave me a day salmon fishing on the River Ribble where he lives. Jo and I did attend the second day at Doncaster. The last race on the card was a fun event with no money to race for in aid of three very worthwhile causes, Bluebell Wood Children's Hospice, Emergency Relief for Thoroughbreds and the Spinal Injuries Association. The riders had to get sponsorship for at least £1,000 as well as having to get a horse to ride in the race. Also, they needed to get punters to fill up the tables, which cost £60 per head. Thankfully, there are many kind people in racing and none of the above conditions created a problem. In the race there were quite a few celebrities who made a come back from their jockey days to compete. With the like of retired amateur and now jockey agent Richard Hales, ex-jockey now trainer, Nigel Tinkler, same with Kevin Ryan, Derek Shaw, Nick Littmoden and Tom Tate. Phil Clark, cameraman for Attheraces, rode in the race which was a first ride for him. Fair do's to Phil, he rode out on a few occasions for trainers and did a course at the Racing College to prepare. Mark Dwyer also rode and he is no stranger to riding winners having ridden the 1985 Cheltenham Gold Cup on Forgiv'n Forget and the same race again in 1993 on the Peter Beaumont-trained Jodami. Former 'cock of the north' flat jockey Mark Birch, who rode well over 1,000 winners, had the leg-up on Dandy Nicholls-trained Mr Rambo. Grand National winning jockey of

1990, on Mr Frisk, Marcus Armitage rode Tarrango, Laura Bradbourne, the racing TV presenter and sister of the jump jockey Mark, plus my neighbour Anne Duffield, wife of jockey George Duffield made up the rest of the field. The race was run in good spirits from a barrier start instead of stalls. Mark Birch on Mr Rambo jumped off and went a good pace only to get collared close to home by Nigel Tinkler on Cryfleld. It was great fun watching the race and all the pilots enjoyed riding. Some possibly carried enough condition and finished a bit out of breath, but on the whole they did well. The riders between them earned the relevant charities in the region of £30,000 for riding in the race. Well done to them.

The Bride and I were on Anne Duffield's table. Michael White of Doncaster Bloodstock Sales conducted the auction, which raised some £17,000. I bought the last lot, which was a day on the set of 'Mersey Beat'. I must say Tim Adams, the Chairman, a great man for good causes organised the day and did a remarkable job, so well done to him. I was sitting next to Billy Parker, the owner of Valuable, the horse that Anne rode, who bought two tickets for our do. Tadcaster trainer and brother-in-law of Michael Dickenson, Tom Tate, also bought six, which left us with a balance of £20,810.

On my return, home in the post was a further £140 cheque for four tickets that I had sold to one of our old owners, Arthur Campbell, for whom I trained the last chase winner to be run on the all-weather at Southwell on 3 March 1992, Miami Bear, ridden by Mark Perrett. £20,670 was now the target. Talking of records, one of our few jumpers, Smolensk, still holds the course record for the two-and-a-half mile chase at Hereford, when he was ridden by Sam Stronge.

On the final day of the Lincoln Meeting, The Bride and I were lunch guests of the big race sponsor Stanley Racing who had agreed to sponsor the Doncaster Lincoln Meeting for the next three years. Bob Bowden was also there. Bob was the managing director of Alpha Meric Red Onion, a firm that specialises in telecommunications and is also a shareholder in Hexham race-course. The idea of the get together at Doncaster, which was with the kind permission of Doncaster Clerk of the Course, John Sanderson, was for Bob to present a Vespa scooter PX125 to me on Channel 4 TV. It was to enable us to take bids on the machine and to have a talk about the scooter during our big day with Leslie Graham. It would then travel up to us for our function on 20 July to be finally auctioned, with the proceeds going to the IJF. Bob is a very generous man indeed; he bought the Vespa bike at the Vision Charity Ball in Dec 02 for £5,400 to swell the kitty of the cause. Two years previously he bought the top lot at the same event, it was a Harley Davidson motorcycle. The auction that day was conducted by the TV personality Jeremy Beadle. I was to have been presented with the Vespa scooter at Hexham racecourse on their sponsor day, Wednesday 30 November, but the meeting was abandoned as the course was waterlogged. On account of that, I asked John Francome if he could arrange the presentation at the Doncaster Lincoln Meeting, which after consulting his boss, Andrew Franklin he duly did. The following Sunday we had dinner with our neighbours George and Anne Duffield. Also, there was Linda Townsend, who gave me a cheque for the five tickets she'd ordered from me the previous Friday at the Doncaster races. All this now reduced our target to £20,495.

In the post I received a nice letter from Dave Lowry, general director of William Hills, with three £100 vouchers for our raffle. I know we often complain about bookies ripping us poor punters off, and hold racing by its short hairs, but anytime I have asked for their help in aiding good causes, not once can I remember any of them refusing, and that's a fact. I have often told the story about bookmakers. During the 1962-63 season, when I was a struggling jump jockey and had recently married, plus of course the missus was in foal, we had the worst weather on record. To make matters worse, I had just packed up my job as Head Lad to the Doncaster trainer Harry Maw. There was no racing for weeks on end and snow lay feet deep over nearly all the country, which was followed by a deep freeze. To help the jump jockeys to weather the storm, the bookmakers countrywide had a whip round for us as well as many others. I was grateful to them for their generosity even though they themselves were struggling… need I say more. It must have been a struggle for William Hill when he first started up as a bookmaker also. He went around on a bike collecting bets from pubs.

The 24 March arrived and the following day Jo and I were travelling from Northallerton with the Duffields as we had been invited by them to attend George's investiture at the Palace to collect his MBE on the Wednesday. I was greatly looking forward to it. If Her Majesty had seen George Duffield in action at a New Year's party, she might have changed her mind. As 'Father Jack' with the Doncaster Sales Bible in attendance, at the same party were the two 'tarts', Jo Berry, Bloodstock Agent Gill Richardson, along with 'nun' Anne Duffield.

I must say George is a great lad now he has retired and lives in the next village. We are often in each other's houses for dinner. Everyone is entitled to a

Left: *Jo, Gill Richardson & (Nun) Anne Duffield.*

Right: *Boy George Duffield and Vicar JB at the Duffield's New Year's Party.*

laugh. Needless to say, as you see by the photos, we do have some fun. In fact, George has ridden a lot of winners for our yard, which included Bri Eden in the the Bovis Stakes at Ascot in 1982. That horse was so fast he could have caught a train. Even I managed to ride a winner on him; in the trainer's race at Catterick.

JB in the plate on Bri Eden riding on to win the Trainers Race at Catterick.

Fair do's to do the job right for such a memorable occasion as George's MBE, Anne booked 1st class tickets on the train to London. We arrived at Northallerton with plenty of time to spare, which is unusual for racing folk, especially the Duffields. Chatting away in the waiting room as the train arrived, Anne told us we were in Coach 'M'. Well, it wouldn't be an exaggeration to say the train with its carriages was a furlong long. As 'M' Coach went flying past us, the new MBE said to his missus, 'you silly so and so why didn't you tell us it was Coach M we were booked in when we were in the waiting room, we could have been right up the platform waiting for the train, instead of all this rushing with the bags and all.' At my suggestion, we dived in an open door halfway up the train and walked through the carriages to M in the 1st class, which was a good job because the train started to roll well before we reached our carriage.

The journey was not all bad. A carer I knew called Diane was once getting off the train at Darlington from London and with her she had a very old lady she was looking after who was wheelchair bound. She was due to be met at Darlington by a porter to give her some assistance in helping the old lady from her seat into her chair and on to the platform and with the cases. Unfortunately, the porter never turned up. At Darlington, Diane managed to get the wheelchair and the cases on to the platform. As she was looking around for the porter, the train doors closed and the train flew out of the station leaving Diane in a flood of tears on the platform. Hysterically, she ran around the station and got someone to alert staff on the train to transfer

Ann & George Duffield at Buckingham Palace to receive his MBE.

her patient to a southbound train for Darlington when it reached Berwick. Imagine how the poor carer felt.

Keeping up the style on our journey, we arrived in a taxi from Kings Cross Station to the Montcalm Hotel where we were staying. Jonathan Orr-Ewing, a friend I met whilst staying at the Montcalm when attending the IJF meetings a few years before, was the General Manager of the hotel. Four days prior to arriving, I asked Jonathan if he could book us a show and hire us a limousine to take the four of us to Buckingham Palace. We went to see the musical *Chicago* at the Adelphi Theatre. It was a great show that we all enjoyed. This was followed by a good Italian meal at the Paradiso Restaurant on the Strand.

The next day the limo arrived to take us to the Palace, all dressed up in our Ascot suits. The cars attending the investiture are all thoroughly searched and checked by the police before they are allowed into the Palace grounds.

Inside the Palace, the sheer splendour and grandeur of the place is breathtaking. I couldn't help thinking 'it doesn't get any better than this'. After having our photograph taken together and George having one taken for the *Racing Post*, we all got back into the limo and headed back for lunch at the Ritz. Nicky, George's son and Linda Townsend joined us, which was great. Going back on the train, I asked George what he said to Her Majesty. Instead of him asking her if she would like to buy a couple of tickets to our 'do' on the 20 July, the selfish beggar told her he hadn't managed to ride her a winner yet. but hopefully he would put that right that year.

Watching Morning Line on the last Saturday of the month, John Francome and Leslie Graham said a few nice words about the Vespa scooter that Bob Bowden had presented to me at Doncaster. They also showed coverage of me sitting on it. John told viewers we were open to bids on the scooter and that it would be auctioned off at our house on 20 July. Within seconds of the flash on the telly John Hutchinson from Ireland rang to raise our original bid of £2000 to £2,800.

Through the afternoon, three or four clowns rang messing about. Then, at 4.20 p.m., Ken Grayson from the North East called to ask what the latest bid was. I told him. He then said he would have a word with his wife and then get back in touch. I wrote the phone number down just in case they needed a call from me to keep them in the picture with the bidding and to make sure it was all kosher and above board and not a tyre kicker. But the man never did ring back.

For the evening of Mother's Day, Jo and I had an invitation from the North West Racing Club to their Annual Dinner at the Quality Hotel in Wigan. The North West Racing Club was the first racing club to start up some twenty-three years previously and was still going strong. Whilst at Cockerham we trained the club's first horse they owned, a two-year-old called The Manor. The horse ran first time out at Wolverhampton in the Turf to finish 4th of 12 with Joe Mercer in the saddle. One of the members said to me, 'Do you think he will win a race, Jack?' 'Of course he will on that run, blimey, if that horse can't win, I have a lot more in the yard worse than him, what chance have they got?' 'You should know,' he said, not convinced. 'Look,' I said, feeling a bit pissed off with this pessimist, 'If The Manor doesn't win a race by the end of the season, come to our yard, pick me up, and take me to Blackpool and I will show my bare arse on the Town Hall steps.' The horse never did win, he turned out a real villain, a bigger rough than Al Capone, the only effort he put into anything was eating! Thankfully, no one took me up on the offer.

There were a number of racing personalities present at the dinner, including Gerry Scott, the ex-jockey who rode the Merryman II to win the 1960 Grand National, and had moved on to become a recently retired starter. Gerry's main claim to fame was that he was the only man to have ridden a Grand National winner and to have started the Grand National. Along with Gerry was the year's Sports Writer Award winner Tom O'Ryan, they were both guest speakers and provided very good entertainment. For the record, Gerry broke a leg eleven times as a jockey. He was also lucky to ride Merryman II in the 1960 National as twelve days before the race he broke a collarbone. Tom was also a jockey before he became a sports writer. In 2001, as I have mentioned before, Tom and racecourse prize-winning photographer Edward Whittaker came with our party to Tenerife for our annual holiday to do a feature on us for the *Racing Post*. Edward took some stunning photos of our beneficiaries' holiday. The write-up and the words Tom wrote from the heart benefited our cause greatly. Extracts from newspaper cuttings of Tom's journey read that on a recent holiday to Tenerife, he found the time he spent with Tim Sprake and Shane Broderick a most humbling experience.

'It strips one to the core of emotions that reminds us how lucky we are, how all the things we whinge about don't matter a toss.' If you didn't read the *Racing Post* account by Tom in the 10 and 11 May 2001, editions you really should try to find the paper and do so.

There were letters later in the paper congratulating Tom on his account of the holiday. Here are a couple of examples of them: John Mariners of Swinton wrote: 'Heart-warming account was so uplifting. Full marks to Tom O'Ryan for his brilliant report on the IJF holiday in Tenerife. I am sure there must have been many like me who had damp in their eyes after reading these heart-warming articles.' Another from Pauline White of Manchester, read: 'I just couldn't allow the moment to pass without acknowledging the pleasure I got from reading the outstanding articles about the IJF holiday. What a read. Tom

O'Ryan's illuminating and uplifting account made it feel as though I was there with all those brave characters. While his articles on Shane Broderick and Tim Sprake almost moved me to tears, at the same time applauding the bravery and positive attitude of two young men who are an example to all.' Finally, Charles Dun from my hometown of Leeds wrote. 'Brilliant! It's the only way to describe the reports from Tenerife on the Injured Jockeys Fund holiday. I don't remember ever reading anything before that moved me quite so much. I say good on yer Tom. Well done!'

At the NWRC every year they have awards for the leading jockeys and trainers at the North West courses, i.e Liverpool, Haydock, Bangor on Dee, Chester and Carlisle. That year's flat trainer was Sir Michael Stoute and the flat jockey was Kieren Fallon. I received the award on his behalf as Kieren was away riding in Dubai. Jump trainer was Jonjo O'Neill, jump jockey was AP McCoy and the Special Award went to the Stable Lads Welfare Officer in the North, Ray Wilkinson. It was a very popular choice as Ray's a star man and does a wonderful job with Racing Welfare for racing lads and lasses. One of the members there was Brian Goodwill, now a racecourse judge. Brian, in 1986, walked to every one of the fifty-nine racecourses in Britain to raise money for the Cancer Research Fund and for the Jane Thompson Memorial Fund. Jane was the lady jockey and daughter of the Stainforth trainer Ron. Jane was killed by a fall at Catterick that year. Brian's walk must have been a lonely ordeal and in order to give him a bit of company, I rode my old pal, OI Oyston, from Haydock Park to Aintree Racecourse with him. For the record, in 1988 Princess Anne rode Ollie in an international race to finish fourth at Newmarket, the closest of our home riders to finish.

We moved into April and IJF Almoner Sarah York rang up to tell me that Frank Dever, the former jockey and one of our beneficiaries (as seen in the photos giving me instructions where to put the plants in our pond while on a vacation at our house), fell out of his wheelchair and broke a collar bone. I was hoping it was an April Fool's Day wind-up. Unfortunately, it was for real. Unlike a story in that day's *Racing Post*, which showed jockey Dean McKeown

Close friends for many years, Frank Dever and JB during his vacation at Well Close House.

sitting on a horse in a pair of Y front underpants on the outside of his racing breeches. It was saying he had got a sponsor and he was happy to wear the Y fronts on the outside of his breeches. It's just like a few years ago, in April, it was reported that lightweight flat jockey, Nicky Carlisle had been relieved of some sperm to be banked so that later it could be inserted into small women as there is so much obesity in this modern age, there was a serious shortage of lightweight male jockeys! On the same day only a different year it was rumoured Desert Orchid had been bought by Harvey Smith to go show-jumping.

Gerry Scott and myself travelled to The West Midlands Racing Club's Grand National Preview in Birmingham. My role was to be evening's auctioneer, the proceeds of which were going to the IJF. Gerry, along with Lord Oaksey were guest speakers. The WMR Club Chairman, Chris Pitt, is a very good pal of mine; he and racing author Sean Magee co-hosted the evening's talk during which the members asked us questions.

It was brilliant. In attendance were: Rex Hamey, whose claim to fame is he rode the good chaser; Linwell when he won the Mildman Chase at Sandown; as were Gene Kelly; and Paddy Connors; all our old weighing room muckers.

Back row: l to r: *Gerry Scott, Chris Pitt, Sean Magee & JB*. Front row l to r: *Rex Hamey, John Oaksey, Paddy Connors & Gene Kelly at West Midland Racing Club.*

So as you can imagine the craic was great and we had a lot of fun. Chris Pitt asked Paddy what was it like when he had his first ride round Aintree, and was he frightened? Paddy answered 'No. I walked round the course early in the morning and thought, I don't know what all the fuss is about. These fences are nice.' He had only walked round the Mildmay Course. When the trainer and Paddy walked the National Course later on, it was a different ball game. He said he was fair messing himself, especially when the trainer said, 'and this one is Becher's Brook'. Paddy said 'it looks more like Beachy Head!'. The racing club members were a good bunch. The auction raised £1,150 for the IJF and our President John Oaksey was presented with the money. The top lot of the night was the print of Martha's Son and Dublin Flyer working in the snow before racing on Gold Cup Day in 1997. It was number 179 of the 285 prints that were produced. For a giggle, which I later corrected, I said, 'This is a unique opportunity to purchase a very rare print of Dublin Flyer and Martha's Son working in the snow on Cheltenham Racecourse with the famous Cleeve Hill in the background from a painting by the famous equine artist, Joy Hawkins no. 917 of 21,500.' Gerry drove Jo's car back, which I will vouch has

JB conducting the charity auction at the West Midland Racing Club.

never run so fast before! I decided to look in the next few days mailbox very carefully hoping not to find one of those horror summonses. If we had, I would re-direct it to Mr Scott.

The cameras were more on the ball when Jo and I stayed in Slough for Royal Ascot. At 21.33 p.m. we were clocked travelling at 35mph in a 30mph zone on the A355 Farnham Road with not a car in sight. The Thames Valley Police charged me £60 and gave me three points on my licence! But they would waive the points if I attended a day's course in Slough, about 260 miles away, and pay £90 for the privilege. What are they on? At least when Dick Turpin robbed folk he wore a mask. Say what they like, it's a blatant tax on the motorist.

There were lots of goodies in the post the following morning, such as the letter from Timeform Chairman Reg Griffin. He had agreed to accept Keith Bradley's racing memorabilia to be auctioned at the Timeform Charity Dinner on Friday 13 June. Another good pal, David Mould and his other half Marion, kindly sent me two signed and framed pictures to auction. One was of himself on Makildar winning in the Queen Mother's colours at Kempton. The other was of Marion on her famous show jumper Stroller. Liz Morley of Boston Spa, whose father Gordon was an international haulier and one of our very first owners even before we trained at Cockerham, paid for her three tickets (£105) as did Turf – £2,000 for their two (£70 face value) reducing our target to £20,110. However, you can't win them all. With the goodies, Fortnum and Mason plc sent a letter declining to donate us a hamper we had asked them for.

Former jockey Lex Kelly was a beneficiary who wouldn't be on our trip the next day to Tenerife. The old jockey has been suffering from depression and he also had a toxic poisoning of some kind. Elaine Wiles, one of our Almoners, asked me if I would pick him up from his house in Harrogate and take him for a head scan at York District Hospital. Lex lived alone and I think half of his trouble was loneliness, but we had a good chinwag on the journey, which perked him up quite a lot. When Lex had finished at the hospital, I took him into town where we had a nice Chinese meal that was enjoyed by the pair of us.

A bundle of fun is Jimmy Uttley, winning jockey in three consecutive Champion Hurdles, 1968-70, on Persian War. Jimmy is a beneficiary of ours; he is a real star and a good pal of mine. He's a bit like Tommy Cooper, you only have to look at Jimmy and you laugh. Not only did I know him from being a jockey and occasionally riding for our yard when I was training, we also served our National Service together in the King's Troop RHA in the late 1950s. I was looking forward to seeing him again. A couple of years ago following our IJF holiday, Jimmy came home and stayed with us here at Hunton. At the time we were doing some gardening which involved moving and levelling some soil. Jimmy, on our next holiday, was telling the rest of the gang that he and Jo were shifting 10 tonnes of soil, working like slaves and all I was doing was telling them where to put it! Which was some joke, as anyone who knows Del Boy, I mean Jimmy, knows there is more working life in a tramp's vest than in him. We also let Jimmy, Paddy and Nan Broderick stay for a holiday at our house in Spain (before we sold it as we didn't go often enough to merit keeping it). When I next saw Jimmy, he said 'God you have a super telly out there in Spain mate haven't you?' 'It's not bad,' I said thinking a telly is a telly. He told me, 'There's no wonder I couldn't get up in the morning, I was up all night watching them at it on Channel 30 every night!!'

It doesn't just happen getting all our beneficiaries together to go to Tenerife, I can assure you. There is plenty of planning to make it happen as they come from all over Britain and Shane Broderick from Ireland. It takes the first day for our team to get settled in, as most of them have been up very early in the morning to catch their flights. However, the minute they meet each other, handshakes, hugs and kisses take place. Although they may ring each other up or exchange Christmas cards, some will not have met since the last time they were in Tenerife because the group differs every year. So as you can imagine, they have lots to tell each other and the craic is great. From time to time I will tell you a little about some of them and fill you in with a few of their tales. While having a chat to Willie Snaith (as a young jockey he was nicknamed 'The Pocket Hercules') and Colin Casey, they had me in stitches. The pair of them were apprenticed to Sam Armstrong when he trained at Middleham. Apprentices didn't get much time off in those days and guv'nors were very strict. One day Willie and Colin ran away by legging it across Middleham Moor to Leyburn and catching a bus to Darlington. Willie then got on a train to Newcastle where he lived while Colin made his way to Birmingham, his hometown. They ran away because they were a bit fed up as it was the middle of winter and they had to sleep in the same bed, snow was inches deep and the window had fallen in and the boss wouldn't get it fixed so they were getting covered in snow. As you can imagine, they were cold.

They needed to cross the Moor to get to Leyburn to catch the bus, because if they had tried to catch the bus at Middleham, the bus inspector would have got on the phone to their guv'nor to ask was it alright that two kids were getting on the bus? It was a regular occurrence for Sam's apprentices to run off. Both were caught and returned to Middleham, which was just as well because they both became jockeys. In fact, Willie was the leading apprentice for two successive years and he became a top jockey having ridden hundreds of winners. When I was an apprentice at Charlie Hall's, I remember he rode the winner of Goodwood's Sussex Stakes on the Queen's Landau, the same year Willie rode the filly Bebe Grand, which was placed third in the 2000 Guineas and second in the Fillies Classic. Willie said that Mr Jack Gerber, a gold dealer, was too ambitious. Had the filly been saved for her Classic and not run the day before in the 2,000 Guineas, she would more than likely have won. Chatting to Willie and Colin brought back many memories.

I remember having a chat with Nicky Pearson years ago when he was riding the odd jumper for Harry Bell, who I also rode for with quite a bit of success. Nicky told me there had been some yearlings delivered to Armstrong's yard, as he also was an apprentice there. One was a real handful, a home bred that hadn't been handled much. It bit and kicked and they couldn't catch it in its box. At feed time, the feeders used to throw its grub in its manger then run out before the brute grabbed them. One day, Nicky was doing afternoon chores as in those days apprentices did, weeding the yard and the like, when he looked over the door at his horse and it was fast asleep standing up. Nicky went into the tack room to get a lead rein, quietly opened the stable door and very gently put a noose around its balls, pulled the rein tight and ran out of the door shutting the door behind him but hanging onto the rein. The horse was going bananas screaming bucking and kicking, but Nicky held tight as it couldn't go anywhere. Eventually, it got so frustrated and knackered it wore itself out. Then Nicky put a head collar on and tied the horse up. When the boss came round at stable time, Nicky earned a few brownie points, but he didn't tell Mr Armstrong how he'd caught it!

Reminiscing away as old racing sweats do, the pair of them were telling me about the 'dung hill bath'. They used to dig a hole and bury the apprentices up to their necks when they had been cheeky. The tales were never ending as in those days, pranks and stunts always went on. During my apprentice days at Charlie Hall's, one of the paid lads asked me to go to the shop for a packet of cigarettes for him. I told him to 'piss off' as we were pulling out in ten minutes and I hadn't got the tack on my horse yet. Also, I had just had a bollocking from Ben Robinson the Head Lad, telling me to hurry up and pull my finger out. Although I must admit, I was a bit worried the bully hadn't given me a crack or a kick up the arse when he'd got the chance. On a bitter cold winter's morning a few days later, just as I had about forgotten it, the big shit was waiting for me as I went down to the stack yard for a couple of loggings of straw to bed up my horse's box. He and another paid lad jumped me and between them they ripped my clothes off right down to the 'nuddy' before they let me go, to get more clothes, because they had run off with those I was wearing. I streaked all the way through the bottom and main yard, which leads out onto the high street, through Towton village to our cottage. A woman called Mrs Warriner, a real nosey old bitch, was always looking through the curtains and she missed nothing, hopefully except that day. Mind you, as I was running that fast with my hand between my legs covering my bits, she could have missed me.

National Day arrived and Johnny O'Hara, his wife Linda, and Anne Harris, widow of Jim, came over. Jim, sadly, died at the age of sixty-six a few years ago and he absolutely loved my song 'The Jolly Farmer' on the 'Off and Running' tape. He played it so often it got stuck in his car and he played it over and over until the day he sold the car in part exchange. He was as sick as a parrot because he couldn't get the tape out of the player, so it went with the car. Jim died, and as he wasn't a God-fearing man, he didn't have a church service. Having been friends with Jimmy for years, his wife Anne asked me if I would say a few words at the crematorium where there was seating for only eighty-five mourners and over 400 turned up. During the service, at which I willingly did the address, the lady vicar who was very nice, said to me, 'When you have finished, press that switch to turn the light off.' After I said quite a few nice things about Jim, when I finished, I hit the switch. Right away, a faint humming sound started up the curtains closed up on Jimmy's coffin and away he went – none of us ever saw him again and the light stayed on. As I was returning back to my seat with my hand over my mouth in shame and shock, although as sad an occasion as a funeral is, most of the mourners could hardly control their giggling on account of Jimmy's premature departure, and once outside, they burst out laughing. Even his wife said afterwards, Jimmy would have loved it and he would have laughed like hell! On our departure from the chapel, the song that was being played was me singing 'The Jolly Farmer'.

From time to time our then Patron of the IJF, the Queen Mother, IJF Trustees, a few guests and beneficiaries, had lunch at the Goring Hotel in London.

The photo is of a lunch with the Queen Mother at Goring Hotel. Jimmy is on the end of the front row in the wheelchair. Jimmy's grand-daughter, Danni, as soon as she could toddle followed Jimmy everywhere, hanging on to his chair as if she was attached to him. He absolutely idolised the kid. At the races, I always gave her £1 to buy an ice cream. To this day she calls me Uncle Jack.

Front row, left to right: *Paddy Farrell, Freddie Winter, HM The Queen Mother, Jack O'Donaghue, Jimmy Harris.*

Middle row, l to r: *Dick Saunders, John Francome, Jack Dowdeswell* (standing)*, Bob McCreary, Jack Berry, Lord Oaksey, David Mould, Richard Dennard, Sir Edward Cazalet, Peter Scudamore and Jeremy Richardson.*

Back row, l to r: *John Winter, Bill Rees, John Smith, Bill Smith, Brough Scott.*

Getting back to National Day, in Tenerife, Linda O'Hara and Anne Harris cut the forty National runners names out of the paper and we all put in a pound to have a sweep. Monty's Pass was the winner at 16/1. He was trained by JJ Mangan in Ireland, but would you believe he didn't see the horse win at Aintree as he

*Jimmy Harris'
granddaughter, Danni.
She followed Jimmy
everywhere and
he absolutely
idolised her.*

missed the last boat crossing over due to bad weather. Cheltenham Festival's leading jockey, Barry Geraghty, rode the horse which was drawn in our sweep by Colin Casey, who received forty Euros for the privilege. Twenty Euros also went to Jane Wicket, for selecting Supreme Glory the 40/1 second. Sammy, who is one of Shane's carers, won fifteen Euros for having picked out the Ginger McCain trained Amberleigh House who came home third at the generous odds of 33/1. First season trainer Andrew Balding's Gunner Welburn ran a big race to finish fourth and Eileen Casey drew him; she got ten Euros. Eileen, I might add, has curbed Colin from running away as they have been married now for forty-seven years. The fifteen Euro booby prize for picking Southern Stop, the last to finish, went to Frankie Dever.

To prove a point and show how much our IJF beneficiaries enjoy and appreciate the Tenerife holiday and the Mar y Sol complex, out of the blue, Colin Casey said to me, 'Do you know Jack, if I ever won the Lottery I would buy this place.'

Churchill's betting shop downtown was crowded out with us ex-jockeys to watch the race on TV with a drink, as it serves as a pub and a betting shop. There was Paddy Broderick, our Sam, Richard Fox, Brian Elder, Tommy Jennings, Sharon Murgatroyd, Dennis Cullen, Frankie Dever and many others and we were all shouting our fancies home. None of us backed the winner except Brod, who invested ten Euros each way, but it was great fun. One of our best lightweight jockeys a few years ago was Desmond Cullen, who can claim more than 700 victories while riding. Amongst those victories, were the Ayr Gold Cup, the Cambridgeshire, and many more big handicaps. For a while, Des was a jockey's valet, whose client's included Lester Piggott. Unfortunately, stress and nerves got to Des and he had to pack the job up. Des told me where, one day at Newmarket, Geoff Baxter and Lester Piggott were at each other's throats having a bit of a 'domestic' in the weighing room, which I can tell you, often used to happen, but it's mainly only 'handbag' stuff. While they were cantering down to the start for the race, Lester rode past Geoff pulled his whip through and gave Geoff two sharp cracks with it on the back, before back protectors were introduced. When the jockeys returned to the weighing room after the race, Geoff, fuming, asks Lester what the 'effing hell he thought he was doing. 'Why, what's the matter?' Lester said. With that, Geoff hit Lester smack in the face and down he goes. When the valets joined in and separated the angry jockeys and Lester had picked himself up, he turned to Des, who, bear in mind, stands about four-foot high and weighs in around seven stone, and said, 'I thought you were supposed to be looking after me. Where were you?' Des started his career off with Kevin Kerr, the son of the famous Irish Bloodstock Agent, Bert. He then left to go to Captain Cecil Boyd-Rochford, then onto Frenchy Nicholson's and finally ended up at Royston with Willie Stephenson.

Charlie 'Jock' Gaston was one of our team out with us in 2003. Charlie is another of Sam Armstrong's apprentices, and has ridden around 400 winners. He was in the yard at the same time as Paul Tulk, Nicky Pearson, Mick Hayes, Josh Gifford, Wally Swinburn and quite a few more good apprentices, in fact, at that time there were twenty-three licensed apprentices in the yard. Without doubt, in those years Sam Armstrong was the king of the kids.

Richard Fox was also present. He had ridden 871 winners in his career, which include just about every big handicap in the calendar. Being a light-weight jockey, Richard didn't have too many rides in Group races. He did ride Boozy when she won the Flying Five at Phoenix Park and she was trained by yours truly. Boozy was his sole Group winner and the last Group race at that Irish meeting before it closed in 1991. Richard is always the life and soul of the party when we are on holiday in Tenerife. He gets about, laughing and joking with everyone. To him it is immaterial what nationality people are; French, German, Swedish, he gets through to them all and has everyone in stitches. Foxy worked on the Harry Potter film as the stand-in for the actor who played Harry. With him being so small, he was ideal for the part. Although he is always fun at breakfast time, Richard was a bit concerned about his son Dominic, who is riding well and with great success at home on the all-weather. The reason for his concern as I write is that, unfortunately, Dominic had a fall whilst riding at Folkestone and fractured a shoulder only a few days before. The worst of it is that the young fella could be on the easy list for a couple of months. Lady Chicky Oaksey, Elaine Wiles, and Sarah York are the three almoners on duty on this year's holiday. Chicky is the wife of our President John, who was one of the best amateur jockeys ever to have put a pair of breeches on. Famous for riding that exceptionally good chaser, Taxidermist, I remember watching him when I went to Sandown Park races whilst in the Army and John won the Whitbread. He beat Taxi's stable companion Mandarin, who was ridden by Dave Dick. The trainer of the pair, Fulke Walwyn, must have had his brains on Mandarin as in the unsaddling enclosure he looked far from being happy (I have since heard John tell the story at

Elaine Wiles, a proper mother hen, of the Northern Injured Jockeys Fund almoner. The IJF beneficiaries lover her to bits.

functions confirming what I thought). Although he rode around 100 winners, John was possibly more famous for finishing second in the 1963 Grand National on Carrickbeg to Ayala ridden by Pat Buckley. John was well clear jumping the last fence only to get collared, up that long Aintree run-in close to home. Later some irate punter from the North, who must have backed Taxidermist at Aintree, saw John and said to him, 'I know you, it's you, the bugger who was second in't National and got tired before 'orse.' Chicky has been an almoner for many years and her input to the fund has been immeasurable.

Elaine worked as racing secretary to Steve Norton and would drive the box, declare, ride and see to the horses. In fact she did anything and everything. Elaine later married Steve Wiles, who trained a small string in Yorkshire. Unfortunately, they split up a few years ago. Elaine is a mother hen to lots of our northern beneficiaries who all think the world of her. She will stand up for their corner and see to their needs day or night. She's a real star but not a soft touch, as was proved when a carer of Shane Broderick wasn't up to the job. She arranged a flight home for him on only the second day of his Tenerife trip. Although she can get so obsessed, wrapped-up and involved in her work wanting to do everything, at times she is so keen and protective she could get accused of not being a team player.

Sarah York is married to northern racecourse steward, Colonel Eddie York, a lovely man and she is also a northern steward. The three of them sort out any problems while on holiday; they and the other almoners arrange the holiday months before it happens. No mean feat, as one can appreciate; our beneficiaries come from all over Britain. Getting them to the airport and flying them to the Canary Island of Tenerife, as I have previously said, doesn't just happen by itself. They have to travel in trains, cars, taxis, lifts and whatever, at varying times, but those IJF almoners arrange it all and it runs like clockwork.

Frank Dever was on the holiday with us. He rode around 40 winners as a jockey mainly for a trainer named William Whewell, who was also the boss of a cargo chemical firm from Bury in Lancashire. Mr Whewell was such a nice man. One year I went to Perth to ride two horses for him, but one went lame before the race and couldn't run and Mr Whewell paid me my riding fee. His son, Joe, and daughter Jean, look after the horses. In fact, Jean married Alan Oliver the show-jumper. Frank went on to train in a small yard near Southwell racecourse and he trained there with a bit of success for about 20 years. He went on to become the main riding instructor at the Doncaster Racing School where he took a real pride in the job and produced plenty of good kids that worked in racing. While he was training, his son Peter rode his main horses and also rode plenty for other people, riding over 300 winners in the process. Taking nothing away from Frank, but perhaps Peter could have become a leading jump jockey had he flown the nest and gone to a bigger yard. He now runs one of the largest wholesale saddlery businesses in the country. Unfortunately Frank contracted MS and is a regular beneficiary with his devoted wife Val on our holiday in Tenerife. Because of the steroids he takes for his complaint, Frank has got quite heavy and is wheelchair bound. On a night when I give Val a hand with Frank, I clean the few teeth he has left with an electric toothbrush and wash him before we put him to bed. Every night Frank is in stitches when I do his teeth. One year I cleaned them for a week when I found one at the very back. Frank cracked up when I told him I'd found another tooth. Frank can't talk but finally got through to me that he'd been trying to tell me about that particular tooth for ages, but couldn't for laughing.

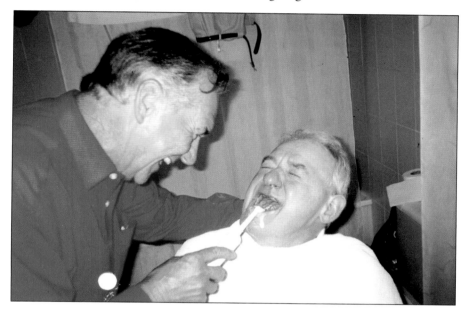

JB giving an industrial clean to Frank Dever's teeth on one of our trips to Tenerife.

In 1969, Bobby Elliott was the leading apprentice. Second in the juvenile list was the diminutive lightweight Ronnie Singer, a great little jockey, until he had the fall from Cross Bill in the Liverpool Spring Mile, which put Ronnie in a coma for three months and left him with head injuries and lameness. In his short career, Ronnie, to his credit rode thirty-nine winners. He lives in an IJF flat in Newmarket, which he keeps absolutely immaculate. In fact he is always very smart and clean. In the cafés in Tenerife or wherever he goes, if there is a 'mike' Ronnie will always get up and give a rendition of 'Peggy Sue'. He is loved by all on holiday whatever nationality and is easily recognised with his sailor cap and welcomes everyone with a 'thumbs up' sign.

Arthur Stephenson's ex-jockey, Paddy Broderick, is a real star on our holiday; he helps with whatever our tribe require – tones up all the old jocks aches and pains with his massages. His wife Nan was a fair point-to-point rider. Unfortunately she contracted MS and was confined to a wheelchair. Although

Paddy had to have a triple heart-bypass a few years ago, he fusses around Nan like a mother hen. Not only did Brod ride Night Nurse to win 1976 and 1977 Cheltenham Champion Hurdles, he and Night Nurse won two Welsh Champion Hurdles, and to make up the nap hand, they won a Scottish equivalent in the same year. Brod in total rode around 550 winners. His old pal Night Nurse was so good to Brod though he was also to blame for ending the jockey's twenty-four-year riding career. On Boxing Day at Kempton in 1977, Night Nurse fell when disputing the lead at the last flight of hurdles. Brod was telling me it wasn't easy for him when he was young in Ireland. His dad was a regular soldier in the Irish Army. Although they didn't see a lot of his father, Brod's mother had eleven kids by him. I said, 'He must have come home at some time,' thinking of all the youngsters. 'He did, he came home every weekend to wind up the clock.' Dennis Letherby rode a staggering 600-plus worldwide winners. His first one was Retreat, when apprenticed to Monty Smyth, who trained at Wantage. His indentures were then sold to Royston trainer Willie Stephenson, when Monty Smyth retired. Stephenson's jump jockeys included Tim Molony and Michael Scudamore. On the flat at the time were Tony Ives, David Goulding, Des Cullen, Bruce Raymond and Dennis Ryan. Dennis Letherby didn't manage to win a home Classic, but he did win the Kenya Derby at Gong Racecourse on Baobab. He also won the Railway Stakes for the Irish trainer Paddy Prendergast Jr on Readjust. Unfortunately, Dennis broke his neck in 1985 and was paralysed for quite some time. His fall was from a horse by the name of Fifth Avenue trained by John Sprake in Kenya, which finished his career. Dennis was a bit cut up about the trainer, as not once did he go to see him in hospital or even made enquiries about his well-being. For the record, Damaris, Dennis's wife is the granddaughter of Billy Bullock, the jockey who rode Signorinetta to win the 1908 Derby and Oaks. The filly was owned and trained by an Italian called Ginistrelli.

Former northern jockey Johnny O'Hara had a moderate hand dealt to him at Newcastle more than forty years ago when he had a very bad fall from Cold Cascade, trained by Bill Murray. That was a spare ride for him on the day. Johnny was first jockey to his father-in-law, Bill Atkinson, at the time, for whom I also had a few rides. As he had only just got going, Johnny rode only fourteen winners before the accident, which left him in a coma for 10 days. He also suffered a broken nose, shoulder, ribs, spinal injuries, a punctured lung and had to have a tracheotomy and two tubes inserted into his chest. He is now in a wheelchair. Married for just six months at the time of the fall, he and his wife Linda have buckled down to make a go of things. Johnny has a small saddlery business. A few years ago while on holiday in Tenerife, I ordered forty canvas-head collars with a ring on the front of the noseband to hook the horses to our walking machines. Within a couple of days of being home in the post came a bill from J O'Hara for the head collars. Jokingly, I rang him up and said that, 'it was the first time I'd had a bill for tack before it had arrived.' He only laughed and I paid it. Johnny and Linda's sons were doing really well, and their parents were really proud of them. Liam, a jockey in the States, rode three winners at Nashville only last week as I write this. The other fellow Seamus is a blacksmith, or should I say 'farrier' down in Lambourn. While we were having a bit of lunch and craic in Brod's apartment, Brod asked Johnny if he could still do it now he's in a wheelchair. Johnny told Brod to mind his own business. It's all good fun.

Mary Bolton, wife of the late Ken, and my old pal the late Paddy Farrell's wife Mary, were both on our trip. Kenny had a fatal fall from Blue Joy at Uttoxeter in 1965. Paddy, Jimmy Fitzgerald and myself went to Kenny's funeral. He was a journeyman jockey nowhere near the top of the jockey table, but he was well liked and respected. Kenny rode for the Tarporley trainer Eric Cousins; he was a quiet and most likeable man. Such a shame, as the horse he rode was a spare ride that Jimmy Morrissey should have ridden; only Jimmy broke a collarbone in a previous race. Kenny was changed and ready to go home when Ivor Underwood, a permit trainer, asked Kenny if he would ride his horse. Even a bigger shame was that Kenny had two more booked rides later on that week. On account of lack of opportunities, after he would have ridden them he was going to retire from race riding and leave to concentrate on the one-hundred-and-fifty pigs he kept to try and make a better living. Kenny received severe head injuries, yet there wasn't a mark on him, but he never regained consciousness and died three days after his fall on the day of his wife Mary's thirty-third birthday, leaving behind two daughters aged five and twelve at the time.

Mary Farrell is the widow of Paddy. He and I worked together when I was an apprentice and he was our stable jockey in the early 50s. Mary was our housekeeper at the yard. Years before they got married they took me on my first holiday abroad to Ireland. I say 'abroad' as that was the first time I had been in a boat and crossed a sea! When Paddy had the fall from Border Flight and got smashed up, most days I took Mary to visit Paddy in Southport Hospital, as Mary didn't drive. She devotedly looked after Paddy who was wheelchair bound up to his death a few years ago. Mary kept herself, her house and Paddy absolutely immaculate. Kate Adie wouldn't have dared gone in there with dirty shoes on. A real disciplinarian, a non-smoker, doesn't swear, doesn't drink – you could say a perfect woman and a real lady. She has two daughters, Geraldine and Eileen, and a son, Patrick. As previously mentioned, her other son Christopher was sadly killed in a car crash on 4th January 2003.

Eileen came out to Tenerife as a companion for her mum but she mucks in and helps. As I have mentioned her before, I may add most of our beneficiaries have Jimmy badges pinned on their shirts for her cause – the kids at

Jimmy's. She has even got a sponsor sheet to run in the Great North Run and there aren't many of us she has missed. Most racing people know it was actually on account of Paddy's injury that our Injured Jockeys Fund was started in 1964. At the next meeting at Wetherby, following Paddy's fall, some of us Northern Jockeys went round with buckets to collect for Paddy, as he had broken his back so badly it was common knowledge he would be wheelchair-bound for the rest of his life. With a wife and four young kids to support, we needed to buy them a bungalow with all the facilities to aid him. I must say people were so generous, even the bookmakers who, I will say again, are so kind when it comes to the crunch. They gave willingly and very generously. *The Sporting Life*, the racing paper of the day, then gave the cause a big lift by publishing the names of all the punters who had sent in donations. Every day there were lists and lists of them. Tenners, twenties, fifties. Even old ladies who couldn't afford much were sending in what they could and they all got a mention. It wasn't very long before enough money was collected to pay for the bungalow. Money kept rolling in. It was then decided that the fearless ex-champion jockey Tim Brookshaw be brought in to help his lot. Tim was a former Champion Jump Jockey who rode the second in the 1959 Grand National on the Ken Oliver-trained Wyndburgh to Oxo without stirrups for nine of those huge fences, on account of having one of his irons broken. Tim had broken his back in a fall from Lucky Dora, when she crashed through a wing, also at Aintree, in a hurdle race not many weeks before Paddy. Therefore, the fund went from being called the Paddy Farrell Fund to the Farrell Brookshaw Fund.

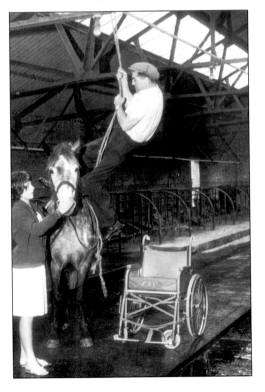

Tim Brookshaw mounting a horse from his wheelchair. He was one of the toughest men I ever met.

Money still kept coming in as the Fund had really got to the hearts of the people. So much so, trustees were found and for the third time in its history the Fund was renamed, this time it was the National Hunt Jockeys Fund. However, as flat jockeys also get hurt, the Fund was finally re-named as it is today, The Injured Jockeys Fund. What a tough nut Tim was even after his accident (as seen in the photo of him mounting a pony from his wheelchair). In the 1964 Tokyo Paralympic Games, he won a silver medal for throwing the javelin. He trained in Shropshire for a time. The first winner trained by him was Dufton Park in a selling chase at Wolver- hampton, ridden by another tough nut, Johnny (Thumper) Lehane.

The founding trustees were: Clifford Nicholson, the man who Paddy was retained to ride for; Edward Courage, the owner and trainer of Border Flight; who himself was a paraplegic in a wheelchair from polio; Wing Commander Peter Vaux, the boss of the northern brewery firm and John Lawrence, now Lord Oaksey. John is still a trustee to the fund and a very valid one at that. As I can tell you sitting on trustees meetings, no jockey need want for anything while Lord Oaksey is there. He is brilliant; all who work with John love him to bits. He is the fairest man you could ever wish to meet. For all those years he had been a most devoted trustee, at the time of writing not a single meeting has he missed (and bear in mind John had a day job to do, but that came second to his mission. I hope I am not talking out of turn, but I can tell you the Fund must have cost him thousands of pounds in travel and costs over the years. He has given many racing talks and done countless things in their aid; he is a true gentleman. All credit is due to John, as in the early years as a trustee meeting he suggested producing an IJF Christmas card, the suggestion of which was received with a lukewarm reception. However, they did it and the Fund made a grand total of £1,000 for their efforts. Today, John's idea along with the Christmas calendars is our main source of income. The year previous to this visit, whilst out here on holiday in Tenerife, Jeremy Richardson, our chief executive and other trustees, invited John to be our President in view of our beloved Patron the Queen Mum leaving us. He nearly had us in tears so on account of people like John the IJF will go on looking after its beneficiaries forever.

When I gave the address at Paddy's funeral, I said then that Paddy Farrell's name would go down in history, as on account of him the IJF was formed. May I also add, that with the generosity of Mr Robert Hitchins of Guernsey

Two greats – Northern Dancer and John Oaksey. (Yours truly on the left.)

several years ago, his gift to our holiday Fund of £1,000,000 made sure that the IJF annual holiday would go on indefinitely. Sadly, Mr Hitchins has since died, so to commemorate his kindness we have now renamed the holiday the Robert & Elizabeth Hitchins' IJF Tenerife Holiday.

That is the story of the IJF starting up. However, things could have been different for Paddy. One day, while talking to him about where we were going and taking stock, he confided in me and said that this would more than likely be his last, or next to last season riding, as he was never going to hit the big time living in the north of England which he loved, and he had no intention of moving down south. He would look for a yard to start training from and he would like me to work for him and ride the horses, a job I would have relished. Therefore, all the good he has done, in a roundabout way for the IJF, has been immense. Its Sod's Law and such a shame that Paddy had to sit and suffer for all those years paralysed in a wheelchair. Throughout the years I trained I didn't have a stauncher supporter than PA Farrell. He followed our horses as closely as if he had trained them himself. So, thankfully, he got lots of pleasure from that.

Dot Kavanach and JB on the Tenerife holiday.

Chapter Seven

Beneficiaries in Tenerife

•

Shane Broderick was on his third Tenerife holiday. He is the most likeable young man you could ever meet. In the past Shane had brought Vincent O'Brien, no relation to the brilliant Irish trainer, and Martin Firey, his very professional carers with him. However, Martin couldn't come on the 2003 trip, as his wife Trish was due to foal any day. To make the numbers up, Shane got David from an agency in Ireland, very highly recommended. However, on his first day there he went into the town and only got knocked over by a car on a zebra crossing, or so he told us. I took him to see the resident nurse who said he should go to the hospital for an X-ray and a tetanus injection, as he had hurt his ribs and he was complaining about and his arm was badly scraped. He said he was not going to hospital and he was not having an injection. I thought then, 'What a soft prat!' He went to his room, got changed and went out again. The next morning, Shane told Elaine and me that he had no confidence in him. It wasn't long before he was in a taxi, escorted by Elaine and yours truly, to the airport to fly via Madrid back to the Emerald Isle. In addition to the pair of carers, Shane had Sammy his pal over with him. Sammy went out on his own on the second night and came back to Mar y Sol in the early hours looking like he'd been in the ring with Sonny Liston for a few rounds. You could hardly recognise him. He had been mugged and robbed of all his money and credit cards. So you could say a portion of Shane Broderick's entourage that year was a bit unfortunate.

The first winner Shane rode was Golden Opal at Thurles in 1993. He rode a total of ninety-four winners in a four-year spell of race riding from some 1,600 rides. Shane started working and riding for Gerry Lynch in Galway, then

The IJF beneficiaries posing at the annual holiday at Mar y Sol in Tenerife.

tried his luck with Tony Redmond at the Curragh until Tony packed up. Then, in September in 1992, he joined Michael Hourigan's stable and partnered Doran's Pride as novice to finish third in the 1997 Gold Cup to Mr Mulligan. The same year when he was having his best season with thirty winners on the board, on 31 March at Fairyhouse, Shane rode Royal Oasis to win the 2½ mile Novice Chase. From a high to a low. The very next ride he had, Another Deadly, crashed and buried him, which left Shane paralysed from the neck down at the age of twenty-two. With the help of some very kind people, Shane now owns an impressive four-bedroom bungalow in Rathcabin with a ten-horse barn, a six-horse walker and a two-and-a-half-furlong circular gallop on twenty-seven acres of land. It's a lovely place. I know; Jo and I have been over and stayed with him.

At the time of our Tenerife trip, all he needed was a decent horse or two to get him a few winners to his name as a trainer. Racing journalist Tim Richards came to join us for a few days during our holiday to do a report for the *Horse & Hound*. On Thursday 10th April, a busload of us were going to Loro Parque. Time didn't half fly, it didn't seem a week since we were setting off from Manchester Airport. At Loro Parque there is an aquarium, Planet Penguin, gorillas and a Chimp Land, all set out as in the animal's natural environment. Shows are held at different times with sea lions and dolphins, which are great. It takes just over an hour on the bus to get to the park at Puerto de La Cruz, but it's well worth the visit. It's always a hit with our team.

Sitting next to Robert Lacey on the bus, he was telling me about his life and his injury. As an apprentice, he first worked for Epsom trainer Boggy Whelan. He didn't have many rides but managed to ride a winner on Nautical William at Brighton for Boggy. Robert then went on to work for Henry Candy, in the years Henry trained Nicholas Bill and Master Willie, when star apprentice Billy Newnes was employed at the yard. He then left Henry to work for jump trainer John Edwards and from there he went to work for ex-champion amateur jockey and IJF Trustee Bob McCreery, on his stud. Moving on from Bob's Stole Hill Stud, he tried his hand at Prince Fahed Salman's Newgate Stud. Whilst there, he was kicked by a brood mare named Daynanarca so badly he had his face disfigured and sustained serious head injuries. So much so that he lost the co-ordination to walk, and it confined him to a wheelchair. His accident was horrific. Robert was taken to Hodstock Hospital by air ambulance and later transferred to their head-injury unit at Bath Hospital. He remained there for four months and it left him with a speech impediment. Worst of all, the accident ended his career. Fortunately, Robert got married to a lovely girl called Jackie who absolutely idolises him and gave up her job to look after him.

One night in Tenerife we celebrated Fred Cheshire's birthday by singing 'Happy Birthday', plus Chicky Oaksey produced a makeshift cake with candles. Fred comes from a family steeped in racing history. His father, who was a very stylish rider, rode the winner of the Ebor Handicap at York and the same year rode in the Grand National. Unfortunately, he died following a fall in a selling hurdle race at Sandown in 1929 on a horse named Cormac. In compensation, his mother received £50 from the Rendelsham Benevolent Fund. Thankfully ill-fated jockeys get looked after better today. Fred served his time with RJ Collings at Newmarket. He moved on from there to ride for Sir Gordon Richards. Over the years, Fred had ridden some 120 winners. His biggest win was the Belgian Derby. He finished his stint in racing as work rider to Peter Walwyn in Lambourn.

A staunch supporter of the IJF and any other worthy cause, Fred for years had put up his little tent at Newmarket Races, selling Christmas cards and other merchandise for the IJF in rain, sleet or snow. In fact, Jeremy Richardson told Fred he had sold over £120,000 worth of IJF goods and done it for love not for wages. So you could say Fred had earned his holiday.

Tommy Jennings came over from Ireland to work for Tom Yeats of Letcombe Bassett and rode his first winner of a career total of seventy-five for trainer Jeff Kennedy, riding his last winner at thirty-four for John Webb on a horse called Indego Jones at Fontwell. Mugga Pura was the best horse Tommy rode to win the Scottish Champion Hurdle in the 60s; he also rode a Cheltenham Festival winner on Beau Caprice, both trained by Fulke Walwyn. The following year, on account of head injuries, the Jockey Club wouldn't pass him fit to ride racehorses, so, like worn out horses, Tommy had to be retired. Tommy Scuse, whose first job was apprentice to Evan Williams, the trainer who, as a jockey rode the 1937 Grand National winner Royal Mail, had a few rides for him without success, then went into the Army for National Service. He then worked for Jeremy Tree as a work rider. That job isn't always as good as it's cracked up to be. More often than not, when the trainers jock the lads off for a jockey, they don't mind but for a work rider they sometimes gets a bit pissed off as a bit of green monster sets in. To get a bit of their own back at times, as work riders are not rated as highly as jockeys, sometimes when the groom gives the rider a chuck up he often throws him up so high, pulling the work rider's leg down often he crushes his nuts on the saddle. By doing so at times, there can be quite a bit of bitchiness among riders and work riders. Tommy went on to join Freddie Maxwell's yard, had a few rides for him again without a winner, but rode many placed and also worked and had a few rides for Keith Piggott, Lester's father. He also rode for Rosey Lomax and for Jack Dowdeswell who rode plenty of winners himself, being Champion Jockey a couple of times, although Jack hates people saying 'Champion'. He says he was just lucky to ride more winners that season than anyone else. Jack actually rode his first winner at Newbury on a horse called Bob. Tommy Scuse rode for years but at the age of forty, the Jockey Club doctor wouldn't pass him fit to ride on account of him losing a kidney through a race-related illness. Now he has a leisurely life in his seventies and tends his wife June, who unfortunately has Parkinson's Disease. While having a dance with June at the karaoke, she told me she used to sing a lot at clubs before she had her stroke, but hasn't got the confidence to do it now. I asked her what songs she liked, so I put the number of the song she said down on a ticket to go on the machine. When it came up I said quietly, 'Come on now June, we'll do this song together', we did and she loved it. She also made a good job of it.

From 1969–74, George Maclean was apprentice to George Todd at Manton, who specialised in great staying horses such as Trelawney, and who won a couple of Ascot Stakes, with its impressive gallops, near Marlborough, where

John Gosden trained in 2004. George then moved on to Ken Cundell's. George rode his one and only winner courtesy of Welsh Windsor, in an apprentice race at Goodwood, from a total of twenty-five rides. Moving on to Peter Walwyn's stable while riding a yearling in the indoor school it reared up and trapped his leg between the horse and the wall boards, breaking it. He was carted off to the Princess Margaret Hospital in Swindon and operated on and the leg was put in plaster for a year. However, it appeared the leg had never been set right and at the time he needed a splint and a stick to get around with on account of the leg muscles wasting. It could have done with being broken and reset. However, it couldn't be done later because there was no muscle and his limb was so weak and thin. George had a wife and two kids to support, so he started riding out again for Peter Walwyn, but a doctor made him pack it up, as he was getting worse. Sick as a parrot, his riding days over, George took up bowling as a career, which proved very successful. As coach for the West of Scotland disabled team, he led them to win the Olympics held in Wales in 2001, when Scotland won eleven Golds, three Silver and five Bronze Medals – a feat surely to be proud of.

Lots of our beneficiaries were in the warm pool one morning in Tenerife as Tim Richards – the newspaper reporter who came on our trip to Tenerife for a couple of days to write and article for the *Horse and Hound* about the IJF holiday – came to say his goodbyes, all dressed up. I shook his hand as I reached out of the pool and pulled him nearer the side, Chicky Oaksey got herself into a flap, 'Oh, no Jack, no don't do it', so I adhered to orders and I didn't. Tim was a bit worried, as he knows me from old. Years ago Jimmy Fitzgerald's owner Tony Budge, was throwing a party in aid of some kiddies charity and the guest speaker didn't turn up. We were all asked in turn to tell a tale of some sort or sing a song. Tim was sitting next to me and after I told my tale I announced that, as the guest speaker was a declared non-runner, Tim would stand in and do the talk to the 100 or more racing folk about the fund. Well he coughed and spluttered his way through and he hadn't a clue what the cause was about. Ever since, wherever he sees me, with a sheepish smile he says, 'You're a bugger, you are.'

One night in Tenerife, we went to our annual trip to the Pig Farm, a place where we either eat chicken or pork chops, and where the portions are huge. Normally, we arrange trips to go on whilst we are here on holiday to various places, which are optional as not everyone wants to go, but the Pig Farm always gets 100% support. On our visit, we had the pleasure of our new IJF Chairman, Sir Edward Cazelet, in attendance along with his son Hal. Hal, along with his pal Ian, who are both classical singers, gave us a rendition of the song from the show 'Oklahoma', 'Oh what a beautiful morning', and a couple more tunes that were really good and appreciated by all. Outside the Pig Farm's dining room was one of those little Postman Pat's vans. We put little Richard Fox in the driver's seat and Ronnie Singer riding shotgun and I put one Euro in to start it up. It was so funny we were all crying with laughter. As you can imagine on the way back in the bus we were in great voice.

Yorkshire girls have a reputation of being tough. Muriel Naughton was the first woman to ride in a jump race in Britain at Ayr in 1976, on a horse named

Ballycasey; but Sharon Murgatroyd is one of the bravest lasses I have ever met. She broke her back at Bangor on Dee racecourse in 1991, marring the year our yard had its best ever season with 143 winners. You talk about Yorkshire folks having grit. This Yorkshire lass, from Keighley, certainly had more than her fair share. That fearful day Sharon broke her neck in five places. She was taken to Wrexham Hospital and was later moved to Oswestry Orthopaedic Hospital. Nosey, and wanting to know everything like she does, she asked the doctor tending her what was the matter with her. Doctor El Masry told her she had badly broken her neck and she said 'but I'm not dead am I?' In Tenerife, she goes out all over and if there is a party you can be sure Miss Murgatroyd will be there in the thick of it with a glass in her hand, and she will stay there till the end! Earlier in our time there, she said in a joking manner, knowing full well my missus rode our flat runners in amateur races, 'You never gave me a ride, did you Jack?' 'No, I didn't, mate,' I said, 'but I didn't get a lot of chances.' I was thinking at the time if I could have looked into the future and known she was going to get hurt so badly, I would have made sure I had given her a ride, and wouldn't have stopped until I had put her on a winner, although The Bride wasn't a bad pilot. Amongst other winners, Jo rode just four times in the Brook Bond Five Furlong Sprint Race at Wolverhampton, Fiona's Pet, 20/1, Bri Eden, 7/1, Relative Ease, 20/1 and Lilac Star, 6/1 and she won them all at those prices, one could hardly say they were good things. Another Yorkshire lass, Jane Thompson, holds a record we could well do without. Jane was the first female jockey to get killed through injuries while riding on a British racecourse. This happened at Catterick in 1986. These brave hearts of the racing world that ride with danger to make their name, do we stop to think, as we choose our horse, of the jockey who may not finish the course?

These are the words of Sheila Henderson of Selkirk in Scotland. Sheila wrote this song and the music about jump jockeys. She has recorded Hal Cazalet singing it and kindly sent the words on to me. I can assure you it is very good. The IJF almoners sell the CD of it on their stalls at the races in aid of the Fund.

The Brave Hearts of the Racing Game

Chorus:
We're the brave hearts of the racing game
We ride with danger to make our name
Through the autumn winds and the winter rain
We'll go out and do it all again.

We come from many a Scottish town
From Tipperary to County Down
The Cumbrian Fells and Yorkshire Dales
The Wiltshire Downs and Berkshire Vales
To ride a winner is our aim
To be just second is not the same

The runners gather out on the track
And there's jockeys shouting from the back
No Sir, No Sir
The sleet is driving in our face
The divots fly as we ride our race
The going's soft and all around
There's jockeys tumbling to the ground
The horses tank on down the straight
A few more runners will meet their fate
There's bumping, boring out here today
And some flowery words along the way
With just two fences left to clear
The winning post coming ever near
A quick look through our legs reveals
The jockey closest on our heels
The tired horses give their all
We're praying hard we won't have a fall
The crowds are cheering us from the rails
Maybe one last crack if all else fails
The ups, the downs, the highs and lows
Are all just part of the life we chose
Though battered, bruised and black and blue
Our spirits down, our dreams in two
But morrow is another day
A new day dawns and we're on our way
The craic, the jokes and the bird last night
With our pals around we'll be all right

Chorus:
We're the brave hearts of the racing game
We ride with danger to make our name
Through the autumn winds and the winter rain
We'll go out and do it all again

With the eviction of David, Shane's would-be carer and Shirley, one of Sharon's carers, the vacancy was admirably filled by Eileen Cullen. Janette Boston, Sharon's other carer is the wife of former jump jockey Noel Boston, who rode in the north at the same time as me. She, like me, is into Country and Western music. One night on our trip we had karaoke on before dinner. Our Sam, his partner Carole, Jo and I had been out together for a meal. As they live in Sparsholt, near Lambourn, we don't see that much of them. The minute I stepped into the dining room bar for a drink our gang were heckling me to sing, so I didn't let them down. I sang, or should I say strangled the Kenny Roger's song, 'Coward of the County'. When the restaurant closed at about 11 p.m. or so, Pepe the waiter at Mar y Sol, who has been there since we first came in 1992, makes sure our glasses are topped up before he closes the bar. We all then sit outside around the tables with our drinks by the poolside talking and

The IJF beneficiaries having a drinks party before dinner in Tenerife.

singing. I would get up in the middle of the night to have a sing song. It often goes on for a very long time, but it's great to see these people having a bit of 'craic' together, as most of them don't see each other from year to year and they don't want it to end. God knows how some of them have suffered.

Brian Elder went from school to the Stanley Wooton yard at Epsom to serve his apprenticeship. When Mr Wooton retired, Brian was sent along with Pat O'Leary, Freddie Hunter and other apprentices to Staff Ingham in Epsom. He was there six years getting plenty of rides for Harold Wallington, Vic Smyth, Matt Feakes, Sam Hanley, Doug Marks, Norman Bertie, who trained Sir Victor Sassoon's 1953 Derby winner, Pinza ridden by Gordon Richards. The versatile George Forbes, the auctioneer, vet and bloodstock agent asked Brian if he would go to India to ride for the Royal West Indian Turf Club which he did for three months, riding a dozen or so winners. He rode a really nice filly while there, called Rainband, which went on the following year to win the Bombay 1,000 Guineas, ridden by Willie Snaith.

Brian came back to Staff Ingham's, but Staff had as many jockeys in the yard as horses. Staff's stable jockey Scobie Breasley, arranged a job for Brian with the Yorkshire trainer Jack Ormston. Brian once had the leg up on Le Garcon D'or, the British sprinter with a record 36 wins. Our old grey fellow Palacegate Touch was 13 years old in 2003. I was trying my heart out to beat Le Garcon D'Or's record with him when I trained, and Archie, as we know him at home, managed to win thirty-four times. On 17 September 1996, at Sandown, Archie on good-to-firm going galloped the five furlongs in 58.82 seconds to break the track record.

Brian was then called up for National Service. Charlie Smirke said to him, 'You're not going to be a jump jockey, as most flat jockeys get heavy in the army. I will get you a riding job in Mauritius.' On and off, he rode and trained there from 1960-1992 with a lot of riding and training successes. Brian had a lot of success for the main man he trained for, Philip Koom from Taiwan. A rival Chinese trainer didn't take kindly to being beaten so often by B Elder, and made a plan with Brian's boss for him to be relieved of his duties. From there he moved on to South Africa as an assistant to the leading trainer Stanley Crick for a couple of years. While there life wasn't just a bed of roses. One day he was robbed off all his possessions; photo's, racing tapes, trophies, every single thing he owned including the mattresses on the beds. The thief even emptied the fridge of food. However the nicest thing was, the South African jockeys who had ridden with Brian in Johannesburg heard about the robbery and rallied round and bought Brian new shoes and clothes, in fact, they completely kitted him out. As you can imagine Brian couldn't thank them enough. Probably the best thing was that Brian wasn't in the house at the time or more than likely they would have killed him.

He then married Jackie, a local girl, and came to England to look after his father who was sick, until he died a few years ago. Whilst in Mauritius in 1962, he attended sixteen meetings, he had eighty-two rides and rode forty-two winners. Brian also had quite a few falls, in one he broke his right leg in ten places. He then, unfortunately, suffered a stroke, which finished his riding career. He is now seventy years old. While here on holiday in Tenerife, he met up with some of his old riding mates, i.e Willie Snaith who he hadn't seen for over thirty years, same with Colin Casey, Des Cullen and so on. As you can imagine, a fair bit of reminiscing went on.

Our last Saturday night in Tenerife was Show Night, and our Chairman's son Hal Cazalet and Ian Bloomfield, both professional singers, accompanied by Susie Allen on piano made our night one to remember. They sang classical ballads, Irish songs, a whole range and invited us all to sing along as Hal's father Edward had brought song sheets with him from England knowing full well that Hal and co. would get us going. I introduced them on stage and as there were a lot of Germans also over here Chicky asked me while I was up on the stage to announce for everyone to be very careful, as Frank Dever, Johnny O'Hara and a couple more had all fallen over on the slippery floors during the last couple of days. So I told them to make sure and be very careful as we have recently had more falls here than there were at that day's Scottish Grand National. Gabby, the complex's Master of Ceremonies, stood behind me and out of sight gave me the cues in German, so I also introduced the artists in German and English. Honestly, our punters were impressed! In fact, Mary Bolton asked me, 'Where did you learn to speak German?' No doubt you are aware, as I have mentioned it before, but in 2003 our top jump jockeys made a tape with the Irish duo, Foster and Allen with McCoy and company singing in the background. This time I sang the song, 'The Fields of Athenry', while Susie played the piano and Ian and Hal sang the choruses with me. Our crowd loved it, unless they were just being kind to us; it could have been that! Whatever, the whole night went down a treat.

Our Chairman, Sir Edward Cazalet, came earlier in the day to stay with us until we went back the following Tuesday, bringing with him some good news. Princess Anne had agreed to be patron of the IJF for a five year period to replace our beloved late patron, The Queen Mum. On the Sunday night our Sam and Carole asked his mum and me to go out to the Over Seas Chinese

Restaurant with them for a meal and if I didn't let them pay, they didn't want to go. It was really good. We got back to the Mar y Sol about 10.15 p.m. Ian and Hal had Shane, Sharon and Ronnie all doing their bit on the mike. I haven't mentioned our Sam much until now, but had it not been for him the Tenerife holiday would not have taken place. Years ago, when Sam was an apprentice, he used to come to Tenerife with his mates on holiday. I dread to think of what they got up to, but no doubt they had plenty of fun and he loved Tenerife. After that awful day, 5 March 1985, when he had the fall from Solares, which finished his riding career, he received some money in compensation. With his money he bought himself an apartment at Mar y Sol, which is a sheltered complex equipped with a gym, a heated swimming pool with a hoist and all the other facilities wheelchair-bound people need. In addition, medical staff are also on site.

When I came to visit him, Sam was swimming with armbands on in the heated pool, really enjoying it. When I had left England the day before, it was a foot deep in snow and freezing cold and I was thinking there are lots of people at home who are injured jockeys who would relish this experience and the Mar y Sol IJF holiday took off from that moment. Sam met Carole there on holiday, but on account of a bit of loneliness and a few problems he had sold his apartment. The pair hit it off and got engaged to be married and live together in a lovely house in Sparsholt, near Lambourn. Carole had been married before and has three children, Kim, Paul and Kelly, who is Fergus Sweeney, the flat-jockey's girlfriend. Doug, Carol's late husband, died a few years ago. Sam rode winners on the flat and over jumps; he was a very stylish and lovely rider. He looked destined to go far as a jockey and I'm not just saying that because I am his dad. That was now twenty-three years ago, so we will never know. He was so keen to get back riding when he was released from hospital, every Wednesday we took him to Christine Pollet's Riding for the Disabled classes at Wrea Green, near Preston. Sam even rode Solares, the horse he got hurt on in our indoor school at Cockerham, but it was awful to see him flopping around like a rag doll, as he had no balance. On account of Paddy Farrell's injury, the IJF was formed and on account of Sam Berry's injury the Elizabeth and Robert Hitchen Tenerife Holiday was set up. The Fund and the holiday will hopefully go on forever. Therefore you could say Paddy and Sam are famous.

Our time in Tenerife, sadly had come to an end. Traditionally, we keep our last night our speeches and our presentations. On our last night I was MC, John and Edward also had something to say.

I started by telling the beneficiaries how relaxed and well they all looked. Nice and sun-tanned. but all good things come to an end. Most of us thought the holiday the best we had had, but they say that nearly every year so it goes to show just how much they enjoyed it. As I said before, Richard Fox is a real star on holiday. He keeps everyone amused whatever breed or creed. In my speech I mentioned the year R Fox didn't come out with us. The captain who flew the plane nearly turned it around when he realised Foxy wasn't on board. I also mentioned a few of the funny things that had happened, like when we were playing games, such as gaining points for kisses, one for a lady and five for a waiter! Tommy Scuse kissed four waiters; needless to say he hacked up. I said all of us ex-jockeys knew he was a bent jockey, I think June his missus had a suspicion he was a bit 'the other way' when he went out at times in her gear. Since the kissing game, the waiters have been all over him like a rash.

Foxy and Ronnie Singer, following their trip in the Postman Pat van, rang the Pig Farm up and tried to buy it! Sarah York, one of our almoners was finishing at Christmas, not to start a family, I told them, 'She's retiring.' We presented Sarah, Chicky, Oaksey and Elaine Wiles with a present each and thanked them for looking after us so well and organising the trip, which took a fair bit of doing. Also, they look after all the beneficiaries brilliantly. They got a well-deserved big round of applause. I told them that birthday boy, Fred Cheshire, who as I mentioned for years has put up his tent at Newmarket races selling our IJF goods, was now, at the ripe old age of seventy-three, calling it a day. Fred asked John Oaksey and myself if we wanted to buy his business, we declined of course.

I asked them to spare a thought for the rest of our almoners who were absent that evening and the office staff who hardly anyone ever sees, and who all contribute to keeping our 'show on the road', and of course not forgetting our Chief Executive Jeremy Richardson who keeps us all under control. I told them: 'By now you will have all met our new Chairman, Sir Edward Cazalet, who has taken that role over from our President, Lord Oaksey. Before I passed them on to John, who I said, 'is going to give you some good news about our new patron', I told them a couple more things, something about our Chairman, who I assured them, 'is not just a city gent as some of them may have thought. Edward is unique as he is the only High Court Judge to have ridden a Cheltenham Festival winner, when he rode Lochroe who beat Taxidermist with John Lawrence aboard, the now Lord Oaksey. In addition to that, he rode another twenty-four winners under rules and sixty-five point-to-point winners. Edward has been a trustee of our IJF for fifteen years and I can assure you he does a good job.' Whilst we were all there together, I asked them to, 'give a warm thank you to all those people who contribute in so many different ways, such as leaving money in wills, holding functions for our benefit, making donations or buying our IJF Christmas cards and calendars. We all rightly know that without them we wouldn't have been there that night.' This request received plenty of support. For the entertainment our thanks went, 'to Hal Cazalet and Ian Bloomfield who sang so well and Susie Allen who played the piano so beautifully. They enhanced our holiday so much, thank you.'

Last, but certainly not least, I thanked our President Lord Oaksey. During his years as a devoted Trustee of the IJF John has served as a Racing correspondent for the *Daily* and *Sunday Telegraph*, written a weekly article for the *Horse & Hound*, been a columnist for the *Racing Post*, a TV presenter, a leading amateur jockey, president of a couple of racing clubs, a JP and more. He has always been busy with work, but that all came a poor second to the IJF. John had earned the Fund many thousands of pounds by giving speeches and attending functions, always with his baby, the IJF and the beneficiaries in mind. As you can see by the ambitious plan below, one day I would hope to get this complex off the ground and name it Oaksey Estate, a sheltered accommodation for our beneficiaries sponsored by the Fund and private individuals. The initial plans were knocked up by Dave Armstrong, an architect pal of mine, and me.

I ended my speech by saying: 'The ex-John Lawrence, now Lord Oaksey, should kick the 'Oaksey' bit into touch and be named Lord Injured Jockeys Fund. There are thousands of beneficiaries who have enjoyed a much better quality of life on account of his help. A true gentleman, Lord Oaksey.' John thanked me for the kind words and was truly moved. Following the speeches Hal, Ian and Susie got cracking and they let us all have a sing with them, even as good as they were. Shane Broderick sang 'Sponsor Hill' with Richard Fox, which was great – very touching and quite emotional.

Sharon Murgatroyd also sang a couple of David Bowie songs and it was all very moving. Simon O'Neill, a Trustee and course starter left me £50 to buy our gang a drink. Whether it was because our party thought it was such a rare occasion Simon coughing up, I don't know, but no one refused. When I went to the bar to get weighed-in, Simon's money paid for about one third of the bill! Chicky stepped in though and paid for the rest. When the restaurant bar threw us out, a party was held in one of our trustee's rooms. In there were the two singers. I am not going to tell anymore tales about it but at 4 a.m. there were plenty of people swimming in the heated pool and not many swimming

An early sketch of the plans for 'Oaksey Estate'.

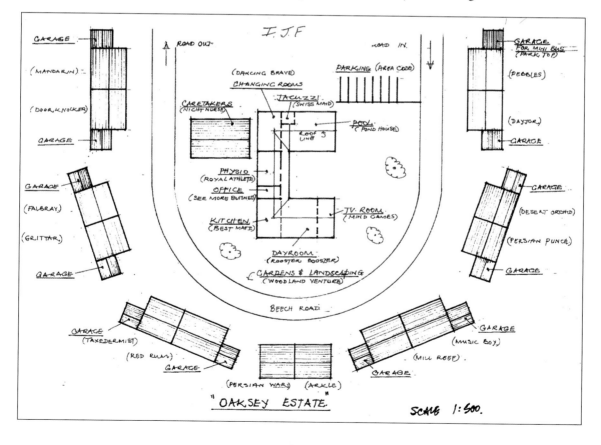

suits were on view! They tell me it was 5 a.m. when the trustee in question went to bed. Next morning we were loaded onto our buses to be at the airport for 11 a.m. with everyone kissing and shaking hands, hoping to see each other, if not before, then next year. I'm sure they will often talk about the Tenerife holiday as they ring each other up and swap birthday and Christmas cards. When you see the camaraderie and the way everyone helped each other, the laughing, the banter, the craic, it was money well spent. On account of Mr Robert Hitchen's generosity, we will never be out of his debt, or him out of our grateful thoughts and hopefully the annual holiday will go on forever.

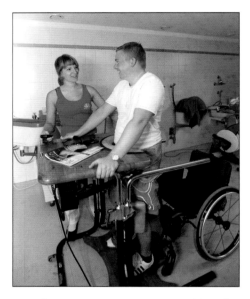

Beneficiary receiving treatment in Tenerfe.

Chapter Eight

Holiday Over – Let's Kick On

•

On my return from the IJF holiday, a fax arrived from Coolmore signed by Christy Grassick's secretary confirming the agreement for two people to visit Coolmore Stud, Fethard, and Ballydoyle racing stables. I waded though the post and, as usual, most of it was junk mail, which we don't waste as it goes in our village recycling bin. However, I did have the good fortune to win a £50 Premium Bond. Also I received £70 for the two tickets Sarah York bought, a £20 donation from a young lady I sold a ticket to at Doncaster Races, though unfortunately she couldn't come. The £100 cheque arrived from the boss of Sterling Fibre, John Connors, who agreed to sponsor the pig for the hog roast. Jo and I in the main absorbed the postage in sending the tickets out and whatever else, we still hoped to send around £10,000 worth or even more raffle tickets in the post,

I put to one side Sarah's £70 and Sophie's £20 towards postage costs. However, I was still crediting our balance with the money as at that moment I still had it. Also in the post was a letter with a credit of £70 from the IJF office, as Sarah Cousins had sent her cheque for two tickets to them instead of me. We took the credit for Sarah's cheque, which now made the target less than £20,000, which was great. I knew that very soon I would need to write out a cheque for around £500 for the eighteen photos and prints that we were getting framed at Frame Plus of Colburn, near Scorton. Graham, the boss, does us a good deal. Our balance was now £19,920.

An outing for the Teenage Activity Scheme and Specialised Outreach Childcare Scheme to Jack Berry's house for their BBQ treat.

On Thursday 17 April, the weather was absolutely scorching, every bit as good as we had in Tenerife. The weather forecaster reckoned it had been the hottest day recorded for that time of year. Very appropriate, as at 11 a.m., fourteen youngsters and their one-to-one carers came to a barbecue we had put on annually for them. They were from the TAS, Teenage Activity Scheme, and SOCS, (Specialised Outreach Childcare Scheme). Both are run under the umbrella of Thirsk and Sowerby District Community Care Association, which was set up to aid young people with a varied range of disabilities.

Martin Wright, Northern Racing Clerk of the Scales, asked me if they could have a day with us at our house when I saw him at a Doncaster meeting. Sue, his wife is the TAS Administrator. Our dogs love them as they threw tennis and golf balls for them as they played in the paddock. The youngsters fed the fish in our pond, where a few of the balls also ended up, and some of them had a ride on the quad bike. We also took them to see the horses, OI Oyston and other company in the field in the village. Ollie was all over the kids. He's always been gentle and loveable with youngsters or people who are just not 100%. That's probably why he and I have always got on so well.

My dad always said a horse in a stable would never hurt a child or a drunken man. The youngsters were 'good doers' at the barbecue. I was in charge of the cooking, so I let them take a turn at cooking which they loved, as did the carers, and we enjoy having the kids. Seeing them enjoying themselves so much is great. It doesn't take a big star to shine to light up their life. The postman dropped a cheque off for £70 into our box from Terri Herbert-Jackson for his two tickets. The jackpot now stood at £19,850. In the same post was a letter from Harrods having a re-think, thanking me for my letter but regrettably they couldn't give us an auction prize on this occasion. Although I received a better result in the evening, John Forsyth and Terry Holdcroft, with their wives both named Margaret, called in to see us after Ripon races, where their horse Golden Nun ran second. He was by Terry's stallion, Mind Games, who we

The youngsters from the TAS and SOCS at the BBQ.

trained to win quite a few Group Races, which included the Palace House Stakes at Newmarket and the Temple Stakes at Sandown twice. We called Mind Games 'Dennis', a name given to him by his breeder Rob Hughes, who used to play football for Crewe Alexander and Rob's idol at the time was Dennis Law. Dennis, gave our yard its first Royal Ascot win when he won the Group Three Norfolk Stakes in 1994, ridden by John Carroll. Dennis wasn't as fast as Indigenous, the sprinter, who in 1960 broke the world record at Epsom, humping 9st 5lbs with a time of 53.6 seconds when ridden by Lester Piggott and trained at Epsom by Dick Thrale; but he was very fast. As we had no brood mares for the following year, and seeing as I had an annual nomination to Mind Games, subject to Terry's approval, I would put my nomination into the raffle, for which I hope to sell a lot of tickets. Mind Games stud fee was £3,500 and there are some other great prizes to be won. Terry and John are very generous when it comes to any charity (except for the day at Haydock when Terry bought just one raffle ticket off The Bride which has a mention later on). They bought and paid for a pair of tickets each, leaving our target standing at £19,710. John asked me if I would conduct the auction at Tern Hill, in aid jointly for the IJF and kiddies hospice in Shropshire on 21 June. I told him I would willingly, as the majority of the punters who would be attending were racing and hunting folk. To help the auction, I gave John one of the hunting prints and one of Martha's Son and Dublin Flyer both by Joy Hawkins. Also a nice little painting of Fidalgo ridden by Joe Mercer when he won the Irish Derby in 1959, which should sell particularly well at that venue. This painting was amongst the memorabilia kindly donated by Joe via Lady Oaksey, who knew Joe he wouldn't mind half the money raised for his painting going to the kids. Joe is a great man. For years he has organised a golf tournament and sent our IJF holiday fund many thousands of pounds.

I had just been on the phone to Jo Bower to ask her how the raffle tickets were coming along as her firm Creature Comforts were sponsoring them. We were hoping to do a run of 20,000 but in batches of A1-1000, B1-1000 and so on. Only the printers said to put the alphabet letters on would mean they have to be on the press twice, cost £480 and that would hold us up for another eight days. In view of that, I told Jo to go for the straight run. Mind you, imagine buying a ticket numbered 17,208; the buyer wouldn't rate his or her chance to win very highly. The thing was to get them so we could crack on and sell them. If we only sold half the tickets, it would put us in good stead to reach our target.

It was Middleham Open Day on Good Friday. I was hoping to sell quite a few barbecue tickets but I didn't want to just sell tickets for the sake of it. Hopefully, we would attract some good bidders for our auction. The weather was brilliant and people came from miles to visit Middleham. Lots of them knew me and although I had been retired for three years at that time, people still asked me to sign autographs, which was nice. It was great to walk around the yards at Middleham. I must say all the horses looked well. There was no chance of going to look round all the yards in one day, as there are so many of them. We went to George Moore's yard, the son-in-law of my old late pal Steve Nesbitt. In the late 1970s, Steve trained a very useful sprinter but dangerous one, named Ubedizzy. The Jockey Club warned the horse off in Britain because after finishing second he tried to savage his lad and any onlookers who came close. When he ran at Newmarket's Craven Meeting, Ubedizzy had quite a bit of form before that occasion, as he actually bit off the finger of Andy Crook, the trainer, when he was a stable lad looking after the horse. Steve and George were looking all over for that finger-end to take to the hospital with Andy, so hopefully it could get sewn back on. Unfortunately, it couldn't be found; the brute probably ate it! George trained the two-year-old Iron Tempest to win at Beverley the other day. So, if he had any horses of shares in horses to sell, the Beverley winner would help him.

Carol, George's wife, is a smashing lady who I have known forever; she always helps us in any way she can for our charities. Carol had also sold raffle tickets in the past. I left ten entry tickets for her to sell for our day on 20 July. Jo and I visited the yard of Kate Milligan whose horses at the moment are in cracking form and are looking particularly well. Kate ordered two tickets for our barbecue, as did Chris and Judy Fairhurst from Glasgow House Stables. Chris, is the son of my old mate Tommy who retired from training a few years ago. Chris always keeps his yard immaculate. It's is steeped in history and is a pleasure to visit. A few years ago Tommy bought a yearling that had a lot of faults with its limbs, not 'correct' as racing folk say, which most of us have done at some time (something most bloodstock agents seldom do which is why they miss a lot of bargains). Provided the faults were minor and wouldn't stop the animal running, I could live with it. We wanted to train race horses, not show horses. Although Tommy's yearling was cheap, he couldn't pass it on at any price to any existing or potential owner, as only Tommy thought the animal would stand training. When the poor little mite was being broken, Tommy would say to it, 'Come on my son, get a grip, Harry's coming', the Harry he was talking about was Harry Atkinson, the local knackerman! He finished up naming the horse Harry's Coming. Thankfully, he did stand up to training and also won races. Thankfully, Harry never did come!

Stan Roberts, a permit trainer and amateur rider for whom I rode a few horses for years ago, was there and he ordered a pair of tickets. I say 'ordered' as until they actually paid, I didn't count on it! We then went on to Anne Duffield's yard at Sun Hill Farm, Constable Burton, whose horses looked even better than anyone's we saw that day and the yard was really immaculate; not a straw in sight – a real credit to her and the staff. For me, she would have won the Best Turned-out Stable, no bother, or be awarded Man of the Match. Anne's Rifleman won a race at Ripon the other day, as I write, at 16/1, which caused quite a lot of interest. Anne works so very hard to get it right, whatever success she gets I can assure you she earns. There, six tickets were ordered and four were bought and paid for by Stewart Adams the owner of Rifleman and Mr and Mrs Nuttall, which left our target figure at £19,570.

These Open Days are great, but I must say an awful lot of work and organising goes into them. You wouldn't believe the moaning that goes on from the occasional punter, which can be a bit rich when we are in the main only trying to help others. One year at Cockerham we were going flat out in all our spare time tidying and painting the place up, when some kid managed to get white paint on her coat and the mother went bananas and threatened to sue us. I think the little madam must have been climbing the gallop rails as it had only been finished a couple of days before the event – you can imagine the paint that went on that! It doesn't take much imagination to work it out, three six-inch rails on each side of the gallops, four feet of a six-by-six post sticking out of the ground to cover every six feet. For the rails alone it's five-and-a-half miles and we painted both sides, making eleven miles of rails to paint, plus the hundreds of posts. If you could have seen the paint on my little apprentice 'Rembrandts' who put it on, that little girl got let off lightly! Some of our 'artists' you could hardly recognise, although I did give them a few extra pounds for doing it. They put their ears back at times and would rather have not done the job. In fact, it would be fair to say if they had been horses, a good half would have had to have been equipped with blinkers with a few stall handlers giving them a push. If and when they had a little moan, I would quietly remind them what we were doing it for. They soon settled down and got on with it.

Our first big Open Day at Cockerham, was held to save the Grand National, jointly with getting a party of terminally-ill youngsters from Morecambe on a trip to Disneyland in America. We had managed to get so much free publicity on TV and our local radio. On one station the DJ would say every hour, 'You know where to go on Sunday at 11 a.m., yes, Jack Berry's Racing Stables at Cockerham.' Then he would give the spiel to his punters. We also got publicity in the papers and on race cards at just about every racecourse in the country weeks before the event, and also had them repeated. My mistake was I never told the authorities, i.e. the police. I didn't know one had to, although the day before the event our team put posters up all over the place giving directions to our yard that were printed and donated by the *Lancashire Evening Newspaper* so you'd think the Police would have seen them. Our event started at 11 a.m., but there were cars, some with caravans attached before we had even mucked-out the horses coming from as far as Devon and Scotland. It was five miles from the M6 motorway on a minor road to the yard. Around lunchtime, all the roads leading to the yard were blocked solid with traffic. We couldn't take the £5 per car entrance fee fast enough, especially as most of the people wanted to chat to our girls clad in our owners racing colours at the entrance gate, with the like of 'what a lovely place you have', 'It took me hours to get here', 'whose colours have you got on?', 'you should have more signs up', 'we got lost at the traffic lights at Garstang', 'did we take a wrong turn?' and so on. There was a family from Liverpool who were just having a day out in the country who got caught up in the traffic and were ushered up to the yard! We still took their fiver and they had a wonderful day.

The law finally appeared at the bottom of our lane, took down the notice board we had erected and waved the traffic straight on into Blackpool so that they could unblock the roads. People who knew the road to our yard were arguing with the police that that was not the way to Jack Berry's stables. One man got out of his car and wasn't going to move, telling the bobby that he and his family had travelled all the way from Yorkshire and had been looking forward to this day for ages. It was absolute chaos. We possibly had in attendance as many people as Haydock Park gets on a race day. It was a sweltering hot day and by 2 p.m one couldn't buy a sandwich, a cup of tea or anything.

Everything was sold out and, bear in mind, we had used outside caterers, certainly not a 'do-it-yourself' job. As luck would have it, the local pub, The Manor, did the bar and they brought plenty of beer, so quite a few people went home hungry, but happy. If the police hadn't interfered, we could have given Old Trafford a run for the day's attendance. Weeks before the event I asked Alan Worthington, our blacksmith, if he would de-nail all our old shoes and racing plates from our horses and bag them up. This was so that we could give the punters one each as we took their money on entering by way of a bit of luck. By lunch time the three sacks full had been dished out. At one time the queue to the ladies toilet must have been a furlong long! When it got a bit quieter, Dave Ashworth, our village bobby, came up and gave me a right bollocking for not informing the police. By the amount of people that came, the police must have been the only ones who didn't know!

The outcome was the Grand National Appeal copped quite a few quid and the Morecambe youngsters got to Disneyland. Except for the girl who got paint on her, everyone had a good time so we were happy. Therefore lawman Dave's dressing down was like water off a duck's back. A bit like the picture and caption Tony Collins gave me.

When you are in deep SHIT,
say nothing, and try to look like
you know what you're doing.

Both Jo and I have always been suckers for the welfare of kids. John Brown, one of our long-standing owners, had read in his local paper that some Manchester youngsters had been turned away from the Royal Manchester Children's Hospital through lack of beds, under the heading 'no room at the inn'. Ringing up the hospital fund-raiser Cath Smith, I told her we would arrange an Open Day at our yard in Cockerham to get her the additional much needed cots. The event was arranged for Sunday 13 August 1989. I thanked everyone involved at the time, all those years ago. It would be nice to thank them in print now for the way they rallied round. In addition, to reaching our targets for the cots, a substantial surplus went towards the running costs.

Following the Middleham Open Day I had another progress meeting at home with Jo Bower, everything was going to plan and the raffle tickets would be ready and printed up for the following weekend. On Easter Saturday, Graham Saxton, the boss of Frame Plus, rang to say the prints and photos we took him to get framed were ready for picking up. Jo was just about to go to Tesco's to indulge in her favourite hobby (shopping), so I told her I would drop her off at Tesco's and drive on to Colburn to pick up the pictures, then double back for her. It would take just over half an hour to meet up again. When I got to Graham's, he had made a great job of the framing and as it was for a good cause he shaved 20% off the proper price. Even so, I was loath to write a cheque out of our fund's book, but I did for £548. Unfortunately for the first time in ages we were above the £20,000; the thermometer had risen to £20,118. As I have already stated, the framing was money well spent. We would not get anything like the value of the goods if we sold them unframed.

My shopaholic was still in Tesco's when I returned. I was mindful of Kempton and Haydock racing on the box and also Carlisle and Newton Abbot jumping on Attheraces. A great day's racing in store, therefore I didn't want to hang about, so I parked up the car, went into the store and walked behind the check-in desk. There was The Bride about halfway up, getting weighed-in with about ten shoppers deep behind her. You should have seen the look on the face of the exceptionally well-made lady waiting for the next turn and the facial expressions she was pulling, when our Jo was dragging a fistful of saver coupons of all denominations out of her pockets, which she had no doubt cut from magazines for various goods she had bought. The old girl behind her didn't know Jo, but it would have taken much more than a mountain of a woman to ruffle her!

We hadn't burnt all the daylight as we arrived back home in time to see the racing and it was good to see on the box our son Alan's Caldy Dancer win at Haydock. It's always nice to train a two-year-old winner first time up and Haydock, being Alan's local course, would have given him a great buzz.

Just a few days before we went to Tenerife, Dave (joiner) and I had washed and painted all the stables. While we were in the mood, we decorated the tack room, which I must say looked great. On the morning of Easter Sunday, we hung the paintings, photos and pictures up in the tack room that we were to auction later at the BBQ. We had made it into an 'art gallery' to enable people to view them prior to the auction. Before the day, we would catalogue the lots in the brochure and get them some publicity. I made quite a big effort that ringing up folk to encourage them to sell the tickets, with a bit of success but I would only put the actual sale down on paper when I received the money. Some people I asked meant well in advance but didn't always follow their intentions through. Although I did receive a fax with the local jokers' names written all over it; Anne and her keen gardener husband, George Duffield. They would have known it was a good time to wind me up because I told them at their Open Day that I would be working on the tickets on Easter Sunday as I had been to Tenerife and had a bit to catch up on. As I never heard from the Swale Valley Stompers, and time was ticking on, I rang Bob Kendal, Country & Western singer from Brough, to invite him to come to our 'do' again on 20 July to entertain us. Thankfully, he said he would. Gary Gibson came and did a good job the year previous. Gary sings and looks like John Lennon, but that kind of music isn't everyone's cup of tea. Bob is good, plus the fact that I get up with him and sing a song or two. In fact we made a tape together called 'Off and Running' a few years ago. Bob dragged me to one or two of his gigs and we also had four of our girls from the yard who were the backing group to one of the songs I sang, 'The Jolly Farmer', and we travelled to Scotland, Wales and all over singing the song.

We even sang it at Lester's at the London Hilton in 1996. We recorded the tape at the Music Farm, Egremont, near Whitehaven. As you can see on the photo, jockeys Brian Storey and Tony Dobin who got up with Jane Molloy and The Bride are giving it some welly at a charity function in Carlisle. Behind me having a bit of a cower is Dave Parker. No doubt lots of people might think he should have stuck to his day job and maybe he would have trained a few more winners.

Back row: l to r: *Jockey Brian Storey, stable girl Jane Malloy, The Bride & jockey Tony Dobin. JB in front. Everyone giving* The Jolly Farmer *some welly at a charity function in Carlisle.*

Sarah York rang me as she couldn't get hold of the trustee, John Smith, who is responsible for one of our beneficiaries, John Trask, or of our Chief Executive Jeremy Richardson. She needed to get the 'all clear' for me to give permission for the IJF to pay for the funeral of John Trask wife's, who had died the previous night in her local hospital ICU. The poor lady had been ill for quite some time with a cancerous growth she had recently had removed from her gullet. John himself suffers from epilepsy, a bad heart and a speech impediment. Therefore, life won't be easy for him in the future. No doubt Sarah would go to visit and sort out some help for him.

As I write, exactly forty-six years to the day, on the Queen's Birthday, I rode my first winner on a little grey horse named Sasta Gri at Wetherby, trained by my old guv'nor, Charlie Hall. It has not rained for six weeks solid; it's been the hottest Easter on record. We have encountered firm going up and down the country on our racecourses for ages. I changed to go to Wetherby races and it's pouring down! Jo and I sold quite a few tickets at Wetherby. All are sending their cheques except for Arthur Slack, the cattle and sheep dealer. Arthur paid me £70 in cash for his two tickets, which now leaves the balance at £20,043. At last year's BBQ we had a 'Guess the Weight of the Bull' competition. As I was about to announce the winner, I said on the mike, 'is there an

Peter Lorimer who played for Leeds United when they had a formidable football team.

Arthur Slack anywhere?' Most of the crowd would know him, his wife Evelyn trains a few jumpers. Arthur waved his ticket excitedly thinking I was going to say he had won. Instead I said, 'Call yourself a cattle dealer? I'm glad you don't buy cattle for me! You weren't within a hundredweight of guessing the bull's weight!' Arthur loves a bit of fun and took it in good part.

The night after Wetherby saw me at the Alexandra Hotel in Sunderland attending a charity evening that raised over £2,500 in aid of Rachel Spence, an eleven-year-old girl with an estimated ten-month life expectancy who was suffering from an inoperable brain tumour. She wanted to fulfil her ambition before she passed on to go to America and swim with the dolphins. Isn't that sad? There weren't many people in the room who didn't feel a lump in their throats. In attendance were quite a few sportsmen who included Bobby Kerr (who played for Sunderland when they lifted the 1973 FA Cup) and Mickey Horswill. When they beat my team Leeds United 1-0, the winning goal was scored by Ian Porterfield. Brian Robe told me he went to Wembley to see the match in an Air Force blue suit he bought for the occasion at a cost of £79. See the team sheet on the team players. Dear me, I wish we had a team like them now, but fair dues to Sunderland, captained by Bobby Kerr. That day they played out of their skins. Peter Lorimer, a good pal of mine who could kick a ball with the power of a horse, blasted a ball just ten yards from the goalmouth and Jimmy Montgomery saved it.

The winning 1993 team carrying the FA Cup.

The Sunderland signed sheet.

On a normal day, a kick like that would have left the goalie in hospital. It was an absolute miraculous save. I often go to see Sunderland play with Brian Robe and after all those years that goal save from Jimmy is still talked about. The only problem on the bus photo is that it should have read: 'Well Done Leeds'. Dave Lawson of Northern Freight had offered Rachel his villa in

Florida at no charge to stay in while she is in America. Jackie Charlton was the guest speaker. Bobby Knoxall and Bob Dunn were the comedians and were very funny. At the auction I bought an England football, not that I intend taking up the game. I didn't own it for long as Brian Robe said he wouldn't mind the ball. I was just keen on making good money for young Rachel, so instead of me paying for it, he did.

I had a bit of banter with Jackie Charlton as he sat opposite to me at dinner. Years ago, when Leeds United were a club to be feared in the 60s and he played for them, I trained a horse owned by some of the players at the time; Peter Lorimer, Mick Jones, Eddie Gray, Jimmy Lumsden, Mick Bates and Terry Yorath that was called 'Zemander'. Jackie remembered her, but he wasn't in with the above lads as he is noted for being frugal and owning racehorses is far from a sure way to earn money. However, he wasn't so frugal at the Alexandra; he donated his speaking fee to a charity close to his heart which is for handicapped anglers, as Jackie is a keen fisherman.

Most sportsmen and women, past and present, are generous to good causes. Not only does David Beckham kick a bag of wind around, recently David gave eighteen-year-old Lisa Brown from Nottingham a £6,000 donation to help buy her a special pair of artificial legs. Lisa contracted meningitis, which led to blood poisoning and the surgeons had no option but to amputate her legs. Not too many people know that, but they all know he once was reported to have worn a thong. It was also not common knowledge that the Manchester United player's Ole Gunner Solskjaer made a donation of £100,000 to UNICEF.

The first person I bumped into at Catterick races the following day was Graham Lyle, the Leeds former bookmaker and staunch rugby supporter. I say 'former' as he had just recently sold his betting shops to Coral. When I was telling him about our BBQ on 20 July at the opening Doncaster Meeting, Graham said he would come if he could, but at Catterick he told me he couldn't make it as he had a rugby commitment. However, he gave me a donation of £100. Making our total now again under the twenty grand bracket; £19,963.

Michael White one of the Doncaster Bloodstock auctioneers, who did a sterling job at our last function, was in attendance at Catterick and was in good form as he had just got the connections of the two-year-old selling race winner, Fortunately, owned by Paul Dixon and trained by our Alan, to fork out £4,200 to buy their filly back in. I asked Michael if he would conduct the auction again this year, he said he would if his diary was clear on that date and would check when he got home. Our little postman also left a cheque for £70 from Eileen and PJ Cullen for two BBQ tickets. £19,863 to go. The postman also delivered a registered parcel that contained the headscarf Dennis and Demaris Letherby promised me in Tenerife for our auction. No ordinary scarf I may add. It was made of pure silk with every Derby winner, starting with the first Derby until 1908, the year Signorinetta won when ridden by Demaris's grandfather. In addition to the scarf which Jo very gently washed, I took up to Graham of Frame Plus to frame, also in the parcel was the original very fine steel plate, made before aluminium plates were invented, worn by Signorinetta that very day he won. It was mounted on a metal background with the words painted on it: '1908 Derby and Oaks winner, Signorinetta.

Owner Cheu Ginistrelli ridden by W (Billy) Bullock'. It was most unusual for a filly to run in the Derby or the 2,000 Guineas because they have their own Classics to run in the Oaks and 1,000 Guineas. For the record, three other fillies have won the Derby and the Oaks. The first being Eleanor in 1801, Blinkbonny in 1857, and Fifinella in 1916. In 1916, on account of the war, the Derby and the Oaks were staged at Newmarket instead of Epsom. It was no mean achievement to win both Classics just two days apart, but a bit discriminatory seeing as colts are not eligible to run in the 1,000 Guineas or the Oaks.

Saturday 24 April was the last day of the jump season – but would you believe the new jump season was starting on Monday? What a joke. I rode jumpers for sixteen years and loved it, but we had a break at the end of the season. Jumping all year round is no good for anyone. The jump horses should be turned out in a field for at least a month and the jockeys should have a few weeks of complete rest so their bodies can recover from all the knocks and bruises they have taken over the proper season. The governing bodies have listened too much to bookmakers and not enough to the industry's hands-on workers. They are saturating the sport with far too much racing to the extent that the staff can't cope, nor can the racecourses. All the watering to 'ease the ground' that courses get in summer doesn't allow the grass roots to search for water. Betting, betting, betting is all they can think of. Even people who work in betting shops will tell you there is far too much racing. The hairy, eccentric monster from Channel 4, John McCririck, advocates there should be racing even on a morning; he's not satisfied with racing three or four meetings a day, night and Sunday racing.

When I trained, persuading staff to partner their steeds to Wolverhampton on a Saturday night on the all-weather we very nearly had to mug them to get them into the horsebox. I can assure you, money didn't come into it. Nowadays, the racing game is all geared up for the bookies and betting, not sport, just money and greed, which may be all very well, but it has taken over and a lot of the fun has gone out of the game.

I gave racing a miss. Instead of going to Ripon, one of our local tracks, I went to watch the football derby, Sunderland v Newcastle, with Brian Robe and the ex-Newcastle Team Coach, Terry McDermot. As we were looking over the balcony in Brian's box, one lady said, 'Oh look, someone has thrown us a coin.' Yes, I thought, there is no doubt that it was a Sunderland supporter throwing at Terry as there is no love lost between those two teams. Luckily it was only a coin. With Newcastle beating the home side 1-0, and that goal coming from a penalty, needless to say the crowd was a bit hostile. Terry was in no hurry to go, I can tell you, until the crowd had dispersed. I dropped Terry off at the Ramside Golf Club, where I had picked him up. As Terry works with the coaching staff and is a big mate of the Newcastle captain, Alan Shearer, I asked him if he could see his way to getting me one of Alan's shirts for the auction. He said it was not a bother and that I would have a signed Shearer shirt delivered to me within the next few days.

Opening the mail there was a cheque for £105 from Andrea Mallinson for three tickets I sold her the other day whilst at George and Anne Duffield's. There was another one from John and Ann Walmsley, the old show jumping family where as a kid my first pony Gamecock came from. I had sold two tickets to them last Monday at Wetherby races. Leaving our total to aim for now at £19,688. Also in the mail was a voucher for two persons for bed and breakfast in one of the Presidential Suites overlooking the first tee and eighteenth green of the Champion Course at Carnoustie Hotel, plus a round of golf for two to be auctioned on our big day, donated by Martin Delaney, arranged by John Foster.

It's great to get people to donate items for our auction. Taking stock and being realistic, if I'm not careful I thought we would have more lots to sell than Doncaster Bloodstock do in the September Yearling Sales. I was not complaining though. People on the whole were so kind. Any surplus items I would keep for another time to take and give to other IJF functions. I do my bit for or give them to other charities when asked, and that's often.

A very successful fifty-year to the day riding and training career ended on a high note when Josh Gifford's eleven-year-old horse Skycab won the 4.40 p.m Attheraces Handicap race at Sandown. A very fitting place to train his last winner. Josh, four times champion jockey, was handing the reins over to his son, Nick. The legend trained many winners on the Esher course and a total of 1,587 winners countrywide, which is no mean feat. Josh gave racing another fairytale story when his Aldiniti won the 1980 Grand National being ridden by my old pal, Bob Champion. Beforehand, Bob received a kick from Fury Boy, a horse that fell with him in a novice chase. While trying to catch the horse, it lashed out and kicked Bob in the testicles, and this is believed to have led to him developing cancer. While Bob was in hospital, Josh went to visit the jockey taking a bottle of brandy. Josh got so depressed seeing Bob so poorly, he drank the whole bottle while there! He never thought Bob would recover. Thank God he did, not only did he recover from the dreaded disease he, as we all know, won the National and has deservedly been awarded the MBE for his charitable work. Bob rode his last winner on Lumen at Wetherby in 1982, fittingly for Josh Gifford.

Jo and I rang around and sold BBQ tickets to Kevin Ryan, Trevor Taylor, Brian Smart, John Nixon and John Weymes.

The Duffields, Lady Bolton, Jo and I went to the Wyville Arms for lunch. Lavinia (Lady Bolton) brought with her two very nice prints for our shindig's auction. One framed and signed by Roy Miller the artist and the jockeys Steve Cauthen and Willie Shoemaker. The print was of the pair when they rode in the 1984 Oaks at Epsom, Steve on Panquite Queen and Willie on Malack, it was number 55/475. The other was a headshot of Desert Orchid taken by AJ Gill. Both prints were in top class condition and should sell well, I thought. Lavinia looked round our 'gallery' and placed £100 bid on the carpet, Billy Maguire, one of Anne Duffield's owners gave us the other day to auction. The good lady also put £100 on the racing plate of the 1955 Triple Crown Winner, Meld who won the 1,000 Guineas, Oaks and St Leger when ridden by Harry Carr, the father in law of Joe Mercer. The plate was mounted on a very nice onyx stand with the filly's name and the Classic races won engraved on a silver plaque also mounted on the stand. For the record, Meld died in Ireland at the ripe old age of thirty-one. Lavinia also started off the bidding with £500 for Joe Mercer's racing lightweight saddle.

The next day on my return from an IJF meeting in London, I couldn't wait to open the mail to see if we had any more cheques. Sadly, I was to be disappointed, just a load of junk mail and two bills.

Brian Robb called to bring me a painting from Nigel Brunyee, the equine artist whom I had commissioned to paint Mind Games to add to our private gallery. Nigel had painted a few of our best horses over the years, which included Ol Oyston, So Careful, Bolshoi, Paris House, Selhurst Park Flyer, Almost Blue and Clantine, which we displayed on the walls of our stairway at home. We had better luck with the mail man the next day, two £70 cheques came in for the BBQ tickets, one from the former jockey Pat Hurley and the other from Mrs JS Kilpatrick, a friend of Pat. The jackpot now stood at £19,458.

While Brian Robb was here David (J) Bowes and I were building a rockery near the bridge in the garden over the pond. As mentioned before, Brian used to work for Spillers and provided our feed whilst training at Arksey. So as you can imagine we go back a long way. Those days he was a fit man and a couple of times a week before he set off for work, he rode out for us. Looking at him as we worked, he must have weighed getting on for two hundredweight and was hardly fit enough to lead a horse around let alone ride it! One particular day, Brian rode out with us on an old selling chaser of ours, called Peter Graham. I was on Ulsterman, Jo was riding Klondike Pete and Robert Earnshaw, a lad who worked for us, was riding the other horse we had out by the name of Autumn Wood. A good lad he was too, not to be confused with Robert Earnshaw who worked for Michael Dickinson and rode Silver Buck to win 1982 Cheltenham Gold Cup and now a racecourse official.

This particular day it was very foggy and our gallops at Arksey weren't the best. A neighbouring farmer, who was a real horse hater, wouldn't even drive steady when he passed us on a tractor, but he had a cracking ten or twelve acre grass field about a mile from our yard. Every time we rode past I used to say I wished that it was ours to ride round as our gallops weren't as good as Manton or Ballydoyle. In view of it being foggy when we tacked the horses up, I said to the team, 'Let's go and have a canter round the old bugger's field. I'll go first, you go second Jo and you Brian next and seeing as that fellow takes a bit of a tug, Rob, you whip-in. We will only go steady but keep each other in sight so we don't get lost.' We had gone a couple of times round this field, 'Paddy' Ulsterman was loving it and no doubt the others were too as the ground was perfect, far better than they were used to. I was thinking, 'I'll get a bit of graft into these horses while I've got the chance,' just as Autumn Wood came flying past me loose! 'God,' I thought, 'I hope he's got better eyesight than me and sees where he's going', and prayed to myself, 'please, please horse, don't get hurt!' We didn't have enough horses to be losing any. I shouted, 'Pull up,' to Jo and Brian, hoping not to alert the farmer as he could be on walkabout, and to enable us to find Rob. We turned round to backtrack, so to speak.

We were in that field for an hour looking for my man. Thankfully, the horse was caught in one piece and no cuts or bark off him. Then I heard this kind of muffled sound coming from my left. I rode over, shouting 'Rob.' By now, I was desperate and had forgotten all about the farmer, I just wanted Rob back. There was a very wide dike with a hedge on either side and Rob was in the bloody thing. Even his mother wouldn't have recognised him he was so shit-up, and absolutely plastered in thick slimy mud! The poor lad was stuck and couldn't climb the bank to get out and was he glad to hear my voice! I say, 'hear', as he had no chance of seeing me his eyes were so full of muck. First of all, I gave my horse to Brian to hold as Jo rounded up Autumn Wood, taking my jacket off and managing to get through the hedge. I then got Rob to hold onto it as I pulled him up the bank. What a state he was in, and he stank like a bloody polecat. As he fell off the horse, he must have gone through the hedge headfirst. His hat was missing and his hair was all caked up and horrible. When we all got home, I hosed him down in the yard and he then went into our house for a hot bath. Thankfully, except for a few grazes, Rob was all right and rode out with the next lot.

On Wednesday the last day in April, Jo, Dave Armstrong and I boarded a plane from Leeds Bradford Airport bound for Dublin heading for Punchestown races. The last time I went there, I was a young fellow at Charlie Hall's, and was taken by my old pal Paddy Farrell while on holiday. This day we were box guests of fellow IJF trustee Simon Tindall and his wife Caroline. It was great seeing so many of the old faces and having a bit of craic with them and we stayed overnight at the Downshire Arms Hotel, Blessington, County Wicklow. Before racing on the second day, Jo and I went to Naas to visit Benny Powell, my old pal of years ago, who is Brendan the Winchester trainer's father. Brendan, known for being the jockey who rode Blue Danube the first horse to fall in a British all-weather steeplechase at Southwell in 1992, but much better known for riding the 1988 Grand National winner Rhyme 'N' Reason. Benny had suffered with heart trouble and a breathing complaint for a few years and has been in and out of hospital so many times he was given a white coat, some people probably thought he worked there. The first horse I bought from Benny was Palacegate Jack, the winner of the Tattersall Breeder Stakes at the Curragh in 1993. I had also bought a few decent horses from him since and we remained the best of fiends.

What a buzz at Punchestown, seeing the horses jump the Irish banks. Simon, Jo and I went to one of the banks during the race and I was thinking what I had missed never having had the chance to ride over them. I would have loved it!

2,000 Guineas day arrived. When Wizard won the very first running of 2,000 Guineas that was the amount of money the horse raced for. This day's first prize was £185,600 – quite a bit different. In time the race may get updated to the 200,000 Guineas. The unbeaten Refuse to Bend owned by the Moyglare Stud, trained by Dermot Weld in Ireland and ridden by Pat Smullen won the event. Refuse to Bend is the half brother of Media Puzzle. Hopefully, this result will put a few extra quid on the photo of Media Puzzle that Dermot kindly gave us to auction following his win in the 2002 Melbourne Cup.

The 20,000 raffle tickets arrived by courier. As Jo went to Haydock races to see Simianna, our filly, run third, I elected to stay at home to meet Karen Bedford who Brian Robb brought to type up this account or 'book' as it is now. While chatting to Brian and Karen, during the conversation I mentioned Jimmy's outpatients and the need for the money Eileen Cullen was raising for them. In view of Karen working for Next the clothes firm (and there are around 3,000 people working there), she told me that they had team leaders and she was one of them. Sowing seeds in her mind, she thought it was a good idea to sell some of Jimmy's badges to the workers via the team leaders. To give it a try, Karen took some of them with her.

Before Jo went to Haydock, I rang my old jockey, John Carroll, to ask him if he would be good enough to sell some raffle tickets to the boys in the weighing room for our cause. Also, Jo took some to sell at the races. I had written a list of all the many people I have asked to sell tickets for us and over the weekend. The Bride and I would parcel the amount each person said they would sell, or try to sell and post them on the Monday. On Jo's return from Haydock she had sold £55 worth, but also left tickets with others to do the business for us. I couldn't believe my ears when she told me she had been up to Terry Holdcroft's box at the races and Terry had bought one ticket! Terry is the owner of Bearstone Stud where Mind Games stands. It was probably true what the old lady said when she peed in the sea, 'every little helps!' I don't want to be ungrateful, but if people like Terry bought just one ticket, it was going to be an uphill climb to get the 20,000 sold. I would be a ripe old age by then. It was a good job that he agreed when I asked Terry if it would be all right to put my nomination to Mind Games up for the first raffle prize. At the rate left to Terry, he probably would have donated a photo of Mind Games as first prize, possibly cut out of the Stud Book of stallions! Only joking! To be fair to Terry, Jo either caught him on a bad day or he was taking the juice, as in my dealings with him in the past, scrounging for various causes, he has been very generous. The cash we collect for the raffle tickets we sold, instead of writing them up straightaway, we intended putting the money in a biscuit tin. Periodically we would bank the money and when we did, we would then write up the amount.

The week saw the end of the road for the world's most winning jockey, Laffit Pincay Jr, with a career that saw him ride a staggering 9,530 winners. Laffit, fifty-six years old the previous December, still wasn't ready to call it a day. A fall in a turf race at Santa Anita in March put paid to that when X-rays revealed two fractures of a bone in his neck. Otherwise, he would have intended to ride on for another couple of years or at least until he had ridden 10,000 winners. In 1971, he was America's leading jockey with 310 winners under his belt. That's going some even by AP McCoy's standards. I didn't know what Laffit intended doing, possibly training. However, when the day came for eleven times champion jockey Pat Eddery to hang up his boots, I knew he intended to train, although he would have been well advised to take up tipping horses for a living. Pat wrote for the *Daily Star* newspaper every Saturday during the flat season, a role I performed for the paper in the early 90s. Last Saturday, as I write, he tipped three selections only and all three won! Today Pat tipped Persian Lighting, who won at 11/1, Needwood Blade won 9/4, Fire up the Band won 4/1 and, finally, Refuse to Bend in the 2000 Guineas won at 9/2. These were the only selections he gave and that's truly incredible. I thought there would be a run on the *Daily Star* newspaper the following Saturday following his four timer this week!

At 3.35 a.m. on Sunday morning 4 May, I was just getting the names and phone numbers ready to have a blitz later on in the day to ask people if they wouldn't mind selling some of the raffle tickets and some BBQ tickets. Looking at four great boxes of them you could imagine how Custer felt when he saw all those 'effin' Indians charging at him and his troops! It was an unearthly hour to be up, but I'd never been one to waste too much of my life in bed. It wasn't a case of me having inexhaustible energy, but as soon as I wake up I like to get out of the pit and do something. Mind you, I like to have something to do. I am thankfully not so 'hyper' that I need to walk around at night. If I go to a hotel or someone's house to stay, when I awake I like to plan and think things out. Without doubt, the best thing I ever thought up – thanks to our Sam – was the IJF Tenerife holiday.

Later in the day, Jo was a great help when we rang around our local trainers and horsemen who we thought would help us to sell fifty tickets each. We rang people such as Chris Thornton (whose son Peter that year ran the London Marathon in aid of Racing Welfare), George Moore, Jed O'Keefe, David Barker, Sally Hall, Micky Hammond, Chris Fairhurst, Gerry Scott, Brian Smart, Kevin Ryan, Sue Smith and others. Not a single one said they wouldn't, couldn't or didn't have time. It's a fact of life, if you want something doing you ask a busy person. Racing people in the main, play the right notes and sing the same tune for any worthwhile cause or charity when asked. All in all, Jo made up thirty-one parcels with brown paper and she used up all the Sellotape! I dashed off to Catterick Sunday market to get some more. While there, I spent £112 on plants for the rockery garden we are building around our pond – but I didn't tell The Bride. In all we packed up ready to post, 3,600 raffle tickets, 16,400 to go. Quite a task, but we were getting there. I would like to think we would make £10,000 from the tickets. When we sent the tickets out we booked the numbers, so if people were slow in returning them, to keep in step and to avoid their memory haunting them, a bit nearer the time I would ring to remind them, if they hadn't already sold them.

Today, as I write, my team, Leeds United beat Arsenal 3-2, which gives Man United the Premier League title. Being an Arsenal fan, Frankie Dettori wouldn't like that result! Alex Ferguson was at his grandchildren's birthday party, but for all that he would have kept his eye on the results. I gave him a ring on his mobile to ask him, 'What about Leeds now?', as Man United and Leeds United supporters don't exactly love each other, but the boss's phone was switched onto answer phone. He had probably left the party and gone to the pub to celebrate!

On the Monday morning I rang him again and he was absolutely delighted. I asked him what he thought of Leeds now, 'They are a great team,' he said laughing. I arranged to see Alex at the training ground on Friday morning to sign the prints and we were going out for a spot of lunch afterwards.

Later in the day, Alan rang to ask his mum and I if we would go to Newcastle to tack up his three runners for him, as he was going to Doncaster. At the time, his horses were running out of their skins. His first runner, a two-year-old Melinda's Girl won, beating another sixteen rivals, which was great for

Alan who had trained three two-year-old winners during the last three racing days. I must also add his horses looked great to boot. Long may it continue.

Victor Roper, one of the recently retired trainer Dennis Smith's owners, paid me for a ticket he bought for our rave-up, which brought the required amount to bring our ambitious total to £19,513. Although I passed on to sell quite a few more BBQ and a lot of raffle tickets to people, including two to ex-jockey, now trainer, Nigel Tinkler who, for the record, rode a winner on the flat, hurdles and over fences by the age of sixteen. Not only trainers retire; we have here in our possession the famous, almost white, thirteen-year-old Palacegate Touch – known to his hundreds of friends and fans as 'Archie'. The other grey is Anselman, 'Marco', with others in their retirement with us. As I write, the old fellow ran at Newcastle ridden by young Paddy Mathers in the seven-furlong apprentice race. Paddy looked after Archie at Cockerham and he thought the world of him. When he ran today in the middle of a big field of twenty, I thought I couldn't see the old lad winning another two races to beat the long standing record of Le Garcon D'or's record of thirty-six wins, as races such as today's are so difficult to win. Therefore, I rang Alan on his yuppie phone to see if we could have Archie dropped off at our house on his way home to give him the retirement I always promised him. Archie was always destined to stay in the family, so to speak. I bought him three times! As a yearling I bought him and sold him to Palacegate Racing Syndicate. When they folded up I bought him again for the Laurel Racing Group, from whom I bought him again when they cut down on the amount of horses they had in training. Never leaving Cockerham, except for the previous year when he came here to Hunton for his winter break, I free-leased half of him to Adrian Parr, a publican, who along with his wife, adored him. During his career he ran 207 times winning thirty-four times, second twenty-four times and third twenty-seven times. Over the years he has won for his owners £144,643. Above all, except for when the vet gelded him as a backward two-year-old, the only other times in his life that the vet saw him was to give him his compulsory annual pre-vac injections. The old boy was as sound as a pound and looked as fresh as new paint. A proper Peter Pan, he didn't look anything like his age. Hopefully, Jo and I will have a lot of fun riding him about when we feel like it, as he is not the sort of horse just to chuck out into a field, Archie will have a long and happy retirement. If he goes on like my old pal Ollie, who was then twenty-seven years of age, and except for the odd occasion when the old fella gets a bit disorientated, looks good and healthy – he would outlive me! Mind you, Archie was still very active.

When Alan's box dropped Archie off, we turned him out in our top paddock with Ollie and our two Falabella ponies, Frankie and Bernie, and they all got on like a house on fire. I took the liberty to ring Jim Gale, the boss of the northern Doncaster Racing School, to get him a job for just two years before he retires here completely following a couple of weeks holiday. Looking at them in the field I asked myself, where on earth could you get two horses together that have won between them fifty-eight races? I knew Archie would like to stay in training; he just wasn't ready for the slippers yet, but at his age I don't want him running just to make up numbers. I knew for a fact those kids at Doncaster would love him as he was an absolute gentleman and a mega ride.

A Mr Clegg rang up while I was in the bath, wanting to know the address and charity number of the IJF, as he was about to make his will and wanted to leave the charity some money. Jo told him and said: 'Let's hope it's a long time away before you need it', which I agreed, unless it was that prat Mr Clegg, our woodwork teacher at the Leeds school I mentioned in *It's Tougher At The Bottom*. That dozy bugger had us kids kneeling down praying to God to ask a haulage firm called Illingworth and Ingham to deliver our wood as we had run out.

On Tuesday 6 May, it was the start of the Chester meeting. The first race on the card was the Joseph Heler Cheshire Cheese Lily Agnes Stakes. One of the first decent two-year-old races of the season in the north, a race I took great pleasure in winning a few times. It was good to see our son Alan, whose horses were still absolutely flying having just had a win with Arabian Knight at Bath, was following suit. At Chester two years before, he won the Lily Agnes Stakes with Simianna and at Chester he won the race with Caldy Dancer, the 9/4 fav, a filly that won her first race in a big field at Haydock seventeen days previously. The race was sponsored by Joseph Heler who I trained lots of winners for. He's a good friend of mine, but unfortunately, Alan doesn't get on with him. He was MFH (Master of the Fox Hounds) for years and is quite old fashioned and set in his ways. In fact, Jo and I were staying at his house after Chester, which is the Heler's local racecourse, where, fortunately we have trained a few winners for him. One of his horses, Ace of Parkes in 1998 broke the six furlong, two-year-old track record in a time of 1min 2secs. We were lunch guests of Joe's and his wife Janet on Thursday at the races as we have been for years. In fact, I do the 'run through' on the form of the horses and the

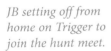

JB setting off from home on Trigger to join the hunt meet.

tips before racing. Joe was very kind to our BBQ last year by giving us a cheese for guessing the weight of the bull, one in the raffle and one for the auction that James Blackshaw of Cantor Sports bought for £300. Joe was also providing cheeses for our day this year on 20 July. For the first time at dinner at the Heler's, dress was casual. In the past we had worn dinner jackets. I don't know what the world's coming to. As usual it was great fun, most of the chat was about horses and hunting. Joe was the sole master of the South Cheshire Hunt for five years, the same time as the famous Johnny O'Shea was huntsman. They will have enjoyed many wonderful days hunting over that superb grass country in Cheshire.

Master Joe had the most beautiful hunting saddle made for him, that carried him over the hedges, walls, ditches, gates and whatever crossed his path for over twenty years. When I retired from training, Joe gave me a set of golf clubs, and his hunting saddle. I don't play golf too often, but I do enjoy going hunting twice a week with The Bedale and we have some great days. (As seen opposite in the photo setting off for a local outing on my hunter, Trigger). The painting is of my other hunter 'Paddy' by Jan Scott. Andrew Osbourne, one of our masters and huntsman, is the cousin of ex-jockey and now trainer Jamie Osbourne who is a nutter, but what fun.

Jan Scott's painting of my other hunter, Paddy.

While there at the Heler's, Janet, Joe's wife, who is friendly with The Bride, told me that she was a bit wary of their dog Blazer, a two-year-old Doberman. It growled a couple of times and curled his lip at her. She was frightened it might have a snap at their grandchildren when they visited. To cut a long story short, I said I would take it as a swap for our Jack Russell, George. Jo, my missus put her ears back when I told her we were having another dog, but settled down a bit when I told her we were also parting with one.

Master of the South Cheshire Foxhounds, Joe Heler (at right) *with his huntsman Johney O'Shea.*

I did the tips and the spiel in the box on Thursday before lunch. In the first race I went for course specialist Damalis, a seven-year-old mare trained by Eric Alston which duly won at 13/2 followed by Ocean Silk 15/8 and Asian Heights at Evens. Not bad – three out of six. Also there, as lunch guests, were Walter Wharton, the ex-trainer Dave and Trish Brown, and Philip and Sandra Arkwright. Philip, before he retired, was the Clerk of the Course at Cheltenham and Haydock Park and Sandra was the racecourse judge, now a steward.

*Jo Berry shares a joke with
my book sponsor's wife, Janet Heler.*

Chapter Nine

Sharp Lads

•

We were talking of the current shortage of staff in racing and yet there were more meetings scheduled for the following year. Where the extra staff needed would come from was a real headache. When I was a kid, racing lads were so sharp that it was difficult to get into a decent yard; nowadays they seem so different. Most trainers are short staffed, not because they want it that way, they just cannot get staff to cope with the amount of horses there are in training today. In fact, they have to be imported from all over the world and we can't breed enough staff to go round, but we are breeding far too many horses, especially from moderate mares. I know for a fact when I trained, if a filly was no good, the owner often sent it to another yard, just to make sure, and often, when proved useless for racing, then they bred from it. Only yesterday, on Channel 4, Derek Thompson had a chat with the four lads who led the horses up in the Chester Vase. The conversation went something like this. Asking the first lad, if he would win he replied, 'I don't know.' Derek asked, 'Where do you come from?' 'France,' said the lad. Second lad he asked, 'Hello big fella, what do you call this fella?' 'Cruzspel,' said the lad. 'Has he got a chance and do you think he will win?' 'I think he's got a big chance and hope he will win.' 'Where do you come from?' 'Ireland.' The next lad your man Derek asks, 'Where do you come from?' 'Pardon?' said the lad. 'Where do you come from?' Derek asked again. 'The Ukraine,' said the lad. 'Oh, the Ukraine.' 'Yes, that is what I said.' 'Yes, but what's the horse called?' 'Pardon?' 'What is the horse called?' 'Dutch Gold.' 'Will he win?' 'I don't know.' 'Oh well, thank you very much.' Last of the four runners, but not least, 'This is a very nice looking horse, will it win?' 'I would like him to but I honestly don't know.' 'Well thank you very much for that, you've been very helpful, and where do you come from?' Half expecting the lad to say he didn't know, but he also said 'France.' 'Oh by the way, what do you call it?' 'Risk Taker.' By looking in the paper I was able to confirm it was 'Risk' and not 'Piss'. Derek possibly didn't ask the lads the right questions but for all that they didn't seem very sharp.

When I was an apprentice, the lads in our yard were really switched on and as sharp as needles. When the boss of the house went out, we used to sneak his Racing Calendar from his office. The Racing Calendar, dating back to 1751 and being in the Wetherby family since 1778, was racing's undisputable bible. It was a weekly that contained everything there was to know about racing. One lad would be in charge of it. We would have a pool, a penny a go for the first round of questions. If you got a question wrong, you would pay three pence to come back in. If you got three wrong, you had to drop out. To help swell the kitty, it cost a penny to stay in after every round. The last one left collected the pot. Whoever started the questions went once round, then it was the next lad's turn. On a typical day it would go a bit like this. The question master with the calendar would say:

'Who trained Pappa Fourway?'
'Bought at auction for 150 Guineas and trained at Malton by Bill Dutton.'
Someone would say; 'Look 'ere you clever prat, before we go any further just answer the bloody questions and stop being so damned big headed.'
'Right, what are Major Holiday's colours?'
'White with maroon hoop.'
'Right, who is the first jockey to Noel Murless?'
'Lester Piggott.'
'Yes but any silly prick would have got that!'
'Right, who trained Gregmore Boy?'
'Horace Cousins.'
'Yes, who is Brian Lee apprenticed to?'
'Ernie Davey.'
'Right, who is the first jockey to Rufus Beasley?'
'Johnny Greenaway.'
'No, it's Joe Sime. I knew you were a dozy bugger, he passes us every day in that blue Jag to ride out at Beasley's, where did you think he was going – to see a bird?'
'You don't need to make a meal of it, I meant to say Joe Sime rode for Rufus Beasley.'
'Well you should have, if you want to stay in, get your three pence in and stop 'effin' whingeing.'
'There's me three pence. I want to stay in.'
'Is Leicester racecourse right handed or left handed?'
'Right.'
'Yes.'

Jockey Joe Sime.

Then one of us would say, 'that was too damned easy and any silly bugger knows that!'
'Who trained Uncle Barney?'
'Herbert Clarkson.'
'Which three-year-old filly won the 1000 Guineas and the St Leger in 1952?'
'Meld.'
'Right, what horse is the sire of Petite Etoile?'
'Petition out of Star of Iran by Bois Russell.'
'You are some brain pot aren't you? If you keep on gloating you are out and not playing any more. Just answer the sodding question.'
'Right, who owns Freebooter?'

'Mrs Brotherton and Bobby Renton trains it and Jimmy Power usually rides for him.'

'I only asked you who owned the bloody horse, clever twat. I didn't want its history. You are always bloody gloating you are! Just like him the next time you are out as well.'

Which as you could imagine often led to arguments and sometimes very near to fisticuffs!

'Where does Captain Rupert Leigh train?'

'Ogbourne Maisey.'

'Yes, Captain C Boyd-Rochford, the Queens trainer; what does the C stand for?'

'Cecil.'

'The 'c' is right alright but you two 'c's must be having it off. Your questions to him are that 'effin' easy!'

Someone else would say; 'Oh come on, man, that's two soft questions he's had. You prats are working together, you've got to be. Even the housekeeper would have known that. You're out next time, you're not playing you cheating sod.'

'What horse won the Irish Lincoln, the Irish Cesarewich and the Champion Hurdle in the same year?'

'It was Hatton Grace, but that's not a fair question because he was trained in Ireland.'

'Alright, I'll give you another one.'

'No, you can piss off. You asked me and I told you?'

'My turn now.'

'Where is the Emblem Handicap Chase run?'

'Manchester.'

'Right, you always reckon you know about colours, what are Mrs Laureline Brotherton's colours?'

'Blue and silver quartered, blue sleeves and a red cap.'

'No, you silly prick, blue and silver halves, not quarters.'

'Oh, I meant halves.'

'Well you should have said halves then, get your money in!'

'Can I owe whoever owns the kitty? I'm skint.'

'No you can't, you know the script, go and make the tea and keep quiet.'

The craic was always great though at times it got a bit heated. Often we had to cut the quiz time short, as we would hear the boss's car coming into the yard. Then one of us would dive into his office with the Calendar and return it. Mind you, we didn't have all the luxuries like we have today. Having said that, did we need them? We had a lot of fun. It was only on major race days or if we had a runner in the odd big race like the King George or the Scottish Grand National that we were invited by Anne, the boss's niece, to watch the telly in the guv'nors house. In there, we would take our shoes off and stand at the back of the room and as soon as the race was over we would say our 'thank yous' and go out. We got our fun from boxing, playing football, ratting, running, fishing or riding the cattle in the fold yard. I'm sure stable lads don't get as much enjoyment out of the game as we did! Today, they are stressed out and wound up like springs mainly due to the acute shortage of staff and a heavy work load. Yet, I read we are to get even more race meetings and there's even talk of some morning fixtures. It won't be long before owners are leading their own horses round the paddock. Until they somehow recruit more stable staff, how can it improve? Having said that, I don't know where they will come from. It won't be any different unless Peter Savill and the BHB can teach these asylum seekers how to ride and get them in the yards as there is not enough British staff to go around now as proved by Derek Thompson at Chester the other day.

Youngsters are leaving school a whole lot heavier than they used to. Possibly they are fed better, or should I say, more. Also kids don't play games or run around so much, instead they are far happier playing with mobile phones, computers and watching telly. Is there any wonder when kids leave school at sixteen a good many of them wouldn't do the minimum jumping weight of 10st, never mind the 8st 4lbs flat, not even taking in a weight allowance! You only have to see the little darlings when their mums take or pick them up from school. A fair proportion of them will be eating something and maybe have a can of pop in their hands. No wonder lots of them look like miniature sumo wrestlers until they are around sixteen when they look like real ones!

Having met up with Alex Ferguson at the training ground, he readily signed the prints of Rock of Gibraltar along with the original painting by Steven Smith, which I left with the manager to negotiate a deal with the artist's agent, Peter Mason. Alex was in good form and of course I again mentioned Leeds United helping his team to win the Premier League by Leeds hammering Arsenal. Alex loves a bit of fun, a totally different man to the one we see on the box being interviewed, or during a game, looking pensive and stressed when he has to keep focused on the job (the photo shows Alex enjoying a day at the races.) On my return from Manchester, I was like a little kid opening his Christmas presents diving into the mail. There were two payments, £70 from Brandsby trainer Peter Beaumont for two tickets and £35 for the ticket I sold Pat O'Gorman at Chester races. Pat, is an ex-owner of ours, whose firm makes the most delicious pork pies you ever did taste. The total required now was £19,408. Also, there

JB & Sir Alex Ferguson at Chester Races.

was a parcel from Terry McDermot with the Alan Shearer signed shirt for the auction as promised.

Lots of footballers enjoy racing as most racing folk enjoy football. During our early days training at Cockerham, one of our owner's had something to do with Bolton FC and he told me that for a realistic fee I could be a match sponsor, which comprised of a couple of banners on each side of the ground and a corporate box for up to ten people. My man was convinced we'd get a spin off and pull a few owners which, at the time I can assure you, were badly needed. Inviting a few potential clients to fill the ten posis up, we had a very good lunch. When we got to our seats before kick off, the pitch looked in tremendous condition and our banners were displayed in red, white and blue. However, when I read them I couldn't believe my eyes. Instead of the printer putting on them: 'Horses to train and potential owners wanted, ring Moss Side Racing Stables', it stated 'Moss Side Riding Stables'. Needless to say, the next day we spent a good half of it telling folks no, we don't give rides, no, we don't do liveries and we don't give lessons. The phone was red hot with enquiries of all sorts, except the ones we would like to have heard – 'can you buy or train me a racehorse!'

Jo and I went to Saturday evening races at Thirsk. We pulled up in the car park next to Dandy Nicholls. Dandy is always good for any cause and tonight was no different. He took two tickets for the barbecue and asked me to send him 200 raffle tickets. Local jockeys, Joe Fanning, Tyrone Williams and Gaynor Garrity of Thirsk racecourse all bought BBQ tickets and will forward the fees on. Although it was not a formality for people to buy, I asked Mick Easterby if he would like a couple of tickets for our event. 'Yes, I would love to,' he said, until I told him it was £70. Then he back-pedalled and said he would think about it and dived for cover! However tight, Mick is good fun, as you can see the way he is performing at a Malton Trainer's Open Day later on. At Thirsk, I was having a chat with Maggie Smith, the wife of the York Clerk of the Course, John Smith. Maggie is absolutely lovely, full of fun and a really nice lady who I love to bits. Two years previously, the Malton racing charity bash was organised by Rose Carter wife of the ex-jockey Ted, who rode around 200 winners. Ted started his career with Val Moore, served his time with Captain Elsey, later worked for Frank Carr and the sprint king of the day, Bill Dutton.

When he packed up riding, he trained for several years in Malton until one day he had a bad fall from a horse on the Malton gallops, while he was on his own. The horse didn't gallop off, it stood near a gate eating grass. At the time there wasn't a soul about. He lay there freezing cold and in absolute agony for over an hour before he finally spotted a jogger. Ted frantically shouted and waved his cap to get the man's attention. The man went for help and an ambulance took Ted to Malton Hospital where he stayed for quite some time. While in hospital it was discovered he had very fine arteries and poor circulation. Due to a combination of these defects and the recently broken bones, he had to have his leg amputated.

This photo is at a northern jockey's dinner at Malton. Colin Dukes, Tommy Kellett, Nimrod Wilkinson, Gerry Scott, Johnny East, Jack Boddy, Bruce Carr,

Northern Flat and Jump Jockey's dinner dance held in Malton in the 60s.

David Sheldon, Gerry Kelly, Jimmy Fitzgerald, Geoff Oldroyd, Percy Wigham, Jack Berry, Ted Carter (who is sat on my knee on account of there being no more chairs; hopefully you didn't think I was the other way, because I'm not. I couldn't be doing with men refusing me as well as women!), Brian Henry and Brian Lee.

Getting back to the Malton racing charity do, I was talking to two Scotsmen in kilts about my retirement. One asked would I autograph his programme for his dad who was an avid fan, and would be chuffed to bits as he had his photo taken with me at a race meeting. It hangs in pride of place in his house. He backed every two-year-old we ran in Scotland. Jo was dancing with John and I was dancing with Maggie, on the floor jigging were the two Scotsmen with their two partners. Jokingly, I asked one of them if it was true that Scotsmen don't wear anything under their kilts. 'Yes, it's true,' he said. 'I don't believe it, let's have a look,' said Maggie, and with that he lifted his kilt over his head and he didn't have a stitch on underneath! Well Maggie and I cracked up laughing. We were uncontrollable and neither of us could spit it out to tell John and Jo for ages why we were laughing, with tears were running down our faces.

The following Sunday I was up really early, champing at the bit and ready for off. I thought I would have another blitz on the trainers to sell our cause's raffle tickets. Knowing Sunday morning before 9 a.m. was the best time, I started at 6.20 am with the ones down south, Conrad Allen and Mick Channon. Then I came up with the idea of ringing them from the *Horses in Training* book in alphabetical order. I rang Hamish Alexander, Alan Bailey, John Balding, Michael Bell, Sue Bradbourne, Milton Bradley, Giles Bravery, Owen Brennan, Michael Chapman, Clive Cox, Robin Dicken, James Eustace, Jimmy Fitzgerald, Merrick Francis, David Gandolfo, Josh Gifford and James Given who between them pledged to sell for us 1,600 raffle tickets. John

Foster visited with a very nice framed print of Mind Games I sold him at one of our Open Day charity auctions a few years ago, on account of John now having a smaller office, and space was at a premium. Also, he paid me for the two tickets he ordered previously, which now left us £19,308 to find. John a great man for jokes, told me the following: A Jewish couple were having a conversation; the hubby asked his missus if she had ever been unfaithful during their forty-year marriage. She said 'to be honest, I have on three occasions.'

'Oh no,' said the husband, 'as I have been faithful to you, tell me when was it?'

'Well, you know when you started off in business and the bank manager wouldn't lend you the money to start with, then four days later he rang you and said you could borrow it?'

'Yes.'

'Well that was on account of me.'

'Oh love, I will forgive you for that. Why the other two?'

'Can you remember when you had a heart transplant the surgeon said you would have to go on the two-year waiting list, then he rang you the following week and said you could go in for the operation in three day's time?'

'I do indeed.'

'Well that was because of me.'

'Thank you so much, I can forgive you for that, but what was the other one?'

'Remember when you were turned down as a member of our local golf club…?'

On Monday 12th May, Michael White of Doncaster Bloodstock called round on his way while visiting yearlings for his firm's sales, mainly to discuss whether he could do our auction again as he had three engagements on 20 July. Thankfully, having seen most of our brilliant auction prizes, he said he would tell the other two functions that he was doing ours on that day. Great news as Mouse, as he is affectionately known, is very good.

Jo and I had been lunch guests of Tattersall's, at York races, which was very nice chatting to some old faces. One doesn't need to be long out of racing before us old sweats are saying, 'Who's he? Where does he train? Who is that jockey?' and the like, although on account of me wearing my customary red shirt this seems to have got me better known than most. At one Leger meeting at Doncaster in the town before the sales started, I was approached by an American who asked me if I was Jack Berry. 'Yes,' I duly said, 'I thought so, I recognised the shirt.' However, there are people who don't know about me always wearing red shirts. Once while staying at Glorious Goodwood, on the third day having breakfast at the hotel, a lady came to the table and said hello to me, then she said, 'we've all done it at some stage. It's nothing to be ashamed of. No doubt you have forgotten to pack other shirts. I noticed the first day you had that red shirt on. Last night I also noticed you were letting it rip on the dance floor. Therefore you must have got warmed up. It must be crying out for a wash. When you come back from the races I will lend you one of my husband's, he's about the same size as you.' I thought she was taking the juice. That night for a change we ate somewhere different. At the next day's breakfast, she handed me a clean shirt and said 'there you are love, try this on.' I could have crawled down a mouse hole.

In the 1990 season we ran a nice little filly in a seller at Folkestone. A nice little filly called, For Real. She wasn't brilliant but she was capable of winning this type of race. Therefore, I didn't want to lose her at the auction, so early in the season, as I was attending another meeting in the north, I rang my Epsom trainer pal Geoff Lewis up to stand in for me to saddle her up and buy her back if she won, which she did. As Geoff was representing me, the berk donned a red shirt and borrowed a Trilby off a punter and mimicking me bought the filly in on my behalf. For a bit of fun the auctioneer called 'bought in by Jack Berry.'

In the post on my return from York races were cheques for £140 from Trevor Taylor. Trevor was part owner of Solares, the horse Sam got hurt on. There was a further cheque for £70 from Graham and Glenda Waters. Graham was the proud owner of Spindrifter, the record breaking two-year-old who won thirteen races including ten on the trot when ridden by George Duffield and trained in Newmarket by Sir Mark Prescott Bt. A third cheque came from Colin Mandel, one of our owners from the 'red shirt brigade'. Colin is a farmer from Cumbria who was a casualty of the foot and mouth disease outbreak and, unfortunately, had to have his entire herd slaughtered. Also, Anne Duffield has sold two tickets at York to one of her owners for cash, making up a total of £350 which reduced out target to £18,956. Joe and Janet Heler came to stay at our house ready for York races the following day and paid for two tickets reducing the amount to £18,785.

It was very sad to read in the morning's of the death of 17-year-old old Danehill, one of the world's best stallions. Bred in the USA by Juddmonte Farms owned by Prince Khalid Abdullah and trained by Jeremy Tree. When he was the champion three-year-old sprinter while standing at Coolmore Stud he was Champion First Crop Sire and Champion Sire of two-year-olds on four occasions. Sire of fifty-one, no less, Group One winners, which included the likes of Danehill Dancer, Mozart, Landseer, and the previous season's champion racehorse Rock of Gibraltar. Liz Morley, who could sell ice packs to Eskimos, managed to sell me two tickets in the car park before racing at York, to attend the Annual Buffet Lunch in aid of MacMillan Cancer Relief. Which was good. I had a long chat with my old pad David Barker. For the record, David Barker was one of the two best horsemen I have ever seen. The other was Ben Jones of the King's Troop. Some of you old sweats will remember David as rider of the great show jumper Mr Softee. John Francome, who during his colourful career as a jump jockey rode 1,138 winners, was doing the run-down on the race card and it was a good job he works for Channel 4 – if he relied on his racing tips he would starve! Only joking! Johnny's a star and does an awful lot behind the scenes for lots of good causes without reward and is always full of mischief and fun. John trained for a short time when he retired from the saddle. His first winner, That's your Lot was ridden by his old pal Steve Smith Eccies at Sandown in 1985.

John Smith, an IJF trustee and Clerk of the Course at York, gave me a £70 cheque for his tickets. Also in the post was a £70 cheque from Lavinia, Lady

Bolton for our bash, which brought the target down to £18,645, a figure at this stage I was very pleased with. Having said that, to reach our target we needed to keep bashing on, as we hadn't sent any raffle tickets to Scotland yet. Linda Perratt, who is a most charming lady and refers to me as Uncle Jack, did her list at 7 a.m., so at that time I rang to invite her down for our BBQ and asked if she would sell some raffle tickets for us. She readily accepted the invitation and would willingly sell some tickets. The date was now getting much closer and there were an awful lot of tickets left to go, so we needed to keep focused. Jo and I had sent out, given by hand or posted something like 16,000 £1 raffle tickets. We were hopefully going to have another blitz at them on the following Sunday to disperse the rest.

A bit of good news arrived on the fax from Eileen Cullen. The Variety Club had agreed to give the Jimmy's kids £20,000 towards refurbishing their department. The following Sunday I was to take quite a few nurses from St James' Hospital to Ripon races to meet the Wooden Spooners and bosses who Jo and I were having lunch with, to hopefully finalise the amount they would donate towards the appeal. Also in the post were two £70 cheques, one from Brian Smart, another old mate of mine, and his missus Vicky and the other from Middleham trainer Don E Incisa reducing the required figure to £18,505.

Talking to Peter Easterby at Thirsk on Saturday 17th, I mentioned to him that we had in our possession a 12 x 12 original painting of 'Night Nurse Winning the 1976 Champion Hurdle' with the jockey Paddy Broderiek on board, and as Peter trained the horse, I asked if he would like to start the bidding, which he did at £200. There were two cheques in the mail, one for £10 along with the stubs of the raffle tickets bought by Carol Mitchell, the other from the Tote for £13 that Jo had won. It was a welcome change to get a cheque from a bookie I can tell you! Really, I thought I should get it framed, it being such a rare occurrence. You would think being in the 'know' so to speak it would be easy to back winners, however, I can assure you that isn't true. One of the most memorable touches I ever had, which did come off, was when betting was illegal and I was an apprentice. The Sherburn in Elmet bookmakers Ray and Geoff Westmoreland, around lunchtime stood outside the village shop at Towton where I worked for Charlie Hall to take bets from punters out of the village. One of us, nearly always the youngsters, would go with all the various bets on scruffy bits of paper the lads from our yard had made out. That was unless on the rare occasion one of them had had a winning bet the previous day he would go himself to pick up the winnings and to make sure of his fair do's as the pair of 'accountants' were very near as sharp as us! For instance, they would say, 'Tommy Lynch owes us £4, there's £1 get the rest from Tommy', and all that sort of thing. Also, when we gave them the slips with the bets on, Geoff and Ray would sift through them like misers, 'Take that one and that one back, and tell those two bloody burglars they can't have another bet until they've straightened up with what they owe us, and tell that bugger Slogatt to cough up with that five bob he had on Star Wings when he got stuffed at Wetherby three weeks ago!' The pair of betting stable lads would have told us what to say to the bookies before we went, as they had heard it all before. 'Tell them prats if they won't take the bet, I will definitely pay them on

Saturday, as I have my present to come from Whitty winning at Manchester the other day.' Making excuses was a path often trod by the lads, but on this occasion this one could have been true, as for every winner we looked after we received £5 in the wages on the next Friday, which in those days was a fortune, especially when apprentices only received five shillings a week.

Although at the Chester May meeting in 1955 by my standards I won a lot of money by having one shilling each way and a shilling win double. The first horse was the champion three-year-old sprinter Pappa Fourway who was having his first run of the season ridden by Harry Carr and trained at Malton by Bill Dutton. Drawn on the outside he won at 8/1, the next horse I had coupled with Pappa Fourway was Prescription to win the Chester Cup the following day when ridden by Bill Rickaby and trained by Jack Jarvis, who also won at 8/1. Possibly Pappa Fourways was such a good price with it being his first run of the season and drawn 9 of 14. The horse went on and won his next seven races and was sold unbeaten as a three-year-old to race in America. My reason for backing him at Chester was that he won by five lengths first time out with Johnny Greenaway on board at Haydock as a two-year-old, therefore he wouldn't necessarily need a race to put him right. As one needs to bear in mind, in those days all-weather gallops were unheard of so it was a lot harder to get horses fit in the early part of the season, as winters were very much harsher than they are nowadays, especially in the north. Drainage wasn't good; often making grass gallops waterlogged and unfit to use. When I picked up my £5.5s from Ray Westmoreland I felt like a millionaire and I certainly had no intention of doing any deals to settle the other defaulters' accounts!

Before I set sail for Ripon Sunday racing, our guests Willie and Wilma Burns bought two BBQ tickets making our target £18,435. It was Willie who the previous year bet me £500 that I wouldn't swim across our pond, needless to say the fund benefited from his brave bet. Wilma, who runs a B&B at their house in Scotland, makes the best scones you ever did taste and always brings me a nice supply whenever she comes to visit. It was not all about just trying to prise the money out of folk for good causes. At Ripon during the Wooden Spoon lunch, we did have some fun as we raised a few quid for disadvantaged youngsters, like last year John Morgan and me ran down the cards for the lunch guests. John told his old jokes, most of them we had heard the year before, and the year before, and at all the other venues John attends, but they always raise a laugh. Between us we managed to find a couple of winners. During the 1993 season, every Saturday I used to give a selection on the days televised racing for the *Daily Star* newspaper. On 31 May, in the four races TV from Sandown, Briar Creek obliged at 7/2 ridden by M Roberts, our own Paris House won the Group 2 Temple Stakes at 9/2 beating the champion sprinter Loch Song. Pay Homage was my next tip and won at the generous odds of 8/1, ridden by Michael Hills. Finally Polar Dancer duly obliged at 11/10.

My job was just to select a fancy on the TV races with half a page of verbal. On this occasion, I said in the paper, 'if you would like to try a nap hand you could do worse than add Mr Men who runs at Redcar to your list. Although it's the colt's debut he's fit and runs a bit.' Mr Men won at 7/1 beating seven winners. A man called Shane Peters followed my selections and won a serious amount of money. The BHB or the taxman needn't worry as Mr Peters didn't send me a bung! The Wooden Spoon Society, like the IJF, has HRH The Princess Royal as their patron. It started 20 years ago when a wooden spoon was presented to a group of English rugby fans mourning their defeat in Ireland. Over a few pints of Guinness, the idea grew to involve others and raise a few hundred pounds for the real losers in life, needy children and in doing so making losing a bit more pleasant to bear. The charity raises up to £20,000 a week for disadvantaged children and young people. One of its sayings is: 'We make a living by what we get, and we make a life by what we give.' At the Farnham Gold Cup in September 1983, the Wooden Spoon Society was launched. A wooden spoon badge with red, white, blue and green stripes depicting the Four Nations was specially commissioned and everyone joined the founder members as associate members of The Wooden Spoon Society, like the one I and many more wore at Ripon races this day, as I did at Royal Ascot one of the days last year along with my 'spooners' waistcoat. Members pay an annual subscription and events like this day's Ripon event raise money for projects that help the Society to live up to its motto: 'Wooden spoons stir smiles.'

David and Laureline Wilmot-Smith paid for their BBQ entry leaving the amount required £18,365. The following day in the post box was a letter from the ex-trainer Bill Watts, inside were the two returned tickets as on 20th July, Bill and Pat will be in Scotland. To help our cause Bill very kindly enclosed a cheque for £50 reducing the target to £18,315.

The next day, Terry and Ronni Herbert-Jackson called round for lunch. They were amongst our owners at Cockerham. We showed them our 'art gallery' and Terry put a bid of £300 on the photo of Rock of Gibraltar that David Fish gave us at Cheltenham and Ronni outbid by £50, Lady Bolton's bid on Billy Maguire's carpet. On Tuesday 20, I was up early in the morning thinking at the rate we were going we would never sell all the raffle tickets. Ringing trainers up to buy or sell them for us just wasn't on as they were so busy and I should know. I sat down at about 6 a.m. and wrote them this letter; got Jo to photocopy is dozens of times on our fax machine which had by now run out of ink! She posted them to all the trainers I hadn't already asked to help us out. Hopefully, if we got a third of them sold this way, it would be a result:

Dear Whoever,

On the 20 July we are holding at the above address a BBQ and a charity function in aid of the Injured Jockeys Fund. In addition we are holding a raffle with some excellent prizes to be won. I hope you don't think me too bold, could I please ask you, would you mind selling the enclosed £50 worth of tickets for me? Would you please keep the money and send a cheque made out in favour of the Injured Jockeys Fund and return it and the stubs to me at the above address.

Many thanks for your help. Good luck.
Yours ever,

Jack

I took the three paintings of Night Nurse, Stalbridge Collonist and Special Cargo to 'Frame Plus' to get some nice frames for them and also to pick up the Derby headscarf I took in to get framed. Unfortunately, Graham the boss couldn't do it. He said that the silk was just too old and fragile and I told him I knew the feeling, but he was serious. Therefore, I intended selling it as it was but I would put it with the racing plate of the 1908 Derby winner, which was mounted up and printed up, and would sell them both together. They were so rare I thought they should make a lot of money.

The following day the postman wasn't so kind to us. Among the bills and junk mail was a letter with three returned tickets from Elizabeth Raine from Cumbria, stating she and her mates were now non-runners due to other engagements but very kindly enclosed a £10 donation bringing our figure to £18,305.

On the following Thursday, Peter Mason came to pick up the signed prints of Rock of Gibraltar. I gave Peter a tour of our 'art gallery' and he was impressed. So much so he made a few phone calls to some of his punters to put bids on some of the auction lots. He got them to put £100 on the signed photo of Michael Owen, £250 on the print of Colonel Collins and £1,000 for the Derby scarf and racing plate of Signorinetta. Jo was busy ringing the trainers we had missed to ask them if they would sell some raffle tickets for us which she thought was the fairest thing to do rather than just drop them on them. Most people were great and answered by saying, 'Yes, send them on.' As previously stated, 16,000 of the 20,000 we had printed had gone out in the post. In fact Peter and Cath Teesdale, owners of our village shop and Post Office, probably hadn't been so busy in their lives with all the little parcels my missus had been making and taking down there daily by the bag full. It was a good job we didn't need to lick the stamps anymore or I would have needed to take Peter out for a couple of pints every night. When Jo rang up Terry Mills's Epsom offices, the lady who answered the phone was bit sharp. Jo being Jo, told her that her telephone manner was not very good. She rang back later after she said she had spoken to Terry, who told her to tell us he wasn't going to buy or sell any tickets but perhaps we could try him next year. Therefore, that must mean never. Following Where or When's gallant second to Hawk Wing in the Lockinge Stakes, I read that at the end of the season that Terry will retire and his son will take over. We must have called the office on a bad day. Having been a trainer I know the feeling well. In addition, I know Terry well and he is a good man.

The mine of racing information, Chris Pitt, rang at about 7.30 p.m. to ask me if I would step in to talk with him on his live show, broadcast from Birmingham which lasted fifteen minutes. His guest had been taken ill and Chris would ring me back at 8.05 p.m. when we would be on air. 'No problem' I said, 'it would be a pleasure.' It was a nice change Chris ringing me for something; it was usually the other way round. In today's *Horse and Hound* was the IJF holiday feature by Tim Richards with a few photographs, which included Shane Broderick, Sharon Murgatroyd, Eileen Cullen, Martina Lemair, Des Cullen, Jane Wicket and Frank and Val Dever. Tim made a good job of the story introducing it with, 'laughter floated across the water.'

Even four days later it still echoed as he sat in a tortuous traffic jam. The road ahead led to Newmarket's Craven meeting, but cars and lorries were stationary as far as the eye could see. Tim was fretting, agitation turned to stress, but the memories of Tenerife returned to put a saner perspective on the frustrating fume-filled journey. 'So what if we miss the first race?' he thought. 'To be in the sunshine with those who have suffered at the hands of Lady Luck in the name of horseracing is humbling and uplifting.'

On 23 May the postman left us three cheques. One was from Johnny and Linda O'Hara for £105 for three BBQ tickets, which was dated 12 May 2003. I don't think you can blame the post for that; it will be Johnny, the tight beggar, who couldn't let go if it. Only joking – Johnny is a great lad. £80 from Owen Watson-Wilson, the man we bought our Hunton home from for two BBQ tickets and £10 for raffle tickets and finally a £50 cheque came from Ian Bolland, our accountant, for raffle tickets. This now left our total to reach £18,070.

In the photo Johnney is seen in the chair having a bit of craic with Des Cullen, JB and Pat Hurley at an IJF function at York Racecourse.

L to r: *Des Cullen, JB, Johnny O'Hara & Pat Hurley at a IJF function at York Racecourse.*

Jeremy Richardson, our Chief Executive of the IJF, sent me a fax saying he has been arranging a charity cricket match for 14 July to be held at the Royal Household Cricket Club, Windsor Castle where Newmarket racehorse trainer Sir Michael Stoute had gathered an Invitation XI to play the Royal Household CC (The Queens Cricket Club) where the Queen would be in attendance or at least would be having lunch. I didn't think I would be able to sell Her Majesty any raffle tickets, I was told she doesn't carry any money with her. Michael's racing team may be so poor that the Queen won't stay to watch it all. Although, to be fair, I had never seen the racing team play cricket though I had heard they were quite good. In the past David Nicholson, Josh Gifford, Ryan Jarvis, Julian Wilson and quite a few other racing men were quite fanatical about it. JR wanted me to be a trustee to represent the IJF, although there was a catch. Dickie Bird, who was going to umpire the match, couldn't drive his car owing to recent cataract operations, so he asked me to pick him up from Barnsley on our way down. I rang Jeremy back and told him I would be delighted to attend and to deliver Dickie Bird to the match. I've carried all sorts in my car but it was a first for me carrying a 'Dickie Bird'.

The next Saturday a host of race meetings were taking place but, as I have done many times in the past, I chose Cartmel as the One to go to, I love it, Cartmel is like racing used to be – 100% enjoyment. Everyone seems to get on with little obvious pressure. It's seldom that there are Stewards Enquiries, but always lots of fun . The day was no exception. Jo and I had a lovely time. It was funny that on the way to Cartmel we stopped the car for fuel. In the filling station shop window were two very life-like dogs, one a red setter and the other a Jack Russell terrier. Always a sucker for anything like that, as I was paying for the petrol, quite innocently I asked the lady serving me 'How much is that doggy in the window?', as she gave me the reply we both cracked up laughing!

Back home in the post box was only one cheque from the Newmarket trainer, Willie Haggas, for £50 along with his raffle stubs. Willie had bought them all and there was an accompanying card which read:

Dear Jack,

Absolutely thrilled to help, huge congratulations to you for continuing all the hard work you do for charity. If by any chance one of these tickets comes out, stick it back in, unless it is one of those free bets in which case I will try to turn it into more money to go to the injured jockeys.

William

Doesn't a letter like that make you feel good? We were not looking for brownie points, but it was rewarding when a letter of encouragement arrived like William's.

David (F) Bowes invited Jo and I to a BBQ that evening. When we arrived, Gerry Scott the ex-starter had been and gone. But not without leaving an envelope with David containing two cheques, one from himself for £70 the other for the same amount from his friends Mr and Mrs Kirby for our BBQ moving our total nearer to our target of £17,880.

As it was Bank Holiday Monday and there were lots of race meetings on, I went to Redcar to put the tack on Alan's runner in the first race, OBE Bold, which finished third. There was no post today, however, I did receive £50 from John Spouse at Redcar for the tickets he had sold for us. John was the very first person I employed even before Cockerham; he was now Clive Brittain's Travelling Head Lad at the races. Not only did he sell the tickets to Brittain's lads and lasses, John asked me for another fifty tickets to sell. That was a first, not many people were asking for more tickets to sell, and just as it happened I had some in my pocket. £17,830 to go. Hopefully, we would make our goal £30,000 at the rate we were going. I would be very disappointed if we didn't, that amount would buy us two Balder wheelchairs.

The Balder chair is a revelation. It is the first wheelchair of its size that can raise its occupant to a standing position and then walk them round the room in an upright position. This chair is a must for lots of our beneficiaries. On 29 April 2003, four wheelchair-bound former jockeys had a demonstration of the chairs at Stoneleigh. They were Jonathan Haynes, who broke his back in a racecourse fall at Southwell in 1980, Jenny Liston, a champion point-to-point rider who can claim to have ridden fifty-five point-to-point winners and five under National Hunt rules. Her career came to an end on 20 February 1993 when she had a fall in a point-to-point race at Larkhill. As she suffered brain damage, she was airlifted to a hospital in Southampton. Lee Davis, is a more game young man than you never did see. When he was a nineteen-year-old apprentice jockey in 1990, he was horifically injured in a car crash. He is a tetraplegic although even that doesn't stop him playing rugby for the Welsh Paraplegic team. Also, Andrew James, another point-to-point casualty of 1981 is now tetraplegic. At the wheelchair trial, Jenny, Lee and Jonathan all raised themselves to a standing position and were comfortable, bearing in mind these people hadn't stood up for years. The delight and wonderment on the faces of these 'test pilots' said it all. Imagine them to be actually in a position to 'eye ball' someone they are talking to instead of being looked down upon. That alone must be a marvellous breakthrough for them. I can tell you, that all of us that have dealings with the IJF are so excited about this chair. Jenny was beside herself with excitement. Jonathan, like many people in wheelchairs, has serious kidney problems, as it is difficult for them to drain sediment away. On his chair trial he was able to stand up for fifteen minutes with the help of the Balder chair, a thing he hasn't done for years. Straight afterwards, his water bag had filled – normally that would not have happened for three or four

more hours. This was a big break-through for paraplegics as they often suffer with kidney trouble and bladder infections. When I was talking to Jonathan at Cartmel races, his reaction to the chair was brilliant and his enthusiasm was infectious. So much so, talking away we missed seeing a race! Typical of the man he said: 'It's great, I can paint the stables and even plait the horses up.' The quality of his life and many others would be enhanced with this great advance, as can be seen in the photo of one of the IJF beneficiaries Angela Hallas at an IJF beneficiaries day at Doncaster Racecourse.

Angela Hallas showing off her new Balde chair.

On Tuesday 29, out of habit, I went to the mailbox to collect the mail. The first letter I opened was a bit bulky. with two 41p stamps postage.I thought: 'I don't like the look of this; someone has returned our raffle tickets.' Some people object to having tickets sent to them through the post. Sure enough, £50 worth of tickets were returned from Henrietta Knight with a card explaining why she had returned them.

The tickets must have caught Hen on a bad day, as she is a giver and to boot one of the nicest people in racing. Hen went on to say it was the last straw receiving the tickets in aid of the IJF, as she had given us the print of Best Mate for our auction and on 21 September she was having an Open Day for the same cause. She also stated that she gets inundated with so many requests for good causes they nearly drive her crazy. She was right too, I do know as I had the same experience at Cockerham. Hen finished off with, 'Will see you at Ascot, love Hen.' Hen, in my eyes, you are still a star and I sincerely hope that Best Mate wins the next three of four Cheltenham Gold Cups for you. In fact, for me the lady can't train enough winners and a minor kick in the balls won't hurt for long. On the whole in racing we all sing in tune from the same hymn sheet – only on some days better than others.

Toby Balding the Andover trainer, sent his raffle ticket stubs with a card wishing us good luck. Leaving our target at £18,780.

The following day, the figure reduced further. Lilo Blum, the lady who was famous for her riding school in Hyde Park a few years earlier, and is a full sister to my old pal Gerry, the ex-Newmarket trainer, sent £20 and her ticket stubs. Also, Amanda Perrett returned her stubs along with her £50 cheque with an accompanying letter from herself and her husband Mark, wishing us all success with the BBQ and auction on 20th July. £18,710 to go.

We finally tracked down Charles Wyville who again agreed to donate for the auction one gun at Constable Burton estate's tenant farmer shoot in January, where a bag of 100/150 birds was anticipated for the day. Lunch at the Wyville Arms was also included in the package which the previous year sold for £500.

An IJF meeting came up, which again was held at the Montcalm Hotel in London.

You wouldn't believe this, but this was one of the rare occasions I didn't attend. The reason being that Jo went a few days earlier to a health farm with a mate of hers, Anne Hartley, and wasn't returning until late that night. Therefore, with all the animals to attend to I jibbed, leaving the other trustees and almoners to sort out the cases. I was certain they could manage without me, which they did. Although I rang John Oaksey, Elaine Wiles and Jeremy Richardson to put my pennyworth in with a number of the cases. Later on, I rang Sarah York and Elaine Wiles to see how everything had gone. The day went well everyone got just about what they wanted, including Jonathan Haynes, who had to go and get measured up for his Balder chair. The postman dropped two cheques in for us that day, one from Chris and Antonia Thornton for £170 for their BBQ and 100 raffle tickets. Alan King sent his stubs back with a £50 cheque, making our goal to get £18,470. Jo returned from the health farm looking big and well. I think she put on about 4lbs, although she went with the intention of losing weight!

On 30 May 2003, just before I set off for our local meeting at Catterick, I caught up with the postman, who this day played a blinder. There was a raffle prize of four complimentary badges into the Club Enclosure for any race meeting in 2003 at Catterick; a cheque for £200 from Dennis and Demaris Lethaby for the raffle tickets they had sold round the pubs in Malton and a £10 cheque from Carol Pipe for a book of tickets. Carol took ten books and had put the others in with some of their owner's bills, who would pay us direct. Clive Brittain's cheque for £50 for tickets arrived as did the same from Mickey Hammond – chiselling our target figure down to £18,160. It wasn't all roses at Catterick either. Alan was racing at Ayr, so Jo and I put the tack on his runner. It was no problem as Catterick is only five miles from Hunton. Frascati finished third which was as near as we got to saddling a winner. In the fifth race Alan's young apprentice, Paddy Mathers, had a fall riding a horse for Roger Fisher and broke a collarbone. The ambulance took him to Northallerton Hospital and we picked him up later and he stayed the night with us.

You may remember it was young Paddy who rode Columbine recently in a race at Musselburgh when he looked as though they were all over the winner, only the kid dropped his hands in the last couple of strides to get done by a short-head in a photo finish, something for which the stewards punished him heavily.

I often attend Catterick which is a cosy little track, with a very friendly feel to it, and looked after so well by Jonjo Sanderson and his team. It reminds me of the time when David Mould, his wife, Marion, and son, Jack, and I went to Old Trafford to watch Manchester United beat my team, Leeds Utd. Dave told me he travelled up to Catterick from the south with Dave Dick who was driving an MG Sports job. Dave was the jockey who rode ESB to win the 1956 Grand National, the year the Queen Mum's Devon Loch looked to have the race sewn up only to collapse halfway up the run-in.

After the racing, Dave Dick stopped his sports car for a squaddie hitchhiking from the camp. He put the soldier and his kit in the back which was a bit cramped for him. It was years before speed cameras, so cops in cars gave one a sporting chance. Dave drove at 100mph plus down the A1 and he stopped for something to eat at a café near Doncaster. As soon as the car door opened, the soldier, who wasn't a bit grateful, couldn't wait to get out and said 'thank f…k for that' and told Dave he didn't want to go any further. He would fight Germans or anyone, he would even be taken as a POW rather than get back into that car the way Dave was driving. 'You're 'effin' mad!'

When one talks about justice, in the *Daily Mail* on 31 May, a teenaged hooligan car driver was fined £200 for killing a young motorcyclist. He had not passed a driving test, had no insurance, had a string of driving offences and had been convicted on nine occasions for driving without a licence and insurance. When he left the court he said to the Press: 'That was a good result as I'd expected to be going to jail' How can one compare the life of this prat to young Paddy who is the most inoffensive little lad one could imagine, clean tidy, exceptionally well-mannered. Yet our justice (if that's what one calls it), read straight out of the tunnel-visioned rule book that has no kind of heartbeat or common sense whatsoever. The Musselburgh stewards gave Paddy twenty-one days suspension. What good does that kind of punishment do to a young lad who is so inexperienced? He hadn't yet even ridden a winner. One could hardly call it a confidence booster. It was a pity some of our heartless officials didn't act as Magistrates in Court to deal with the like of the aforementioned offender, whose name the Press couldn't even print as the yob was protected! Paddy could have done with a bit of protection from the lads in the yard taking the piss out of him when he got back. In addition, his name was splashed in every paper, not to mention Attheraces who talked about it in great detail.

I saddled up for the second day on the trot for Alan at Catterick and took Paddy back so he could go home in Alan's horsebox. Catterick being local gave me the chance to open the mail before setting off. Julia Routledge Martin sent a £50 cheque for raffle tickets. Devon trainer, Rod Miliman, who we asked to sell some tickets for us, said, 'Yes send me 250,' as they were having an owner's lunch party and it wouldn't be a problem. Rod actually sent a cheque for £308, which included £58 from their raffle. Newmarket trainer, Charles Egerton, sent a £10 cheque for a book of raffle tickets and returned the other four books. At least we are a tenner better off than we were the day before! Sir Michael Stoute the Newmarket handler of 190 horses found the time to send a cheque for his £50 worth of tickets together with a very nice accompanying letter signed by Michael wishing us well with our event, proving again a busy person gets things done. Peter and Lisa Teasdale sent a cheque to the value of £140 for four BBQ tickets and Kevin Linfoot sent a cheque for £70 for his BBQ tickets. Finally, in a recorded letter there was a £20 note for two books of raffle tickets I sent to John Yeoman of Wolverhampton. John, who loves his racing, is a night porter at one of the town's hotels where we stayed some twenty years earlier and he had kept in touch ever since. George and Carol Moore who, I will say again, are great at helping out for any worthwhile cause, sent a cheque for £140 and a cheque to the value of £70 from Mrs Mary and Miss Susan Hatfield, owners of Anne Duffield's. The total received was £858, which left us £17,312 to ring the bell.

It was a scorching hot day at Catterick. John Brown, for whom we trained ninety-nine winners for in twenty-five years at Cockerham, was there. He is not to be confused with John Brown the ex-boss of William Hill the bookmaker, although we did train for him also. John was always a bit upset we retired before we trained him the magical one-hundred winners and would you believe it, he was still on ninety-nine three years later! We invited his racing partner John Shaw and Gino Bernacchi with his wife, Meme, to our house for a BBQ after racing had finished. We had a great time, the Hall of Fame benefited. After their viewing, they placed their bids on various items ready for our auction.

The next Sunday 1st June, I had been asked by Val Thewlis to conduct the auction at the Middleton Park Equestrian Centre, Middleton near Leeds. It was to be a Fun Day in aid of Riding for the Disabled. A fun day it was too. Spen Valley Brass Band gave it plenty of oomph! There were two riding demonstrations that were very good. The kids did riding competitions that were brilliant. There was a 'bucking bull' which I kept well away from, but the youngsters couldn't get on the beggar fast enough, also some kick-boxing, the trainer who was in charge of it must have weighed getting on for four hundredweight – if he had told me it was Saturday last Sunday I would have believed him. I wouldn't have liked a kick from him! Two of the nicest looking young girls, about eighteen/twenty years old with lovely long hair had the whole lot shaved off all in aid of the Riding for the Disabled. The girls earned the cause £4,800 from sponsorships and they deserved the support they got. Well done. Twenty-five lots were donated to be auctioned, ranging from a four-hour drive in a chauffeur driven limo, a case of special reserve Merlot, an adult's scooter, to a framed picture of Stroller and Marion Mould. It was a really nice sunny day with lots of people in attendance. My job started at 2.30 p.m., which finished just in time for me and Jo to go the eighteen miles to Pontefract in time to watch our filly Simmiana run fourth of seventeen in the 4.20 p.m. race and collect £891 for her efforts. At Pontefract, Harry Cook, a member of the Hillside Racing Group, and one of Alan's owners, mentioned to Jo he had sold the raffle tickets which she had sent to him and thought he would sell another five books without a problem. It wasn't long before the 'old lady' was legging it to the car to get Harry another five books! Chris Grant, the father of Chris Grant, the ex-Arthur-Stephenson jockey, now a trainer, gave Jo £10 for a book of tickets he had sold, leaving our balance to get £17,292.

The following night a foursome, we Berrys and Jill and Dave Armstrong, went to Adrian Maguire's testimonial and celebration of a great riding career. The Newcastle venue was the first of a series. Hopefully, Adrian, a really nice fellow, would get enough out of his testimonial year to finance the point-to-point yard himself and his good lady, Sabrina Maguire, intended to buy in Ireland to set up training there. As I have mentioned, Adrian's retirement earlier I won't go overboard, although I would just mention what Toby Balding said of 'A' as Toby called him, when Adrian came over from Ireland to work at Fyfleld, Toby's yard. Adrian has an amazing C.V. He had already ridden six winners in one day at Drommahane point-to-point, ridden Omerta a Cheltenham Festival winner and the Irish Grand National. Adrian must have given Toby 'many, many portions of pleasure and excitement' as the trainer said of the boy prodigy! A joy to work with and a team player with true talent. When Henry Beeby, MD, of Doncaster Bloodstock Sales Ltd, one of the best auctioneers around conducted the auction, he had no trouble raising £13,100 for just eleven auction items. The top lot of £2,500 being a chance for two to go 'behind the scenes' – with lunch thrown in – with Morning Line on Channel 4 at York racecourse. Adrian's whip, used when he rode Sibton Abbey, winning the 1992 Hennessey, and the boots he wore when he kicked home Paris Pike to win the Scottish Grand National in 2,000, raised £2,000, Dave Armstrong won a Magnum of Taitinger Champagne in the raffle and was presented with it by Tony McCoy, but Dave gave it to me to put into our raffle on 20 July. Northern Champion jockey, Tony Dobbin, and I arranged to get all the jockeys up when the band came on, to sing the Irish song that the jump jockeys had recorded with Foster and Allen, 'The Fields of Athenry'. However, when the band started up it was just a loud thudding racket, hammering out arrangements for younger persons than yours truly! Tony looked at me and said, 'We'll give it a miss and do it some other time!'

The following day saw our target reduced to £17,172 on account of Mary Reveley sending £50 for raffle tickets and Len Shears forwarding on his £70 BBQ cheque. Brian Robb brought for our auction a very nice pastel of Rock of Gibraltar donated by the artist Nigel Brunyee. Brian was taken by it and opened the bidding with £200. Michael Chapman, the Market Rasen trainer, rang to tell me that his stable jockey Billy Worthington had suffered a racing fall some months ago when he broke three small bones in his neck that were not healing. He had just returned the previous day from paying a visit to a bone specialist who had given him the bad news. In addition, there was a chip of bone floating about in his neck very near to his spinal cord, which was extremely worrying. The specialist said he needed to have an immediate operation, as it was so serious. The cost, including aftercare, would be in the region of £12,000. The operation was a complicated one, as the surgeon would have to work through his mouth to retrieve the chip and fix the bones. It sounded awful and Michael was quite upset. I told him not to worry and that I would ring our president, Lord Oaksey, who would get things moving quickly, and he did. We knew it would not be many days before Billy had an appointment with a specialist with the result being a visit to the operating table.

I opened the post on Wednesday 4 June before setting off for Perth to stay at Willie Burns house ready for the following day's racing, where I was conducting the auction in aid of the British Red Cross and the Queen Mother Memorial Fund in support of the Tracing and Message Service. This provides much needed support to the families torn asunder by conflict, with many enquiries even now, from World War II to the present day and post-war Iraq and Afghanistan. In the post were three cheques. The first came from Peter Airey for £70 for raffle tickets, the other two were both for £50, the first from Ponty Pridd-trainer Derek Haydon Jones for raffle tickets. The other, from Sir Mark Prescott, contained a nicely written card congratulating our team for its efforts. The figure now stood at £17,002.

As soon as we got to the Burns' house, we enjoyed a lovely meal prepared by Wilma, a superb cook. Before retiring for the night, she gave me a £50 cheque and stubs from the tickets she had sold making our target figure £16,952.

When we arrived at Perth racecourse about 12 p.m. for their Charity Race Day, The Queen Mother Memorial Fund in aid of the British Red Cross, we sat straight down for lunch. At 12.45 p.m. I started the auction. I have conducted several charity auctions but I would not be in the same league as the likes of Mouse White or Henry Beeby. Lot one was a beautifully framed, Joy Hawkin's print of Martha's Son and Dublin Flyer cantering in the snow, one we acquired from Joy but gave to Carol Mitchell to help with their fundraising. It made £750. Lot two was the horserace thriller-writer Dick Francis's book, *To the Hilt*, which raised £250. The print of the Queen Mother's horse Makaldar ridden by my old mate David Mould, donated by Tony Collins, sold for £400. David rode Tom Jones's brilliant horse, Tingle Creek, to win the Benson & Hedges. Finally Polly Pullar's book, *Rural Portraits: Scottish Native Farm Animals, Characters and Landscapes*, sold for a further £250. Guest Speaker was the ex-Newbury trainer, the 1959-60 champion amateur jockey, Gay Kindersley, who was good and very funny. Jockey Mick Fitzgerald was tipster and at 1.30 p.m. there was a Charity Race. Edward Sackville rode the winner beating the recently retired jockey Brian Storey. Brian, a good all-round jump jockey, at that time a Jockey Club Starter, never really hit the big time, but he did ride Mighty Mark to win the 1988 Scottish Grand National. Although only second in the Charity Race, Brian was really chuffed, smiling away. In fact, he was so pleased with his ride, I thought when he entered the enclosure he might do a Frankie Dettori 'flying dismount', an act most racing people love to see, as in the picture overleaf taken by Alec Russell of the great man after winning the Ascot Gold Cup on Papineau. Alec Russell produced the picture and some others in aid of the Asian Tsunami Disaster of 2005.

Although I couldn't help thinking if it was 'Fanny Rowbottom', a 7lbs claimer on permit trainer 'Joe Smith's' selling hurdler winner at Carlisle, this procedure may have been stopped by the powers that be! At 3 p.m. in the paddock there was a parade of the Queen Mother's horses with Lord Oaksey giving a run-down of their past glories, followed by a display arranged by the Shetland Pony Society, in the centre of the racecourse. There was one occasion when Frankie tasted the wrath of the stewards when he went into an enquiry chewing gum. They told him the steward's room wasn't a fast-food store.

In between all these events there was some very good racing. In the evening after racing, there was a hog roast and real hand-clapping, knee-slapping country dancing. It was great to revisit Perth, the first time I had done so in years although I had ridden round and enjoyed many days racing there as a jockey. Needless to say, as soon as I arrived home I dived into the mail, which proved a big help toward reaching out target. First of all, I opened a letter from York Race Committee Chief Executive offering two County Stand tickets for York October meeting for one of our raffle prizes. Former jump jockey Dave Parker, who now worked for the racing press, sent a cheque for £105 for three BBQ tickets. Trainer Giles Bravery forwarded a £100 cheque and stubs from his raffle tickets. Philip Hobbs, the Minehead trainer, sent £90 and the stubs from his tickets because inadvertently we had sent Philip nine books instead of ten. A further £70 cheque arrived from Wilf Storey, Brian's father, for his two entry tickets. A cheque also came from my old pal Shane Broderick for 150 Euros for his ten books of raffle tickets; I would enter here £100. A further £100 arrived from my ex-show jumping pal John Walmsley for tickets he and his wife Anne had sold. Roundgrey Limited sent a cheque also for raffle tickets as did Emma Balding, the mother of Andrew Balding. Andrew was in his first year training in his own right, had his first treble that day at Epsom, but not just an ordinary treble. Casual Luck ridden by Martin Dwyer won the £240,700 Vodafone Oaks. Finally, a cheque for raffle tickets came from the Scarcroft trainer Richard Whittaker. It all added up to £715 – three cheers for the postman! Our target figure was now £16,237.

It was lovely to see eighty-nine-year-old ex-champion-jockey Scobie Breasley on the box as a guest of Epsom racecourse on Derby Day, being introduced to all the jockeys riding in the great race. Australian-born Scobie won the Derby on Santa Claus in 1964 and again on Charlottetown in 1966. Scobie rode his first winner way back in 1928, on Noogee. When the old jockey retired from riding in 1968, his racing boots and saddle were auctioned for £750 in aid of the Stable Lads Welfare Trust. It was also good to see Kieren Fallon win the Derby for the second time on the Sir Michael Stoute-trained Kris Kin. Keiran won on Oath in 1989.

In the post that day, Noel Chance sent a cheque for £100 for tickets he had bought himself, along with a £50 cheque from another old pal, Michael Jarvis, the Newmarket trainer with whom we had spent some great times when our two families shared a rented house in Barbados (where we invariably we met up with ex-trainer and Manchester City footballer Franny Lee and a lot more racing folk). The figure now stood at £16,087.

At 9.45 p.m. Derby night I wrote a letter to Mrs Thompson of Cheveley Park Stud in Newmarket, where the last season's champion sprinter Kyllachy was then standing as he had retired to stud. My writing was so bad I thought that Mrs T, a lovely woman, probably wouldn't be able to read it.

Anne and George Duffield had invited Jo and I to a barbecue the following

Frankie Dettori doing his flying dismount on the Ascot Gold Cup winner Papineau.

day, therefore I would take it with me to get it typed by her secretary, Ian. It showed what initiative us ex-trainers can have. I changed my mind, I would post it as it was! As I had just recently come out of hospital having had key-hole knee surgery, when Jo and I got to the Duffield's, the mischievous old jockey asked me, really concerned,' How's your knee, mate? 'Alright, just a bit sore,' George added; 'That's good. You'll be alright to play the piano now.' 'Too right I will!' I said. George replied, 'that's great, because you couldn't play it before!' What's he like?!

Dear Mrs Thompson,

Please don't think too bold of me but I am bringing to your notice that in July we are holding a barbecue and a charity auction in aid of the Injured Jockeys Fund. Last year we raised £21,000 for the IJF plus £2,000 to buy a nine-year-old spastic blind girl a new wheelchair. Hopefully with the generosity of people like yourself we hope to better that total.

I am writing this letter to you personally as when your stallion Kyllachy won the Nunthorpe Stakes, I wrote to Henry Candy asking him if he would be kind enough to give our cause an actual plate that the horse wore on the day, to be accompanied by a letter of authenticity, which Henry very kindly did. Since we received the plate, we have had it mounted on a very nice piece of oak (polished) with the horse's name and details of his Nunthorpe victory engraved on a silver plaque.

Please, Mrs T, may I ask you if you would be willing and good enough to place a bid for this wonderful auction item? Michael White, of DBS, is the auctioneer on the day. I would gladly give him your instructions.

I wait with anticipation for your response. Also may I take this opportunity to wish you every success for the rest of the season.

Kindest regards, yours ever,
Jack Berry

Cheveley Park owned the good sprinter Music Boy when he retired to stud. I loved that horse. I liked him a lot when he was in training with Snowy Wainwright, the father of John, who trains at Malton. When Music Boy's youngsters went to the Sales, there weren't many of his yearlings I didn't take a look at. In fact, I bought some really good horses sired by him. The majority were tough and sound. They also trained on and would go on any ground. Some that come to mind are; Prohibition, Clantime, Food of Love, Antonia's Folly, Fylde Flyer and Dancing Music. When Northern Command won the Killingworth Maiden Stakes at Newcastle for us on 27 March 1989, he was the 500th winner Music Boy had sired. To commemorate the occasion, the Thompsons presented me with a lovely photo of Music Boy galloping round his paddock at the stud, mounted and engraved in a beautiful silver frame, a photo I treasure that stands on our sideboard. Just about every time I visited Newmarket I went to Cheveley Park Stud to see Music Boy. A few years ago when the old fella died, Cheveley Park held a Memorial Service there for him and I was invited. It was a sad day. Although Cheveley Park had lots of horses in training, unfortunately they were all down in the south, although we were lucky enough for them to send us a couple of horses for us to train at Cockerham.Thankfully, these won races.

I rang up Dave Pollington. Dave was Kieren Fallon' s agent, to tell him I was thinking of making a comeback and would he act as my agent – only joking

A group photo of racing folk in Barbados. L to r: *Michael Jarvis, Neville Callaghan, JB without the customary red shirt (as you can see, I don't suffer from anorexia), John Akehurst, Jo Berry, Willie Carson, Pat Eddery & Elaine Carson.*

of course! Really it was to ask if he could send a good signed photograph of Kieren riding Kris Kin at Epsom for our auction. I would have rung Julie, the champ's missus, only I didn't want to bother her at that time as she had enough on her plate, with her father having died the other day and the funeral being the following day.

With the help of the IJF, Billy Worthington had the operation to remove the chip in his neck and set the bones. The operation was performed by the top surgeon in this field, Professor Crockhard at the Wellington Hospital in London. Thankfully, it was successful. The NHS certainly wouldn't have performed it as quickly.

One of my favourite stallions, Music Boy. He bred his stock tough and sound – they would gallop on any ground.

To get our place smartened, up Dave (J) Bowes and I made a rockery all around our pond and planted it all up with shrubs and plants. Every bit of my spare time when I hadn't been attending functions or going racing over the last few weeks, I had spent on the project. Most mornings we had had the cement mixer on the go by 7 a.m. Using tonnes and tonnes of stone that mainly had been given to me by Dave (F) Bowes, Dave (J) had done the majority of the mixing while I had laid the stone and done the pointing. Most of the time I worked with my shirt off, as it was very hot weather ideal for sun bathing. Dave (J) was a non-runner that day. I laboured and laid the stone and we managed to completely finish the job. All of the people who came to our BBQ the year before would certainly notice the huge difference to the place.

On 10 June, David Nicholson, the ex-jockey and trainer, rang to invite Jo and me to lunch in the car park the following Tuesday at Ascot. The Duke, as we all call him, had been under the surgeon's knife recently having had a hip replacement. David sounded in good form and he said he was much better. David and his wife Dinah, had invited us to the Ascot lunch for years, a thing we always look forward to. Dinah valets our top hats for a note donation in aid of a charity of her choice, which is usually for retired racehorses. John Spearing, the Kinnersley trainer, sent our cause a cheque for £75 and £50 for raffle tickets he had bought but for which he had not returned the stubs. Hopefully, John would send them on later as there were some really good prizes to be won in the raffle and he deserved his chance to win. The total now stood at £16,012.

Our sincere thanks go to Lisa, the secretary to Chester racecourse, who rang and had arranged a paddock ticket for two with lunch included for their big

David Nicholson with his wife, Dinah, in the Royal Progression at Royal Ascot.

meeting in August, as an auction or raffle prize and would be sending the invitations and badges on.

Some trainers enter their horse many times in different races, shot-gun style. Then when they see the entries published in the they decide to run in what they consider to be the easiest race, or the one that appeals best. That's all very well, but not only has the owner several entry fees to pay; he also has a surcharge for each entry made. All in all this can amount to as much as a week's training fee.

With the yearlings, I suppose it is easier to pick out potential winners than it is with the young jumpers. One can sort out the sprinting types against the journeymen. Then sort out the sharp ones amongst the sprinters. As early on in the season, five furlongs is the maximum trip they can run, one has to make sure the youngsters can see the five furlongs out without getting too revved up and then blowing their minds; especially the fillies. Everything has to be done quietly during breaking with no rush attached. It's most important to have the staff who break and ride them off not to lose their rag with the youngsters the minute they do something wrong, as they are only babies. Like us, some learn faster than others. Having said that it helps if the teacher knows what he or she is doing, unlike those Musselburgh stewards reading straight from their rule book. Taking advice from elsewhere, one needs to have a heartbeat or feel the pulse. That's the trouble with the country today. As Ben Robinson would say, no common 'effing sense. Bad habits are soon picked up, often sooner than good ones. The very word 'habit' is an awful word and hard to get rid of.

HABIT

Cross the 'h' off and you still have 'a bit'
Cross the 'a' off, you still have 'bit'
Cross the 'b' off you still have 'it'

Therefore, it's very important that teachers don't teach bad habits to whatever or whomever they are teaching.

Once the youngsters have been lunged and driven in strings plenty of times and have got confident, they just about tell you when it's time to get on their backs. Many people are of the opinion that its better to ride them off in a couple of weeks, I always thought it was better to drive them for at least that long. Don't rush to get snaffie bits on them, start with a straight breaking bit with 'keys', then change to a broken bit with keys. Mouths are made on the floor, not on their backs, and if a yearling starts off with a good mouth, it's a good start to its racing life and thereafter.

While the driving or the lunging is taking place, it's very important to talk to them. Ask the yearlings to walk, trot, or canter. Don't demand it. When one asks them to stop, the person in charge should ask them to come by quietly reeling the horse in. When the youngster comes to the handler, make a fuss of him/her. Don't go to the yearling and make a fuss of him or her and never eyeball them as they walk towards one. The youngsters get confidence and relax. If it's possible, pipe some music into the school while the breaking is going on.

Have a dog or two around and if someone wants to come into where you're working the youngster, let them stand in the middle with the teacher. You can't take the people out of the stands on a race day. The more they see the better; they cope later on when it matters.

If one has an indoor school or a manège and the youngsters are ridden round to get them going, trotting in circles and figures of eight, keep them going but after every other turn change the leader. It's always important to have someone on the ground, e.g the trainer or head lad while this procedure takes place. In the event someone gets dropped, he can give the pilot a leg-up, also he or she can give the instructions when to walk trot or whatever. At the end of the session when the riders dismount, it's a good thing to lead the horse for a turn or two then as the horses follow the instructor in single file, he throws the riders back up onto them and, if possible, walks them through a set of open stalls. When the riders dismount, lead the yearlings for a pick of grass. It's money well spent to place a set of stalls at the entrance to the yard. Every time the horses go in or out of the yard they get used to them as, let's face it, stalls are not horse friendly and, with all the noise and rushing about at the start of races, if the youngsters don't get familiar with the stalls they will resent them.

So they can switch off and unwind by doing things this way, the youngsters will start to enjoy their schooling. Then their workload can be increased. I don't mean by chasing them on, but by furthering their education by hacking them round a canter ring, lobbing up the gallops and bunching them up and cantering in pairs. By now they are looking more like racehorses. Even when the weather is bad, once the youngsters are cantering, I liked to keep them going – as seen on the gallops at Cockerham in December. As long as they are well fed, kept warm, given a portion of TLC, they will come to no harm. To make them grow-up even more, when the bunch gets to the top of the gallop, spread them out like a fan and walk back. Further to their education, send the

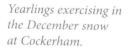

Yearlings exercising in the December snow at Cockerham.

yearlings out to canter two minutes apart to hack up the gallop on their own and walk back. When they can do all this without shouting for each other, they have grown up and they become independent. During all the time we trained we never gave a yearling a lead on the gallops with an old horse. They led each other. Then, when their time comes to race, they are fit and well tutored and they jump out of the stalls. They will keep going and not hang about waiting for leads.

Let them grow up. When a two-year-old goes racing and it's shouting and bawling nine times out of ten, the animal isn't ready to run. It's not independent. It's what the jockeys call 'green'. I hated it whenever jockeys said that about our two-year-olds. It's reported one owner was said to have heard the jockey say that the horse was 'green', the owner said to the trainer, 'You told me it was a chestnut when I bought it.' When John Carroll rode our youngster's first time out early in the season, he would let them canter down to the start in the middle of the track without a lead. Look at one of the all-weather gallops on an Open Day at Cockerham; note the punters waiting for a bunch of our two-year-olds to come up. One would hardly say they were green, some spectators got so close they could have stroked the youngsters as they passed.

When they ran, if they hit the gate and got a flyer, he let the two-year-old go and didn't take any prisoners and very often won because they were educated. We have had some wonderful open days at the yard with some famous celebrities present with Desert Orchid and Red Rum.

Stable-Jockey John Carroll leads the string on one of our many open days at Cockerham.

The following day, I thought I had cracked it when I received two payouts from the Premium Bonds; like the late WA Stephenson used to say when he poached small races with decent horses, 'little fish are sweet.' Both were £50 each. Pat Murphy the East Garston trainer sent his cheque and stubs with a very nice message. £15,962 to go.

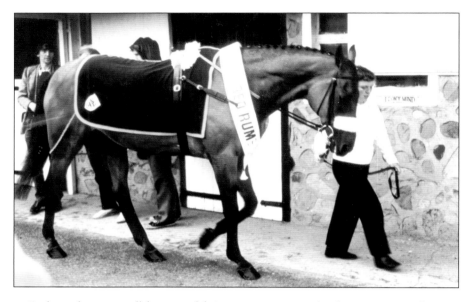

Perhaps the most well-known celebrity to grace our yard – during an open day – three times Grand National winner, Red Rum.

Chapter Ten

Some Operator – Mouse

•

It was 3.20 a.m. on Thursday 12 June. It was not unusual for me to be up at this hour; when I was at the yard, it was a regular thing. When it was quiet and peaceful, I could work on the entries for the horses. Once you have got your horses fit and well, for me that is the most important part of training. Any silly bugger can enter and run the horses – it's placing them in races they can win; that's the key. This morning I was up because the BBQ was on my mind and I wanted it to work. With only five weeks to go there was so much still to do. I was working on the brochure putting the auction items in order of sale, choosing which to sell because we had dozens of lots. We had no chance of selling them all on the one day. I needed to catalogue a maximum of eighteen to twenty. Any more and the punters would lose interest, start talking amongst themselves and the seller loses control. Having said that, Mouse White is some operator.

As you can see from the photo of Mouse, he's auctioning the winner of the selling race at the now defunct Teeside Park as a mere nineteen-year-old. Holding the horse is the Malton trainer Nigel Tinkler with his mother, Marie.

While he was selling, I am sure he wouldn't let the punters lose their concentration. Therefore, I decided we may auction off twenty-to-thirty items. The

A young Mouse White about to offer the winner of the Selling Race at the now defunct Teeside Park for auction.

rest would go in the raffle, mind you, I have never seen or heard of a raffle with such good prizes on offer since Barney Curley raffled his house. Hopefully, we would get a lot of ticket money in during the following two weeks. The last thing we needed was people paying on a day and bringing hundreds of raffle tickets stubs to fold up! It would take too much time on the day that we want to devote to everyone having an enjoyable day and above all they would need to feel part of it. We wanted them to know that because of them, we would be able to take a lot of our gang to Tenerife for a holiday, buy some more Balder chairs, pay for urgent operations and help in many other ways. All the entry tickets and the raffle tickets had been catalogued and had been accounted for as they had been paid. Therefore, on 1 July, I decided I would ring all the slow-to-pay punters to remind them to kick-on, settle-up and send in their stubs. Most people are good and mean well, but when they receive their tickets they get put aside and forgotten, so they sometimes need a friendly reminder.

It's 4.30 a.m. now, as I write. Lots of people ask me every week; 'Do you miss the training?' 'Life is not a cardboard cut out.' I tell them, 'not really as I did it for three decades and everything has a sell-by date, I feel I went as far as I could go.' What I do miss are the horses.' By now, often I would be having a cup of tea at Cockerham, then at 4.45 am I would catch up with Neville Hill, our feed man, and feed the horses with him. That was a nice part of the day; they were always pleased to see us, as soon as they heard Neville and I pushing the feed barrow around. I do really miss that. It was a lot nicer sound than that bloody racket we listened to at Adrian Maguire's Newcastle Testimonial! I would then have another cup of tea, look through the lists of runners and riders that Jo, Allen and Flash and Kevin, the head men, had arranged the previous evening and change a few about.

We would turn on the Radio 2 programme where the sound was piped round to the three yards, the horses walkers, the lunging ring, the fold yard and the indoor school. Often in the dark, we would turn on the lights. Everyone would be dashing about with tools and tack, singing away to the sounds, or chatting away. The place used to really buzz. I loved it and I do also miss it.

The lads would put their horses on the walkers, tack up and ride their first lot out round the roads for three-quarters of an hour. We would then work them while the ground staff mucked-out. They would quickly do them up and ride the horses off the walkers. Everyone would re-load the walkers up and then have breakfast, do the same again and then go racing. Working with the horses is great, and it's good at the races, especially when the horses are running well. The worst part of the job is the travelling every day, often six and eight hours a day in a car. That was the main reason I bought a new car every year. I got so fed up of seeing the same car. Having said all that, racing has been good to me and I would do it all again, although with all the red tape, rules, regulations and protocol that's in force now a lot of the fun has evaporated from the job and it has deprived the sport of a lot of characters.

The postman must have thought he brought us enough the previous day with the Premium Bonds, because the following day we received a bill for £218 from Simon Winstanley, a local firm, for mending the ride on grass mower, two returned entry tickets from Peter Beaumont, trainer of Jodami, the 1993 Gold Cup winner, who had paid for them but told me up in Perth he couldn't get to the day but would send the tickets back to sell on and wouldn't require a refund. At least doing that we didn't have to increase our target figure by writing him a cheque. Good man he is, Peter, he comes from a really good jumping family. He is also the father of Anthea Moreshead, the Perth Clerk of the Course, her husband Sam being the course's General Manager. Between them they do a remarkably good job. To boot, both were jockeys before they took these posts. A further pair of tickets arrived back from Robin and Brenda Johnson of Penrith, declaring themselves as non-runners.

Friday 13 is unlucky for some. It's our youngest son Sam's birthday. The day before was an unlucky one for him. From time to time following his accident at Sedgefield, he periodically suffers from convulsions and Sam had one the previous day. Carole, his partner, felt it was coming on as they were in the car and she drove straight to the doctors, where he had the fit in the surgery. An ambulance then took him to hospital, but he was out the following night for a couple of hours at the party Carole had arranged for him. Tough as old boots that lad.

What a difference a day can make. The following day was the first day of York races, but we didn't go as The Bride had arranged to have her hair done, it being the Timeform dinner that evening. Missing the races also meant not seeing our filly Simianna run fourth once again, producing a payday of £1,080. The postman did a good job that day leaving a few cheques for our cause in the box. The first one being for £70 from Bill and June Robinson, friends and neighbours of our when we lived at Cockerham, for their tickets. Brian Robb sent £100 cheque and stubs for raffle tickets he had sold. Nerys Dutfield, the Devon trainer who usually trains a good two-year-old or two, always good for a worthwhile cause and a lovely lady to boot, sent her cheque for £50 for the tickets she sold with a few nice encouraging words. Brighton trainer Gary Moore sent his cheque for raffle tickets and stubs as did my old friend and colleague, Reg Hollinshead, the Rugeley trainer, a former jockey renowned for producing good apprentices such as Kevin Darley, Tony Culhane and a host of others. Kevin rode for our yard after serving his apprenticeship. It was great to see him become champion jockey in 2000. I always knew there was a brilliant jockey inside that body of his trying to get out; even as a kid he had everything and was so keen. Reg, born in 1924, I believe, was the oldest trainer still training at that time and a true gent. He's one man no one ever says a bad word about. He wrote a nice letter enclosed with his £50. In all, that was £320 for the day, that got our total under £16,000, to £15,642, which was well on course. John Dunlop OBE, himself a great man for his charity work especially for Stable Lads Welfare, sent a cheque and a letter showing appreciation for our efforts.

As stated above, Jo and I were invited to the Thirty-third Timeform Charity Dinner by its Chairman, Reg Griffin. The first Dinner and Charity Day in 1971 raised £24,186 for Cancer Relief. The previous year, a staggering £176,239 was raised and the grand total from the start to the time of me writing, not counting the previous night's proceeds, is a colossal £3,128,446 raised by the Timeform Organisation. The Timeform Directors, Reg Griffin and Jim McGrath, need to be applauded. I for one would cast my vote for the pair of them to be knighted.

Everyone and all the top people with racing connections at some point get invited to the Timeform Dinner, a very prestigious event. At this time Rodney Tennant conducted the auction, whereas in the past Sir Peter O'Sullivan took the role, and very good he was too. Having said that, Rodney wasn't bad either! He recently won an award for auctioneering. There were eighteen lots that evening which raised £84,300. Lot Five was very nice being *The Race Of My Life* memorabilia, a beautifully presented package which is the end product of a marathon autograph hunt. It involved a journey of 13,000 miles and took no less than two and a half years to complete. It was by Sean Magee, his personal account of the most memorable races of thirty of the world's greatest jockeys. It spanned the four decades and was inspired by jockey's agent, Keith Bradley, who set about obtaining the autographs of all those featured, photographing each of them holding the book. These photographs were then framed and autographed. The book was leather-bound and the package also included the Cross fountain pen used by the jockeys to sign their autographs. As I mentioned earlier, Keith wanted the *Race of My Life* funds to go to the IJF, so I arranged with Reg for the package to be auctioned there that night instead of at our BBQ. Therefore, we were claiming the £1,400 paid by David Wosskow for the package which brought our target figure down to a more realistic amount £14,242. Well done, Keith and Sean, and thank you David for buying it!

At the dinner I was seated opposite John Forsyth, one of my old owners and we were chatting away as one does. John was telling me a story about a horse he had in training with Mark Johnston. Mark rang John up and told him he had entered the filly in a seller at Newcastle and he would like to run her. It was a poor race and he couldn't see her getting beaten. 'Hold on,' John says, 'I'm not too sure of that, running in a seller, my missus Margaret really likes her and we don't want to lose her in a seller.' 'There's no chance of that,' the

L to r: *Lennie Peacock (in profile), JB, Sally Haggis, Princess Anne & Reg Griffin having a chat at the Timeform Charity Dinner at York Racecourse.*

trainer said, 'as she's a good thing and we'll buy her back if there's a bid.' After a bit of pestering, 'Go on then,' said John, relishing the thought of having a little touch. On the day, the traffic was really heavy and it was a big rush to get there, as John had to attend a meeting at work beforehand. In his own words he said, 'It was pissing down with rain.' The journey took him four hours to complete. His horse was hot favourite at 1/2. John weighing up the situation thinking that's a poor price, but Mark insisting it couldn't get beaten. Therefore, he put £1,000 on the good thing, reasoning, 'at least I'll win a monkey (£500).' Darryl Holland took the ride and a furlong out the filly was absolutely hacking up. When close to home, Kim Tinkler's mount found a bit of foot and mugged John's filly right on the line. There was no bid for the winner, but would you believe John's filly was subject to a claim. John was sick as a parrot, wet through, feeling like a drowned rat and worrying like mad because Margaret had lost her pride and joy. As he was leaving the course to make towards the car park, he bumped into the Newcastle boss, Sir Stanley Clark, who I might add, has done wonders for the Tyneside course. He is a very jubilant man who tries to please and always has time to chat to everyone. He said to John, 'Hello have you had a nice day?' 'Have I had a nice day? I've been stuck in traffic for hours my bloody horse was odds-on in the seller and got stuffed, I lost a grand on it and some prat has gone and claimed it, I'm 'effin' soaked to the skin, and you ask me have I had a nice day?!' Sir Stan listened with interest and then says to John, 'Well the food was alright!'

In addition to raising lots of money for good causes, the highlight of the evening was to choose the Timeform Personality of the Year, which was a great honour to receive, as looking down the list there had been some great people who had received the award. The very first in 1972 was awarded to Major Leslie Petch OBE, who at that time was acting Clerk of York racecourse. Major General Sir Randall Feilden KCVO CB CBE, followed the Major in 1973. Sir Peter Sullivan in 1974, one of the best racecourse commentators ever, took the award, and in 1975, Lester Piggott was next in line. Lady Beaverbrook received the award in 1976. Northern jockey (Cock of the North) Edward Hide took the award in 1977, Newmarket trainer Sir Noel Murless in 1979, Sir Noel had the privilege of training nineteen Classic winners during his long career. Five times Champion jockey Willie Carson OBE, 1980. Peter Easterby one of the best trainers to put a saddle on a horse, flat or jumping took the award in 1981, Bob Champion the Grand National winning jockey in 1982. In 1983, northern Clerk of the Course, John Sanderson took the award. Dr Vincent O'Brien, possibly the best trainer of all time, (in fact it would be fair to say he *was* the best trainer of all time), as he came out tops in a competition held recently for the best racing personality who had achieved the most in racing. Michael Dickinson won in 1985, and what a training achievement he performed to train the first five home in the Cheltenham Gold Cup. In 1986, the seven times champion National Hunt jockey John Francome MBE won the award. Jonjo O'Neill, one of the most likeable and courageous jockeys I have known, took the honour the following year. Son-in-law of Sir Noel Murless, Henry Cecil, the Newmarket trainer was the recipient in 1987 followed by another Newmarket trainer, Luca Cumani, National Hunt champion jockey Peter Scudamore was the holder in 1989. In that year, he set up a new record for the number of winners ridden by a jump jockey when Arden won at Ascot that gave him his 1,139th success passing the previous record set by John Francome. Peter was stable jockey to the most winning trainer ever, Martin Pipe CBE, who took the prestigious prize the next year. With Peter riding and Martin training the horses, they had the first five winners on a six-race card. Peter had by now retired, but I thought it wouldn't be long before Martin trained all six winners on a card somewhere! The man has broken every other record in the book. In 1991, it must have been a struggle to find an outstanding recipient, as I picked up the award, which I am privileged and honoured to have done. The President of our IJF and my old friend Lord Oaksey OBE, very deservedly was awarded the trophy in 1992. Senior Steward Lord Hartington collected the award in 1993 followed by Middleham trainer Mark Johnston the next year. Mark has done wonders for northern racing and has come a long way since he trained his first winner Hinari Video at Carlisle in 1987.

The then BHB boss Peter Savill, one of our former owners, was the lucky award winner in 1995. However, I doubt that would have happened if G Duffield had been chairman of the panel of judges. Godolphin and their team took the next year's honour. The two past award-winners, Sir Peter O'Sullivan and Willie Carson, both retiring from their roles, jointly took the honour in 1997. Most winning jump jockey Tony McCoy, probably the greatest jump jockey to ever have sat on a horse, who last Friday, as I write, was quite rightly awarded the MBE in the Honours List, carried off the prestigious award in 1998. There followed another champion jump jockey in 1999, Richard Dunwoody MBE, who rode his first winner on Game Trust at Cheltenham in 1983. In the year 2000, aptly, it was awarded to John Dunlop OBE, a man as busy as he is training one of the biggest yards of horses in the world, finds time to work tirelessly for racing charities; a truly great man. Evergreen ex-champion jockey Pat Eddery (but not as old as Harry Beasley who at the age of eighty-five rode a winner at Ballydoyle in Ireland) took the podium the following year, followed by fellow trustee of the IJF, John Smith, Clerk of the Course at York, where he has been responsible for the impressive stand being built at a cost of over £20 million. Hopefully, the stand will stand as a monument to John for the dedication and hard work he put into his job. John retired in 2003 from that post but when he looks back, or passes the racecourse he must feel proud of what he has achieved there.

His successor, William Derby is a very nice fellow and I wish him well, although he does have a hard act to follow. This year, 2003, for the second time only, it was a joint award to a couple of racing's most beloved people, Terry Biddlecombe and Henrietta Knight. There wasn't a single person in the room who wasn't pleased for them. Many times I have attended that dinner and never before have I seen a standing ovation like it, not only for their training of Best Mate. They are two good eggs.

The next day, Saturday, Jo and I were lunch guests of Timeform at York races, where the weather was warm and sunny and a crowd of 30,700 flocked to see some great racing. There was talk at that time of closing Ascot racecourse to get it refurbished to build a new stand. The Royal meeting would have to go to some other course whilst Ascot was worked on. Sandown, among other courses had been suggested; even Cheltenham had shown an interest in staging the great meeting. Not just because I am a northerner, but being realistic, where would you go better than York to stage Royal Ascot? Whilst at York, David Dicker paid me £70 for his two BBQ tickets.

On our return from the races, we had a £50 cheque in the post box along with tickets stubs from Newmarket trainer, Ben Hanbury. This reduced our target down to £14,122. Before diving off to stay with our Sam and Carole on our way to Ascot, I called to check our post where we found one cheque for £30, accompanied by a nice letter from Myra Nesbitt for raffle tickets she had sold for us. £14,092 to go.

There is always a great buzz at Royal Ascot. On the Tuesday, as we were car-park lunch guests of David and Dinah Nicholson. We arrived early and, as always, it was great. Our IJF new patron, as usual, attended the Nicholson lunch and was in good form. To see so many good horses is always a pleasure. In the Owners and Trainers bar I was talking to the Irish jump jockey Ruby Walsh and Con Marnane, a pin hooker from whom I had bought yearlings in the past. Ruby told me Shane Broderick's trained a second called We're Just Friends, in Ireland the other day. As bad as Shane could do with a winner, it was Sod's Law his horse was beaten by a horse trained by his old boss, Michael Hourigan, who Ruby said was as sick as a parrot for beating Shane's horse. Everyone in racing was desperate for Shane to train a winner. Timmy Murphy, the jockey who rode the winner, after dismounting walked to the weighing room and threw his tack on the floor and said, 'That's one 'effing winner I didn't want to ride.' Con gives money every year for the IJF. This year was no different, he put his hand in his pocket and gave me two £50 notes saying, 'That's for your IJF holiday.' This left £13,992 to reach our goal.

Mind Games, winner of the 1994 Norfolk Stakes at Royal Ascot.

Royal Ascot has been a very lucky meeting for our yard in the past and holds many wonderful memories. It took our yard quite a few years to train its first Royal Ascot winner, Mind Games in 1994, in the Norfolk Stakes.

To be fair, it was quite frustrating having so many placed horses without just getting there. However, three years ago training that magic treble, Bolshoi in the Kings Stand, Selhurst Park Flyer in the Wokingham and Rosselli in the Norfolk was, to say the least, some feeling. When I bought Rosselli at the Newmarket Yearling Sales, I rang Terry Holdcroft of Bearstone Stud and partner in Mind Games to ask if he would like to buy him, as he was by Puissance the same sire as Mind Games. Terry came to view him the following Sunday and liked what he saw and said he would buy half of him on one condition; that I kept half and promised not to sell him. As he liked the horse so much, I told Terry I wouldn't mind training as many horses as John Dunlop, but I didn't want to personally own as many as Sheikh Mohammed. Surely, he could buy all of him, but the Bearstone Stud boss said, 'No, that's the deal.' Half a loaf is better than none. Thankfully, I had risen above the days when I needed to ring our bank manager to honour the cheque I had written out to pay the wages, so I agreed and we shook hands on the deal. Rosselli won his maiden as a two-year-old first time up at Newcastle. His second race we stepped him up in class; to win the Robert Massey Condition race at Beverley. Rosselli's next run was in the Group Three Norfolk Stakes at Royal Ascot, which he won.

Bloodstock agent David Metcalfe rang me up to ask if the youngster was for sale as he would like to buy him for Sheikh Mohammed's son, Rashid. 'What's the offer?' I asked. '£500,000' was the reply. I told David I would come back to him after having a word with my partner. When I spoke to Terry, he said, 'Remember we shook hands on the deal and you promised you wouldn't sell.' I said, 'I know I did, but this amount of money is obscene. We only paid 34,000gns for him, and he has paid us back already and more, as he has won all his three starts.' However, Terry wouldn't move. Sod's Law, the horse only won once again. It's not my style to welsh on any kind of deal, good, bad or indifferent, but this one time I should have dug my heels in. My share would have very nearly bought our new retirement home in North Yorkshire.

Rosselli, winner of the 1998 Norfolk Stakes at Royal Ascot.

However, Terry rang me one day and said his mate, Terri Herbert-Jackson, who also has several horses in training with him, would like to buy my half but would only give me £30,000 for it. 'Tell him to write the cheque out,' I said. And he obliged.

This year, 2003, Jo and I stayed with an old friend during Ascot, the Radlett trainer, Ken Ivory, for the first three days only, as on the Saturday I was auctioneer at a Summer Ball in Shropshire in aid of the IJF and Hope House Children's Hospice. I needed to get home. At Ascot I did bump into

Mrs Thompson of Cheveley Park Stud who told me she had put a bid in for Kyllachy's racing plate and it was in the post. So I was quite keen to see her bid. Mrs T is a very nice lady and I have a lot of time for her. I am always pleased for her when I see those familiar red with a white sash and blue cap colours pass the winning post in front.

In the post on my return from Ascot was a £70 cheque from David and Helen Hodgson for their BBQ tickets, a £100 cheque as a donation from David Wosskow with his BBQ tickets returned, as unfortunately he had to go into hospital on that day. David was a lively participant at our previous year's BBQ and he was also at the recent Timeform Dinner. I hoped his problems were not serious and he was soon well again. It's typical of David's kindness to send the tickets back and to donate the £100. Simon Sherwood, the Hereford trainer, kindly sent me £50 for tickets as did the Kinross trainer Lucinda Russell both with nice messages. Linda and Geoff Lucas kindly sent me a cheque for £100 for the raffle tickets they had sold and inside was a note wishing us well on the day. Reducing our aim to £13,622. Great!

Sure enough, our friendly postman dropped the letter from Mrs Thompson, true to her word, with a staggering £5,000 bid for the Kyllachy plate on behalf of herself and her husband, David. What a result! Aren't there some kind folk about? That generous boost greatly reduced our target figure. I couldn't see that £5,000 being bettered on the day. I must say our target was looking good.

On Friday 20 June, I arranged a meeting with Jimmy Andrews, our top BBQ man, to arrange additional food to the hog roast that we need to cater, such as; sausages, burgers, salmon, salads, potatoes, sweets, etc., also plates, chairs tables and the like. Jimmy's a good man who really enjoys helping any worthwhile cause. With him he also brought £280 for BBQ tickets he sold, shaving a further slice off our target to £13,442.

Later in the afternoon, in between televised races from Ascot, Jo Bower from Creature Comforts, our sponsors, came to arrange the order and format and brochure with me. Jo, and our Jo and I shouted the Cheveley Park Stud filly Russian Rhythm home in the Group One Coronation Stakes, where the winner collected £156,600. After Mrs T's kind bid on the Kyllachy plate, I hoped someone was looking down on her and she was being rewarded for her generosity. Jo Bower also gave me a further £100 and the stubs for the raffle tickets she had sold leaving the score at £13,342 to go.

Saturday, on the final day of Royal Ascot, the old Cork and Orry six-furlong sprint, was renamed The Golden Jubilee Stakes. I sincerely hoped Henry Candy's flying machine, Airwave, did well. She was only a three-year-old but what an engine she had! The postman must have been kicking on today to get finished to watch Royal Ascot on the box, as he was early. Leaving us three cheques, one for £200 from Pat O'Grady trainers, David Wintle and John Norton both sent £50 for raffle tickets accompanied by a nice letter from John, which reduced our figure to £13,042. No chance of Jo and I watching Royal Ascot on the box, as I was to meet Rob Hughes, who owns a stud in Shropshire and bred Mind Games. He sensibly kept a share in the horse throughout his racing career. Mind Games, whose stable name was 'Dennis', was a very good horse, being champion three-year-old sprinter, and from two

-to-four-years old won seven races; the Brocklesby, the Norfolk Stakes Group Three, the GRP Massey Stakes, the Temple Stakes Group Two, the Palace House Stakes Group Three (twice), and the Listed Fieldmarshall Stakes. A kinder, sounder, good-looker would be hard to find. The meeting with Rob at 4.30 at the Tern Hill Hall Hotel was to view the lots I was to auction at the Hall's Midsummer Night's Charity Ball in the evening.

Travelling down we listened to the Royal Meeting on Radio 5. Delighted that Tim Easterby's horse, Fayr Jag, won, or should I say dead-eated, but I was really sorry my nap of the meeting, Airwave, got beaten by the Australian horse Choisir. The same horse won the Kings Stand Stakes on the Tuesday ridden by Johnny Murtagh, the first horse to pull off the sprint double for eighty-three years. The Ball had been arranged in memory of the Shropshire Gentleman's Clubs late chairman, David James, who sadly passed away the previous August. David's two favourite charities were the IJF and Hope House, a local hospice for children. Imagine what it must be like for the kid's parents when they take them to the hospice knowing it's a 90% certainty that they won't be coming out again. The event MC was John Morris, the retired International cricketer, who played his domestic cricket for Derbyshire, Durham and Nottinghamshire. John was more famous for being David Gower's co-pilot flying over the wicket in Queensland than for his cricket. I'm not trying to compare John with Eddie the Eagle, but he was the bowler when Brian Lara scored his world record first class score of 501 in 1994.

Some 160 people attended the ball that was held in a huge marquee, the ladies in long gowns, the gents in evening suits. Ball was the appropriate word. There was an Abba tribute band playing which was exceptionally good. Everyone had a ball and carried on dancing well into the night. No doubt a lot of people would remember it for a long time. I didn't know David James, but if he had been looking in he would have been pleased at what he saw. A class act where on account of Rob and his team's sterling efforts, the two deserving charities received over £5,000 each.

On the Monday, Sarah York brought a dozen bottles of very good mixed wine that her husband, Colonel Eddie York, sent for our auction. Sarah also brought a £35 cheque from Rita Myatt of Evelyn Stud for her entry ticket. Also in the post was a £70 cheque from Malton trainer Tim Etherington for raffle tickets. Steve Curtis, one of Mick Easterby's owners sent his BBQ tickets back, because of business commitments, he couldn't make it. It was a shame as Steve is a fun loving fellow who would have enjoyed his day with us, but the generous man that he is, still sent us his £70 cheque.

Chapter Eleven

Tickets and a Dickey Bird

•

A few years ago at a Malton Open Day, Steve Curtis and Mick Easterby were dancing on a trailer at his yard while I was singing 'The Jolly Farmer', a right laugh and it was shown on the racing channel. Some man is Mick. Things were looking good, £12,837 was the current figure.

In the post on Tuesday was the first bill we have had for some time. It was for £82 from Frame Plus for the framing of the three prints of Stalbridge Colonist (Stan Mellor), Night Nurse (Paddy Broderick) and Makaldar (David Mould), which Karen Hatton had dug up from our IJF office archives for our auction and raffle. However, on a brighter note there were two other cheques to compensate. One for £100 from Auriol Robinson. Auriol is Walter Wharton the ex-trainer's sister, and no mean point-to-point rider in her day; the cheque was for raffle tickets she had sold. The second cheque was from one of Sharon Murgatroyd's carers, Shirley Marshall, also for raffle tickets. Leaving the total target at £12,769. I noticed in the the eleven-times champion jockey, Pat Eddery was to quit racing at the end of the season. Pat is the second most winning jockey in British racing, who at this time had ridden no less than 4,586 winners. Pat rode his first winner Alvaro in Britain for Michael Pope.

Pat rode some of the greats in his time. Horses he rode that were voted Horses of the Year were, Grundy 1975, Pebbles 1985, Dancing Brave 1986 and Bosra Sham in 1996. Riding fourteen British Classic winners in total, I thought he would have ridden on for another few years. He was only fifty-one and hand on heart, I can say he was riding as well as ever. In fact, the Maestro himself, Lester Piggott, said when he was asked to pay Pat a tribute, 'Pat has had a great career as a jockey, I can't understand why he's giving up when he's so young; he must have made more money than I did!' Some people would have you think that Lester had to have a smile first thing in the morning to get it over with. Like the enclosed card I can assure you that's not true; he was always amusing.

Eleven times champion flat jockey, Pat Eddery.

> Start each day with a smile
>
> and get it over with.

In the early 90s, when we trained a lot of two-year-olds so that we didn't have to run two or more in the same race, we had them fit early on and well schooled. To avoid them clashing, we would run them all over the country as in those days every racecourse was compelled to stage a two-year-old race every day of their meet. Nowadays, racecourses are encouraged not to run early two-year-old races on their cards. God knows why, because lots of people love two-year-old races. I certainly did. When John Carroll was up north, Pat stepped in on lots of occasions to ride our youngsters in the south. In doing so, he rode quite a number of our early winners. He was a most honest jockey regarding explanations. One day at Bath he finished second on one of our youngsters and when he came back into the paddock, unlike most jockeys when they cock-up and get beat and blame everything and anyone except themselves, Pat said, 'That one got away Jack. We should have won.' He thought he had gone a stride too fast and cut its throat. Although I could also say Pat also rode winners for us that we should not have had, if we had not had Pat on our side. A very strong, focused, hungry and determined jockey. I knew whatever he did in the future he would make a go of; he gives it 110% every time.

In thirty years of training, I am ashamed to say we have never trained a Group One winner. The King's Stand Stakes at Royal Ascot used to be a Group One race. However, the year we won it with Bolshoi in 1999 the race had been demoted to Group Two status. Pat rode our Distinctly North in 1990, second to Lycius in the Group One Middle Park Stakes at Newmarket. The same year he rode Sid (Distinctly North) again second to Mac's Imp who was trained by

We're smiling – Jack and Lester Piggot.

Bill O'Gorman in the Group One Heinz 57 Stakes at the now defunct Phoenix Park racecourse in Ireland. The following year we took rather a brave step in running our two-year-old, Paris House, in the Nunthorpe Group One Stakes at York. Paris House was the first two-year-old to have run in the Nunthorpe in thirty-four years. Our man was ridden by Darryl Holland when he was an apprentice to Barry Hills. Paris House finished second to Sheikh Albadou.

The same horse went on to win the Group I Vernon Sprint at Haydock Park and the Grade One Breeders'

Cup sprint in America. Who rode the winner? Pat Eddery. As it happens, Lyric's Fantasy trained by Richard Hannon won the race the following year. In 1994, Paris House was flying, winning the Group Two Temple Stakes at Sandown, despite carrying a penalty for winning the Group Three Palace House Stakes at Newmarket. On both occasions he beat Loch Song. When the pair met at Goodwood in the King George Stakes, our man finished second, beaten by just a head to the flying filly giving her eleven lbs. When they met again in the Nunthorpe, with me thinking we had a really good chance of training our first Group One winner, Paris House ran out of his skin but finished second to the Ian Balding-trained-lady, Loch Song. Our fellow didn't run after that as he retired to Corbally Stud in Ireland and he did himself very well by siring lots of decent winners. Loch Song went on and won two Prix de L'Abbayes and ended up Champion sprinter. When we were in the second enclosure in York, congratulating Jeff Smith, Loch Song's owner, I said to him, 'When these two flying machines go to stud why don't we let them meet up?' Jeff said it would be a great idea, but unfortunately, it turned out to be a damp squib and it never happened. I would have loved to have the chance to train the offspring from those two, no doubt the Balding family would have too. Paris House could catch pigeons, but on her day Loch Song was so fast she would have caught 'Bin Laden'!

I bought Paris House, by Petong out of Foudroyer, at the Newmarket Yearling Sales for 5,000gns. Those days we bought lots of yearlings on stock, but mainly they were owned by the Midland Bank and the Sales Companies, until I sold them. You could say we were sleeping partners so to speak. Only they often sent me fan mail trying to reduce their commitment. One day, out of the blue, Peter Chandler the chef from the Paris House Restaurant, Woburn Abbey Estate, rang. He asked me if he could come to the yard and buy a horse

Paris House was so fast and was so unlucky to keep on having to race Loch Song. Paris House was so fast she could have caught Bin Ladin.

from me. We arranged a day for him to view some of our yearlings for him to choose from. I put six of them in the price range 4,000–10,000gns in nice paddock sheets and had our staff to lead them round our main yard, so I didn't influence him in his choice. I invited Peter to choose one without telling him which was which or the price of them. I wasn't concerned in making a profit, I wanted to train winners and the benefits arrive when winners arrive. The horses would stay in the yard for me to train. I sold them all for the sales price plus their expenses and keep. Peter reminded me he was a chef and wouldn't have a clue, he just wanted a horse as an interest because he liked racing and wanted to get involved by owning a racehorse. Therefore, I said, 'You may as well take the grey fellow, at least you will have a fair chance of recognising him in the paddock and in the races being a grey!' It's now history.

Paris House was an exceptionally good horse and won a stack of good races which included, the Group Two Flying Childers, the Newbury Super Sprint, the Group Two Temple Stakes, the Group Three Palace House Stakes and others. Sold, he then went to stud sound as a bell for a considerable amount of money where, at this stage, he had sired the winners of around 350 races.

On Thursday 26 June, one of our old owners, Jack Clayton, said he couldn't make it to our shindig. Therefore he sent his tickets back but also donated a cheque for £100. Mrs Terri Herbert-Jackson and trainer, Linda Ramsden, both sent their £50 cheques and raffle stubs. Jo went to Thirsk races this day to put the tack on Alan's runners and whilst there Peter Dunn, the former jump jockey who now drives a horse ambulance at the races, gave her £60 for raffle tickets he had sold. This reduced our target to £12,609.

The Vespa scooter PX125 which Bob Bowden, the director of Alphamerica Red Onion Ltd, gave us for our auction was delivered. While it was in transit going to the launch at Doncaster racecourse, it somehow got a scratch on its mudguard. Bob had it returned to its maker to have it put right. What a star! It was absolutely brilliant and so kind of Bob to donate such a valuable prize.

Friday 27 June, Jo and I were working on finalising all the required information for the brochure. Time was getting on and it would take two weeks for the printers to produce, which gave us just two weeks to get the copy to them. Owen Watson-Wilson sent his £70 cheque for his additional two tickets he had ordered, chiselling the required figure to £12,539.

We had a bit of luck with our filly Simianna going in at Newmarket, not winning out of turn, as this was her first win for two years since she won the valuable Joseph Heler Lily Agnes Stakes at Chester. For all that, she had been a dream to own. The filly had run some great races in defeat, always knocking on the door. In fact, in her three seasons racing for us she had only on two occasions not had a pay day. This was her fourth win in all. When Alan bought her for us as a yearling, bred by the Cobhall Stud, she cost just 1,000gns at Doncaster sales.

John and Tim Conway, David Sleater, an MBE for his charity work, Noel Delaney and Jo and I are the remaining members of the Monkey Partnership which we started years ago at Cockerham. John Conway looks after the accounts department, we each put into the account £1,700 to start with when Simianna was first bought. The cost of buying her and keep also had to come

OI Oyston on duty at a Cockerham open day.

out of that. Since then she had given us no end of fun running at all the big race meetings up and down the country, including finishing fourth at Royal Ascot as a two-year-old and also as a three-year-old. Her win and place prize money to that date was £56,687 – not bad for a grand!

On our return from Newcastle on the Pitman's Derby day, Saturday, where we had been lunch guests of Brian and Donna Robe, looking in the post-box there was quite a bit of junk mail and a £70 cheque from Kevin and Debbie Darley for their entry tickets for our day. £12,029 to go. When Kevin comes to our BBQs, I would kid him on and tell him he couldn't have a ride on our old Ollie. When Kevin did on the odd occasion ride him at home, the old horse took the juice out of him something rotten, as he did when most jockeys rode him work! One day, when hacking to the start of the gallop, the old boy nipped

Ollie at Newmarket the day in 1988 that Princess Anne rode him.

off with KD. Ollie also bolted in the piece of work he did. When Kevin finally pulled him up, he gave himself a bit of a breather then hacked him back to where I was standing only to get carted off with him again, nearly knocking me over in the process! Kevin at this time was the Vice President of the Jockeys' Association of Great Britain. I thought he might have a word with his boss Michael Caulfield to set up a 'Dodgy and Dangerous Ride Committee!' Having said that, Kevin rode the horse to win eleven times and like us all loved him to bits. It was just Ollie having his bit of fun.

See the photo (previous page) of Ollie being led up by his groom Wally Hagger at Newmarket the day Princess Ann rode him to finish fourth in a Lady Jockey's race in 1988, and me on him at one of our Open Days at Cockerham. The punters loved him, especially the kids. During the auction a little fellow asked if I could bring Ollie back and give him a ride on him.

On the last day of June, Jo and I went to meet Jo Bower at Rufford Park in Nottinghamshire, mainly to list up the auction and raffle prizes and to put the finishing touches to the brochure's format and in what order things should run, just about a full day's job! When we left, after a fair bit of juggling, thankfully everything was ready to go to the printer, who now required about ten days from start to finish. On our return, Preston trainer Eric Alston and his wife Sue had sent a cheque for £170 for their BBQ tickets and their 100 raffle tickets they had sold. Leyburn trainer Karl Burke sent £120 for his BBQ and raffle tickets. Colin Stud at Newmarket also forwarded a £30 cheque for raffle tickets they had bought reducing our target figure to £12,149.

Sam and Carole were getting married on 3 August. Sam phoned his wheelchair-bound mate Charlie Williams, who he met in Tenerife quite a few years ago, to invite him to the wedding. Sam had been going out with Carole for a few years then and Charlie was full of wit and a very funny man. He said to our Sam, 'Are you sure you're doing the right thing? There's still time to get out of it!' Charlie is a very knowledgeable man, very near unbeatable in the pub quizzes answering general knowledge questions. When the programme 'Who Wants to Be a Millionaire' comes on the box 'yer man Charlie' has most of them answered before the four options appear on the screen. Charlie is also a

Neither could this little fellow. He asked if I would bring Ollie back so he could have a ride on him.

very confident fellow who would not crack-up under pressure and would be an ideal candidate for the show. Everyone tells him he should get on the programme, as he would take some beating. Apparently he has been trying to get on it for years – all to no avail.

When Charlie rang me I asked him, 'When are we going to see you on the telly trying to be a millionaire then?' He told me he would love to go on the show, as he honestly thought he could do well. I cracked up when he said if he got stuck answering any of the questions, he could rely on Sam in the audience coughing-up the answers.

July 1 arrived. Jo went with George Duffield to Hamilton to watch our two-year-old, Presumptuous, run. I stayed at home to meet Jim Gale from the Doncaster Racing School as I told him he could have Archie (Palacegate Touch) for the youngster to be taught to ride on. Honestly, I believed he missed being ridden out. Now he had had a nice break he wanted to be off again. Jim liked him so I made arrangements for the horse to go for a while to see how he got on. He could always come back if he didn't suit. I couldn't see that happening, as he was a mega ride and a real gentleman to boot. Although I knew I would like him back in a couple of years. I didn't want him being ridden too much when he's an old man.

Anne Duffield had just rung up inviting me down for a meal that night, Jo and George would go straight to the Duffield's from the races. GD rode three winners the previous night at Musselburgh and the first at Hamilton the following day, so we have a good chance of eating meat at our meal! The post was again kind to us. John Berry, the Newmarket trainer, sent his cheque for £50 for the raffle tickets with a nice letter. Another cheque arrived for £32 from the Carluke trainer Ian Semple for tickets sold. One of our old owners Scarborough Estate Agency boss, Norman Jackson, who thrives on a bit on fun, not only sent a cheque for £50 for the tickets he sold, but also sent £100 donation. Our figure now stood at £11,917. We were getting there.

It took Jo Bower and me about half the following day to finalise the format of the brochure, exchanging many faxes and answering each other's phone calls. The lots in the order we auctioned them on the day. We tried to mix them around, and, as you can see in the picture of brochure (page 250), there are some good items all donated by some very kind people and the same can be said about the raffle. They would be drawn in order as they are printed on the sheet, rather than in order of value.

John Brown, the boss of William Hill Ltd, sent his cheque for BBQ tickets. Mr M J Sakal sent a £10 cheque for raffle tickets. Eric Wheeler the Oxfordshire trainer, sent a £50 cheque and his raffle stubs, (Eric and I were Officers Grooms in the Kings Troop RHA and great mates), Norman Chamberlain the County Durham trainer also sent £50 reducing our target to £11,737.

Friday 4 July arrived and there were only 16 days to countdown! Andrea O'Keefe, Jed's wife, rang up to ask me to send her another 10 books of raffle tickets to sell. The ones we had sent her sold like hot cakes. Chris Morris, one of our old girls who looked after our first Group winning sprinter, Bri Eden, and is married to the ex-jockey Stuart, rang to ask if we had a couple of tickets she could buy for the BBQ. In the post were quite a few cheques. There were four £10 cheques from Marlborough Electronics, Mr PH Bells, MG Podmore and MP Bowing, one of Mark Tompkin's owners, with an enclosed complimentary card and a £10 note.

Roger Charlton, of the famous Beckhampton stables, sent his £50 cheque, one of our many former apprentices, Alan Daly, sent a £150 cheque along with a £50 cheque from Patrick Harold for the tickets he had sold. A real star is Alan, nothing is too much trouble for that man. Alan was just the same when we were working the horses. If ever there was an odd horse left that needed riding out, Alan always volunteered, no matter how many horses he had ridden work on or how late it was. For me he can't ride enough winners.

Margaret Roberts from Lancashire sent two BBQ tickets back with a donation of £25. This reduced our total to £11,412. On Saturday 5 July, it was Eclipse day at Sandown and I watched Luca Cumani's Falbrav beat the favourite Nayef, while The Bride went to Beverley to saddle up for Alan. The postman was really good to us this day, he left us a £70 cheque from Tim Palin, of the Middleham Park Racing Club, and an £85 cheque from Ferdy Murphy of Wynbury Racing Stables. I knew we had a hiccup or misunderstanding with Ferdy on the BBQ tickets the previous year. However, I can assure you there was no better man to rally round a cause than Ferdy Murphy.

Helen Davey, the young lady who ran the northern marathon in aid of the St James' kids, also runs in the Flora London Marathon in aid of Rehab UK, the brain injury charity and whose Vice President is Claire Balding. It was nice to see that the racing world had got behind Rehab UK by providing challenge teams of runners from the yards of John Dunlop and Venetia Williams. To raise money for Helen's ordeal, our village committee put on a hot-pot supper and sing-along. The food was prepared by none other than our local masterchef, Ian Vipoint. The music was provided by Tony Hill on guitar and Lily Wright on the fiddle. I was the MC and auctioneer for the night and our aim was to raise a couple of grand for our star runner. When I asked Ferdy Murphy if he would like to buy a couple of tickets for the event that cost £7.50 each; no hesitation: 'I will take six and bring a few of the lads and have a bit of fun.' There was a great deal of support for the effort to make it a success and everyone enjoyed themselves, and Rehab UK benefited by £2,640. Also in the post that day was another £15 from D A and L M Askew, some of Ferdy's owners. Two further cheques from Miss MA Lake and Mr Loakey for raffle tickets. A cheque to the value of £50 from the Welsh trainer Bryn Pailling with a nice letter, £10 from RM Levitt, a chartered accountant from Newmarket, £30 from Adrian Parr, Colin Mandle of the old Red Shirt Brigade sent a cheque for £50. PM Rickett one of Mark Tompkins' owners sent a cheque for £10. My old pals Frank and Val Dever sent £80, Anne Harris, the wife of the late trainer Jimmy, sent her £100 cheque for tickets, Dennis Aitall and Jane Bailey both sent in their £10 cheques and Henry Brown of Peterborough forwarded £20. My old King's Troop army buddy, trainer Barry Hills, sent £200 for the Mark Huskinson cartoon I sold him at York with a further £50 for raffle tickets and a few words from Desi Wylde, his secretary, on a compliment slip where he asked if I would send two more books of raffle tickets, which I did.

Lots of lads, racing and sports' people, were posted to the King's Troop for their National Service. Whilst I was there in 1959, Cliff Jones of Tottenham Hotspur and other footballers were there, but not riding the horses. They worked in the stores and on transport. Until 24 October 1947, the King's Troop was called the Riding Troop. Its name changed when King George VI visited the barracks at St John's Wood. As the King was very proud of the outfit, over lunch in the Officer's Mess that very day the troop was re-named, The King's Troop RHA. On the death of His Majesty in 1952, as a tribute to her father, Her Majesty Queen Elizabeth II decreed that the title should remain during her reign.

The cream of the whole British Army – the King's Troop Royal Horse Artillery.

We were proud to do our National Service in the King's Troop. The photos show the horses and more recently a reunion at the barracks of St John's Wood.

Reunion at the King's Troop barracks in St John's Wood, London.

When Jo returned from Beverley, she handed me £150 in cheques and cash that Sue Townsend, Alan's secretary and partner, had given her for raffle tickets that she had sold to Alan's owners. Ticket-wise it was the biggest post-bag to date which added up to £837, leaving us with a near guaranteed target to reach, £10,577.

Ian Bolland, our Cockerham accountant, is a great fellow who sees humour in most things. When I wrote my *One to Go* book a few years ago, Ian heard that we trustees of the IJF had been to lunch with the Queen Mother. He takes the juice out of me something rotten as often as possible. He invented a myth, which I included in my book, that hearing of my impending retirement, the Queen Mother visited the yard and I was showing her round the stables when a two-year-old let go with a resounding fart that registered eight on the Richter Scale. As it rattled the windows and frightened the dogs I just could not ignore it. 'Oh dear,' I said to the Queen Mum, 'I'm sorry about that, Ma'am.' 'Think nothing of it, Jack,' she said, 'I thought it was one of the horses!'

Trainer Mark Johnston had written a weekly column in the *Racing Post* for quite some time, often in a contradictory and opinionated manner. However, over the past few weeks, the writer David Ashforth had vigorously fought for a better deal for stable staff welfare and it had rattled the Middleham Maestro's cage. So much so that he had thrown his toys out of the pram and packed up writing for the newspaper. Below is a letter Ian Bolland sent me, which he said he sent to the to publisher. However, I didn't see it appear, so more than likely they didn't print it although I couldn't see their crime writer Graham Green bottling out.

The Editor
Dear Sir,

JUDGEMENT DAY

I greet the news that Mark Johnston is to retire from his column in the *Racing Post* with a mixture of emotions, starting with sheer delight and working upwards.

It reminds me of a rumour I heard some time ago concerning the great and the good. On Judgement Day, God decides to take only the greatest examples from every walk of life and eventually He turns his attention to racing. For the jockeys, He calls up John Francome, a great rider but also a man of honesty and wit; for the owners, He calls up Jim Lewis, a man with passion for life and passion for his horses; God turns to the question of trainers, but as He starts his announcement Mark Johnston strides up the gilded stairway.

God pauses, confused; 'Er... I'm sorry Mr Johnston, I was just about to make the award to Mr Jack Berry...'

'Never mind all that,' snaps Mr Johnston, 'What the hell are You doing in my chair?'

Yours sincerely, Ian A Bolland

On Sunday, 6 June 2003, I wrote to Dr Bruce McClaine, the northern race-course doctor, to make sure he was attending our day as promised. One has to take precautions nowadays. You never know if some berk might fall in the pond or get bitten by one of our dogs and need Bruce's assistance. After our first Open Day at Cockerham, as mentioned earlier, I try to do everything by the book now.

On Monday 7, at around 10.20 p.m,. I had just finished my tea after the IJF meeting I attended in London. For sure, there were some sad cases, but hopefully after that day's meeting, a lot of their lives will have improved considerably. I was just going through the mail. Midlands trainer, Norma Macauley, sent a £50 cheque for raffle tickets. Ex-jockey now saddler, Peter, son of Frank Dever, sold £85 worth of tickets and enclosed his cheque reducing our target to £10,440. The next day in the post were four cheques. The first was from Anne Barlow, the wife of Midland racing steward, George, the very lady from whom I bought a Jack Russell pup we called Spud. He was now fourteen weeks old and so old fashioned it wasn't true. We love him to bits. Thankfully, so did all our other dogs! He's seen below helping me to do a bit of stone-walling. I have put so much stone walling around our house and the horse walker, some of our locals now call me Hadrian! Anne sent a £20 cheque for tickets she had sold. The second cheque came by registered post and it was for £80 from Owen Brennan, the Worksop trainer. The other two £10 cheques and stubs came from NA Fuller and Roalco Ltd, owners of Mark Tompkins. When we told Mark Tomkin about our event a few weeks earlier on the phone, he said, 'send me 400 tickets and I will put a book in with each of my owners' bills' hence the reason we were receiving so many cheques for £10. Mark you're a star. The figure to reach was now £10,320.

Giving Spud a cuddle whilst stone walling at home. I have put up so much walling that some locals call me Hadrian.

Jed O'Keefe's wife, Andrea, had really got behind us to make a go of our day and she rang to ask for a further ten books to sell. She was doing a brilliant job! Phil Burn, the man who hires out toilets, came to work out where to put the portable toilets and how many we need to cater for everyone. Phil said six would be enough. Half would go in the field shelter for the colts and geldings and the other in the field below the house for the fillies and mares. Both places had been painted out only the previous week so I knew they should be fine.

We went to Catterick on Wednesday 9 July, a glorious sunny day and most enjoyable. After the last race, I waited for George Duffield to change from his racing gear as I was giving him a lift home. Anne was at Newmarket. Ian Watkinson, the old jump jockey who went around the tracks when I did and now had a racehorse transport business, said to me; 'By Jack, this place brings back memories to us, don't it mate?' One of his tales he told, as Ian was in great form and I could hardly get a word in was this: in the days when you had to declare jockeys no earlier than three-quarters of an hour before the race, at Catterick, Freddie Milburn, a northern trainer, asked Ian to ride a horse in the Novice Chase and maybe one in the Handicap Hurdle. Well the chaser was a bit of a bone breaker, but Ian badly wanted to get going and also wanted the easy ride on the hurdler, so he jumped the chaser off up with the leaders, gave it a really brave and positive ride and got the horse into the race and jumping well, getting a great tune out of the horse. Then they jumped the last open ditch where the poor horse collapsed and died of a heart attack. When Ian came back to tell Milburn how sorry he was, he asked 'Do I ride your hurdler in the last, Mr Milburn?' 'No you don't,' he snapped, 'Roy Edward, a proper jockey who rode a Champion hurdler winner, rides and he will more than likely win.' Although Ian had finished riding for the day, he stayed at the races to watch the horse run in the last to see what he had missed. It only finished in the middle. Ian couldn't resist going up to Mr Milburn saying, 'Your horse

A bit more of my stone handiwork around our horse walker at home.

didn't run all that well, Guv'nor, he only finished in the middle. Roy Edward wasn't that good, I could have done just as well.' 'Maybe you could, but he didn't kill the 'effing horse though, did he?'

Quite a few cheques arrived in the post again. When I sent the raffle tickets to the trainers to sell on, Carol Pipe, the Somerset trainer, Martin's wife, said that like Mark Tompkin she would put a book in with their owners' bills and ask them to send their money direct to me, hence a lot of the £10 were from Mark's or Carol's punters. Mr Frewen, one of Martin's owners even donated £100 to the fund and enclosed a few nice words, as did two of Martin's big owners, Peter Deal and David Johnson. Isn't it rewarding and all worthwhile when someone as busy as Martin Pipe can write and send a letter as he did with the enclosed tickets to his owners. I know the man has some who knock him, but he has come a long way since he sent out his first winner Hit Parade to win a selling hurdle at Taunton in 1975 when ridden by the now Dumfriesshire trainer, Lennie Lungo. As a forty-five-year-old, Martin was the youngest trainer to train 1,000 winners. Catch the Cross in 1990 at Kempton Park and there was a lot more to come. When himself and AP McCoy teamed up, they were a hard act to beat. If he had ever decided to do a Vincent O'Brien and get rid of his jumpers to concentrate on the flat, I would have had just one word for the flat trainers, 'Beware!'

Beryl McCain, wife of Don, trainer of the famous Red Rum, forwarded a £32 cheque for raffle tickets. Five separate £10 worth of raffle ticket money arrived including one from BA and EM Kilpatrick all the way from Jersey. That would be a long way to take the ton of wood shavings if they win it! Also, a cheque from Chris Fairhurst, the Middleham trainer, and another from Huntley Forster Association for entry tickets. Brian Robb gave me a further cheque for £70 for tickets for Derek Shaw, who trains his horse. Unfortunately, we had to write a cheque out from the funds account for £109 to Makro of Teesside, as Jo went there to buy some dishes for the sweets, serviettes and plastic knives and forks as we had decided against hiring as we did at the previous year's BBQ. The balance to reach was now £10,017.

I love to attend the July meeting at Newmarket and especially to see the July Cup which, for me, is one of the best races in the flat calendar. Therefore, when Jo Bower arranged our final meeting to see on screen how the brochure would look and to make the very last additions and alterations at the Creature Comforts stand at the National Stud Fair, I chose the Thursday of the famous meeting to enable Jo and I to see the Darley Stallion Parade, for which we had an invite, before racing. At the parade the stallions looked absolutely superb. What a pleasure to see so many great horses on the same day, such as Polish Precedent, champion miler and sire of Pilsudski, Singspiel, father of Moon Ballad, In the Wings, a famous son of Sadler's Wells, Cape Cross another champion miler, Xaar who was a very fast two-year-old and a champion three-year-old leading first crop sire in France, Lord of Men, the unbeaten champion two-year-old Tobougg, Gimcrack winner Josr Algarhoud, Kings Best a great middle distance horse, Kayf Tara another by Sadler's Wells who merited a Timeform rating of 130. Noverre won and was placed in Group I races. Fantastic Light, Breeders' Cup Turf winner Diktat, son of Warning, and the old favourite Mtoto, even as a twenty-year-old he looked a picture and was still siring winners, Duke of York winner Lend a Hand, Mark of Esteem one of the highest-ever rated milers, Lomitas boasted 11% stakes winners to foals; a remarkable average, and the old fellow Machiavellian, sire of eight Group One winners. Except for Coolmore in Ireland, where on earth would you get to see better? It was a very hot day and Darley Stud as always looked after everyone very well with lots of food and drink. In fact, one of our former owners was there and when I saw him later at the races he definitely looked the worse for wear! Was it the complimentary drinks or was it the heat? On my return when I opened the mail, the trainer of Persian Punch and Desert Orchid, David Elsworth, kindly sent his £50 cheque along with twenty Christmas cards and envelopes with Desi and Persian Punch on for us to sell at our 'do'. The recently-retired flat jockey Lindsey Charnock sent a £70 cheque for tickets, we had two £20 cheques from Messrs Pipe and Stutt, and a £10 cheque from Mr KP Hall. Our target figure was now less than £10,000! In fact, it was £9,847. I couldn't have been more pleased.

It was York on Friday 11 July 2003, but I didn't go as, at the time, I had seemed to be doing more travelling than Alan Whicker. The postman left us £220 including a cheque for £45 for raffle tickets from one of our ex-owners Gino Bernacchi, who owned an Italian restaurant in Scotland. Bill Turner, the Sherborne trainer, sent £50 as did Epsom trainer, Simon Dow, both including nice messages. Simon is a game chap who loves a bit of fun. However, if he wants to race you for a little wager, don't take him on! In 1976, he was rated the top juvenile athlete over 800 metres in the UK. Tom and Nan Bibby our ex-owners and friends from Cockerham days, sent us a £70 cheque for two more tickets they had recently received and a further £50 for raffle tickets. Finally, Seamus O'Neill the ex-jump jockey sent £50 for his tickets which now reduced the required figure to £9,532.

It was Magnet Cup Day at York and what great racing it was on the box. I would love to have gone to York, but with our big day only nine days away, we had enough on getting things organised, but I did miss it. Our neighbour, fifty-six-year-old George Duffield, the oldest flat-jockey riding at that time, could still boot the horses home. He had a good day riding the first race winner on Sir Don for Dandy Nicholls and the second last race for his boss Sir Mark Prescott on First Order. My missus had a touch, having had a fiver each way on Far Lane which won at 7/1 and a fiver each way on Hugs Dancer at 11/2.

Brook Sanders, the Epsom trainer, sent her £50 with a nice letter. When Jo was a lady jockey a few years ago along with Brook, they had some fun. Brook was as hard as nails and a very good rider. She rode in the region of forty or so winners. My old mate Jonjo O'Neill sent the other £50 cheque that arrived and a nice complimentary letter. Newmarket trainer, Stuart Williams, clearly is not a fan of the IJF. In a letter he sent to me he said he didn't approve in what I was doing. It's his right to say what he thinks. Like our Alan says, even a broken clock is right twice a day.

At least he sent us the tickets back in plenty of time to sell on. I wondered how many of others went straight to the bin with all the junk mail we get these days. £9,432 was the current figure we were aiming at.

Brian and Donna Robe called in on their way back home from Chester races. Brian said he would get twenty-four bottles of wine delivered for our day on July 20, which would be a big help and take a bit of expense off John Stephenson who was sponsoring the alcoholic bottle tombola and the beer for the bar. Brian was always generous when helping charities. Recently when the Sunderland Echo launched their appeal in aid of Children of Courage, in support of Grace House Children's Hospice, he invited and paid for a party of us to see the show Chuckles for Charity show, held at the Empire Theatre in Sunderland. The cast included Frank Carson and Bobby Knoxall; they had the whole theatre in stitches. In addition to that, Bobby and the rest of the cast worked for nothing ensuring every penny went to the hospice.

On Monday 14 July, I didn't have time to wait for the mail. Jo and I set off to pick up the famous cricket umpire Dickie Bird at 4.30 a.m., to take with us to the charity cricket match where the Royal Household Cricket Club would play against Sir Michael Stoute's XI and Dickie would be umpire. When we arrived at Dickie's house, you could have mistaken it for Fort Knox. Every window had bars in diamond shapes so close a rat could not have got in, let alone a burglar! There was a metal cage-type folding door behind the front and back doors and lights and a camera were installed on the entrance. I didn't ask Dickie if he wore a belt and braces as well to make sure his pants didn't fall down! The day was very hot we had a good run down in the car, Jo drove and Dickie was in the front riding shotgun, as he didn't travel well in the back of a car. I didn't mind as I had a bit of a kip in the back. Dickie is a very interesting man and we had some great laughs. He tells a good tale. It was a good job Freddie Trueman couldn't hear some of them though. There didn't appear to be a lot of love lost between the pair of Yorkshiremen.

A rat would be hard pressed to get into Dickie Bird's house; never mind a burglar.

When we reached Windsor it was about 11.00 a.m., we were offered a Pimm's following our car inspection when the number plate was checked. There were quite a few people in attendance from the racing fraternity, e.g Lester and Sue Piggott, John and Lady Carolyn Warren, Harry Herbert, Chris and Anne Richardson of Cheveley Park Stud and many more. On the way down, Dickie told me he had just recovered from surgery to his eyes, they had been leaking and had became jellyfied. and As result, he lost his sight for a while. Jeremy Richardson at our IJF meeting the previous week told me my old mate Lester had just about lost his sight in one eye as it had been leaking like Dickie's. Dickie had never met Lester before, so I introduced them to each other and told Dickie to tell Lester who did his eyes so they could exchange notes to try and get the old-jockey's eyes sorted out, as he was clearly worried about them. For lunch we had a very nice BBQ inside a marquee. I was drawn on Prince Philip's table and it was great fun.

The Newmarket XI were Michael Stoute, Jeremy Richardson, Willie Haggas, Julian Wilson, Ed Dunlop, Willie Jarvis and a few others and assisted by Michael Holding, Graham Cowdrey and Rory Bremner. For the ladies who didn't want to watch the cricket, there was a tour of Frogmore House and the Royal Dairy. For security reasons only 100 guests were invited. Lunch was served at 1 p.m. and the cricket started at 2 p.m.` This was the ground's centenary year as it was opened in 1903, the same year the brothers Wilbur and Orville Wright tossed a coin in a field to see who would attempt the first manned flight.

Since then a lot of water has gone under the bridge, and the picturesque ground of the Royal Household Cricket Club has come a long way and grown from strength to strength. Matches are fought keenly and competitive sportsmanship is paramount. It was a brilliant game played in good spirit and on an extremely hot day. The Newmarket XI beat the home team by five wickets. Jeremy Richardson stumped particularly well, he was really sharp. Julian bowled well, but the star of the match was Michael Stoute despite carrying a fair bit of gut and looking in need of a race or two. He batted really well. When his team needed just three runs to win Michael hit the ball with some force to land a four and clinch the match.

At the auction, which was in aid of the IJF, four items were sold and realised £2,450; the main one being a big portrait of Lester in Charles St George colours which was bought by Geoff Ammas for £1,600. Lester and I gently took the picture out of the frame so Lester could sign it for Geoff. The auction was brilliantly conducted in a very light hearted manner by Rory Bremner who took the water out of Lester by saying, 'if you buy his portrait, put it through the business and claim the tax.' He also had a few good humoured 'pops' at the establishment. Planes flew over every ninety seconds or so and Rory said that they have had their house up for sale for thirty years, but on account of the noise they can't get any takers. Recently, in fact, it was nearly burnt down! He was so funny, but the Queen and the Duke took his humour as it was intended, in good spirit. Talking about our intended auction to Geoff Ammas, although he had no chance of coming all the way from Maidenhead, he very much liked the Derby scarf and the racing plate of Signorinetta and told me to put him a £2,000 bid on it and to fax him a list of the auction items. Needless to say I did.

Returning home and opening the mail, I found John Quinn, the Malton trainer, had sent a cheque for £50 as did trainer David Barron from Thirsk and the Melton Mowbray handler, Kevin Morgan. The target total now was £9,282. In the post on the same day was a letter I could have done without. It came from the North Riding Police, a speeding fine for £60 and three points on my licence. I picked it up when travelling to Beverley races recently as I passed through Bishop Burton village just a few miles before the racecourse at 42mph, following every other car going racing. As you can imagine, I mentioned a few choice words about those North Riding officers at the Duffield's BBQ the following day.

The next day's post thankfully didn't contain any more nasty letters. Michael Chapman returned his stubs and £100 cheque for tickets. Also Pat Hurley, the ex-jump jockey sent £20 and European Steel Sheets Ltd sent a £10 cheque – both for raffle tickets. Finally Peter Mason of Sporting Fine Art forwarded a £40 cheque also for raffle tickets he sold for us while in Ireland recently. This made the wanted figure now £9,112.

On Wednesday 16 July, Dave (J) and Dave Armstrong were busy putting up one of the pagodas and cutting the middle out of our paddock trees as they had grown very tall. I was sweeping, painting and generally tidying up until the afternoon when I had to go to Catterick races to pick up a cheque for £250 for the second year running in favour of the IJF. It was very kindly donated by the 5th Regiment Royal Artillery stationed at Catterick. Whilst there I was asked if I wouldn't mind signing a race card that was handed to me. The man asked if I would write a few words on it, as it was his wife's birthday and she was a great fan of mine in my riding days.

For the Injured Jockeys Fund benefit the Fifth Regiment Royal Artillery stationed at Catterick hold an annual raffle. For the second year I have been invited to receive the cheque on behalf of the IJF.

JB returning to the winning enclosure at Manchester Races in 1961 following a win on Happy Dene in the two-mile chase. The trainer, George Stanley leads the mare in.

One of my mounts she followed was Happy Dene, shown on the photo being led in after winning a two-mile chase at Manchester in 1961, by his trainer George Stanley. Note the crash helmet, no goggles or back pad.

'What's your wife's name?' I asked, and he told me, 'and how old is she?' 'Ninety,' he said. Now, here I was three years retired and people still asked me for autographs; it can't be bad. I said to the man who asked me, 'she possibly followed my mounts at Manchester, Birmingham, Bogside, Rothbury, Teesside or Woore, as there aren't too many people around who remembered that far back.' If they remember these meetings and me riding they are knocking on a bit. The other day I went to the doctor with chest pains. It's true, I said, 'Oh no, not yet, I haven't had our open day or finished my intended book on it.' The doc sounded my heart out, lungs, and blood pressure. Thankfully, I wasn't having a wobbler; he said it was indigestion. It probably started when I was a kid. There were eight of us youngsters in our house and we had to rush the food down to get a fair share of it. Then being in racing the rest of my life, riding and training, I gobbled the food down, often on the hoof, always in a rush. Looking at the instructions inside the packet of pills I picked up on prescription from the chemist, it read in the small print 'possible side effects; swelling of the breasts and being unable to get an erection.' What's new!

On my return from Catterick I went through the post. There was a lot if it. Wilma Burns sent £40 for raffle tickets as did Alan MacTaggart, the Scottish trainer; John K Brown, one of our ex-owners, sent £20 for raffle tickets. Brian Robb had been a wonderful help to us and sent a cheque for £50 for yet more raffle tickets he had sold. John Forrest of Bury in Lancs, sent £20 for raffle tickets. Miss Wilson from Doncaster also sent £30 cheque for her tickets. The ex-Warwickshire and England fast bowler, David Brown, sent a cheque with a few words on the back of a picture postcard of their good horse, Bolshoi, the winner of the Group Three Sandown Temple Stakes and the Group Two Kings Stand Stakes at Royal Ascot in 1998. I mentioned to Dickie Bird the previous day that Dave was a big friend of ours and he was coming to stay with us on Saturday ready for our 'do'. 'Be sure to remember me to him,' he said, 'Grand lad, Brownie.' We had plenty of drink in as he could down quite a fair drop. A good mate for my missus he was. Dave was by now the Chairman of the British European Breeders' Fund, of which I recently became a Trustee. Vicky Jones, the rep for Red Mills horse feeds and daughter of the late trainer Arthur

Jones, who sent out Merry Deal to win the 1957 Champion Hurdle forwarded a £50 cheque for tickets sold accompanied by a nice letter. Malton trainer Tim Easterby sent a cheque for £68 for raffle tickets. Tim received two entry tickets, but there was no cheque for them. It looked as though he probably wouldn't be coming, which was a shame, as I was looking forward to him being here. We could still hope. Johnny O'Hara sent £20 for the tickets he sold, he always does his bit for any cause we have going, a star man is Johnny. There was a card also stating I had to pay £1.14 and go and collect a letter from Northallerton Post Office. So I trudged off to pick it up, it being a cheque and stubs from Josh Gifford MBE the ex-champion jump jockey and recently retired trainer. He only put a second-class stamp on the envelope so it was 14p underpaid and the other £1 was for Revenue Protection. Mind you, that's not as bad. Former jockey, Richard Pitman, whose father certainly brought his son up to look after his money, once sent me a letter with a grubby stamp stuck on the envelope with Sellotape. Now that was mean, although I will admit I have been known to re-use unmarked stamps on occasions. The day's tally added up to £538, which brought our commitment to well below £9,000, at £8,574. The following morning Chicky Oaksey rang to say she had forgotten to give me the raffle ticket money and stubs at our last IJF meeting but would send on the money. She thought our BBQ was last Sunday so she was sending it on first class.

In the news it said the Post Office lose something like four million letters a year. I wondered how many of those were carrying raffle tickets to the trainers and the like as we still had got quite a lot to come in. Cheques came today from Lambourn trainer Jamie Osbourne for £50 (Jamie was also a very good jump jockey; at the 1992 Cheltenham Festival he rode five winners), £80 from Linda Stubbs from Newmarket who sold them with the help of her apprentice jockey daughter, Christy. Mrs Cook from Hillside Racing kindly sent a £70 cheque. Finally, Merrick Francis, trainer and racehorse transporters and son of the famous thriller writer, Dick, sold £100 worth of tickets. £8,274 was the target figure now. We should have hacked it up to reach the £30,000 now. I thought: surely the rest can be made in the auction?

Three days left to go and it rained today, the first time for two weeks. Please God don't let it rain on Sunday!

Janet Sayer, our neighbour along with her daughter Catherine, came to collect jellies and sponges to make up some trifles. Dave (J) Bowes, Jimmy Andrews and John Tunstall were busy putting up the food pagoda. Jo had been last minute shopping. The wine that was donated by Brian was delivered. Dave (J) and I cut all the lawns and smartened up all gardens, there was not one weed in sight! We even bought plant feed to brighten all the little darlings up for Sunday. Charlie Dimmock would be proud of us. A few years previously Dave (joiner) Bowes had some rides as an amateur. The nearest he got to riding a winner was six of twenty-eight in a novice hurdle at Newcastle while riding Superscope. His first-ever ride was on a horse called Snow Meg that he trained himself on a permit in the two-and-a-half-mile Hurdle at Wetherby. During the race, at a hurdle round the back, a horse pushed him approaching the jump and carried him out. Instead of pulling the horse up

Dave thought he would have his money's worth. So he carried on in the race to finish. The Stewards had Dave in and didn't take kindly to his actions and fined him five sovs. You can tell that was a long time ago. Nowadays, it's £100 before they open their mouths.

A load of barley straw bales was delivered to use as seating. Dave (F) came up and told me he'd put 50 small bales of good seed hay on a trailer to auction and would bring it up on the Sunday morning. In addition to that, he would deliver it up to a fifty-miles radius free of charge. Doesn't it make you feel good when everyone gets their teeth into the job and they genuinely want to help? And it's very much appreciated.

Friday came and only two days to countdown. Honestly, we were not flapping, but we had a few problems. For starters the central heating oil had run out, which is a must for the Aga and water. The front porch got flooded with the previous night's storm and gale force winds. Linda Townsend sent us a pagoda, which took nearly half a day of Jo's and Dave (J) Bowes time to put up. It was flat to the floor with its legs bent and twisted. The car had been booked in to go to a Stockton garage as its rear end got scrubbed and bruised the Monday previous while reversing into a low wall I couldn't see. Presumably, the wall was there to trip up burglars in the dark at Dickie Bird's house, but it will cost a couple of hundred pounds to make it better.

That night, for the twelfth consecutive year, we were going to go to Pontefract evening races where we stage our Annual Red Shirt Night in aid of the IJF Holiday Fund. We had managed to get five of the six races sponsored and we also received from Pontefract clerk of the course Normal Gundill £30 for each runner in all the races. This night there were seventy-five declared to run. Linda Townsend, Chris and Antonia Deuters, Brett Oils, Messrs Weatherby and the Tote had very kindly sponsored our races. Three of our races were sprints and Pontefract had been very kind to us over the years and we had won many of this type of race there. Often people ask me, why do I always buy sprinting-bred and sharp-type yearlings? My answer to that is I found out horses got slow fast enough without me buying slow to start with. The journeymen or stayers, often stay in the same place too long for my liking. Before we set off, I opened the mail and there was lots of it! £115 from the Lambourn trainer Clive Cox, in the same letter were two more cheques for £25 and £20 from Sally Bruce and Jane Rawlinson for raffle tickets they had sold; £50 from Ian Wood the Lambourn trainer for his contribution. Andrea O'Keefe, Jed's missus, had been an absolute star for our cause, sent her £70 for BBQ tickets plus a stack of cheques from the O'Keefe's, their owners and friends who sold the raffle tickets. There was £90 from Jed, £10 from Mr A Henderson, £10 from Mr & Mrs Saddler, the same amount from Anne and Harry Roberts, Mr and Mrs Noule, Paul Chapman, Mr PT Blackburn and Mr B Hickson. £50 from CJ Lloyd and Miss Gough, £30 from M Chapman and, finally, £10 from Fluorocarbon Co. Ltd. Linda Redmond sent a £100 cheque for raffle. She's a lady we have trained for who had the good fortune to part own that Group-winning mare a few years ago, Bunty Boo, when trained by Brian McMahon. Sharon Murgatroyd sent a cheque for £20. Sharon wrote, amongst other books, *Jump Jockeys Don't Cry*, if you haven't read it, you should. In 1991, as a jump jockey in a man's world, she got an awful hand dealt to her when her mount fell with her at Bangor on Dee racecourse. She has been in a wheelchair ever since. A £100 cheque arrived from John Balding, the Doncaster trainer, himself an ex-jockey and a neighbour of ours when we first started training at

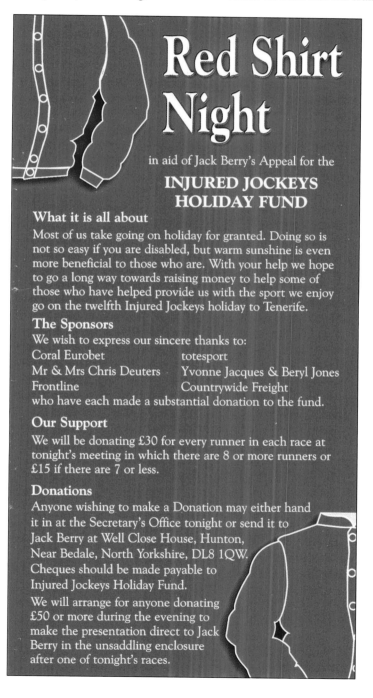

Red Shirt Night

in aid of Jack Berry's Appeal for the

INJURED JOCKEYS HOLIDAY FUND

What it is all about

Most of us take going on holiday for granted. Doing so is not so easy if you are disabled, but warm sunshine is even more beneficial to those who are. With your help we hope to go a long way towards raising money to help some of those who have helped provide us with the sport we enjoy go on the twelfth Injured Jockeys holiday to Tenerife.

The Sponsors

We wish to express our sincere thanks to:

Coral Eurobet	totesport
Mr & Mrs Chris Deuters	Yvonne Jacques & Beryl Jones
Frontline	Countrywide Freight

who have each made a substantial donation to the fund.

Our Support

We will be donating £30 for every runner in each race at tonight's meeting in which there are 8 or more runners or £15 if there are 7 or less.

Donations

Anyone wishing to make a Donation may either hand it in at the Secretary's Office tonight or send it to Jack Berry at Well Close House, Hunton, Near Bedale, North Yorkshire, DL8 1QW. Cheques should be made payable to Injured Jockeys Holiday Fund.

We will arrange for anyone donating £50 or more during the evening to make the presentation direct to Jack Berry in the unsaddling enclosure after one of tonight's races.

Arksey, near Doncaster. A very nice hard working bunch the Balding family, having worked in the game all their lives. Arthur, the father who sadly died at the age of eighty-one, rode the 1927 1,000 Guineas winner, Cresta Run. When he was a trainer he used to wear a very old battered trilby every time he went racing. When his son John took over, I think he carried on the tradition, but I haven't seen it for a while – it must have rotted!

Brian Robb, sent in yet another cheque for £20 accompanied by a further £30 cheque from Ms June Halliday for raffle tickets. Janice MacPherson who along with her husband Kenneth had horses in training with quite a few trainers and who owned a good handicapper, Periston View, when trained by Peter Calver, sent me a £10 cheque for a book of tickets she had received via Mark Tompkin. Jim Old, the Wiltshire trainer, enclosed £50 for raffle tickets. Paul Nicholls, the ex-jockey, and now one of our top racehorse trainers, sent a cheque for £40 and enclosed another from Mr and Mrs Baker for £12 worth of raffle tickets. Finally a £50 cheque arrived from Jim and Helen Goldie the Glasgow trainers. Which all added up to £972, leaving us with a target of £7,302 to reach.

Paul Jackson, the pro from Richmond Golf Club, rang to tell me that he was coming to our BBQ on Sunday, also that he won a golf bag in a tournament the previous day and would like to donate it to our auction; he would bring it down before the event. Our IJF northern almoner, Elaine Wiles, asked me if I would pick up Lex Kelly, one of our beneficiaries at Wetherby, on my way to Pontefract races as she was treating Lex to a meal before racing and wanted to have a chat with him. Lex was in really good form, which was great to see. The previous time, when I took him out to York for a bite a few months earlier, he was very depressed. He and I rode at the same time. Passing the old gallops of Wetherby Park the old boy reminisced, 'Do you remember all the trainers who used that Park to work their horses – Tommy Sheddon, Walter Wharton, Percy Vasey, Billy Newton, Tony Doyle, Donald Oates, and Jack Hanson. Wetherby was a great racing town in those days. That brings back memories,' he said. I agreed; it did. 'Remember old Harry Woodruff, what a character.' 'I remember him well, Lex, he couldn't pass a phone box. He used to carry change for the phone boxes in an Air Lingus bag.' 'That's right, 'eff knows who he used to ring.' That's how the craic went all the way to the races; it was great. At Pontefract, Norman Gundill, Clerk of the Course, told me there were more than 11,000 paying customers attending our Red Shirt Night, the second largest crowd ever for an evening fixture in the course's history, and what a good night it was too. Lots of the race-goers had donned a red shirt, which by now had become tradition. There was a great feel to the evening and the weather was very hot and sunny and could not have been better. Below gives a few details of the RS Night and what it was all about.

The fifth race was won by Begin the Beguine trained at Newmarket by Willie Jarvis. Rocky Reppin beautifully turned out by Claire Balding, trained by her father John, was judged the best turned out for which Claire received £30. Harry Grandfield gave Jo a cheque for £30 for raffle tickets and Elaine gave me £39 for the same, bringing our figure down to £7,233. At the end of racing as always, Norman Gundill invited sponsors, guests and friends up to

Looking after us for the past eighteen years on Red Shirt Night at Pontifract, waitress Iris Chapman.

his director's box for a good meal and chinwag about how the night had gone and so on. Iris Chapman, one of the waitresses there, has looked after us for years on Red Shirt night.

Saturday before countdown arrived, and the first call of the day was from Bill Robinson from South Africa who had been intending to come back to England for a holiday and whilst here was coming to our BBQ. Alas, he had to declare himself a non-runner with a vet's certificate as he had only come out of hospital the day before following a heart attack ten days earlier. This was a real shame Bill is a staunch follower of the IJF. A few years earlier before he retired to South Africa and was the landlord of the Talbot pub in Bishoptown, he rang me up. Over the years he had collected a full set of Twelve Grand National Martell Toby jugs, one for every year the brandy firm had sponsored the race and asked me if I would like to auction them off at an IJF event. Apparently, there were not too many made which make them quite rare. I arranged for them to be in a silent auction on the racing channel and they made no less than £40,000, bought by Robert Hitchens from Guernsey. Mr Hitchens, the generous man he was, told me to sell them again for the Fund, which we did at Lester's in London. For the second time round they realised a further £10,000 for the Fund. In view of Bill doing so much for us, it would have been lovely to see him again. I was hoping he would make a full recovery and looked forward to seeing him again the following year.

David Gandolfo, the West Country trainer, sent a cheque for £60 for raffle tickets, our Sam and his partner Carole came to stay and brought a cheque for £290, for raffle tickets they had sold, plus a £10 from trainer Henry Candy for raffle tickets. My old pal from Cree Lodge Stables at Ayr, Linda Perratt sent £150 cheque for raffle tickets and a £75 donation to the cause. Miss JM Saunders sent a £20 cheque and Mrs KE Ryecart sent £10 for tickets. Lyn

Bill Robinson 'glasses' a big supporter of the IJF. A few years ago, he gave me a set of twelve Martell Grand National TobyJugs to auction for the fund. They made £40,000.

Siddall, the Tadcaster trainer, sent her £50 cheque in. Mary Lofthouse, whose late husband Bob was a good supporter of the Fund and didn't forget our cause in his will either, sent a £25 donation. In the past I had trained a couple of horses for Bob. I must say Bob was the unluckiest owner, as his previous trainer, Jimmy Fitzgerald, agreed. The home-breds he sent were moderate. Horses often can't help being slow, but that couple abused the right; you couldn't have sighted them in a race with the telescope from Jodrell Bank! In sheer frustration Bob had a clear out and asked me to buy him a nice sharp yearling from Doncaster St Leger Sales. In all fairness, he allowed me a fair wedge to spend on it. Me thinking I would change Bob's luck as we have bought some class acts at those sales. Sod's Law. The yearling I bought for Bob wasn't one of my better buys. It turned out to be a good-looking, slow beggar. In fact, it was as slow as a boat. I could cry faster than it galloped. It never looked like winning a race. Poor old Bob would ring me up a couple of times a week to ask me how the crab was. I felt awful for the poor man.

Brian Rothwell, the Malton trainer, sent £135 for his three BBQ tickets and three raffle ticket books. Finally, Sir Alex Ferguson sent a £100 donation.

The target to reach was now £6,358. Mike Sayer, from next door, is a farm contractor and at this time of year he worked all hours God sent. To make it nice for the do, at his expense he slashed all the lane hedges, cut all the verges both sides, borrowed a road sweeper and swept the lane. It looked absolutely immaculate.

Chapter Twelve

The Big Day!

•

A new day arrived, 20 July 2003. The big day!

The previous night Jo and Colin Bower brought the pig and two spare legs of pork along with the portable oven to cook him and the legs in. Jo also brought the stack of brochures she had printed which were beautifully done; they looked great and said it all. At 2 a.m. we put the pig in the oven to start him cooking slowly, as we needed to start to carve at 1 p.m.. Although we stated on the entry tickets from 12p.m., our first arrival came at 10.20 a.m. and by 12.30, lots of people had arrived. Gary Gibson was doing a good job entertaining with his music. The smell of the pig being roasted around our party area was something different. It was absolutely brilliant. Everyone enjoyed the feast with not one single complaint. At about 2 p.m. just before we started the auction, we rounded up a few of the jockeys and ex-jockeys, Pat Hurley, John Carroll, Gerry Scott, Tyrone Williams, George Duffield along with Bob Kendal and we sang the 'Fields of Athemy', which put them in good spirits for the auction. It was, thank God, a beautiful warm sunny day. The bar was free

It's where it all happens – our spread at Hunton.

and there was a great buzz, as always. Doncaster Bloodstock auctioneer, Mouse White, was in great form.

Lot 15, Kyllachy Plate was top, at £5,000, beating Lot 31, the 1908 Silk Scarf and shoe, by £500. In Anne and George Duffield's house is a beautiful painting hung in the prime spot above the fireplace in the sitting room of Prince Fahid Salman, Sir Mark Prescott and George in the paddock at Royal Ascot before George went out to ride Last Second in the Coronation Stakes at Royal Ascot. Needless to say, it's George's pride and joy. I asked Anne if she would bring it to our place on the 20th in the middle of the auction when Mouse was selling. I would hold George's painting up and I was going to ask Mouse if anyone would start the bidding on this painting of these three at a tenner, as it was there to be sold and we didn't want to be hanging around too long trying for bids on the three old farts. It was for a laugh and to see the look on George's face when he saw it. Unfortunately, it didn't happen, as Anne couldn't get the chance to get it here without George noticing. Personally, I think Annie bottled it. George can easily get upset and start an argument with himself.

On the Sunday Jo and I were having a stroll around Catterick Sunday Market where I saw a very lifelike head of a hippopotamus, which floated on water, which I bought. That night we had been invited to the Duffield's for supper. I popped the hippo in his pond. Asking the old jockey, 'how's the fish doing mate?' 'Great,' he said. Of course the mention of the fish meant we had to go and have a look at them. As soon as a leaf dropped in his pond, yer man George fishes it out. When he saw the head of the hippo, he said, 'what the 'effing hell is THAT?' as he automatically jumped over the wall to get a closer look. Needless to say we were cracking up laughing.

Mouse White, the auctioneer, was absolutely brilliant. In a joyful, joking and amusing manner he had his audience keenly interested and eating out of his hand, with punters wanting to help our cause. The previous year, Willie Burns offered £500 to the cause if I swam across our pond, but this year I thought it was someone else's turn. At the end of the auction I presented Mouse with a very nice Joy Hawkin's print, but he said that at DBS Co. Ltd they had a strict rule that they did not take money or any kind of reward for auctioneering at any charity event. Therefore Mouse declined our offer. Not to miss a trick I said, 'If that's the case, let's have it up for sale!', which we did and it was very kindly bought by Kevin Horsley for £500. As Mouse was such a star and he wouldn't take anything, I took the mike again to thank him and informed the crowd that, 'last year someone gave £500 for a certain person to hack it across our pond. Now I am not going to ask any one person to give £500 for Mouse to swim across it. I will ask five of you to give £100 each.' Linda Townsend, John Carroll, George Duffield and Simon Hogg, the jockey's valet, were quick to raise their hands to get him in! Fair do's to Mouse, he straightaway was off with his clobber and in!

Our Sam and his girlfriend Carole, while staying with us for a few days, gave Jo and I an invitation to their wedding on 3 August. Sam was in good form at the auction, he gave £250 for the Newcastle captain, Alan Shearer's shirt. He has followed Newcastle for years, in fact he himself and his old jump jockey pal, Neil Doughty, used to go to watch Newcastle a lot before Sam moved down south. Sam is an avid supporter of Newcastle, as seen on the photo of Sam, Carole, Jo and me at the ground.

In addition, Sam also gave £400 for the signed print of the two American champions Steve Cauthen and Willie Shoemaker. As the Swale Valley Stompers never got back to me with their music, Bob Kendal was a perfect substitute who had the party in stitches while on the mike with his banter as he was the subject of the 'Guess the Weight of Bob' competition, which raised £169 in cash. Bob weighed in at 24st 8lbs. It was won by a lady who was spot-on with her estimate and duly received £100 betting voucher from John Brown of William Hill's Ltd, who was in attendance with his wife Chris. Bob was a really good sport that day as he stood in as a ringer for

JB, The Bride, Sam's girlfriend Carole & JB's son Sam at Newcastle Stadium.

Colette Dolan's carthorse. We decided a few weeks previously to make the switch, just for a laugh. Besides, Bob didn't make as much mess as the horse would have! Second prize went to another lady who received a CD and tape of Bob's singing. The third prize was a bottle each of red and white wine that went to another lady, proving women are better judges of weight than men.

We drew the raffle. Colin Bower told me he had a spare leg of cooked pork left over, so we auctioned it together with the golf pro's bag which raised £250 and was bought by Mr Mallinson. One of my old school friends, Cliff Johnson, who was a Leeds market fruit trader, made up a lovely basket of fruit, which Mouse auctioned as extras at the end (after he had showered following his swim) which the Middleham trainer George Moore bought for £100. We had a silent auction where Pat Fullalove was also selling raffle tickets on the day. There were two pictures, one of old jockeys and trainers in the 50s, which was bought by Mr D Coward for £150; the other was a very old framed picture of Lester Piggot and Steve Cauthen for which the £285 final offer shown on the sheet came from another mate of mine, the ex-Radlett trainer, Ken Ivory. Both pictures were kindly donated by Mrs Myra Nesbitt, wife of the late trainer, Steve. Lot 16, the Vespa scooter donated by Bob Bowden of Aiphameric Red Onion Ltd, failed to top the £2,800 bid placed by Jim Hutchinson of Dunadry of Co. Antrim when Leslie Graham of Channel 4 Racing put it up for silent auction at the Doncaster Lincoln meeting (which was televised). The alcoholic bottle tombola, always a great success, raised £2,400 of which we gave £1,400 back to John Stephenson for a charity of his choice. This was to take on holiday a party of disabled children from Blackburn in Lancashire.

The day of Tuesday 22 arrived and Jo and I were trying to contact the prizewinners of the raffle, which was more difficult than one would think. Lots of people were not in, but we were leaving messages on their answerphones, so we were getting there. Jo had just taken £3,280 in cash to the bank, £1,000 of it came from the bottle tombola, the rest was from raffle tickets and some auction items. Being quite busy, I had only just opened the previous day's mail. We had cheques for raffle tickets sold. The first was for £80 from Lady Oaksey, our President's good wife. £100 for his sterling effort was from Jonjo O'Neill's jockey, Liam Cooper, £50 from Anne Hartley one of our friends from Cockerham and partner in a two-year-old we jointly owned that unfortunately has a touch of slows. There was also £30 from Mr and Mrs Nuttall from Manchester and finally £100 from Derek Shaw, the Newark trainer. These £360 worth of cheques and the money Jo has just banked, left us with just £2,718 to reach our target.

There were also these monies to bank, which were from people who paid for entry tickets on the day. Cheques for starters, first one from David Brown for £70, JM Smith from Aura Public Relations Ltd £70, Colin Bradford-Nutter £70. Mr GA Wilkinson £70, jockey Tyrone Williams £35, GJ and LD Harper £140, J Hope £70, SM and KD Atkins £70, Mr EW Pearson £70, the next £70 cheque came from Stuart Morris and his missus Chris, who I also mentioned before also worked for us for years from leaving school up to the time she married Stuart. An absolutely fabulous girl, she broke horses in, clipped them, drove the box, anything. She looked after Bri Eden, the first Group winner we trained, and also the old horse Ollie. Seeing him again was the highlight of her visit.

Chris was absolutely brilliant at turning out horses at race meetings. During her time at our yard she won dozens of best-turned-out (BTO) prizes, often with good money for the reward, at one time given by the *Racing Post*. A commemorative plaque was also presented to the stable with the most BTO in the month and the winning-most groom received a further monetary bonus.

Unfortunately, some yards, instead of genuinely crediting the person who looked after the horse, credited the travelling head person. This led to the withdrawing of sponsorship, which was a real shame as it gave the staff and the yards a big incentive and buzz.

Steve Parkin and Jeanie Trotter sent a cheque for £70. The next £70 was from Graham Rutter, a local farm contractor, who had done a bit of digging for us when we were shaping up our pond and there was also £70 from WE Sanderson. £70 from Claire King, the prison warden from the TV series, 'Bad Girls', who is a good friend of ours and is a star for any good cause. She attended the BBQ with her m.um, Angela, and dad, John, like the previous year. Also, £5 from Gill Richardson the bloodstock agent that was missing from her original ticket payment. Gill buys a lot of Lambourn-trainer Mick Channon's yearlings. David Sellers who gave our cause lots of help last year as well as sponsoring the race on Red Shirt Night at Pontefract left a cheque for £455 for entry and raffle tickets. This adds up to £1,965 and taking that from our last totting up leaves us with just £753 to go!

In the post the following day was a cheque for £500 paying for Lot 17, the print of Rock of Gibraltar and also nice letter from John and Angela Seed, Claire King's parents. Also a £240 cheque from Willie and Wilma Burns for an additional lot we had auctioned, which was a whole prize-winning Cheshire cheese kindly donated by Joseph Heler, as he had the previous year. Dave Whiteman, Preston Area Manager for the Bank of Scotland, wrote a nice letter stating due to family reasons, he was unable to attend our function. Finally, in the post was a very nice card from David and Laureline Wilmot-Smith, racing friends of ours, who bought Lot 32; a day's shooting, saying what a nice day it had been. We were almost there with lots more to come in only £13 to go and we have reached our target figure.

I had just finished washing all the tables down that we borrowed from our own and the next village's hall, as Dave Armstrong was taking them back at 3.30 p.m. Jo got in touch with the *Racing Post* to put a list of raffle prize winners in the paper. This they kindly did, as already a couple of punters had rung the IJF office to see if they had won anything. When Jo rang the *Racing Post,* she spoke to a very nice lady called Lynne and asked her if she would also add a few of my words to thank all the people who had bought and sold tickets, especially the busy trainers I had hounded, and to let them know that they could come out of hiding and talk to me now as I wouldn't be asking them for anything for the next few months! Well, weeks.

Jo parceled Kyllachy's racing plate up and posted it off to Mrs Thompson of Cheveley Park Stud as her successful top lot bid of £5,000 had secured it. Now I would count the other box of cash and cheques that came in during the activities. A £760 cheque from Donna Robe for raffle tickets, what a star Donna was, a £20 cheque from Eileen Cullen, £30 from Tim Adams. Tim is a good man who does a lot for charities who was recently awarded the MBE for his charity work. John Morgan, the press man of fifty years who lives near Tim, couldn't make it so sent £20 as a donation. John and I go back a long way as we both originate from Leeds. Over the years he and I have often appeared on the same bill at functions. His son died a few months ago of peritonitis; John and his wife Maureen must have been gutted. John himself is an absolutely brilliant fellow, he works his butt off for any worthy cause and has done for years. So sad. Dave Armstrong paid a £350 cheque for Lot 8, the print of Best Mate. Our Sam left us his £650 cheque for Lot 2 and Lot 65, Alan Shearer's shirt. Ripon director David Wilmot-Smith left us a cheque to the value of £850 for his days shooting, Lot 32. Tim Adams bought last year's St Leger winner, Bollin Eric's plate, Lot 19, for £300.

Tim also had a draw in the raffle and won the Emmerdale memorabilia. Mr D Roper bought Colonel Eddie York's wine, Lot 4, for £250. My old riding pal Paddy Broderick who rode Night Nurse to win the Champion Hurdle 1976 and 1977 will be pleased when he gets to know Mr Harper of Doncaster bought the painting for £550, which was Lot 6. Liz Morley from Boston Spa always good to be around at charity auctions to make sure that no-one gets anything under its value as she was under bidder on so many lots, gave £400 for Lot 14, a print of Martha's Son and Dublin Flyer. My old pal, David Brown, paid £650 for a made-to-measure suit which was Lot 23. Brian Robe, in addition to his missus Donna selling all those raffle tickets, bought Lot 28 for £500, a Joy Hawkins print of

Cheltenham in the snow, as well as the Beef or Salmon plate and photo for £400, and also the absolutely brilliant Brunyee painting of Rock of Gibraltar for £2,100, spending a total of £3,000. Mr Mallinson bought Lot 7 the very nice top quality carpet for £200 and in addition bought the golf bag, which was auctioned with the leg of roast pork, for £400. Good for him. The silent auction photo donated by Myra Nesbitt was bought by Mr D Coward for £150. Including the £169 from the 'Guessing the Weight Competition' all these cheques added up to £8,769 – well above our target figure. We have a fair amount to come making the healthy sum of £38,816. I am delighted, but it isn't possible to win them all as we have a few bills to pay. Seeing as Jo, Tracy and Colin stayed overnight to prepare and roast the hog we had planned to put them up in our house, but as Ken Ivory and his partner Val, our Sam and his partner Carole were also staying, we put the 'hog-roasters' up in the local pub instead. Although they actually paid the bill, which was £121.40, we have reimbursed them. When Colin picked the pig up, he was a bit worried we may not have enough meat so he bought another two sets of hindquarters at £75. When John Connor said he would sponsor the pig, he paid £100 which we have banked, but we hadn't paid Colin. Therefore, £175 has to be paid for the pork. Mind you, seeing as Mouse White auctioned a spare leg – granted it went with Paul Jackson's golf bag – which realised £250, it must more than even itself out. Jo Bower had taken the trouble to contact the man who looks after the tapestries and renovates them for Chatsworth House. Jo arranged with him to frame the pure silk 1908 scarf, which was very frail and needed a lot of love and attention by way of special acid-free mounts and a certain kind of untreated wood for the frame. As it was for charity and Jo can charm ducks off the water, she was only charged £100. Our final bill from Frame Plus came to £188.06, but I won't add the pence. Therefore £584 needed to come off our last figure. You can appreciate it was money well spent, especially as the specially framed scarf realised £4,500. I wish Gordon Brown could do as well with our country's money – £38,232 was the up-to-date figure.

On Wednesday 23 July, Mouse White came to pick up the cheese he had won in the raffle. I checked the post, which I was dreading in case there were raffle ticket stubs that were late, I needn't have worried. There were two really nice cards from Nan Bibby and Liz Morley saying what a good day they'd had. Young Steven Bowes handed me £120 cheque today after delivering a fifty-bale trailer load of hay, which his father gave us to auction. Gerry Scott bought it. This boosted our figure to £38,352.

On the Thursday after the 'do' we had a cheque for £250 from Mouse White for a picture he had delivered for us. In the post was a cheque for £10 with a very amusing letter from Tracy Kirkham from Creature Comforts. Also there was a £500 cheque from Kevin and Denise Horsely with a complimentary letter. The money was for the late auction prize, the Joy Hawkins print we wanted to give to Mouse, proving it was money well spent on that print. Finally a £50 cheque arrived from the sale of one of my books and also included a donation. Jo has added up and banked today £2,109 (including the raffle money taken in the day amounting to £1,299 in all). This got us over the £40,000 mark to £40,461.

On Friday 25 July, Ferdy Murphy proved he was a star. Not only did he sell the £50 worth of tickets we sent him, at the auction he also bought for £450 the original cartoon of 'Only Allah is Perfect' (Lot 22). He also purchased for £350 Lot 34, the other cartoon donated by the same artist Mark Huskinson. As Ferdy didn't take them with him when he left on Sunday, Jo and I took them to his yard this afternoon and collected the money that now takes our total to £41,291. Lady Bolton had left a message on our answer-machine; she has put the £500 cheque in the post for Joe Mercer's saddle, as even though she wasn't present on Sunday, her bid was the still the highest. Unfortunately, Lot 16, the Vespa scooter, didn't better the £2,800 silent bid put on by John Hutchinson of Co. Antrim, so it will be emigrating to Ireland in due course.

In the evening I donned my auctioneer's cap, as it was Alan's charity night for the IJF, which was held at the Bay Horse pub near his yard at Cockerham. There was a very good crowd in attendance. The BBQ was really good and at the auction there were some very nice lots. One in fact one quite special. It was a very large bronze horse and jockey by the French sculptor PJ Mene and it must have weighed ten or twelve stone, nearly big enough to ride! Gavin Lees who donated it said he wanted £1,000 for himself and the rest could go to the cause. There was some spirited bidding between Fred Done, the book-maker, who owns a horse with Alan, Brian Robe and Mike and Angela Slater whose final bid of £3,750 clinched it. In all £7,500 was raised for the Fund, which was great. Well done Alan and your team. I must say, it was nice to go back to where we had lived for so long and see some of the old faces again. John Wilding, Alan's yard sponsor passed me one of my books, *It's Tough at the Bottom,* and asked me if I would sign it for a pal of his who knew I was going to be there. He insisted I took the £40 he offered for doing it, for the Fund. He wouldn't have it any other way. Our Alan never gets up to dance but Donna Robe, Anne Hartley and Jo put £20 each in a kitty and bribed our Alan to get up and the £60 would go to the cause. Sure enough he did, and I might add he was a fairly good mover! There were plenty of people still there when we left at midnight. We would have stayed overnight at Alan's but we had to set off the following day, Saturday, as we were going to a wedding at Giggleswick. Before we set off for anywhere, I have a lot of mouths to feed. Horses, pigeons, bantams, dogs, cats, fish, a pony and the wild birds. Mind you, it's nice to get invited to a wedding occasionally and I can't remember the last christening I went to, but I go to plenty of funerals! A bit of a worry at my time of life because lots of the people we're planting are out of the same pen. The wedding was between the son of John and Coral North, good friends of ours from when we first started training at Doncaster and a girl called Alison, who is a relation of Stuart Curry, the owner of the swimming pool at Giggleswick where we sent horses on a regular basis to have a dip whilst at Cockerham.

Before we set off for the wedding, in the mail from Jill Ryan, trainer Kevin's missus, sent a £65 cheque for her entry and raffle tickets. Mrs Thompson of Cheveley Park sent her £5,000 cheque for Kyllachy's racing plate. Well done Mrs T and thank you. Owen Watson-Wilson, from whom we bought our Hunton property, from sent his cheque for £600 having bought Lot 22, the golfing stay in Wales. Owen is a keen golfer, I hope he's better than George

Duffield or it's a waste of time going all the way to Glamorgan. George asked me if I wanted to play on Sunday at Bedale but I said, 'No thanks, it's not really my scene. If I wanted a good laugh I would go to the Embassy Club and listen to Bernard Manning.' Finally in the post was another £100 betting voucher for 'Guess the Weight of Bob'. John Brown kindly said he would get David Lowry, his Group Director, to send this in addition to the other £300 his firm, William Hill, had already donated. Our total now rises to a marvellous, one would hardly believe it possible, £46,956. Great, just great and we still have more to come!

Following a nice leisurely sort of day, in the evening Jo cooked our beef and made the Yorkshire puddings that we took down to the Duffield's for our and their Sunday dinner. Also we took the pair of Joy Hawkins prints that GD bought for £525 and George duly wrote out a cheque to cover it. Our figure was now £47,381. Over the weekend I had personally handwritten fifty-nine letters thanking people for their support.

One could say writing thank you letters is a menial job, but it needs to be done and a lot of people gave, bought and helped and to thank them was the least we could do. This morning, as I write, a letter arrived from Mike, the landlord of our local The Countryman's Inn, who was having a pop at me on account of some of our punters having booked three rooms and not turning up. To be fair, he needed compensating as he could have booked the rooms. Perhaps they changed their minds and went home. We compensated the pub with £100 putting our account back a fraction to £47,281.

On Tuesday 29 July, nine days after our event, there were still many loose ends that needed tying up – like letting the raffle prize winners know that they had won. One could ring them often and leave messages on answer machines for a week before one can get through to them. There were just four race-courses we asked for a day's racing badges, York, Cattenck, Chester and Doncaster who readily obliged, and, would you believe it, Antonia Thornton, the wife of Leyburn trainer, won the four tickets to Cattenck races out of the thousands we sold, and it was their local course! Also Neil Cawood, the guy who sells racing photos and memorabilia at Doncaster at every meeting, won a pair of paddock tickets there, which he needed like a hole in the head! At the moment we have just a few auction items to be paid for, then we can wrap up this year's BBQ day complete all the necessary paperwork and draw the final cheque from the building society for the IJF. As a trustee, I can assure you the money will be put to good use.

Mrs Barbara Wilkinson, is a director of Wilkinson hardware stores. The family opened their first store in Leicester in 1930. Barbara is a staunch supporter of the IJF and did well at our auction as she bought Lot 5 for £400, the Colonel Collins print, Lot 11 for £250, the cricket print of 16 living 'greats' which was dug up from the IJF archives, and Lot 18 for £400. Had Barbara seen the photo of George Duffield at a New Year's Party, it's debatable whether she would have paid so much for his autobiography *Gentleman George*? If the picture had been on the front cover, the book could have been entitled *Slapper George*! Lot 27 for £250 and Lot 31 the original silk scarf of all the Derby winners from 1798— 1908 along with the actual racing plate of Signorinetta worn

*Barbara Wilkinson
enjoying a bite to
eat at Well Close House..*

in 1908 when he won the race. It's got to be unique and worth a fortune. Like Mouse said when he put the scarf up for sale, 'this item should probably be hanging in a museum.' Barbara paid £4,500 to acquire the Lot. Her cheque arrived on Wednesday 30 July for a whopping £5,800, making Barbara the day's top bidder. Since our BBQ day Barbara has jointly sponsored with Trevor Hemmings an (IJF) Beneficiaries Day at Aintree and has contributed substantially with an IJF project that's taking place at this very moment as I write in Lambournes at Market Rasen. She also arranged and sponsored a race which included an IJF Beneficiaries Day. On that same day Barbara brought over from Ireland the parents of the two young jockeys, Shawn Cleary and Kieran Kelly, who got killed. Roger Tindall's cheque for £500 arrived to pay for Lot 20, a day's fishing on the river Ribble. In the past we trained a decent sprinter called Restless Don for Roger. Talk about Jim Lewis being proud and excited when Best Mate wins, Roger would give him a few pounds for enthusiasm. In fact, Jim wouldn't be in the same league as my man Roger, who is extremely hyper. The day Don won a race at Pontefract, no sooner had he won than his owner was on that course leading him in, so excited and chuffed he was all over the horse and jockey! Any minute now Roger will be riding Don into the winner's enclosure and my jockey, John Carroll, will be leading Roger in! Finally Jed O'Keefe and his other half, Andrea, kindly sent a £200 cheque as a donation. They weren't successful at the auction but their entry ticket No. 99 was drawn, which won them a Joy Hawkins hunting print. This brought the total up to £6,500 giving our already impressive figure a massive boost to £53,781.

There were only two or three more cheques to pay into the bank for auction items. I will give the people a few more days to get them in. If they don't, I intend to close the IJF building society account, get the cheque and send all our accounts to the office. When all the other cheques arrive, I will then send them on. I would like to add the money we earn from our share of the auction at Tern Hill.

On Saturday night, the last day of Glorious Goodwood, where we went to see our filly Simianna run six of twenty-nine in the Stewards Cup. On our return I found in the mail two cheques, one for £10 the other for £30 from Hamish Alexander's yard for the raffle tickets he sold but, unfortunately, too late for the chance to win a prize. Any day will do for Hamish, the £30 cheque was dated 15/5/03 from Miss HJE Michael. Poor Henrietta wouldn't be very pleased if she knew! For all Hamish' s lack of sense of urgency, he's a really good lad and would do anything for anyone.

Years ago I bought the good sprinter Clantime from him at Doncaster Sales as a yearling. You wouldn't believe Clantime by the Cheveley Park stallion, Music Boy, who was a Group horse, was sold as 'pedigree unknown on the dam side'. Our office staff did all the spade work to get it put right. Not only was Clantime a class act as a racehorse, he also bred some good horses when he went to stud. At Doncaster Sales that day I thought he was as nice a year-ling as any there. I gave 10,000gns for him without an owner to buy him for. Had the youngster's pedigree been registered he probably would have doubled his money. In the end we sold him to Jeff Beddis and the horse absolutely trot-ted up the first time he ran as a two-year-old at Ayr in very heavy going. He also won the Surrey Stakes at Epsom, ridden by Willie Carson in 1983, the year Teenoso won the Derby.

On 4 August, yet another cheque arrived from John and Gaynor Garrity for £570 for the print of Gimcrack Lot 36, making our figure look even more impressive at £54,541. There were only a couple of cheques to come in and I wanted very much to get the money in before our next IJF meeting at York racecourse on 18 August, so that we could close the account and give the cheque and all the paperwork to Karen Hatton, our Chief Executive's secre-tary. We would be giving our fundraising for the IJF a miss the following year. Often I get the feeling, not so much a cold shoulder but a sheepish look from friends and trainers and so on, I can imagine them thinking, 'Oh no, not that scrounging prat again, what's he going to tap me for this time?' If I can go for a few months without asking for their help, they may come out in the open and speak to me again! Although, as I have previously mentioned, I would love to get enough funds together to build a really big complex with lots of bungalows, wheelchair friendly with sheltered accommodation with lawns to enjoy and on-hand nursing staff, in-house doctor, physios, a heated swim-ming pool, TV lounge and a games room. Like a kind of village where the beneficiaries can bring their own furniture, hang their own photos on the walls, somewhere they can feel free and above all safe. With a nice Social Club attached so they could reminisce about old times have their own minibus and driver to go on outings, or just shopping. Also to supply them named racing badges to get them into race meetings, all to make them feel proud that they or their partners have given their life to racing. Then racing people would look on them like we look on the Chelsea Pensioners, but instead of having been in the Forces they would be proud to be ex-members of the Turf who had given the great sport their best years. As our President, Lord Oaksey, has freely given so much of his life to the IJF, ideally the chosen pla e if and when it gets off the ground, hopefully while John is still alive, would be named in his honour, The Oaksey Estate, with a life-size bronze sculpted by the likes of Willie Newton, Philip Blacker or Caroline Nunnery, at the gate entrance. If I ever win the Lottery, it's on this project that the money would go. If there is such a thing as a God, you never know He may grant me my wish. Mind you, I suppose I should meet him halfway and buy a ticket first! In the past, Jo and I bought £5 worth of Lottery tickets every week until the old lady found out money was given to things she didn't approve of.

Dave Armstrong and I designed and drew the plans up to give us a bit of an idea. There is room for improvements and amendments. It looks quite ambitious but it would be great if it came to pass. Even better, we could purchase a few acres of land, get the bungalows, buildings, roads, car park and such sponsored which could be named after the sponsor (name, firm) or their horses. I am a believer in sponsoring and adverts. I was the first trainer to put adverts on the horse box. I also drove a car sponsored by the *Daily Star*. SAAB sponsored our yard. I have never heard of a book being sponsored before, however, with a bit of luck or, as the Irish say, a rub of the green, this one could be the first.

My sponsored wheels when I wrote a weekly column for the Daily Star.

Neighbour George Duffield I knew for a fact was thinking seriously about retiring from race riding, only now he may have second thoughts as today, 6 August, he rode the first four winners at Newcastle. To commemorate the occasion, Jo and I were invited to the Duffield's for a BBQ and a few jars. Let's hope GD doesn't get a random alcohol test, as Joe Fanning and Keith Dalgleish were stood down from riding as they tested positive. Fortunately, they were let off with a caution. Linda Townsend was also present at the BBQ. Remember,

Linda was one of the five who paid £100 for Mouse to swim across our pond at our BBQ, for which she duly gave me a cheque that took our figure to £54,551.

Yes, the postman, as I write, was good to us, he delivered a cheque from the Dowager Lady Lavinia Bolton to the value of £500 for Lot 9, Joe Mercer's racing saddle, and a cheque for £200 from Mr Brack, as his pal had won the ton of Creature Comforts shavings in the raffle. Mr Brack had bought them and somewhere along the line the IJF came in for £200 out of the deal which brought our figure up to a remarkable £55,251.

On Friday 8 August, we had just about got all the money in by now. The one big cheque for £5,050 (I must admit I had been waiting for) came in the post today from Rob Hughes of Lowstock Manor Stud for conducting the auction on 21 June in Shropshire. This gives our Fund a great boost and brings our total to date to £60,301. Therefore, we will close our account with the building society and get one final cheque for the money and send it to the IJF office. No doubt more monies or cheques would continue to arrive. As they did, I would send them on to the office.

On Saturday 9 August, while watching our filly Simianna run in the Perrault Shergar Cup Distaff Handicap at Ascot, Tony Newcombe, the Bamstaple trainer, gave me a £20 and said, 'put this in your Fund with my compliments', boosting the figure to £60,321.

As we had closed our account with the Alliance & Leicester Building Society, we would draw the final cheque from them and I would enclose Tony's £20. We were lucky to get to Ascot; Dave (J) Bowes fed all our creatures as we left Hunton at 6.30 a.m. to enable us to be at Ascot around 12 p.m. without rushing. We were stuck on the M40 for two hours in sweltering heat as there had been an accident. Apparently, a car had run under a wagon and caught fire, killing the driver. We arrived at the racecourse right on 2 p.m. just in time to saddle up our runner in the second race at 2.15 p.m. The Blue Square Shergar Cup meeting had been hosted by Ascot for four years running where the greatest jockeys from Britain and Ireland go head to head with the top jockeys from the rest of the world over all six races. The result is decided on a points system. This year, as I write, the home team was captained by Pat Eddery. Our other riders were Kevin Darley, Kieren Fallon, Daryll Holland, Mick Kinane and Johnny Murtagh. Frankie Dettori captained the away team and the rest of the team comprised, Shane Dye from New Zealand, Frederick Johnson from Sweden, Andreas Suborios from Germany, Yutaka Take from Japan and, finally, Doug White of South Africa. £260,000 prize money was on offer. No entry fees for runners. Ten runners in each race; even the last horse to finish receives at least £420. Wouldn't it be something if all our racing was like that? The stable staff that led up the horses were given nice jackets and baseball caps and there was £250 for the best turned out horse in every race. Helen Cooper who looked after Simianna was the lucky lady, but unfortunately, the filly could only finish eighth in the race, though she was rewarded with £840 in prize money for doing so. To differentiate between the jockeys riding round, the home team jockeys wore red breeches and donned red caps, leaving the rest-of-the-world jockeys riding in white breeches and caps. It was great racing and in a nice and friendly atmosphere. To give the jockeys more incentive to try harder individually rather than 'gang up' to collect points for their team, £100 per point was given to them in addition to their percentage of winnings at the end of the day. The home team scored 98 points with the away side easily winning with 146 points. I had already arranged with Jason Weaver the home team selector, to get me a pair of one of our jockey's red breeches signed by both teams to enable me to sell them in one of our auctions at a later date, as I did the previous year when Brian Robe kindly bought them for £1,000.

Friday 15 August arrived, and I was now waiting for the final cheque to come from the building society so I could take it to our IJF meeting at York the following Monday. In the post were two cheques, £35 from Jimmy Fitzgerald the ex-trainer and £10 from his secretary, Noel, for raffle tickets he sold – boosting the figure even further to a staggering £60,366!

The days continued to fly by and Monday 18 August arrived. I was hoping the final cheque would be in the post to take to the IJF meeting which was to be held at 1 p.m. in the Steward Room at York racecourse. But it wasn't to be. Jo rang the building society up to get the final figure of the money we had stashed in there, so at least I could tell the other trustees the amount, which was £45,064.37 as the rest, as previously mentioned, has already been sent on to the IJF office. As you can imagine the trustees were 'made up'. I can assure you it's all worth the effort doing such things when people on the whole are so generous, especially if you could have been at York to witness some of the tragic cases on the agenda that came before us. It is only on account of the goodwill and support of the kind people who contributed in whatever way, that we manage to make our Open Day and other functions held throughout the year, such a success. The money will change the lives of some beneficiaries dramatically for the better.

To have received more than twice as much as the £30,000 we initially set out to raise, was marvellous and I would like to thank all the people, for whatever part they played, from the bottom of my heart on behalf of our beneficiaries. On our York agenda was a report on one of our beneficiaries, Anne Hartley, who was blind. In addition to being blind for years, she also suffered badly from kidney trouble. Three times a week she had to travel from the home she lived at to a hospital to go on a dialysis machine. It was a day's job every time and all the travelling and the treatment made her feel rotten. Poor Anne had had enough and refused to have any more of it. During her final week without the dialysis treatment she had a couple of gin and tonics in the evening. One night, she just quietly went to sleep and didn't wake up. Elaine Wiles not only went to her funeral but also arranged to have her ashes collected following the inquest and have them buried beside her parent's grave. Racing is a great sport but a very dangerous one. We are reminded of that when only last Friday Kieran Kelly, the twenty-five-year-old Irish jockey was buried at Derrinstown church in Co. Kildare. He had died a few days beforehand after suffering severe had injuries from a racecourse fall at Kilbeggan on 8 August. It was in 1996, at Tipperary, that Kieran rode his first winner on a horse called Angel from Heaven. At the church many hundreds of mourners gathered, a lot of them were unable to get a seat inside the church, so they listened to the mass outside on loud speakers. Kieran's boss, an emotional Dessie Hughes, reminded the congregation of the horse's name Kieran rode his first winner on and said that's what and where he is now.

My old mate George Duffield has finally hung his boots up and retired. Hence the photo of his riding pals (Fergal Lynch, John Carrol, Robert Winston, Joe Fanning, Deam Mernagh, Adrian Nichols, Franny Norton, Tony Culhane, Joey Brown) presenting the 'old fellow' with a garden seat at Thirsk races.

Hurray, hurray, brilliant! I thought to myself. The cheque from the building society finally arrived, £45,064.31, which I sent straight on to Karen Hatton of the IJF. Over the next few days, in order to tie all the loose ends up, I would be sending the remaining letters of thanks to the contributors who hadn't yet been told of the final figure we had raised, like the trainers who sold raffle tickets. To finalise this write up, I have given you a fair and truthful account and a run down of what's happened from day one. Soon we would be able to settle the account and put it all to bed.

Wednesday August 30 arrived. Carol Moore brought a cheque for £100 for the basket of fruit she and George, the Middleham trainer, bought at our auc-

George Duffield calls it a day. His fellow jockeys buy him a seat, a pipe and a pair of slippers.

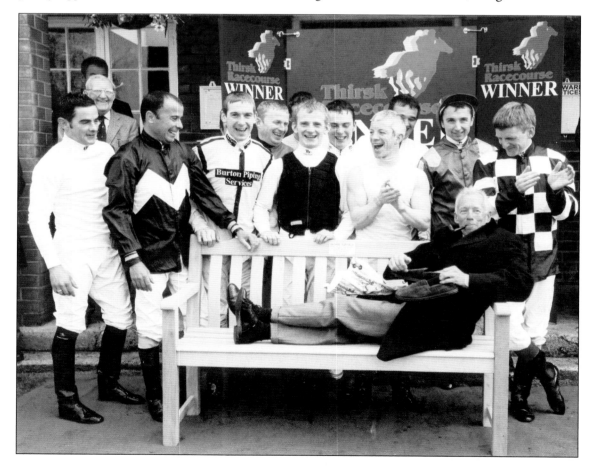

tion. I was not complaining; we could have kept the account open for a bit longer and it was only fair that contributors get a mention. The new figure was now £62,266, quite remarkable, far greater than I could ever have hoped for.

On my return from having a brilliant day at Cartmel where The Bride and I went to saddle-up Alan's rare jumpers (Long Meadows Boy won and his other runner Peter's Imp was second), on opening the mail there was a £500 cheque donation from Brett Oils Ltd who are good supporters of the IJF and who kindly donated the same amount at the beginning of the year. This brings the total now to an astronomical £62,766!! I was fairly confident of reaching our target of £30,000, but this amount was out of this world! To wrap things up, I thought you may as well see the whole brochure of the day's event.

I will say once again, people, on the whole, are so generous. All our beneficiaries throughout Britain, past, present and in the future have you kind folk to thank for making it possible. I soon forget what a bad day is when I am here amongst my friends in Tenerife. When you see the like of Sharon Murgatroyd and many others, who are trapped in a wheelchair the result of a racing fall, and who can for one minute forget about their fate, it's wonderful. It's great seeing Sharon having a good laugh like this when I showed her my imitation dog – you know what – that I had just picked up while having a bit of fun on our annual holiday in Tenerife. And that's what it's about. Having a bit of fun.

Auction Lots

1 2 nights B&B for 4 people in the Player Suite, with full use of the leisure facilities at the famous Carnoustie Hotel, Golf Resort and Spa in Scotland.
Donated by Martin Delaney, Director. Organised by John Foster.

2 "Two Champions" limited edition print by Roy Miller no. 55/475, signed by Willie Shoemaker and Steve Cauthen.
Kindly donated by the Dowager Lady Bolton

3 Four mounted photographs commemorating A P McCoy's record 1700th win on 'Mighty Montefalco'.
Kindly donated by J J O'Neill

4 A mixed dozen bottles of high quality wine
Kindly donated by Colonel Eddie York

5 'Colonel Collins' multi-signatured Limited Edition print. Signed by A K Collins and Robert Sangster (Owners), John Reid (Jockey) and Peter Chappel-Hyam (Trainer) This print is No.1 of only 120.
Kindly donated by owner Mr A K Collins.

6 Oil painting of 'Night Nurse', Champion Hurdler 1976
Donated by the Injured Jockeys Fund Archive

7 Beautiful top quality carpet from Franks Factory Flooring
Kindly donated by Mr W Maguire

8 'Best Mate' winner of 2 consecutive Cheltenham Gold Cups (2002 & 2003) He could win more! This print is signed by his proud owner Jim Lewis, his Jockey, Jim Culloty and his outstanding Trainer, Henrietta Knight who has very generously donated this print to help the Injured Jockeys Fund.

9 Joe Mercer's saddle
Kindly donated by Joe especially for this event

10 A pair of Artist Proofs by Joy Hawken of 'The Ledbury crossing Pidgeon House' and 'The Pytchley Saturday'.
Kindly donated by the artist, Joy Hawken

11 'Sixteen Living Greats'. A print of 16 Northamptonshire and England cricket players brought out in 1999 in conjunction with the Nick Cook Benefit Year. The players depicted are DJ Capel, RM Prideaux, D Brookes, W Larkins, DJ Steele and JR Taylor, P Willey, KV Andrew, FH Tyson, RMH Cottam, RJ Bailey, G Cook, JDF Larter, AJ Lamb, R Subbaron, NGB Cook.
Donated by The Injured Jockeys Fund Archive

12 2 nights B & B for 2 people at the Vale Country Club in Glamorgan, plus a round of golf or a spa treatment.
Kindly donated by Adrian Davies, organised by John Foster

13 Signed photo of Michael Owen, an outstanding player and racing enthusiast.
Kindly donated by Michael Owen

14 'Martha's Son' and 'Dublin Flyer' working in the snow with Cleeve Hill in the background. A lovely Limited Edition print by Joy Hawken No.317 of 385.
Kindly donated by the artist

15 Mounted racing plate worn by 'Kyllachy' when he won the Group 1 Nunthorpe with a letter of authenticity from Trainer, Henry Candy.
Kindly donated by his Trainer Henry Candy

16 A Brand New Silver Vespa Scooter PX125. An absolutely fantastic lot and its ready to ride away!
Generously donated by Bob Bowden Director of Alphameric Red Onion Ltd of Chester-Le-Street

17 Print of 'Rock of Gibraltar', a remarkable racehorse. Signed by Sir Alex Ferguson.
Kindly donated by Dave Fish

18 'Gentleman George'. George Duffields' autobiography signed by the author with an inscription, this is the first book of the press.
Kindly donated by the Author

19 The mounted racing plate of 'Bollin Eric', St Leger Winner 2002 ridden by K Darley, with a letter of authenticity from his Trainer, Tim Easterby.
Kindly donated by Tim Easterby

20 A day fishing on the River Ribble at Dinckley, Lancashire
Kindly donated by Mr & Mrs C Bradford-Nutter

21 'We Three Kings' This must be the most memorable print ever produced. Arkle, Red Rum and Desert Orchid.
Kindly donated by Mrs Sarah York

22 An original cartoon by Mark Huskinson of Newmarket Sales entitled 'Only Allah is perfect'.
Kindly donated by the artist

23 A Made-to-measure Suit for a Lady or Gent in quality cloth of your choice, from Master Tailor David Pipe.
Kindly donated by David Pipe

24 Mounted racing plate of 'Invincible Spirit' worn when he won the Group 1 Stanley Leisure Sprint Cup ridden by John Carroll. A signed photo of him winning the race with signatures of Jockey, John Carroll and Trainer John Dunlop. With a letter of authenticity.
Kindly donated by John Carroll & John Dunlop

25 Alan Shearer's football shirt signed by Alan. A remarkable player for Newcastle and England. A footballing legend.
Kindly donated by Alan Shearer himself

26 Oil painting of 'Parthia' winner of the 1959 Derby, ridden by W H Carr.
Kindly donated by his daughter, Mrs Joe Mercer

27 Signed photograph of 'Media Puzzle' the winner of the 2002 Melbourne Cup. 'Media Puzzle' is half brother to the 2003 2,000 Guineas Winner 'Refuse to Bend'. Signed by Dermot Weld.
Kindly donated by Dermot Weld

28 A Limited Edition Print by Joy Hawken entitled 'Cheltenham in the Snow'. No110 of 275
Kindly donated by the artist

29 A tour of the exclusive Coolmore Stud. A chance to see the worlds best stallions and also a tour of Aiden O'Briens impressive Ballydoyle Racing Stables in Ireland. For two people.
Generously donated by Christy Grassick of Coolmore

30 Photograph of 'Grandera', signed by Frankie Dettori when he won the Irish National Stakes.
Kindly donated by Godolphin

31 A 'once in a lifetime chance' to bid for an original 1908 Silk Scarf depicting all the Derby Winners from 1798 to 1908, along with the racing plate of the 1908 Derby Winner 'Signoretta'.
Very kindly donated by Demelsa Letherby, the grand-daughter of W Bullock, the rider of Signoretta in the race.

32 2 days shooting for 1 gun on the Wyvill Estate at Constable Burton. Date to be arranged. Lunch at the Wyvill Arms is included.
Kindly donated by Charles Wyvill

33 A collage to commemorate A P McCoy's all time record breaking 1700th win at Uttoxeter on 'Mighty Montefalco' trained by Jonjo O'Neill.
Kindly donated by A P McCoy

34 'The Handicappers Welcome' an original pastel cartoon by Mark Huskinson.
Kindly donated by the artist

36 A Limited Edition print of George Stubbs famous painting of 'Gimcrack'
Donated by The Injured Jockeys Fund Archive

37 An original head study of 'Rock of Gibraltar' by Nigel Brunyee. An artist specialising in highly detailed and accurate portraits of racehorses.
Kindly donated by Nigel Brunyee himself

Injured Jockeys Fund · Charity Auction 2003

Looking on are Barbara Hancock one of the IJF almoners, Jo Berry and Janet Boston, Sharon's carer.

Hope you enjoyed the journey. Thanks again for your help and support. Jack.

L to r: Barbara Hancock, JB, Sharon Murgatroyd, The Bride & Janet Boston having a laugh in Tenerife.

Index

Numbers in **bold** refer to illustrations.

Abdullah, Prince Khalid, **178**
Adams, Tim, 117, 239
Addie, Kate, 133
Airey, Peter, 191
Aitall, Dennis, 218
Aizpur, Xavier, 53
Akehurst, John, **195**
Albadou, Sheikh, 212
Alexander, Hamish, 176, 244
Allen, Conrad, 176
Allen, Susie, 144
Alston, Eric, 170, 216
Ammas, Geoff, 226-7
Andrews, Jim, 19, 114, 209, 229
Anne, Princess, 122, 144, 181
Arkwright, Philip, 22-23, 170
Arkwright, Sandra, 22-23, 170
Armitage, Gee, 18, 22, 55
Armitage, Marcus, 18, 117
Armstrong, Dave, 22, 147, 164, 189, 227, 239, 245
Armstrong, Jill, 189
Ashforth, David, 220, 239
Ashworth, Dave, 154
Atkins, KD, 238
Atkins, SM, 238
Atkinson, Bill, 132
Atkinson, Harry, 152

Bailey, Jane, 218
Baker, Mr & Mrs, 232
Balding, Andrew, 128
Balding, Arthur, 232
Balding, Claire, 13, 218, 232
Balding, Claire, 232
Balding, Emma, 192
Balding, Ian, 13, 30, 62, 213
Balding, John, 176, 231, 232
Balding, Toby, 77, 186, 189
Barker, David, 166,
Barker, David, 178
Barlow, Anne, 221
Barlow, George, 221
Barnes, Simon, 110
Barrett, John, 55
Barrett, Ruth, 55
Barron, David, 227
Barry, Ron, 41, 51
Bates, Mick, 160
Baxter, Geoff, 129
Beadle, Jeremy, 117
Bealby, Ben, 56-57
Beasley, Harry, 206
Beasley, Rufus, 172
Beaumont, Peter, 40, 116, 174, 202-03
Beaverbrook, Lady, 205
Beckham, David, 60, 160
Beddis, Jeff, 244
Bedford, Karen, 164-5
Beeby, Henry, 189, 191
Bell, Harry, 26, 126
Bell, Michael, 176
Bells, PH, 218

Bernacchi, Gino, 188, 224
Bernacchi, Meme, 188
Berry, Alan, 20, 36, 71, 102, 160, 166-7, 168, 187, 189, 214, 218, 220, 224, 241
Berry, Carol, 32, 67, 98, 111, 142, 144, 145, 203, 207, 216, 233, 236-7, **237**, 240
Berry, Frank, 29, **31**
Berry, Geoff, 29-30, **31**
Berry, Harry, 29, **31**
Berry, Jo (The Bride), 9, 15, 18, 26 20, 22, 28, 32, 35, 36, 39, 45, **45**, **46**, 48, 49, 51, **52**, 54, 57, 60-61, **60**, **61**,64, 67, 72, 75, 82, 96, **96**, 98, 99, 102, 105, 106, **106**, 111, 112, 113, 115, 116, 117, 118, **118**, 121, 124, 138, 141, 142, 145, 149, 151, 152, 155, 157, **157**, 162, 163, 164, 165. 166, 167, **170**, 175, 176, 177, 179, 181, 182, 184, 186, 187, 189, **195**, 196, 202, 224, 225, 229, 230, **237**, 250, **250**
Berry, John, 217
Berry, Sam, 11, 32, **32**, 55, 67, 70, 71, 98, 100, 111, **111**, 128, 142, 144, 145, 155, 178, 207, 216, 217, 233, 236-7, **237**, 239, 240
Bertie, Norman, 143
Bibby, Nan, 224, 240
Biddlecombe, Terry, 206
Birch, Mark, 56, 116, 117
Bird, Dickie, 184, 225, **225**, 226, 228, 230
Blackburn, Paul, 230
Blacker, Philip, 245
Blackshaw, James, 21, 169
Blake, Derek, 25
Bloomfield, Ian, 144, 145, 146, 147
Blum, Gerry, 22, 67, 102
Blum, Lilo, 22, 67, 186
Boddy, Jack, 91, 175
Bolger, Jim, 62, 73
Bolland, Ian, 220
Bollard, Ian, 113, 220
Boston, Noel, 142
Botham, Ian, 48
Bolton, Ken,133
Bolton, Lady Lavinia, 19, 162, 178-9, 181, 241, 246
Bolton, Mary, 133, 144
Boston, Janet, 250, **250**
Bowden, Bob, 117, 120, 214, 237
Bower, Colin, 104, 235, 237
Bower, Jo, 104-105, 114, 115, 151, 155, 209, 216, 217, 223, 235, 240
Bowes, David (joiner), 22, 34, 37, 43, 45, 47, 58, 95, 100, 155, 163, 196, 227, 229-30, 246
Bowes, David (farmer), 43, 184,
Bowing, MP, 218
Boyd-Rochford, Captain C, 173
Brack, Mr, 246
Bradbourne, Johnny, 54
Bradbourne, Laura, 117
Bradbourne, Mark, 117
Bradbourne, Sue, 176
Bradford-Nutter, Colin, 105, 116, 238
Bradford-Nutter, Jean, 116

Bradley, Graham, 69-70
Bradley, Keith, 124, 204
Bravery. Giles, 176, 192
Breasley, Scobie, 143, 192
Bremner, Rory, 226
Brennan, Owen, 78, 92, 176, 221
Brittain, Clive, 98, 184, 187
Broderick, Nan, 125, 131-2
Broderick, Paddy, 125, 128, 131-2, 179, 211, 239
Broderick, Shane, 16, **17**, 30, **30**, 58, 70, 103, 113, 121, 122, 125, 130, 137, 142, 145, 182, 192, 207
Brookshaw, Tim, 13, 51, **134**
Brotherton, Laureline, 173
Brown, Chris, 237
Brown, David, 48, 102, 217, 228. 238, 239
Brown, Gordon, 240
Brown, Henry, 218
Brown, Joey, 248
Brown, John, 155, 188, 237, 242
Brown, John K, 228
Brown, Lisa, 160
Brown, Philip, 97, 98
Brown, Trish, 102, 170
Bruce, Sally, 230
Brunyee, Nigel, 163, 190, 240
Bryne, Jimmy, 93, 94, 95, 115
Byrne, Jose, 93
Buckley, Brian, 108
Buckley, Pat, 130
Budge, Tony, 140
Bullock, Billy, 132, 161
Burke, Karl, 216
Burn, PHil, 222
Burns, Jimmy, **93**
Burns, Willie, 26, 180, 191, 236, 239
Burns, Wilma, 26, 180, 191, 228, 239

Callaghan, Neville, **195**
Calver, Peter, 232
Campbell, Arthur, 117
Campion, Andrea, 10-11
Campion, John, 10-11
Candy, Henry, 15, 20, 32, 38, 64, 111, 138, 194, 209, 233
Carlisle, Nicky, 122
Carr, Bruce, 175
Carr, Frank, 56, 175
Carr, Harry, 162, 180
Carroll, John, 20-21, 27, 43, 105, 108, 151, 165, 199, **199**, 212, 235, 236, 243, 248
Carroll, Tracy, 21
Carson, Elaine, **195**
Carson, Frank, 225
Carson, Willie, 56, 108, **195**, 205, 206, 244
Carter, Roy, 38-39
Carter, Rose, 175
Carter, Ted, 175, 176
Casey, Colin, 125, 128, 144
Casey, Eileen, 128
Caulfield, Michael, 215
Cauthen, Steve, 55, 162, 237

Cawood, Neil, 242
Cazalet, Lady, 108
Cazalet, Sir Edward, 26, 38, **48**, **127**, 140, 144, 146
Cazalet, Hal, 140, 141, 144, 145, 147
Cecil, Henry, 114, 205
Chamberlain, Norman, 217
Champion, Bob, 38, 162, 205
Chance, Noel, 192
Chandler, Peter, 213-4
Chang, TC, 104
Channon, Mick, 176, 238
Chapman, David, 11, 27
Chapman, Iris, 233, **233**
Chapman, M, 230, 227
Chapman, Paul, 230
Charlton, Bobby, 70
Charlton, Jackie, 160
Charlton, Roger, 218
Charnock, Lindsey, 224
Cheshire, Fred, 138-9, 146
Clark, Phil, 116
Clark, Stanley, 205
Clarkson, Herbert, 172
Clayton, Jack, 19, 100, 214
Cleary, Shawn, 243
Clegg, Mr, 168
Collings, RJ, 139
Collins, Colonel, 182
Collins, Colonel Tony, 26, 154, 182, 242
Connors, John, 149, 240
Connors, Paddy, 123. **123**
Connorton, Brian, 56
Conway, John, 214
Conway, Tim, 214
Cook, Harry, 189
Cook, Mrs, 229
Cook, Nicky, 34
Cooper, Helen, 246
Cooper, Liam, 238
Cooper, Tommy, 124-5
Coughian, Sean, 102
Cousins, Eric, 29, 133
Cousins, Horace, 172
Cousins, John, 29
Cousins, Sarah, 29, 31, 149
Coward, D, 237, 240
Cowdrey, Graham, 226
Cox, Clive, 176, 230
Crawford, Sue, 25
Crick, Stanley, 144
Crisford, Simon, 21
Crockhard, Professor, 195
Crook, Andy, 152
Crump, Captain, 78, 91
Culhane, Tony, **54**, 203, 248
Cullen, Dennis (Des), 128-9, 132, 144, 182, **183**
Cullen, PJ, 82, 160
Cullen, Sister Eileen, 29, 35, 49, 56, 82, 142, 160, 165, 179, 182, 239
Cullinan, Tommy, 61
Culloty, Jim, 40, 76-77
Cumani, Luca, 205, 218
Cundell, Ken, 140
Cunningham, Anne, 29
Curley, Barney, 202
Curry, Stuart, 241
Curtis, Steve, 210, 211

Dalgleish, Keith, 246
Daly, Alan, 218
Darley, Debbie, 34, 215

Darley, Kevin, 23, 24, 33-34, **33**, 41, 43, 46, 203, 215, 246
Dasmal, K, 24
Davey, Helen, 9, 36, 218
Davis, Bob, 51
Davis, Lee, 185
Davis, Rebecca, 31, 79
Dawes, Geoff, 51-53, 71-72
Dawes, Keith, 71
Dawes, Landa, 72
Dawson, Les 99
Dawson, Tom, 62
Deal, Pamela, 13
Deal, Peter, 223
Delaney, Martin, 162
Delaney, Noel, 214
Dennard, Richard, **127**
Derby, William, 206
Dettori, Frankie, 21, 35, 60, 166, 191, 192, **193**, 246
Deuters, Antonia, 23, 49, 81, 111-12, 230
Deuters, Chris, 23, 49, 81, 111-12, 230
Dever, Frank, 122, **122**, 128, 130-131, **131**, 144, 182, 218, 221
Dever, Peter, 130-1, 221
Dever, Val, 131, 183, 218
Dewey, 112
Dicken, Robin, 176
Dickenson, Michael, 205
Done, Fred, 241
Dowdeswell, Betty, 51
Dowdeswell, Jack, 51
Dick, Dave, 187
Dickenson, Michael, 117, 163
Dicker, David, 207
Dillon, Mike, 22, 100
Dimmock, Charlie, 229
Dinkley, Lord, (*see* Bradford-Nutter, Colin)
Dixon, Paul, 19, 56, 115,160
Dixon, Yvette, 19, 115
Dobbin, Tony, 54, 57, 72, 103, 157, **157**, 189-90
Dobbin, Vicky, 57, 58, **58**
Dolon, Colette, 47
Dolon, Laurie, 47
Doughty, Neil, 236
Dow, Simon, 224
Dowdeswell, Jack, 51, **127**
Doyle, Tony, 232
Duffield, Anne, 18-19, 28, 35, 39, 53, 55, 56, 75, 80, 117, 118, **118**, 119, **120**, 152, 156, 161, 162, 178, 193, 217, 222, 236, 242, 245
Duffield, George, 20, 28, 32-33, 35, 38, 40, 55, 56, 79, 117, 118-19, **120**, 161, 162, 188, 193, 206, 217, 222, 224, 236, 236, 241-2, 248, **248**
Duffield, Nicky, 120
Dukes, Colin, 175
Dun, Charles, 122
Dunlop, Ed, 226
Dunlop, John, 16, 21, **21**, 24, 34, 43, 46, 54, 96, 203, 206, 208, 218
Dunn, Bob, 160
Dunn, Kim, 57
Dunn, Peter, 54, 57, 70, 214
Dunwoody, Richard, 17, 44, 206
Durak, Seamus, 54
Durcan, Jill, 72, 73
Durcan, Ted, 72-73
Durcan, Tom, 72, 73
Durack, Seamus, 72, 115
Durr, Frankie, 24

Dutfield, Nerys, 203
Dutton, Bill, 112, 172, 175, 180
Duxbury, Betty, 76
Dwyer, Chris, 56
Dwyer, Mark, 116
Dwyer, Martin, 192
Dye, Shane, 246

Earnshaw, Robert, **163**
Easley, Captain, 175
East, Johnny, 175
Easterby, Mick, 15, 78, 175, 210, 211
Easterby, Peter, 20, 179, 205
Easterby, Sarah, 57
Easterby, Tim, 20, 23, 42, 57, 210, 229
Eccleston, Clive, 56
Eddery, Pat, 27, 46, 108, 165, **195**, 206, 211, 212, **212**, 213, 246
Edmonds, Pete, 40
Edwards, John, 138
Edwards, Lionel, 74, **74**
Edward, Roy, 222-3
Egerton, Charles, 188
Elder, Brian, 128, 143-4
Elder, Jackie, 144
Eldin, Eric, 56
Elliott, Bobby, 131
Elsey, Bill, 24
Elsey, Captain Charles, 24
Elsworth, David, 224
Etherington, Jimmy, 56
Etherington, Tim, 56
Eubank, Nita, 57
Eustace, James, 176
Evans, Richard, 72, 76

Fahey, Richard, 115, **116**
Fairhurst, Chris, 152, 166, 223
Fairhurst, Judy, 152
Fairhurst, Tommy, 152
Fairley, John, 13, 38
Fallon, Julie, 195
Fallon, Kieren, 42, 61, 122, 192, 194-5, 246
Fanning, Joe, 175, 245, 248
Farrell, Christopher, 87, 91, 133
Farrell, Eileen, 133-4
Farrell, Geraldine, 133
Farrell, Mary, 133
Farrell, Paddy, 13, 25, 29, 47, 65, 67, 83, 92, **92**, 106, **127**, 133, 135, 136, 145, 164
Fawcett, Anne, 19
Fawcett, Peter, 19, 22
Feakes, Matt, 143
Feilden-General Sir Randall, 205
Fenwicke-Clennel, Johnny, 41, 107
Ferguson, Sir Alex, 16, 17, 22, 29, 30, 62, 95, 113, 166, 174, **174**, 234
Finlay, Alan, 108
Firey, Martin, 137
Firey, Trish, 137
Fish, David, 113, 181
Fisher, Roger, 187
Fitzgerald, Jane, 56
Fitzgerald, Jimmy, 56, 133, 176, 234, 247
Fitzgerald, Mick, 21, 115, 191
Forbes, George, 143
Forrest, John, 228
Forsyth, John, 19, 101, 102-103, 150, 204
Forsyth, Margaret, 150
Foster, Eddie, 20, 80, **80**
Foster, John, 162, 176-7
Fowler, George, 35

Fox, Dominic, 129
Fox, Richard, 128, 129, 140, 145-6
Francis, Dick, 51, 191, 229
Francis, Merrick, 176, 229
Francome, John, 7, 13, 22, 38, 44, 51, 63, 69, 117, 120, **127**, 178, 205, 206, 220
Franklin, Andrew, 117
Frewen, Mr, 223
Fullalove, Pat, 58, 237
Fuller, NA, 221

Gale, Jim, 167, 217
Gandolfo, David, 176, 233
Garrity, Gaynor, 175, 244
Garrity, John, 175, 244
Gaston, Charlie, 129
Geraghty, Barry, 128
Gerber, Jack, 125
Gibb, Maurice, 94
Gibson, Gary, 40, 58, 115, 156, 235
Gifford, Josh, 51, 129, 162, 176, 184, 229
Gifford, Nick, 162
Gifford, Ted, 56
Gilbert, Johnny, 101
Gill, AJ, 162
Gillon, Mario, 26
Ginistrelli, Cheu, 132, 161
Given, James, 31, 176
Godson, John, 42
Goldie, Helen, 232
Goldie, Jim, 232
Goodwill, Brian, 122
Goodwin, Dave, 62
Gosden, John, 139-40
Gough, Miss, 230
Goulding, Dave, 132
Gower, David, 210
Graham, Leslie, 117, 120, 237
Graham, Peter, 163
Grandfield, 232
Grant, Chris, 189
Grant, Chris, (Sr), 189
Grassick, Christy, 102, 149
Gray, Eddie, 160
Grayson, Ken, 120-1
Greally, Phil, 78-79
Greally, John, 79
Green, Graham, 220
Green, Raymond Anderson, 59
Green, Richard, 62
Greenaway, Johnny, 20, 172, 180
Greenly, Brian, 42
Griffin, Reg, 63, 124, 203, **204**
Grossick, John, 54
Grubb, Murray, 108
Guest, Richard, 40, 77
Guiry, Paddy, 92
Gundill, Norman, 232-3

Haggas, Sally, **204**
Haggas, Willie, 24, 28, 184, 226
Hagger, Wally, 216
Hales, Richard, 116
Hall, Charlie, 56, 66, 179
Hall, David, 105
Hall, KP, 224
Hall, Sally, 166
Hallas, Angela, **185**, 186
Halliday, June, 232
Hallis, Lesley, 37
Hamey, Rex, 123, **123**
Hammond, Micky, 166, 187

Hanbuy, Ben, 207
Hancock, Barbara, 250, **258**
Hanley, Sam, 143
Hannon, Richard, 67, 213
Hanson, Jack, 232
Harding, Brian, 54
Harold, Patrick, 218
Harper, GJ, 238
Harper, LD, 238
Harper, Mr, 239
Harris, Anne, 126-7, 218
Harris, Danni, 127, **128**
Harris, Jimmy, 107, 109, 126-7, **127**, 218
Harrison, Audley, 21, 22, 34, **34**
Hartington, Lord, 206
Hartley, Anne, 55, 186, 238, 241, 247
Haslam, Pat, 19
Hatfield, Mary, 188
Hatfield, Susan, 188
Hatton, Karen, 50, 211, 244, 244, 248
Hawkins, Joy, 30-31, 37, 46, 58, 67, 96, 102, 151, 191, 236, 239-40, 243
Haydon Jones, Derek, 191
Hayes, Mick, 129
Haynes, Jonathan, **53**, 185
Hayhurst, Stan, 91
Haynes, Jonathon, 53, 107, 109, 186
Heaton-Ellis, Mike, 106-107, 109
Heler, Janet, 168, 178
Heler, Joseph, 11, 168-9, **170**, 178, 239
Hemmings, Trevor, **53**, 243
Henderson, A, 230
Henderson, Sheila, 141
Henry, Brian, 176
Herbert, Harry, 226
Herbert-Jackson, Ronni, 181
Herbert-Jackson, Terri, 150, 181, 208, 214
Hewitt, Ann, 22
Hickson, B, 230
Hide, Edward, 205
Higgins, John, 56
Higson, Ken, 108
Hill, Neville, 202
Hill, Tony, 218
Hills, Barry, 16, 212, 218
Hills, Michael, 24, 180
Hitchen, Elizabeth, 145
Hitchen, Robert, 145
Hitchens, Robert, 135-6, 148, 233
Hobbs, Philip, 192
Hockenhull, Dave, 114
Holdcroft, Margaret, 150
Holdcroft, Terry, 101, 150, 165, 208
Hodgson, David, 209
Hodgson, Helen, 209
Hogg, Simon, 236
Holding, Michael, 226
Holland, Daryll, 35, 205, 212, 246
Hollinshead, Reg, 24, 203
Hollowood, Dr, 24
Hollowood, Mrs, 24
Hope, J, 238
Horrocks, Alan, 56
Houlker, Steve, 79-80
Horsely, Denise, 236, 240
Horsely, Kevin, 236, 240
Horswill, Mickey, 158
Hourigan, Michael, 78, 81, 103, 112, 113, 138, 207
Howey, Gordon, 44
Howey, Mary, 44
Hughes, Dessie, 248

Hughes, Richard, 61
Hughes, Rob, 150, 209-10, 246
Hume, Rachel, 62
Hunter, Freddie, 143
Hurley, Miriam, 58
Hurley, Pat, 58, 163, 183, **183**, 227, 235
Hurt, John, 38
Huskinson, Mark, 218, 241
Hutchinson, Jim, 237
Hutchinson, John, 120, 241
Hyde, Timmy, 22
Hyndley, Myra, 93

Incisa, Don E, 179
Ingham, Staff, 143
Ives, Tony, 132
Ivory, Ken, 95, 96. 102
Ivory, Ken, 208, 237, 240
Ivory, Val, 95, 240

Jackson, Norman, **217**
Jackson, Paul, 232, 240
James, Andrew, 185
James, David, 210
Jarvis, Gay, 40
Jarvis, Jack, 180
Jarvis, Michael, 192, **195**
Jarvis, Ryan, 184
Jarvis, Willie, 226, 232
Jennings, Tommy,128, 139
Johnson, Brenda, 203
Johnson, Cliff, 237
Johnson, David, 223
Johnson, Frederick, 246
Johnson, Margaret, 204, 205
Johnson, Mark, 61, 204-5, 206, 220, 221
Johnson, Richard, 18, 53
Johnson, Robin, 203
Johnson-Houghton, Fulke, 64
Jones, Arthur, 228-9
Jones, Ben, 178
Jones, Cliff, 219
Jones, Karen, **33**, 34
Jones, Tom, 191
Jones, Vicky, 228

Kearsley, James. 105
Keegan, Jean, 27
Kellet, Tommy, 175
Kelly, Gene, **123**
Kelly, Gerry, 176
Kelly, Kieran, 243, 247-8
Kelly, Lex, 124, 232
Kendal, Bob, 156, 235
Kennedy, Jeff, 139
Kerr, Bobby, 158
Kerr, Dr, 31
Kerr, Dr Robin, 31
Kerr, Hilary, 31
Kettle, Sally, 57
Kilpatrick, BA, 223
Kilpatrick, EM, 223
Kilpatrick, JS, 163
Kinane, Mick, 21, 246
Kindersley, Gay, 191
King, Alan, 186
King, Angela, 238
King, Claire, 238
King, John 238
Kirby, Mr & Mrs, 184
Kirkham, Tracy, 240
Knight, Rev. Harold, 63

Knight, Henrietta, 19, 45, 50, 62, 77, 113, 186, 206, 244
Knoxhall, Bobby, 160, 225
Koom, Philip, 143

Lacey, Jackie, 138
Lacey, Robert, 138
Lake, MA, 218
Lara, Brian, 210
Lavelle, Patrick, 10
Law, Cynthia, 46
Law, Dennis, 151
Law, Digby, 46, 103
Lawrence, John, (see Oaksey, Lord)
Lawson, Dave, 159 Leason, Kevin, 56
Leatham, George, 108
Leggat, Mr & Mrs, 56
Lee, Brian, 172, 176
Lee, Francis, 70, 192
Lees, Gavin, 241
Lehane, Johnny, 134
Leigh, Captain Rupert, 173
Lemair, Martina, 182
Lennon, John, 156
Letherby, Damaris, 132, 160, 187
Letherby, Dennis, 132, 160, 187
Levitt, RM, 218
Lewis, Jeff, 178, 243
Lewis, Jim, 65, 112, 113, 220
Lewis, Lennox, 60
Lewis, Wade, 21, 34
Linfoot, Kevin, 188
Liston, Jenny, 185
Liston, Sonny, 137
Llewellyn, Carl, 21, 40
Lindley, Harry, 87
Littmoden, Nick, 116
Lloyd, CJ, 230
Loakey, Mr, 218
Lofthouse, Bob, 234
Lofthouse, Mary, 234
Lomax, Rosie, 139
Lorimer, Peter, 70, 158, 158, 160
Lowe, John, 56
Lowry, Dave, 118, 242
Lumsden, Jimmy, 16
Lucas, Geoff, 209
Lucas, Linda, 209
Lungo, Len, 57, 223
Lunn, Sarah, 35
Lye, Tommy, 62
Lyle, Graham, 160
Lynch, Fergal, 248
Lynch, Gerry, 137
Lynch, Tommy, 179

Maclean, George, 139-40
MacPherson, Janice, 232
MacPherson, Keith, 232
MacTaggart, ALan, 228
McCain, Beryl, 223
McCain, Don, 94, 128
McClaine, Dr Bruce, 57, 221
McCoy, AP, 13, 50-51, 55, 61, 61, 92, 165, 223
McCoy, Tony, 17, 18, 19, 21, 44, 54, 60-61, 73, 115, 122, 189, 206
McCreery, Bob, 127, 138
McCririck, John, 63, 161
McDermot, Terry, 161, 175
McGrath, Jim, 203
McGuire, Adrain, 115

McKeown, Dean, 122
McMahon. Brian, 230
McManus, JP, 113
McNeill, Simon, 13, 25, 38
McCrea, Bill, 97
McVririck, John, 63
Macauley, Norma, 221
Magee, Sean, 123, 123, 204
Magnier, Sue, 43
Maguire, Adrian, 43, 44, 189, 190, 202
Maguire, Billy, 162, 181
Maguire, Sabrina, 189
Major, Larry, 91
Maktoum al Maktoum, Sheik, 62
Mallinson, Andrea, 161
Mallinson, Mr, 237, 240
Malloy, Jane, 157
Mandal, Colin, 178
Mandle, Colin, 218
Mangan, JJ, 127
Manning, Bernard, 34, 110, 242
Mansell, Jimmy, 18, 31
Mariners, John, 121
Markham, Johnny, 92
Marks, Doug, 143
Marne, Con, 207
Marshall, Bill, 84
Marshall, Brian, 51
Marshall, Connie, 114, 114
Marshall, Pam, 84
Marshall, Shirley, 211
Martin, Julia Routledge, 188
Mason, Norman, 77
Mason, Peter, 95, 174, 182, 227
Massarella, John, 87
Mathers, Paddy, 167, 187-8
Maw, Harry, 87, 118
Maxwell, Freddie, 139
Maxwell, Robert, 105
Mellor, Dana, 97
Mellor, Elaine, 97
Mellor, Linda, 97
Mellor, Stan, 44, 53, 97, 98, 211
Meme, PJ, 241
Mercer, Joe, 84, 111, 112, 113, 151, 162, 241, 246
Mernagh, Deam, 248
Metcalfe, David, 24, 208
Michael, HJE, 244
Miff, Jimmy, 72
Milburn, Freddie, 222-3
Miliman, Rod, 188
Miller, Roy, 162
Milligan, Kate, 152
Mills, Terry, 33, 33, 182
Minton, David, 109
Mitchell, Carol, 179, 191
Mohammed, Sheik, 208
Molloy, Jane, 18, 157
Molony, Tim, 51, 132
Montgomery, Jimmy, 158-9
Moore, Gary, 16, 203
Moore, Carol, 152, 188, 249
Moore, George, 16, 55, 151, 152, 166, 188, 237, 249
Moore, Val, 175
Moreshead, Anthea, 203
Moreshead, Sam, 203
Morgan, John, 36, 49, 50, 180, 239
Morgan, Kevin, 227
Morgan, Maureen, 239
Morley, Gordon, 124

Morley, Liz, 124, 178, 239, 240
Morris, Chris, 217, 238
Morris, John, 210
Morris, Reg, 108
Morris, Stuart, 217, 238
Morrissey, Jimmy, 133
Mould, David, 108, 124, 127, 187, 191, 211
Mould, Jack, 187
Mould, Marion, 124, 187
Muir, Brian, 22, 34
Murgatroyd, Sharon, 128, 141, 142, 145, 147, 182, 211, 230-1, 249, 250
Murless, Sir Noel, 101, 205
Murphy, Ferdy, 218, 241
Murphy, Pat, 200
Murphy, Timmy, 207
Murray, Bill, 132
Murtagh, Johnny, 210, 246
Myatt, Rita, 210

Naughton, Muriel, 140-1
Nesbitt, Myra, 207, 237, 240
Nesbitt, Steve, 55, 151, 152, 237
Nevit, Willie, 74, 74
Newcombe, Tony, 246
Newnes, Billy, 38, 69, 138, 232
Newton, William, 24, 245
Nicholls, Adrian, 27, 248
Nicholls, David (Dandy), 16, 27, 27, 35, 116, 175, 224
Nicholls, Paul, 232
Nicholson, Clifford, 65, 135, 184
Nicholson, David, 196, 196, 207
Nicholson, Dinah, 196, 196, 207
Niven, Peter, 44, 77
Nixon, John, 162
Noland, Donald, 34
Norris, William, 13
North, Bob, 31
North, Corol, 89, 99, 241
North, John, 89, 99, 241
North, Phyllis, 31
Norton, Franny, 75, 248
Norton, John, 209
Norton, Steve, 56
Noseda, Jeremy, 62
Noule, Mr & Mrs, 230
Nunnery, Caroline, 245
Nuttall, Mr & Mrs, 152, 238

Oaksey, Lord John, 13, 25, 38, 51, 108, 123, 127, 129, 135, 135, 146, 147, 186, 191,192, 206, 229, 245
Oaksey, Lady 'Chicky', 25, 50, 111-112, 129, 138, 140, 144, 146, 147, 151, 2389
Oates, Donald, 232
O'Brien, Aiden, 16, 21, 30, 42, 96, 97, 102, 104, 123, 135, 223
O'Brien, Dr MV, 16, 16, 30, 137, 205
O'Donaghue, Jack, 127
O'Gorman, Pat, 174, 212
O'Grady, Pat, 209
O'Hara, Johnny, 57, 58, 132, 144, 183, 183, 229
O'Hara, Liam, 133
O'Hara, Linda, 57, 58, 126, 127, 132-3, 183
O'Hara, Seamus, 133
O'Keefe, Andrea, 217, 222, 230, 243
O'Keefe, Jed, 166, 217, 222, 230, 243
Old, Jim, 232
Oldroyd, Geoff, 176
O'Leary, Eddie, 22
O'Leary, Pat, 143

Oliver, Alan, 130
Oliver, Damian, 48-49
Oliver, Jason, 48, 49
O'Neill, Jackie, 19, 112
O'Neill, Jonjo, 205, 224, 238
O'Neill, Seamus, 224
O'Neill, Simon, 147
Oliver, Jean, 130
Oliver, Ken, 134
O'Neill, Jonjo, 41, 51, 54, 72, 76, 100, 101, 103, 112, 122
O'Shea, Johnny, 169
Ormston, Jack, 143
Orr-Ewing, Jonathon, 120
O'Ryan, Tom, 61, 121-2
Osbourne, Andrew, 169
Osbourne, Jamie, 69, 115, 169, 229
Osbourne, Michael, 62
O'Sullivan, Peter, 204, 206
O'Sullivan, Steve, 100-101
Owen, Michael, 36, **37**, 182
Oxx, John, 102

Padgett, Brian, 32
Pailling, Bryn, 218
Palin, Tim, 218
Parker, Billy, 117
Parker, Colin, 58
Parker, Dave, 157, 191
Parker, Isobel, 58, **59**
Parkin, Steve, 238
Parr, Adrian, 167, 218
Peacock, Lenni, **204**
Pearson, EW, 238
Pearson, Nicky, 126, 129
Peebles, Roy, 108
Perratt, Linda, 179, 233
Perrett, Amanda, 186
Perrett, Mark, 117, 186
Petch, Major Leslie, 205
Peters, Shane, 181
Pickering, David, 108
Pickering, Martin, 94
Piggot, Keith, 139
Piggot, Lester, 23-24, **23**, 27, 55, 60. 112, 128-129, 139, 151, 172, 205, 211, **212**, 226, 237
Piggot, Susan, 24, 226
Pincay Jr, Laffit, 165
Pipe, Carol, 187, 223
Pipe, David, 20
Pipe, Martin, 17, 58, 62, 92, 206, 223
Pitman, Richard, 229
Pitt, Chris, 123, **123**, 182
Podmore, MG, 218
Polglase, Mark, 115
Pollet, Christine, 145
Pollet, E, 83
Pollington, Dave, 194-5
Pope, Michael, 211
Porterfield, Ian, 158
Powell, Benny, 164
Powell, Brendon, 164
Powell, David, 63-64
Powell, Jonathon, 10, 13, 38, 38
Power, Jimmy, 92, 112, 173
Prendergast, Paddy, 132
Prescott, Sir Mark, 20, 28, 32-33, 178, 191, 224, 236
Pullar, Polly, 191
Pym, David, 94

Queen Elizabeth, the Queen Mother, 26, 127, **127**, 135, 144, 187, 191, 192, 220
Quinn, John, 227
Quinn, Niall, 46, **47**

Radcliffe, Paula, **60**
Rawlinson, Jane, 230
Raymond, Bruce, 132
Rainbow, Howard, 106, **106**
Rainbow, Lisa, 106, **106**
Rainbow, Sue, 106, **106**
Raine, Elizabeth, 182
Ramsden, Linda, 214
Redmond, Linda, 230
Redmond, Tony, 138
Rees, Bill, **127**
Rees, Geraldine, 106, 107, 109, 113
Renton, Bobby, 173
Reveley, Mary, 32, 190
Richards, Sir Gordon (GW), 19, 41, **41**, 51, 73, 101, 139, 143
Richards, Nicky, 41
Richards, Tim, 138, 140, 182,
Richardson, Anne, 226
Richardson, Chris, 226
Richardson, Gill, 118, **118**, 238
Richardson, Jeremy, 25, 26, 50, **127**, 135, 139, 146, 183, 184, 186, 226
Rickaby, Bill, 180
Rickett, PM, 218
Righall, Dizzy, 91
Robb, Brian, 9, 10, 101, 103, 114, 163, 165, 190, 203, 223, 228, 232,
Robe, Brian, 22, 47, 64, 158, 159, 160, 161, 215, 225, 239, 241, 247
Robe, Donna, 64, 215, 225 239,
Roberts, Anne, 230
Roberts, Harry, 230
Roberts, Margaret, 218
Roberts, Paul, 40
Roberts, Stan, 152
Robertson, Bill, 34
Robinson, Auriol, 211
Robinson, Ben, 66, 67, 126, 197
Robinson, Bill, 83-84, 106, **106**, 203, 233, **234**
Robinson, June, 83-84, 106, **106**, 203
Robson, Bryan, 22
Roper, D, 239
Roper, Victor, 167
Rothwell, Brian, 234
Rubin, Major Jack, 74
Russell, Alec, 191
Russell, Bois, 172
Russell, Lucinda, 209
Rutter, Graham, 238
Ryan, Dennis, 132
Ryan, Jill. 241
Ryan, Kevin, 47, 116, 162, 166
Ryecart, KE, 233

St George, Edward, 35
Sackville, Edward, 191
Saddler, Mr & Mrs, 230
Sakal, MJ, 217
Salman, Fahid, 236
Sanderson, Jonjo, 187
Sanderson, John, 117, 205
Sangster, Robert, 26
Salman, Prince Fahed, 138
Sanders, Brook, 224
Sanderson, WE, 238
Sassoon, Sir Victor, 143

Saunders, Dick, 26, **127**
Savill, Peter, 27, 28, 79, 174, 206
Saxton, Graham, 149, 155, 160, 182
Sayer, Catherine, 229
Sayer, Mike, 234
Sayer, Janet, 229
Scott, Avril, 91
Scott, Brough, 13, 38, **127**
Scott, Gerry, 91, 121, 123, **123**, 124, 166, 175, 184, 235, 240
Scott, Jan, 169
Scudamore, Peter,13, 38, 44, 51, 65, 74, **127**, 132, 205-6
Scuse, June, 139
Scuse, Tommy, 139, 145-6
Seagrave, John, 56
Seed, Angela, 239
Seed, John, 239
Sellers, Christine, 19
Sellers, David, 238
Semple, Ian, 217
Shand Kidd, Bill, 108
Shaw, Derek, 115, 116, 223, 238
Shaw, John, 188
Shearer, Alan, 161, 175, 236, 239
Sheddon, Tommy, 232
Sheldon, David, 176
Sherman, Wilfred, 11-12
Sherwood, Simon, 209
Shoemaker, Willie, 162, 237
Siddall, Lyn, 233-4
Sime, Joe, 172, **172**
Singer, Ronnie, 98, 131, **132**, 140, 145, 146
Slack, Arthur, 158
Slack, Evelyn, 158
Slater, Angela, 241
Slater, Mike, 241
Sleater, David, 214
Smart, Brian, 115, 162, 166, 179
Smart, Vickie, 179
Smirke, Charlie, 71, 143
Smith, Alan, 107-108
Smith, Bill, **127**
Smith, Cal, 155
Smith, Dennis, 167
Smith, Harvey, 96. 115, 122
Smith, Jeff, 13, 213
Smith, John, 22, 38, 47, **127**, 175, 176, 178, 206
Smith, JM, 238
Smith, Maggie, 175, 176
Smith, Steven, 174
Smith, Sue, 96, 115, 166
Smith Eccies, Steve, 178
Smullen, Pat, 164
Smyth, Monty, 132
Smyth, Vic, 143
Snaith, Willie, 125, 143, 144
Solskjaer, Gunner, 160
Sommerbee, Mike, 70
Spares, Charlie, 74
Spearing, John, 196
Spence, Rachel, 158, 159, 160
Spencer, Jamie, 16
Spouse, John, 184
Sprague, Harry, 65
Spouse, John, 98-99
Sprague, Harry, **107**, 108
Sprake, Gary, 80
Sprake, John, 132
Sprake, Tim, 121, 122
Stack, Tommy, 51, 93-94

Stanley, George, 228
Stephenson, Arthur, 131
Stephenson, Gail, 27
Stephenson, John, 19, 27, 89, 225, 237
Stephenson, Willie, 74, **74**, 200
Stewart, Peter, 40
Storey, Brian, 157, **157**, 191, 192
Storey, Eric, 83
Storey, Lily, 83
Storey, Wilf, 192
Stott, Billy, 108
Stoute, Sir Michael, 122, 183, 188, 192, 225, 226
Stronge, Sam, 117
Stubbs, Linda, 104, 229
Stud, Colin, 216
Suborios, Andreas, 246
Sullivan, Peter, 205
Supple, William, 24, 54
Sweeny, Fergus, 145
Swinburn, Wally, 129

Take, Yutaka, 246
Tate, Tom, 77, 116, 117
Taylor, Scott, 53-54, **53**
Taylor, Trevor, 32, 162, 178
Teasdale, Lisa, 188
Teasdale, Peter, 188
Tebbit, Michael, 30
Teesdale, Cath, 182
Teesdale, Peter, 182
Tennant, Rodney, 204
Thewlis, Val, 188
Thompson, David, 209
Thompson, Derek, 69, 103, 171, 174
Thompson, Jane, 122, 141
Thompson, Marcus, 57
Thompson, Mrs, 192, 194, 209, 239, 241
Thompson, Ron, 122
Thorner, Graham, 51
Thornton, Antonia, 186, 242
Thornton, Chris, 166, 186
Thornton, Peter, 166
Thornton, Robert, 53
Thrale, Dick, 151
Tindall, Caroline, 164
Tindall, Roger, 243
Tindall, Simon, 38, 164
Tinker, Colin, 102, 114
Tinkler, Kim, 205
Tinkler, Nigel, 116, 117, 167, 201
Tinkler, Marie, 201
Todd, George, 139
Tomkin, Mark, 218, 221, 223, 232
Townsend, Gill, 76
Townsend, Linda. 46, 53, 76, 117-18, 120, 230, 236, 246
Townsend, Sue, 220
Townsend, Tim, 46, 53
Townsend, Tom, 62
Tree, Jeremy, 139, 178
Trotter, Jeanie, 238
Trueman, Fred, 48, 225
Trueman, Veronica, 48
Tuck, Phil, 101, 108
Tulk, Paul, 129
Tufnell, Meriel, 37-38
Tunstall, John, 229
Turnell, Andy, 24
Turner, Bill, 224

Ulsterman, 'Paddy', 163

Underwood, Ivor, 133
Uttley, Jimmy, 124

Vasey, Percy, 232
Vaux, Wing Commander Peter, 135
Vipoint, Ian, 218

Wainwright, John, 194
Wainwright, Snowy, 194
Wallingham, Harold, 143
Walmsley, Ann, 161
Walmsley, John, 161, 192
Walsh, Ruby, 113, 115, 207
Walwyn, Fulke, 129-30, 139
Walwyn, Peter, 140
Ward, Bob, 83, **88**
Wardby, Bill, 103
Warmsley, Anne, 84
Warmsley, John, 84
Warren, Lady Carolyn, 226
Warren, Sir John, 226
Warriner, Mrs, 126
Waters, Glenda, 178
Waters, Graham, 178
Watkinson, Ian, 222-3
Watson-Wilson, Owen, 183, 214, 241
Watts, Bill, 102, 181
Watts, Pat, 181
Waugh, Jack, 33
Webb, John, 139
Webben, Peter, 73
Weld, Dermot, 48, 62, 164
Westbrook, Lady, 23, 26
Westbrook, Sir Neil, 23
Westmoreland, Geoff, 179
Westmoreland, Ray, 179, 180
Weymes, John, 162
Wharton, Auriol, 106, **106**
Wharton, Walter, 83, 84, **84**, **85**, 88, 106, **106**, 170, 211, 232
Wheeler, Eric, 217
Whelan, Boggy, 138
Whewell, Joe, 130
Whicker, Alan, 224
Whitaker, Edward, 121
White, AP, 19
White, Doug, 246
White, Michael (Mouse), 160, 177, 194, **201**,236, 237, 240, 243, 246
White, Pauline, 121-2
Whiteman, Dave, 114, 239
Whittaker, Edward, 34, 61, 191
Whittingham, Charlie, 113
Wicket, Dennis, 38
Wicket, Jane, 38, 128, 182
Wicket, Oliver, 38
Wigham, Percy, 176
Wilding, John, 241
Wiles, Elaine, 31, 124, 129, 130, **130**, 137, 146, 186, 232, 247
Wilkinson, Barbara, 242, 243, **243**
Wilkinson, GA, 238
Wilkinson, Johnny, 60
Wilkinson, Jumbo, 91
Wilkinson, Len, 94
Wilkenson, Nimrod, 91, 175
Wilkinson, Ray, 122
Williams, Charlie, 216-17
Williams, Evan, 139
Williams, Stuart, 62, 224
Williams, Tyrone, 175, 235, 238
Williams, Venetia, 218

Williamson, Jackie, 57
Williamson, Norman, 54, 72
Willis, Bob, 48
Wilmot-Smith, David, 181, 239
Wilmot-Smith, Laureline, 181, 239
Wilson, Julian, 184, 226
Wilson, Miss, 228
Winstanley, Simon, 202
Winston, Robert, 248
Wintle, David, 209
Winter, Fred, 51, 91, **127**
Winter, John, **127**
Wolf, Steve, 48, 49
Wood, Ian, 230
Wood, Tom, **127**
Woodruff, Harry, 232
Wooton, Stanley, 143
Worthington, Alan, 154
Worthington, Billy, 190-1, 195
Wosskow, David, 204, 209
Wright, Lily, 218
Wright, Martin, 150
Wright, Orville, 226
Wright, Rachel, 10
Wright, Wilbur, 226
Wylde, Desi, 218
Wyville, Charles, 186

Yeats, Tom, 139
Yeoman, John, 188
Yorath, Terry, 160
York, Colonel Eddie, 130, 210
York, Sarah, 57, 122, 129, 130, 146, 149, 186, 210

Zetland, Lord, 48

George Duffield, the gardener.